Almost forty volumes*!!* Thank you so much for reading for so long. I couldn't have made it this far without your support. I am very grateful and will keep working hard.

— Takeshi Konomi, 2007

About Takeshi Konomi

Takeshi Konomi exploded onto the manga scene with the incredible **THE PRINCE OF TENNIS**. His refined art style and sleek character designs proved popular with **Weekly Shonen Jump** readers, and **THE PRINCE OF TENNIS** became the number one sports manga in Japan almost overnight. Its cast of fascinating male tennis players attracted legions of female readers even though it was originally intended to be a boys' comic. The manga continues to be a success in Japan and has inspired a hit anime series, as well as several video games and mountains of merchandise.

THE PRINCE OF TENNIS
VOL. 39
SHONEN JUMP Manga Edition

STORY AND ART BY
TAKESHI KONOMI

Translation/Joe Yamazaki
Touch-up Art & Lettering/Vanessa Satone
Design/Sam Elzway
Editor/Daniel Gillespie

VP, Production/Alvin Lu
VP, Sales & Product Marketing/Gonzalo Ferreyra
VP, Creative/Linda Espinosa
Publisher/Hyoe Narita

Printed in Canada

Published by VIZ Media, LLC
P.O. Box 77010
San Francisco, CA 94107

10 9 8 7 6 5 4 3 2 1
First printing, October 2010

PARENTAL ADVISORY
THE PRINCE OF TENNIS
is rated A and is suitable
for readers of all ages.
ratings.viz.com

THE WORLD'S
MOST POPULAR MANGA

www.shonenjump.com

www.viz.com

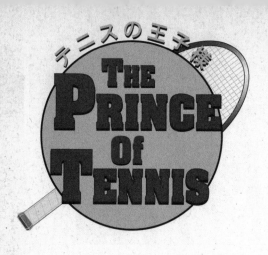

THE PRINCE OF TENNIS

**Flare-up!
Barbecue Battle!!**

**Story & Art by
Takeshi Konomi**

VOL. 39

NNIS CLUB

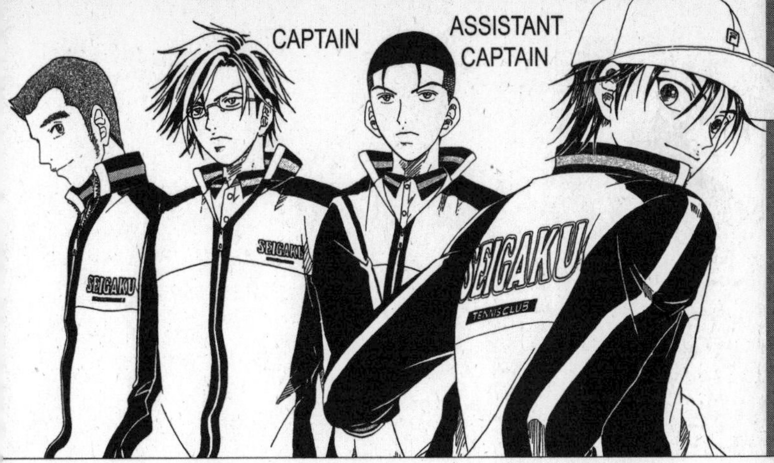
CAPTAIN
ASSISTANT CAPTAIN
SEIGAKU
SEIGAKU
SEIGAKU
TENNIS CLUB

TAKASHI KAWAMURA • KUNIMITSU TEZUKA • SHUICHIRO OISHI • RYOMA ECHIZEN •

STORY & CHARACTERS

Seishun Academy student Ryoma Echizen is a tennis prodigy, with wins in four consecutive U.S. Junior Tennis Tournaments under his belt. He became a starter as a 7th grader and led his team to the District Preliminaries! Despite a few mishaps, Seishun won the Dirstrict Prelims and the City Tournament, and earned a ticket to the Kanto Tournament. The team came away victorious from its first-round matches, but captain Kunimitsu injured his shoulder and went to Kyushu for treatment. Despite losing Kunimitsu and assistant captain Shuichiro to injury, Seishun pulled together as a team, winning the Kanto Tournament and earning a slot at the Nationals!

With Kunimitsu recovered and back on the team, Seishun enter the Nationals with their strongest lineup and defeat Okinawa's Higa Junior High in the opening round, Hyotei in the quarterfinals, and Shitenhoji in the semifinals. They're about to advance to the finals! But first, Rokkaku, Higa, Hyotei, and Shitenhoji crash Sheishun's *yakiniku* party celebrating their victory. An eating contest erupts between the schools! How will this battle end?!

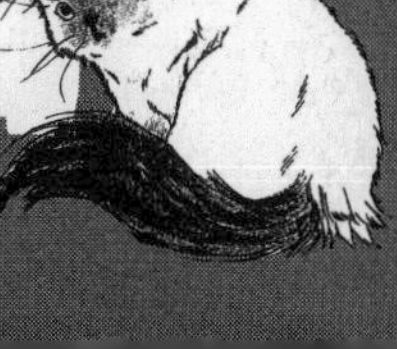

SEIGAKU I

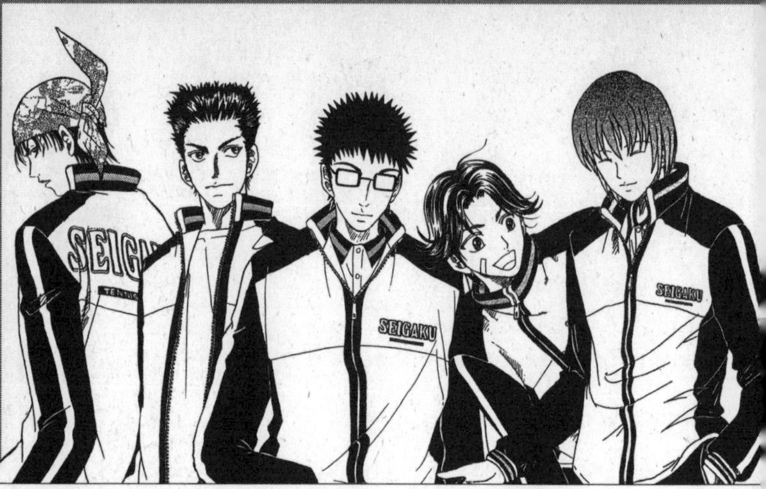

SEIGAKU
TENNIS
SEIGAKU
SEIGAKU

• KAORU KAIDO • TAKESHI MOMOSHIRO • SADAHARU INUI • EIJI KIKUMARU • SHUSUKE FUJI •

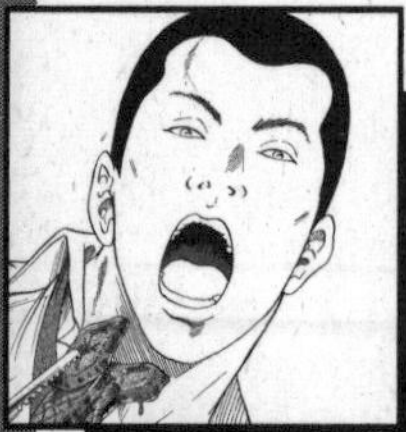
HYOTEI ACADEMY
MUNEHIRO KABAJI

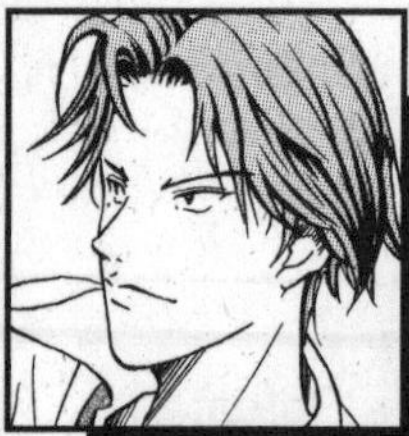
HYOTEI ACADEMY
KEIGO ATOBE

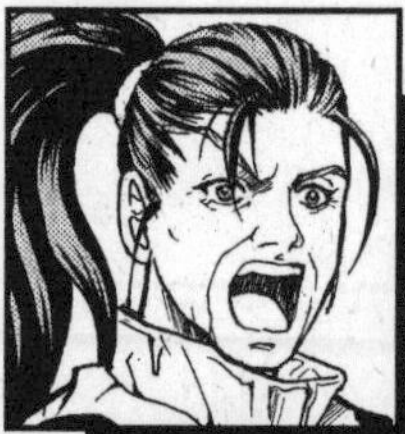
SEISHUN ACADEMY TENNIS COACH
SUMIRE RYUZAKI

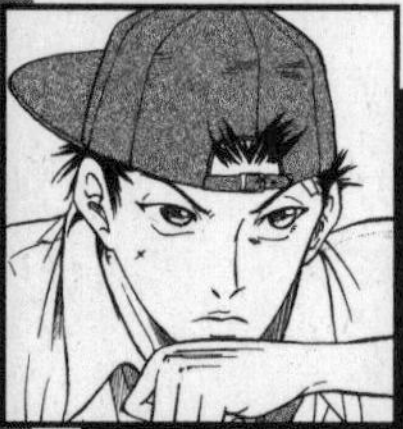
HYOTEI ACADEMY
RYO SHISHIDO

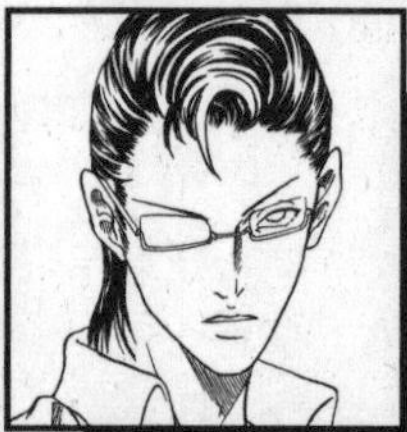
HIGA
EISHIRO KITE

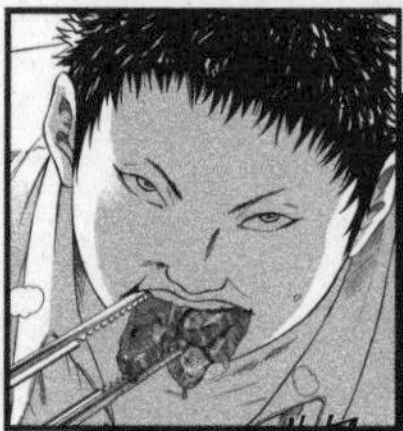
HIGA
KEI TANISHI

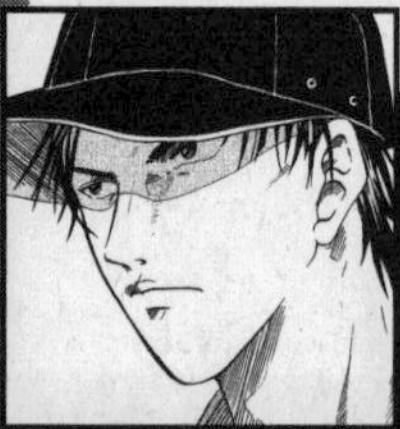
RIKKAI
GENICHIRO SANADA

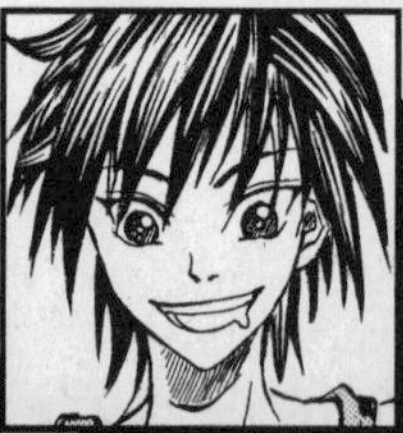
SHITENHOJI
KINTARO TOYAMA

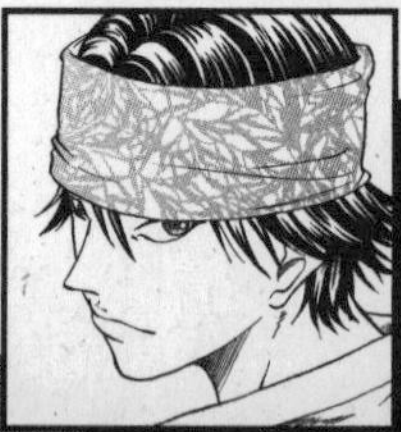
SHITENHOJI
YUJI HITOJI

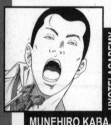

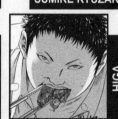

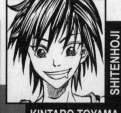

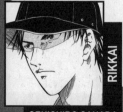

CONTENTS

Vol. 39
Flare-up! Barbecue Battle!!

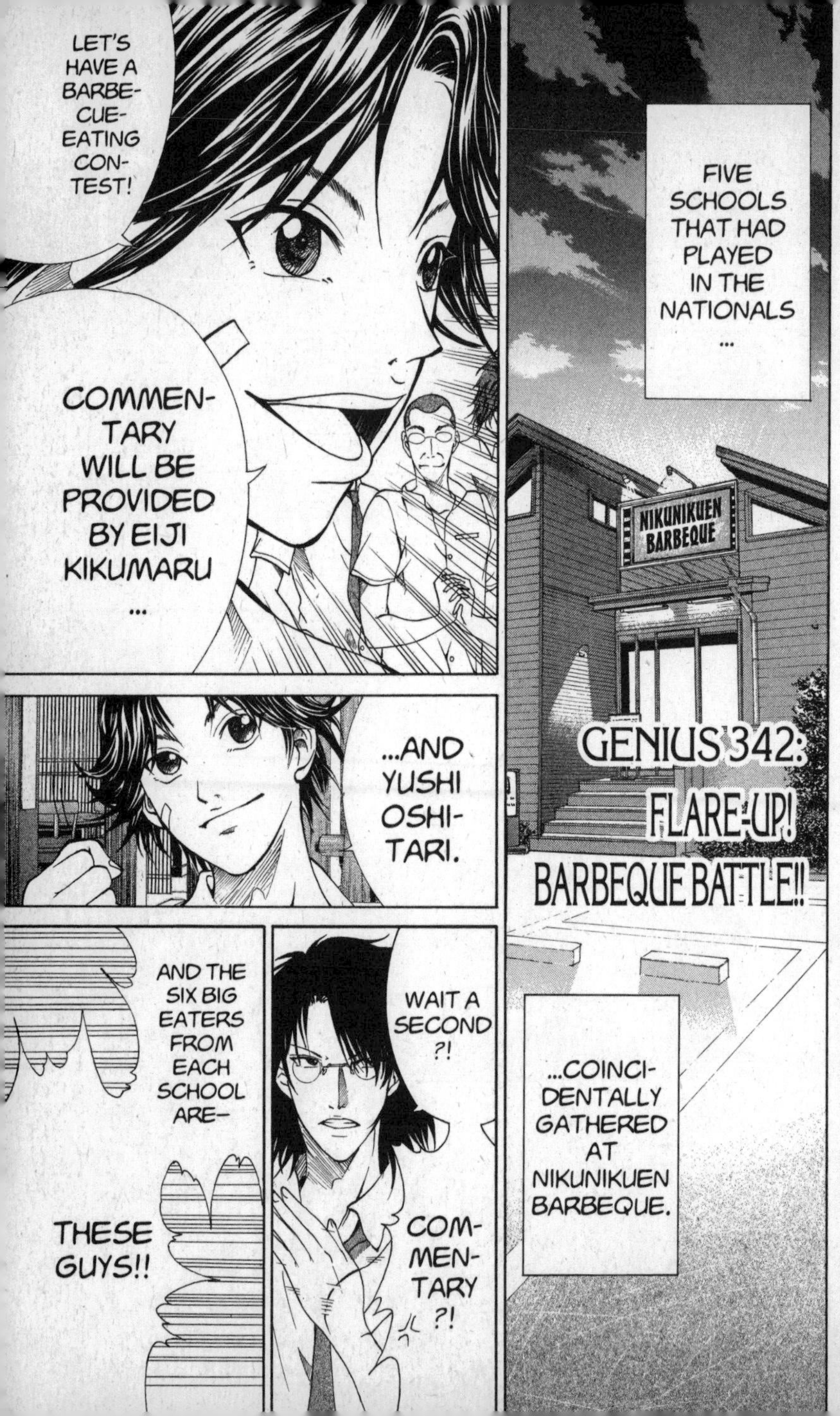
FIVE SCHOOLS THAT HAD PLAYED IN THE NATIONALS ...
NIKUNIKUEN BARBEQUE
GENIUS 342: FLARE-UP! BARBEQUE BATTLE!!
...COINCIDENTALLY GATHERED AT NIKUNIKUEN BARBEQUE.
LET'S HAVE A BARBECUE-EATING CONTEST!
COMMENTARY WILL BE PROVIDED BY EIJI KIKUMARU ...
...AND YUSHI OSHITARI.
WAIT A SECOND ?!
COMMENTARY ?!
AND THE SIX BIG EATERS FROM EACH SCHOOL ARE—
THESE GUYS!!

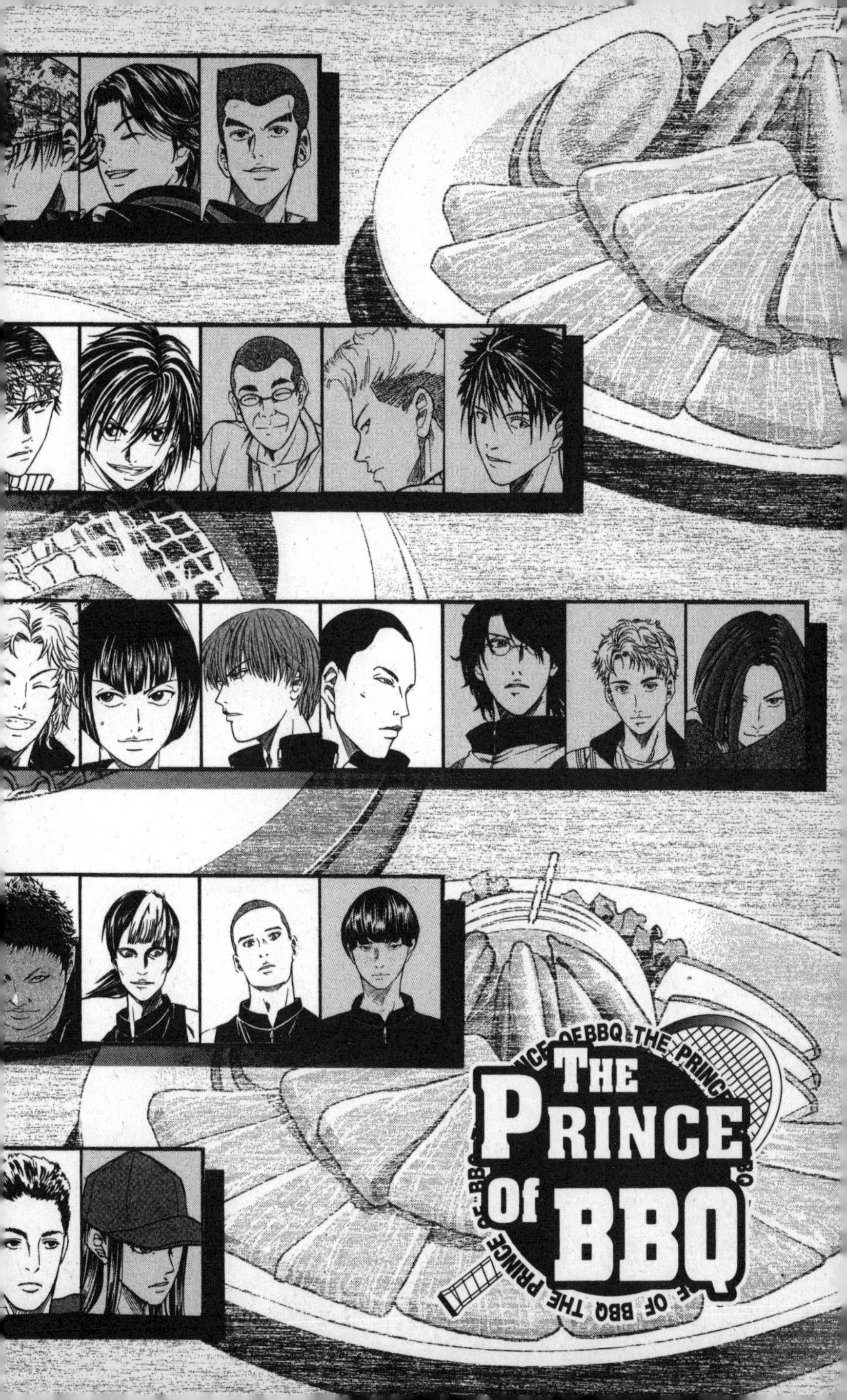
THE PRINCE of BBQ
THE PRINCE OF BBQ THE PRINCE OF BBQ THE PRINCE OF BBQ

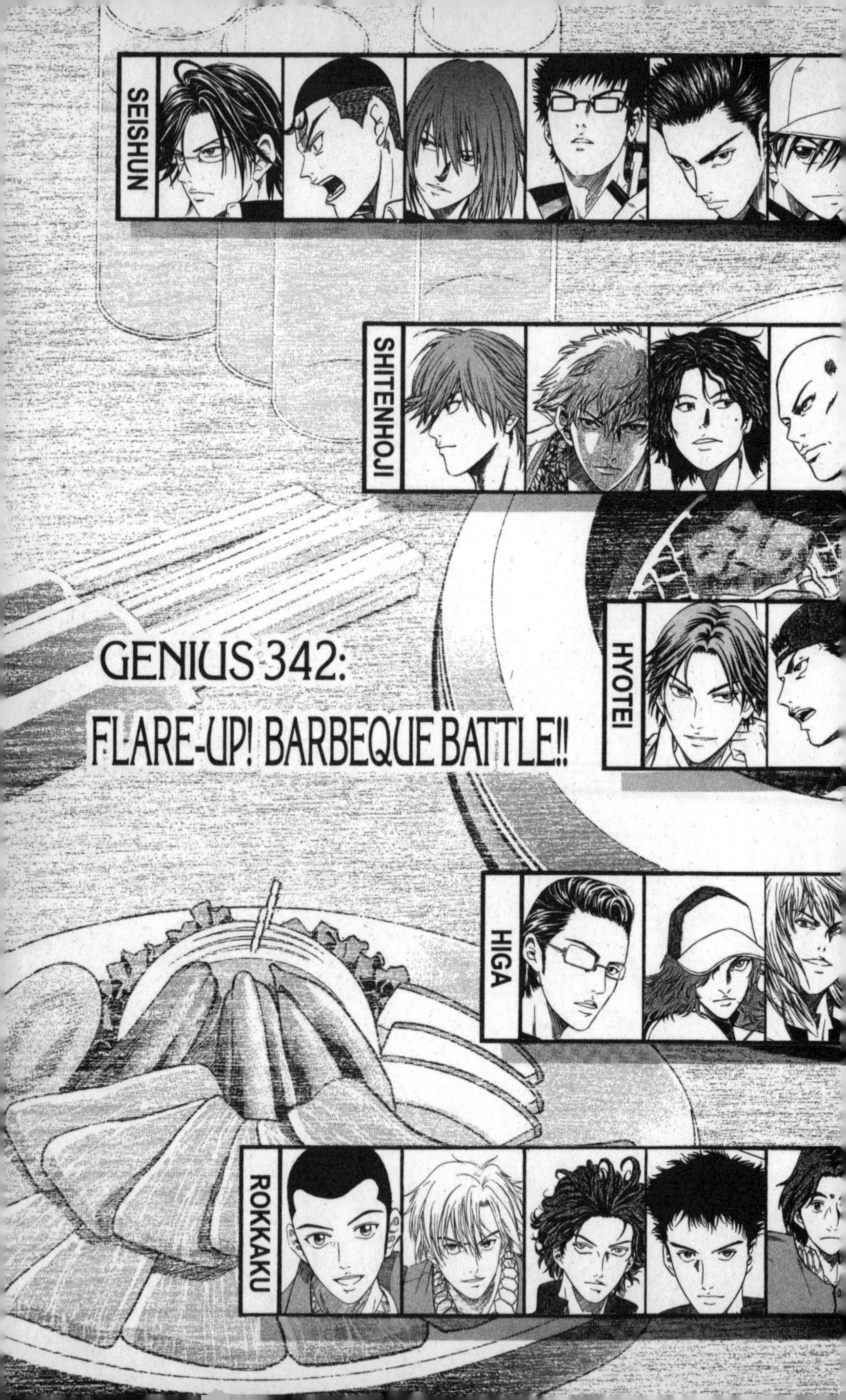
SEISHUN
SHITENHOJI
GENIUS 342:
FLARE-UP! BARBEQUE BATTLE!!
HYOTEI
HIGA
ROKKAKU

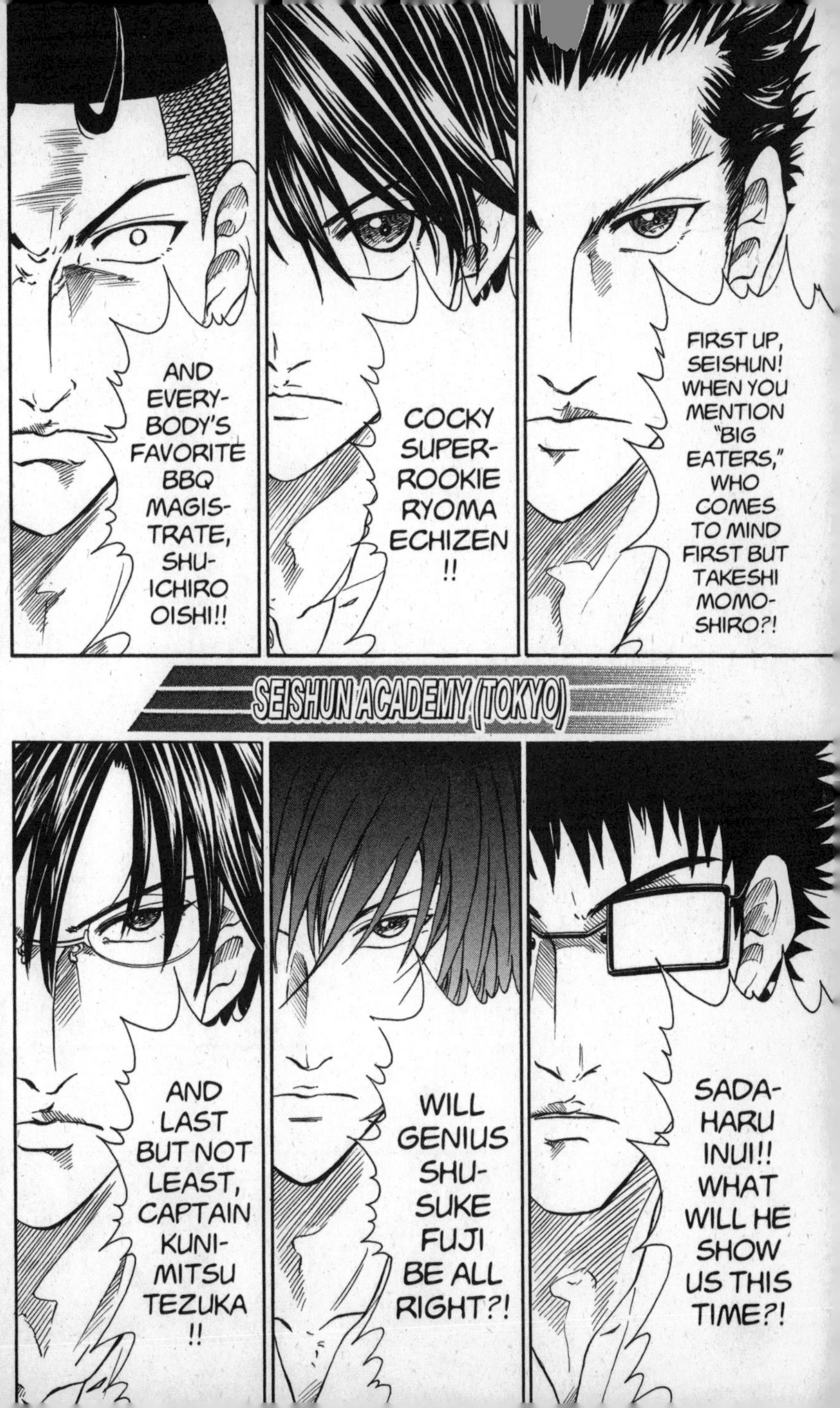
FIRST UP, SEISHUN! WHEN YOU MENTION "BIG EATERS," WHO COMES TO MIND FIRST BUT TAKESHI MOMOSHIRO?!
COCKY SUPER-ROOKIE RYOMA ECHIZEN!!
AND EVERYBODY'S FAVORITE BBQ MAGISTRATE, SHUICHIRO OISHI!!
SEISHUN ACADEMY (TOKYO)
SADAHARU INUI!! WHAT WILL HE SHOW US THIS TIME?!
WILL GENIUS SHUSUKE FUJI BE ALL RIGHT?!
AND LAST BUT NOT LEAST, CAPTAIN KUNIMITSU TEZUKA!!

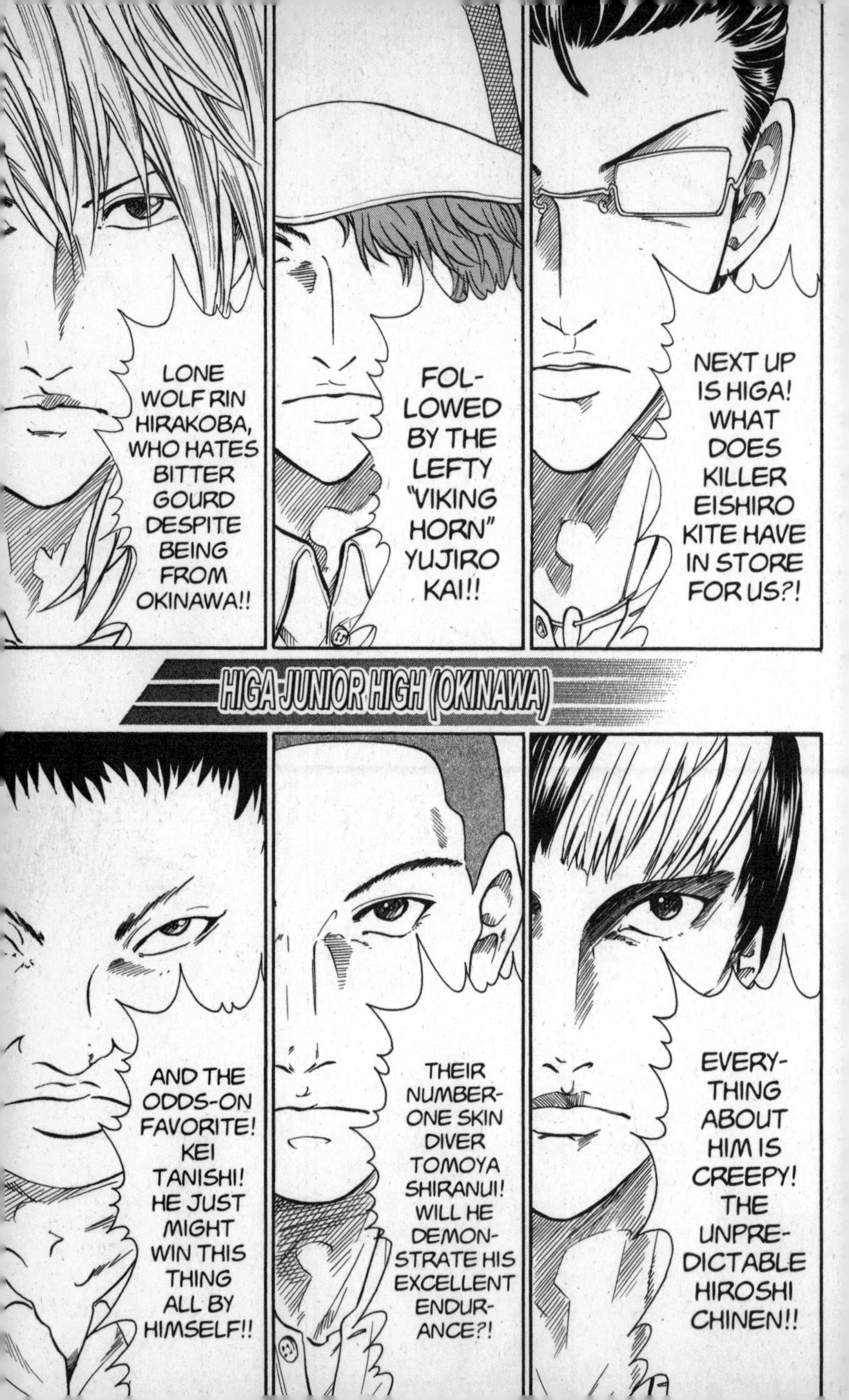
NEXT UP IS HIGA! WHAT DOES KILLER EISHIRO KITE HAVE IN STORE FOR US?!
FOL-LOWED BY THE LEFTY "VIKING HORN" YUJIRO KAI!!
LONE WOLF RIN HIRAKOBA, WHO HATES BITTER GOURD DESPITE BEING FROM OKINAWA!!
HIGA JUNIOR HIGH (OKINAWA)
EVERY-THING ABOUT HIM IS CREEPY! THE UNPRE-DICTABLE HIROSHI CHINEN!!
THEIR NUMBER-ONE SKIN DIVER TOMOYA SHIRANUI! WILL HE DEMON-STRATE HIS EXCELLENT ENDUR-ANCE?!
AND THE ODDS-ON FAVORITE! KEI TANISHI! HE JUST MIGHT WIN THIS THING ALL BY HIMSELF!!

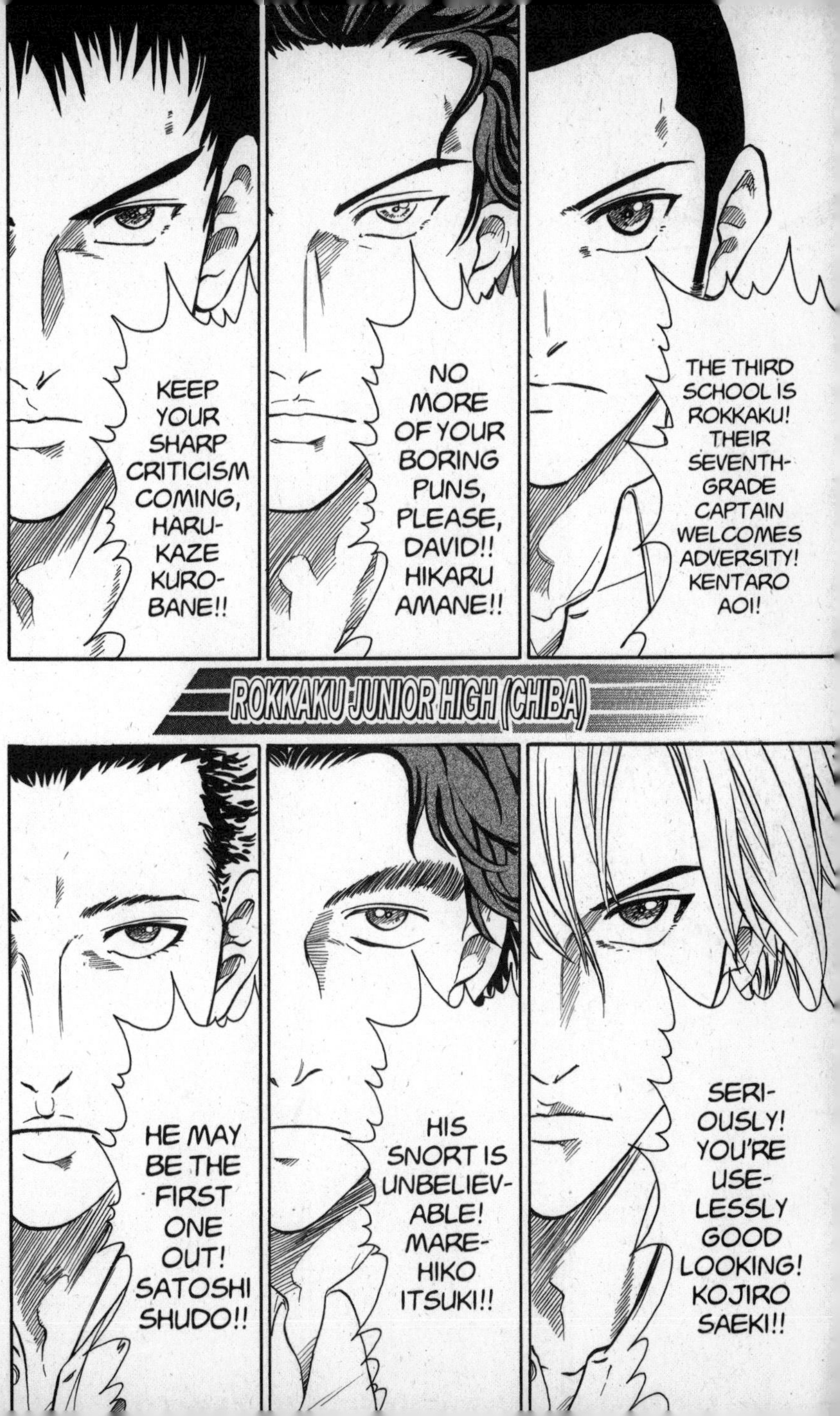
THE THIRD SCHOOL IS ROKKAKU! THEIR SEVENTH-GRADE CAPTAIN WELCOMES ADVERSITY! KENTARO AOI!
NO MORE OF YOUR BORING PUNS, PLEASE, DAVID!! HIKARU AMANE!!
KEEP YOUR SHARP CRITICISM COMING, HARU-KAZE KURO-BANE!!
ROKKAKU JUNIOR HIGH (CHIBA)
SERI-OUSLY! YOU'RE USE-LESSLY GOOD LOOKING! KOJIRO SAEKI!!
HIS SNORT IS UNBELIEV-ABLE! MARE-HIKO ITSUKI!!
HE MAY BE THE FIRST ONE OUT! SATOSHI SHUDO!!

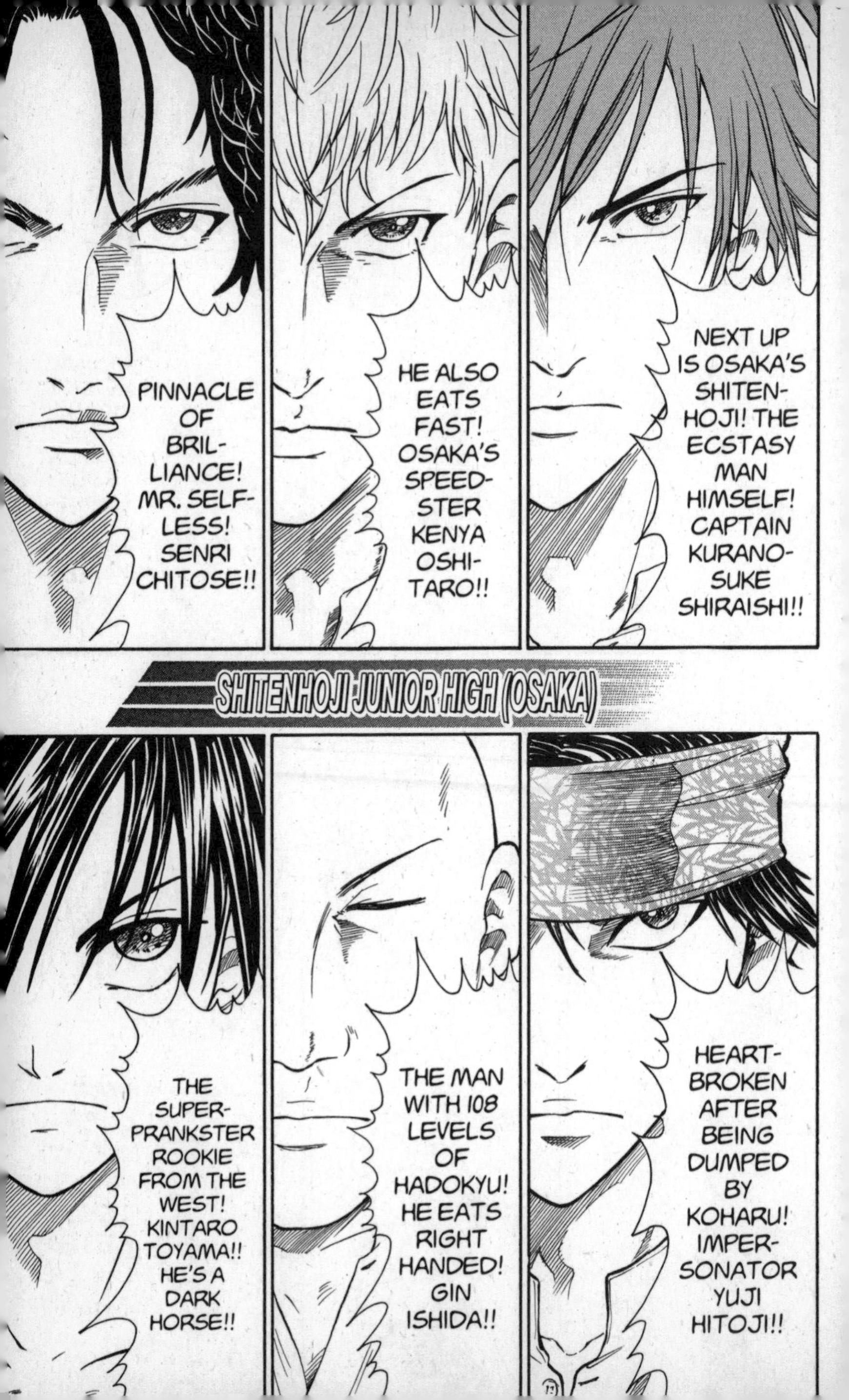
NEXT UP IS OSAKA'S SHITEN-HOJI! THE ECSTASY MAN HIMSELF! CAPTAIN KURANO-SUKE SHIRAISHI!!
HE ALSO EATS FAST! OSAKA'S SPEED-STER KENYA OSHI-TARO!!
PINNACLE OF BRIL-LIANCE! MR. SELF-LESS! SENRI CHITOSE!!
SHITENHOJI JUNIOR HIGH (OSAKA)
HEART-BROKEN AFTER BEING DUMPED BY KOHARU! IMPER-SONATOR YUJI HITOJI!!
THE MAN WITH 108 LEVELS OF HADOKYU! HE EATS RIGHT HANDED! GIN ISHIDA!!
THE SUPER-PRANKSTER ROOKIE FROM THE WEST! KINTARO TOYAMA!! HE'S A DARK HORSE!!

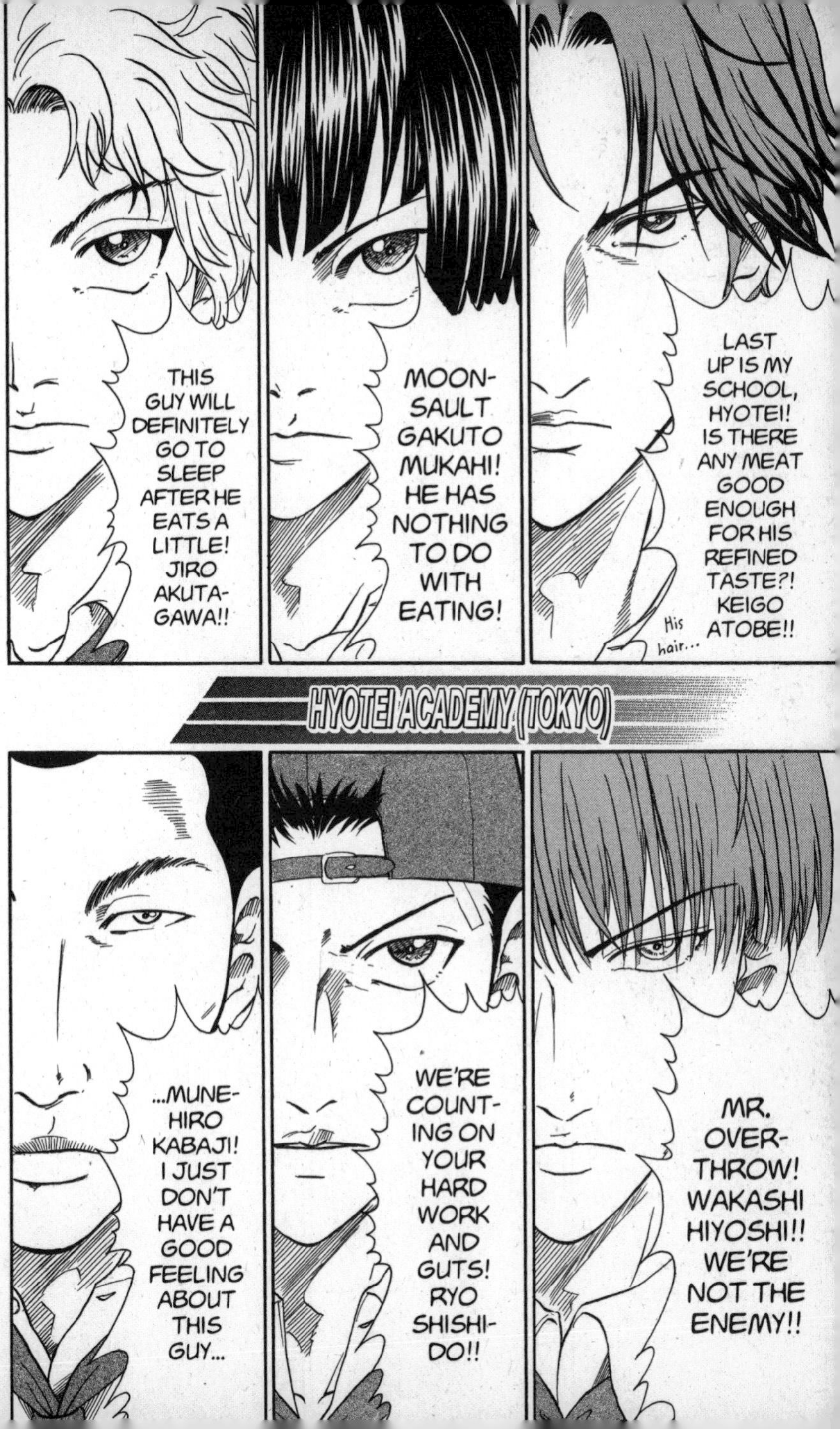
LAST UP IS MY SCHOOL, HYOTEI!! IS THERE ANY MEAT GOOD ENOUGH FOR HIS REFINED TASTE?! KEIGO ATOBE!!
His hair...
MOON-SAULT GAKUTO MUKAHI! HE HAS NOTHING TO DO WITH EATING!
THIS GUY WILL DEFINITELY GO TO SLEEP AFTER HE EATS A LITTLE! JIRO AKUTA-GAWA!!
HYOTEI ACADEMY (TOKYO)
MR. OVER-THROW! WAKASHI HIYOSHI!! WE'RE NOT THE ENEMY!!
WE'RE COUNT-ING ON YOUR HARD WORK AND GUTS! RYO SHISHI-DO!!
...MUNE-HIRO KABAJI! I JUST DON'T HAVE A GOOD FEELING ABOUT THIS GUY...

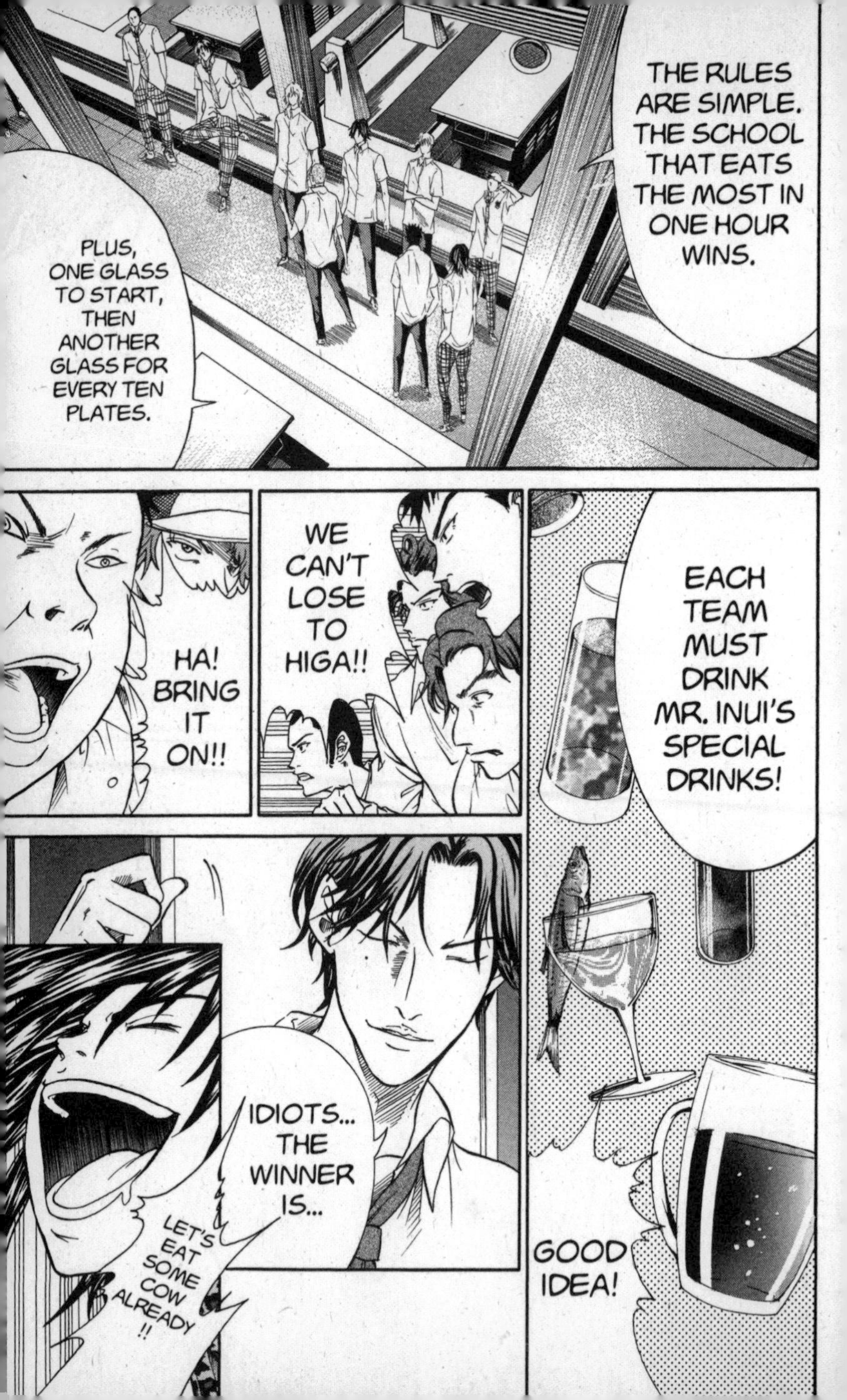
THE RULES ARE SIMPLE. THE SCHOOL THAT EATS THE MOST IN ONE HOUR WINS.
PLUS, ONE GLASS TO START, THEN ANOTHER GLASS FOR EVERY TEN PLATES.
EACH TEAM MUST DRINK MR. INUI'S SPECIAL DRINKS!
GOOD IDEA!
WE CAN'T LOSE TO HIGA!!
HA! BRING IT ON!!
IDIOTS... THE WINNER IS...
LET'S EAT SOME COW ALREADY!!

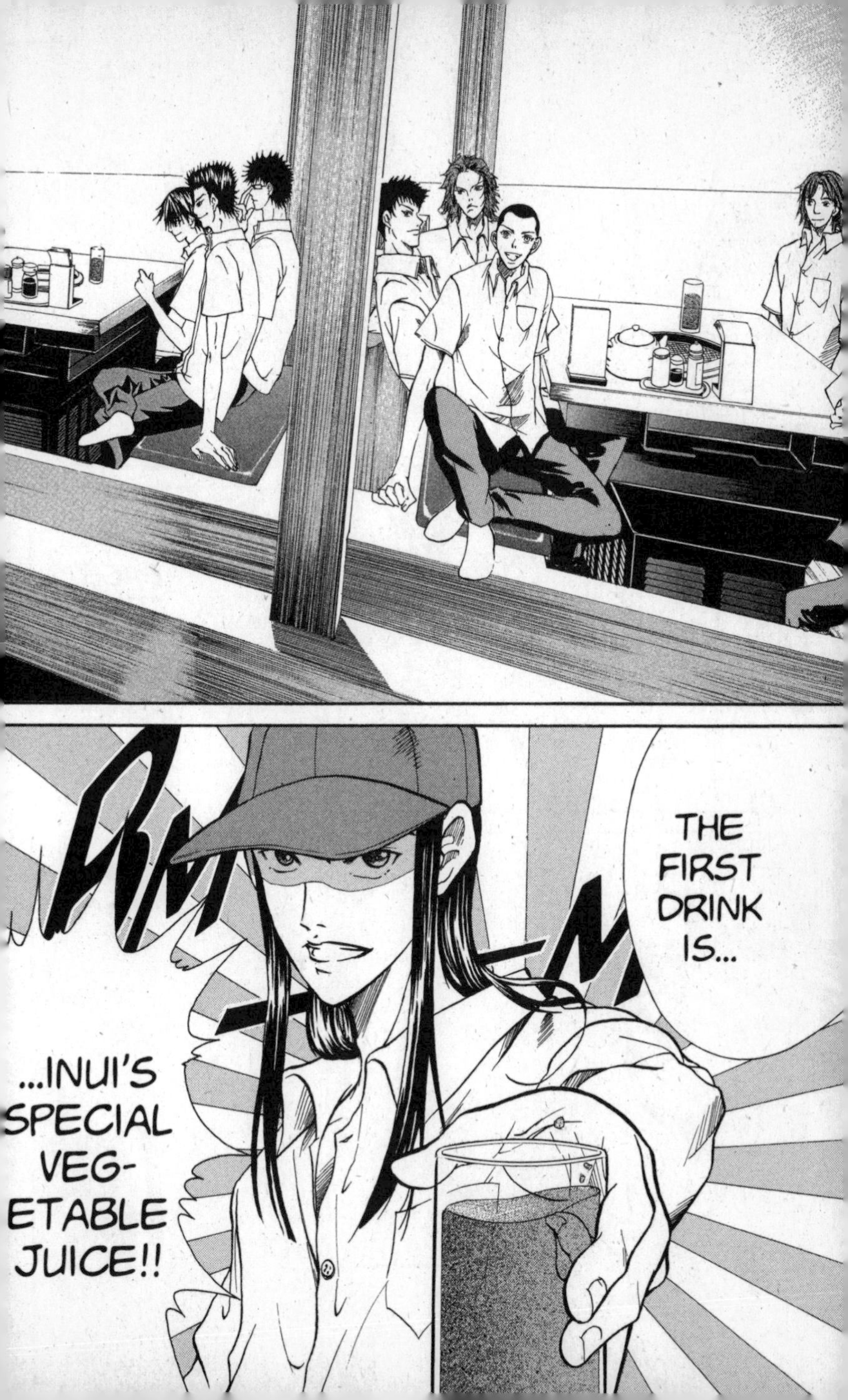
THE FIRST DRINK IS...
...INUI'S SPECIAL VEG-ETABLE JUICE!!

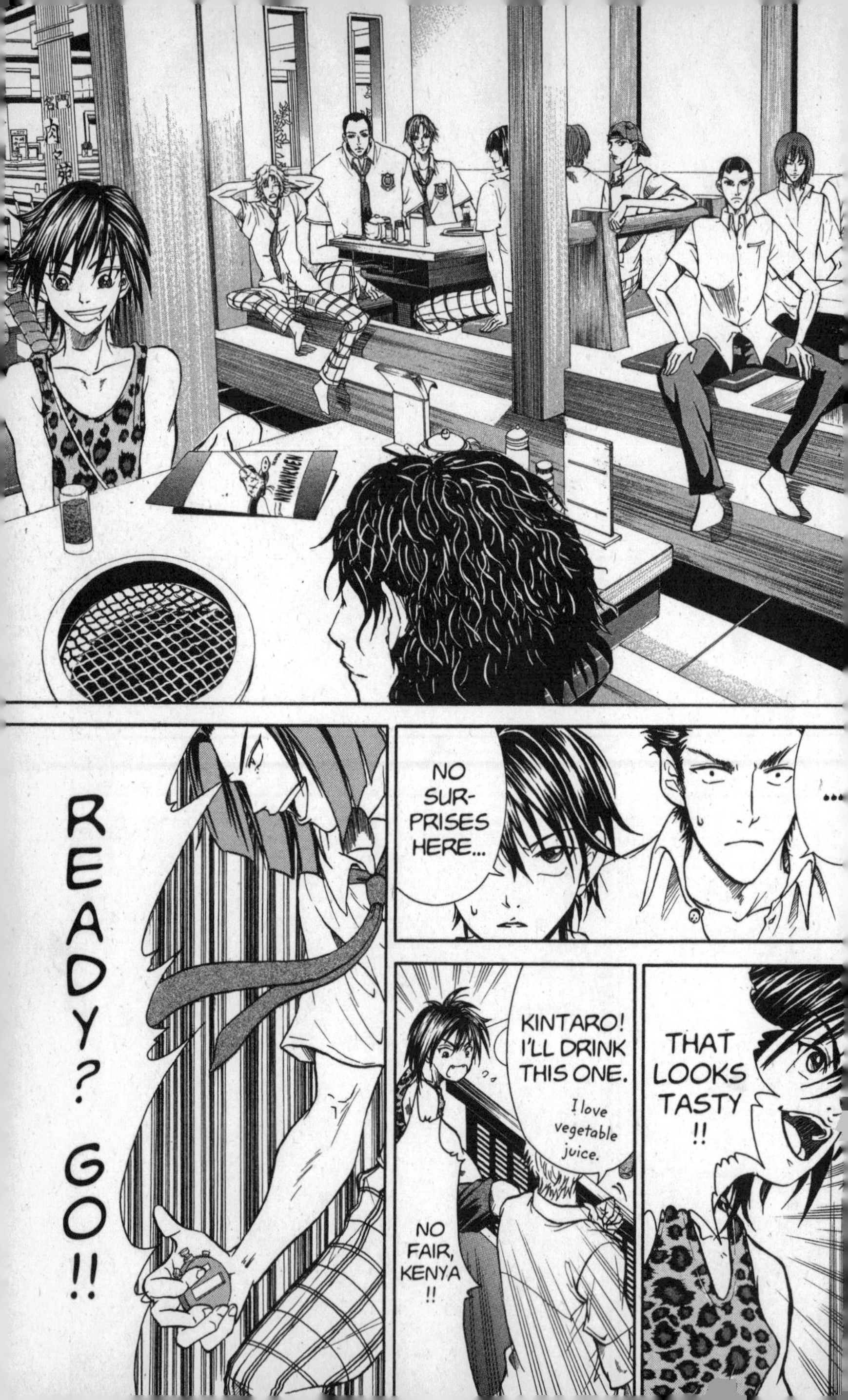
...
NO SUR-PRISES HERE...
THAT LOOKS TASTY!!
KINTARO! I'LL DRINK THIS ONE.
I love vegetable juice.
NO FAIR, KENYA!!
READY? GO!!

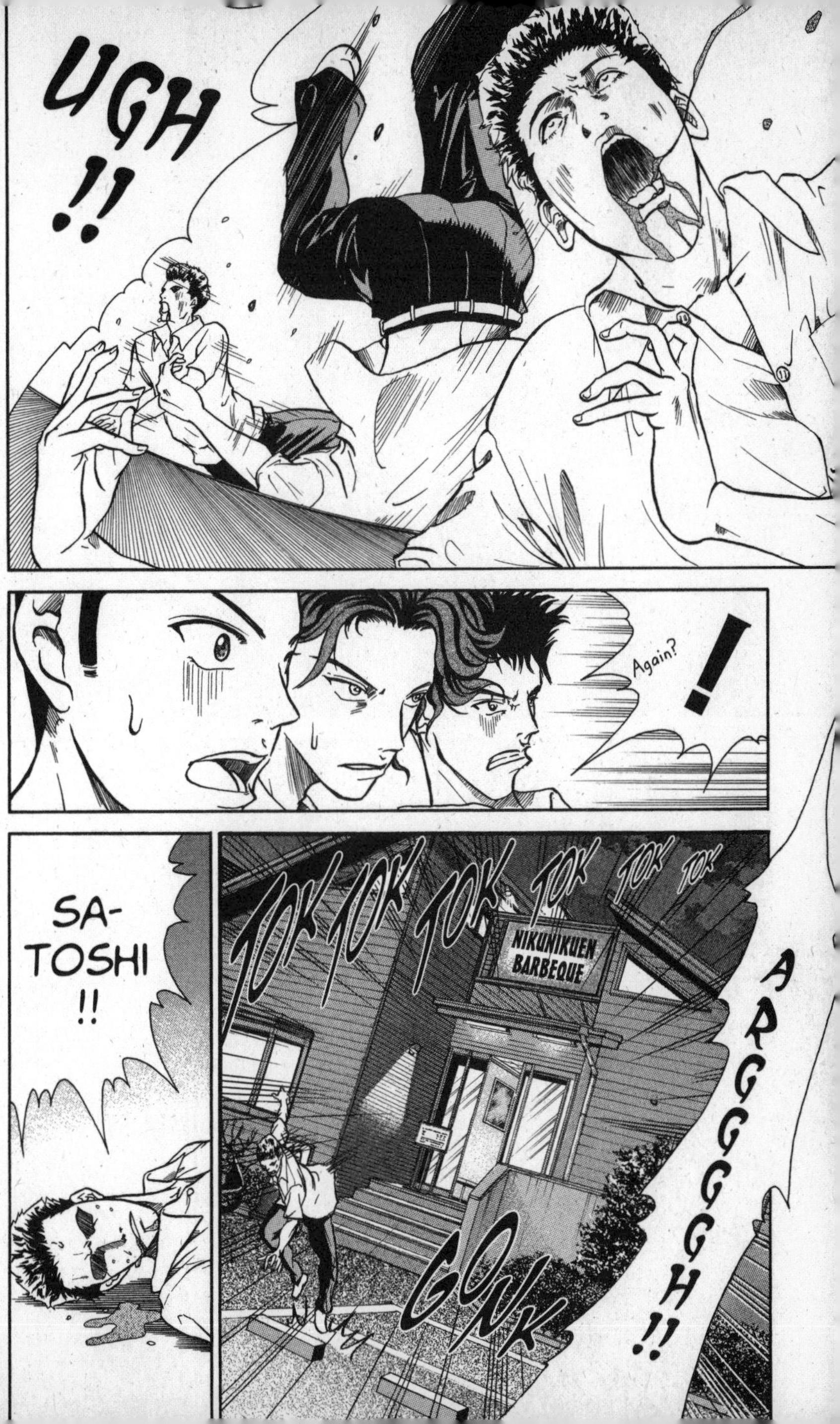
UGH!!
Again?
!
TOK TOK TOK TOK TOK TOK
NIKUNIKUEN BARBEQUE
ARRGGGGGH!!
GONK
SA-TOSHI!!

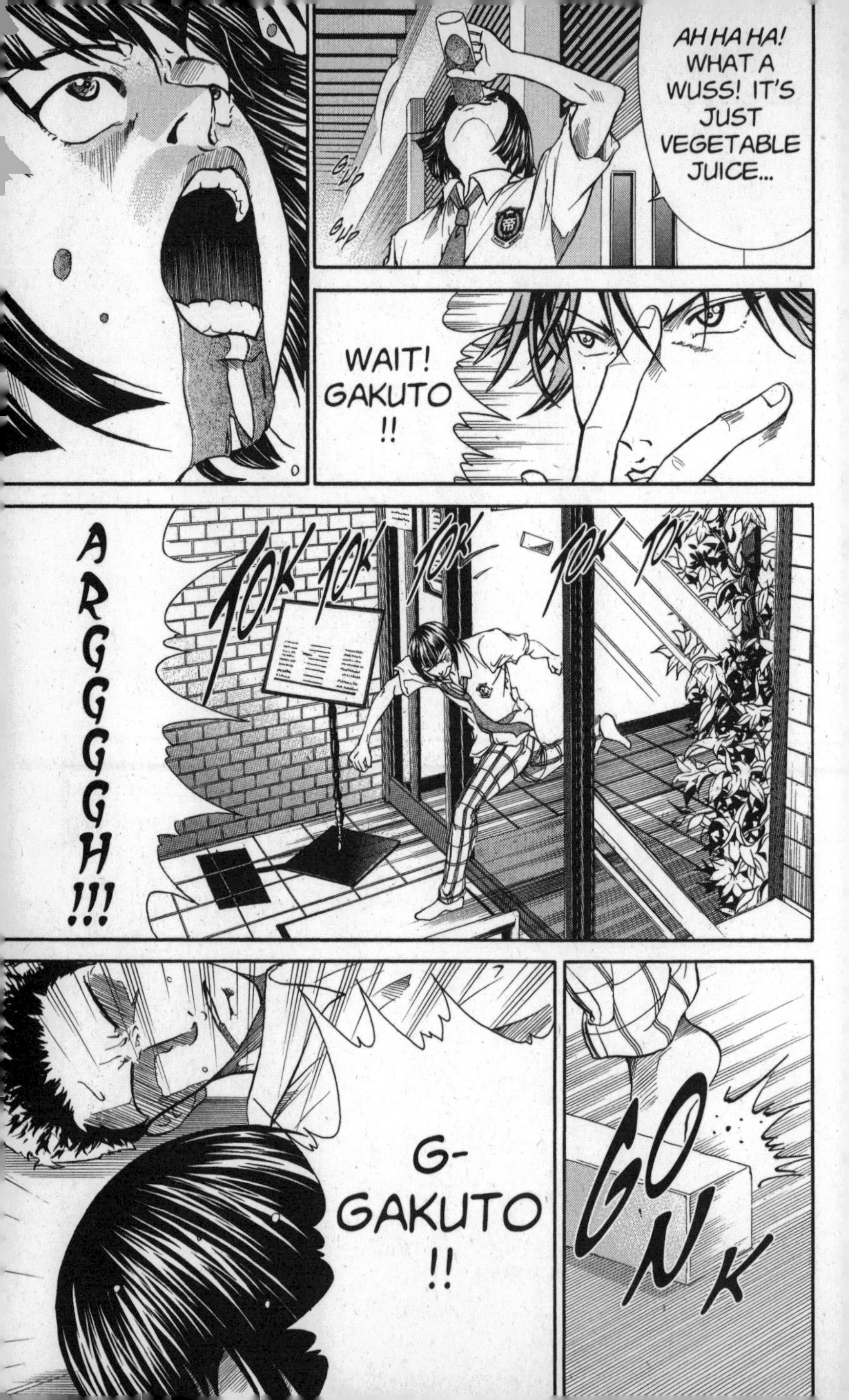
AH HA HA! WHAT A WUSS! IT'S JUST VEGETABLE JUICE...
GLUP
GLUP
WAIT! GAKUTO !!
TOK TOK TOK TOK TOK
ARRGGGGH!!!
GONK
G- GAKUTO !!

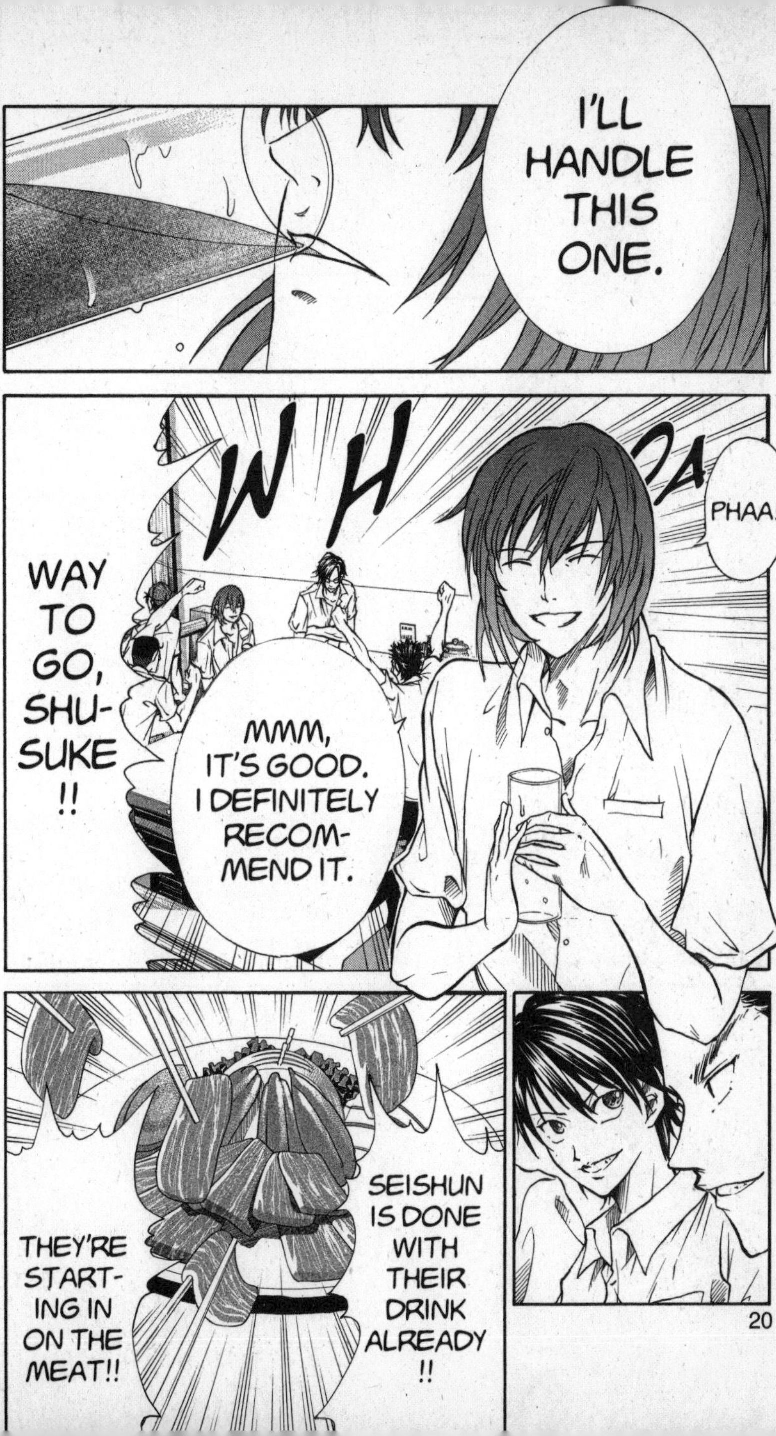
I'LL HANDLE THIS ONE.
PHAA!
WH OA
MMM, IT'S GOOD. I DEFINITELY RECOMMEND IT.
WAY TO GO, SHUSUKE!!
SEISHUN IS DONE WITH THEIR DRINK ALREADY!!
THEY'RE STARTING IN ON THE MEAT!!

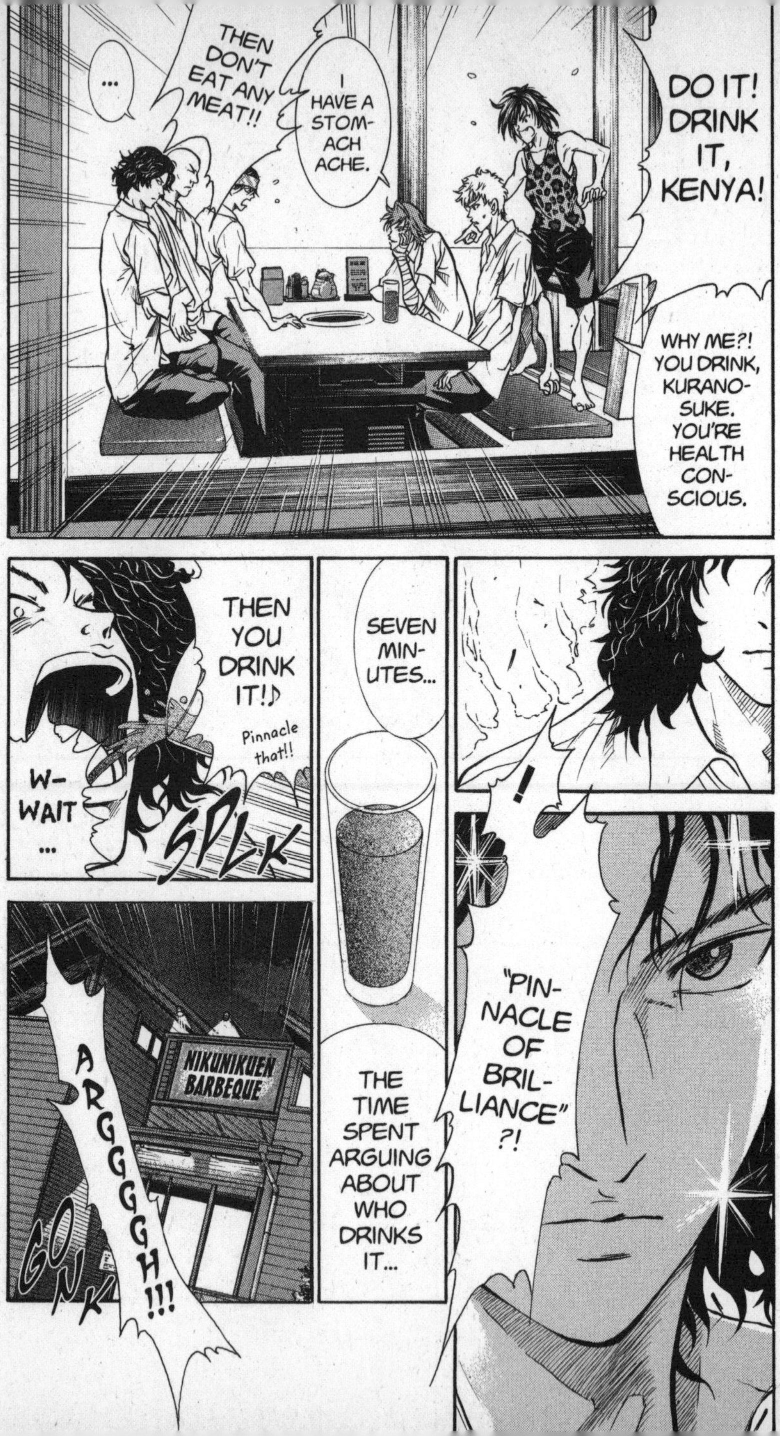
DO IT! DRINK IT, KENYA!
WHY ME?! YOU DRINK, KURANOSUKE. YOU'RE HEALTH CONSCIOUS.
I HAVE A STOMACH ACHE.
THEN DON'T EAT ANY MEAT!!
...
!
"PINNACLE OF BRILLIANCE"?!
SEVEN MINUTES...
THE TIME SPENT ARGUING ABOUT WHO DRINKS IT...
THEN YOU DRINK IT!♪
Pinnacle that!!
W-WAIT...
SPLK
NIKUNIKUEN BARBEQUE
ARGGGGH!!!
GONK

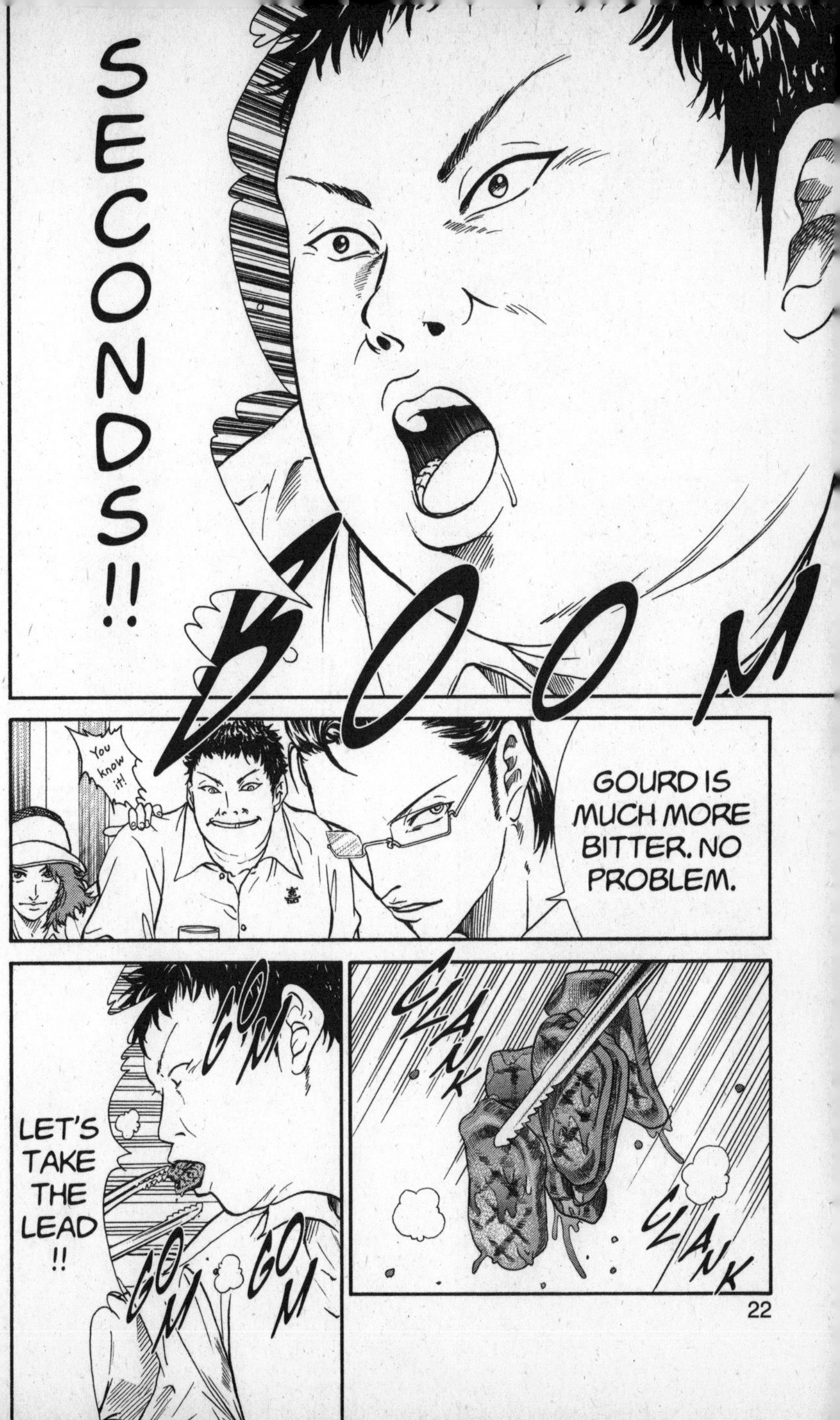
SECONDS!!
BOOM
GOURD IS MUCH MORE BITTER. NO PROBLEM.
You know it!
CLANK
CLANK
GOM
GOM
LET'S TAKE THE LEAD!!
GOM
GOM

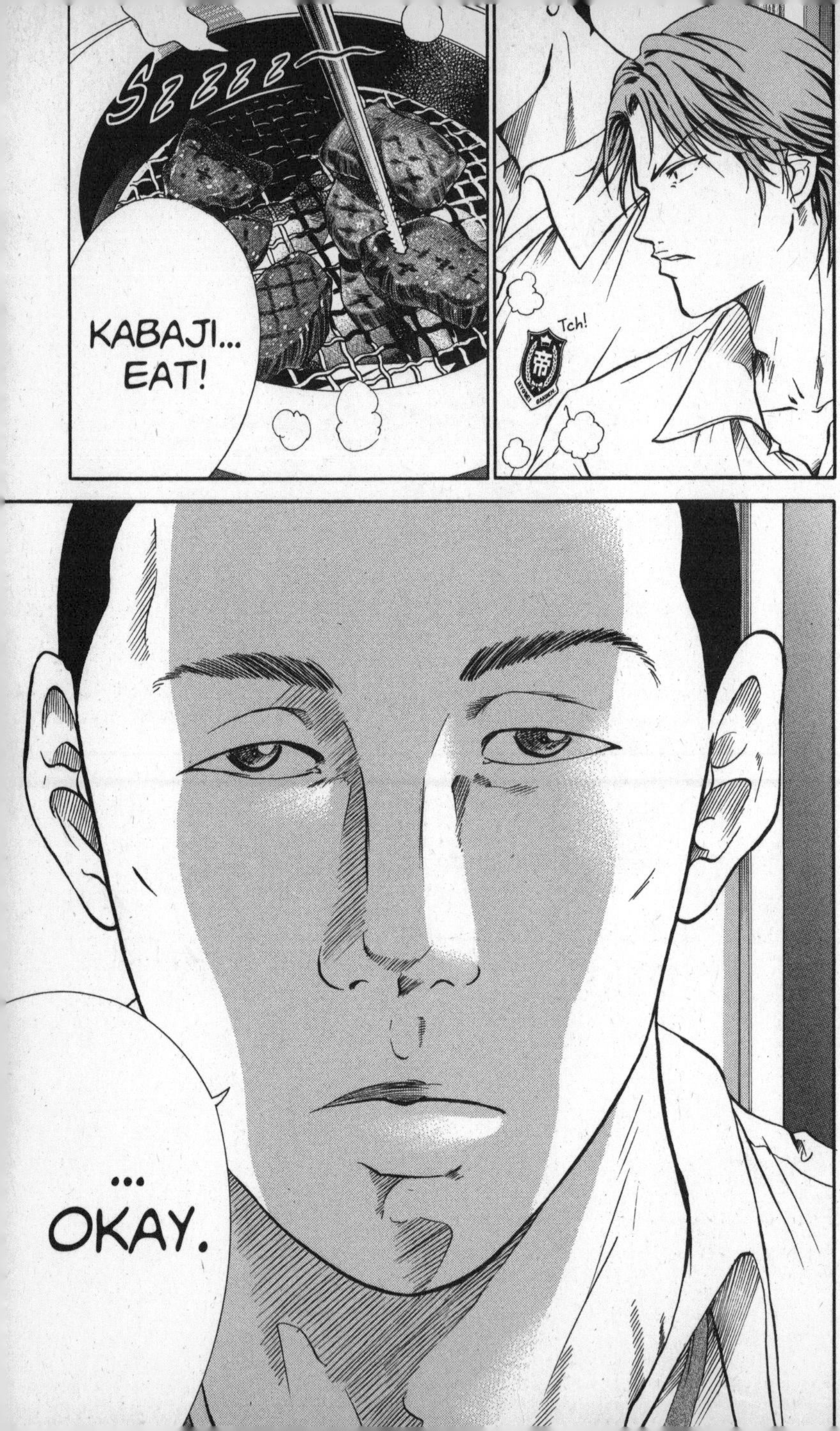
Tch!
Szzzz~
KABAJI... EAT!
... OKAY.

テニスの王子様

THE PRINCE OF TENNIS

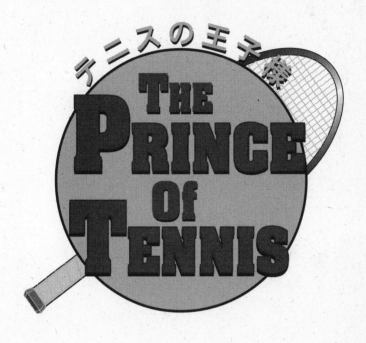

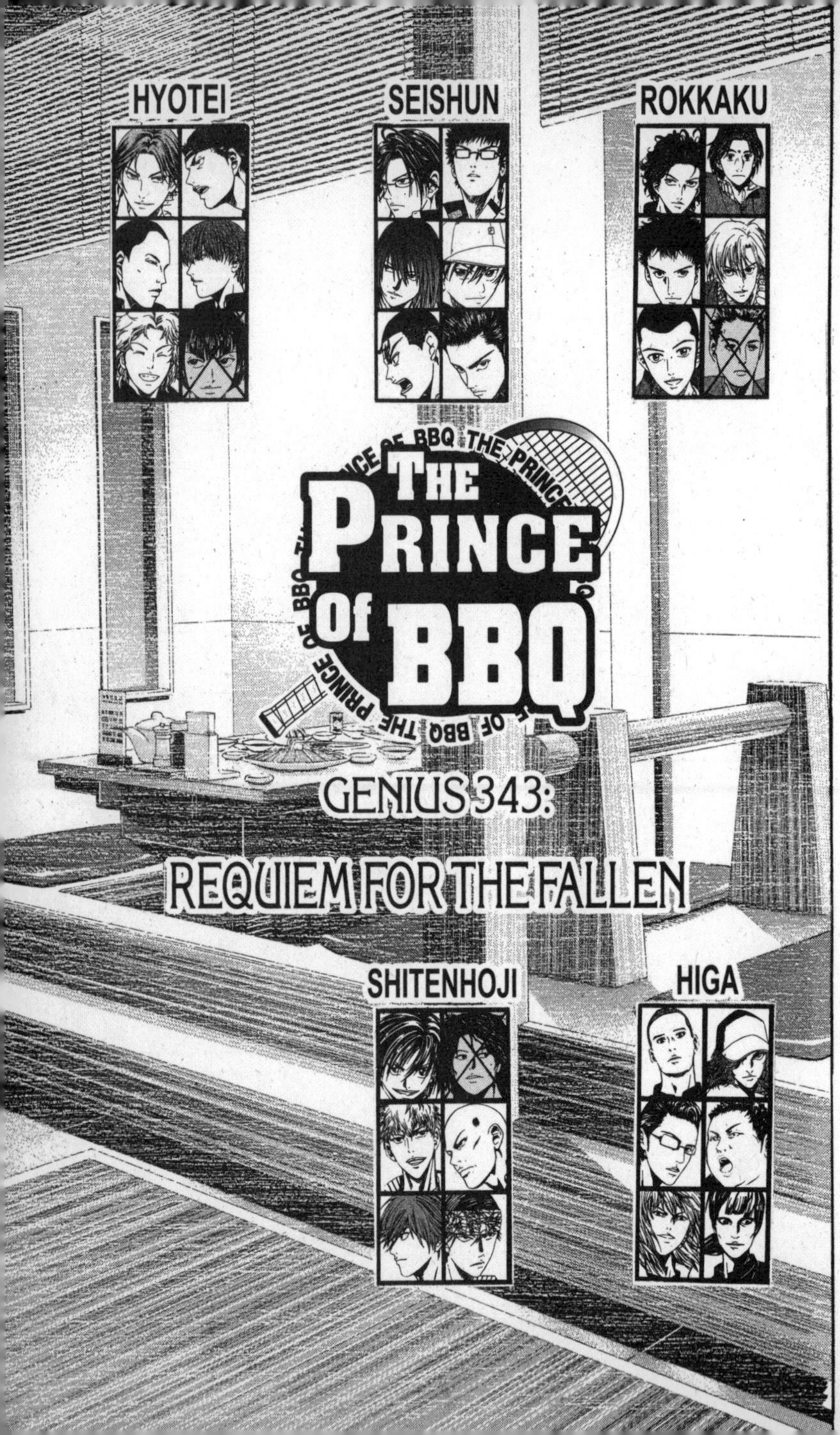
HYOTEI
SEISHUN
ROKKAKU
THE PRINCE OF BBQ THE PRINCE OF BBQ THE PRINCE OF BBQ THE PRINCE
THE PRINCE of BBQ
GENIUS 343:
REQUIEM FOR THE FALLEN
SHITENHOJI
HIGA

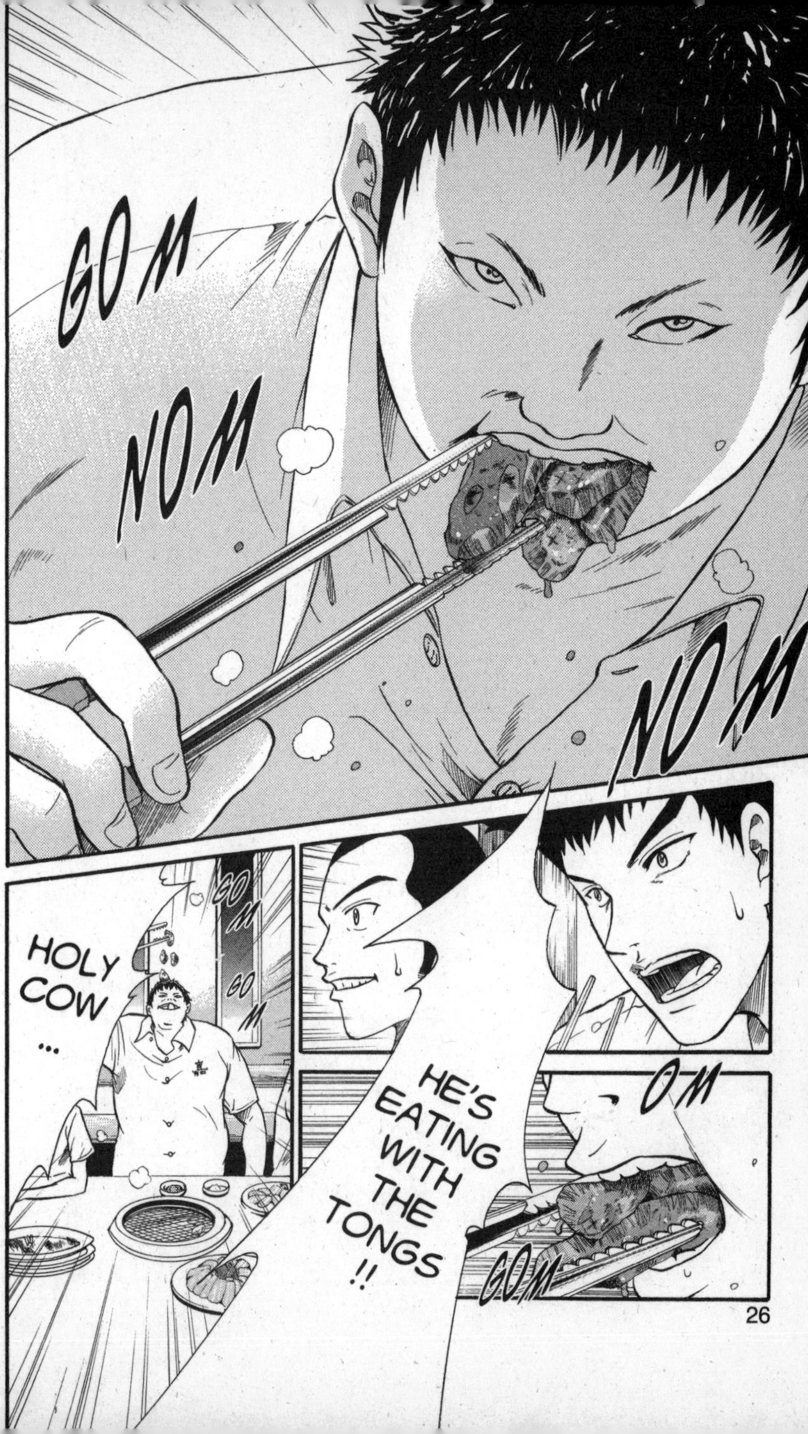
GOM
NOM
NOM
HE'S EATING WITH THE TONGS!!
OM
GOM
GOM
GOM
HOLY COW...

READ THIS WAY

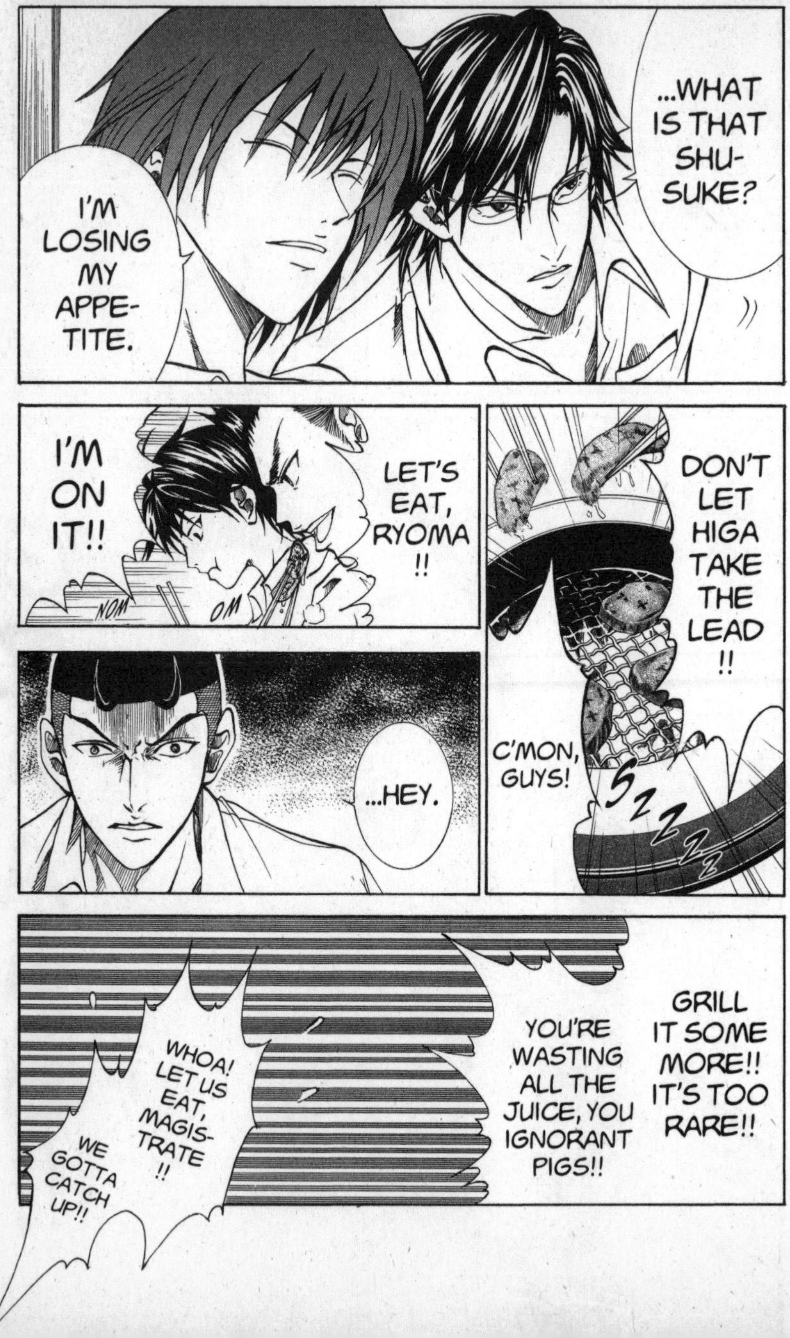
...WHAT IS THAT SHUSUKE?
I'M LOSING MY APPETITE.
DON'T LET HIGA TAKE THE LEAD!!
C'MON, GUYS!
SZZZZZ
LET'S EAT, RYOMA!!
I'M ON IT!!
NOM OM
...HEY.
GRILL IT SOME MORE!! IT'S TOO RARE!!
YOU'RE WASTING ALL THE JUICE, YOU IGNORANT PIGS!!
WHOA! LET US EAT, MAGISTRATE!!
WE GOTTA CATCH UP!!

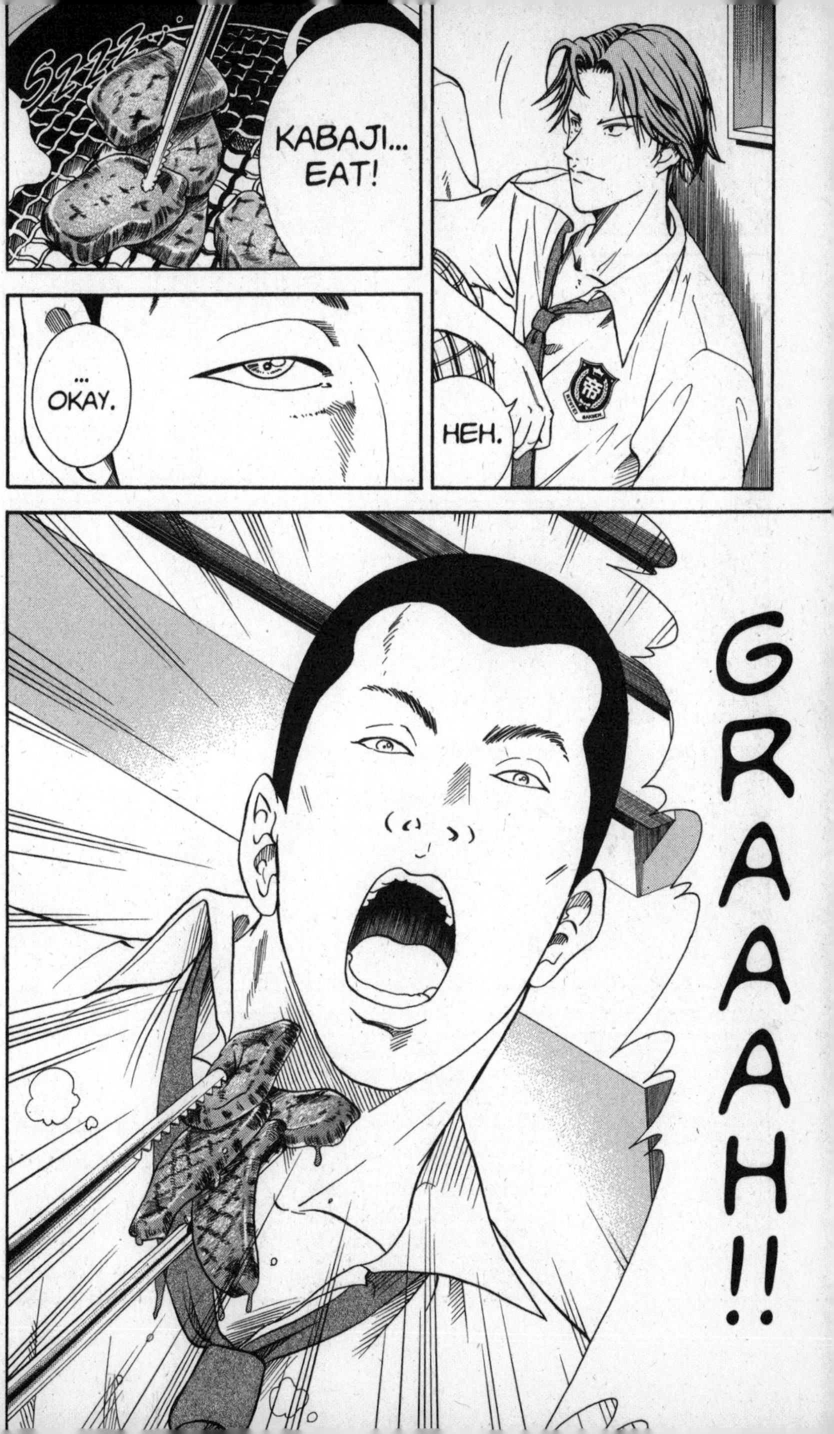
HEH.
KABAJI... EAT!
SZZZ
... OKAY.
GRAAAH!!

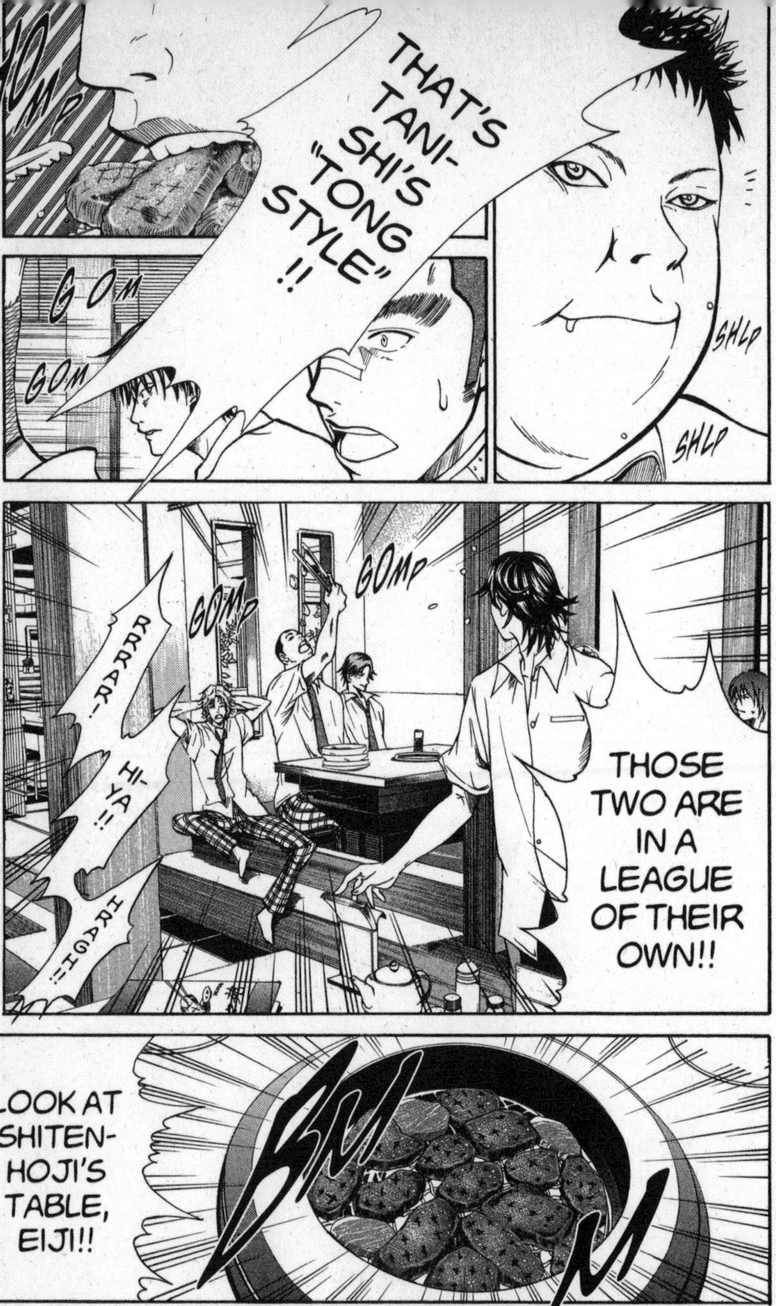
HOMP
THAT'S TANI-SHI'S "TONG STYLE"!!
SHLP
SHLP
GOM
GOM
GOMP
GOMP
THOSE TWO ARE IN A LEAGUE OF THEIR OWN!!
RRRRAR-!
HI-YA!!
HIRAGH!!
LOOK AT SHITEN-HOJI'S TABLE, EIJI!!

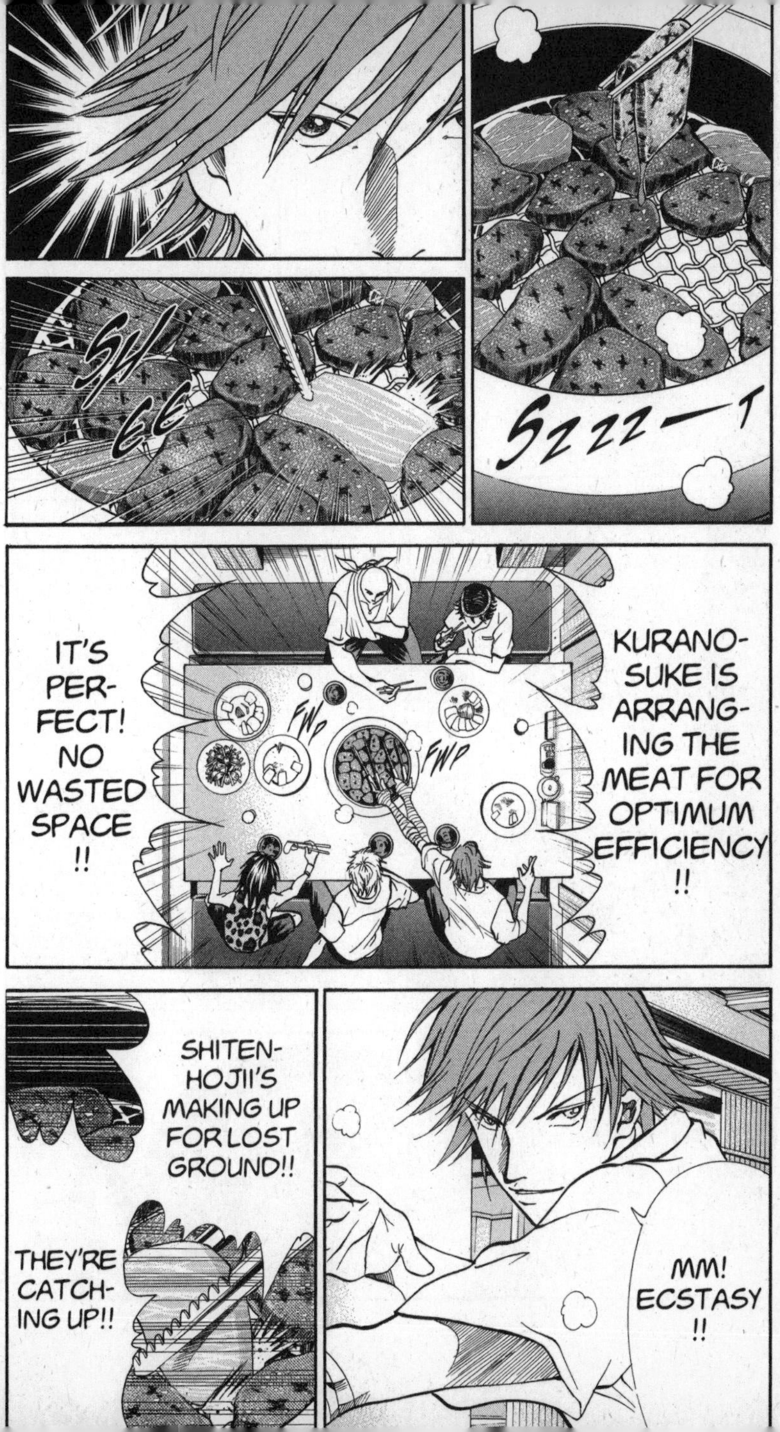
SZZZ—T
SWEE
FWP
FWP
KURANOSUKE IS ARRANGING THE MEAT FOR OPTIMUM EFFICIENCY!!
IT'S PERFECT! NO WASTED SPACE!!
MM! ECSTASY!!
SHITENHOJII'S MAKING UP FOR LOST GROUND!!
THEY'RE CATCHING UP!!

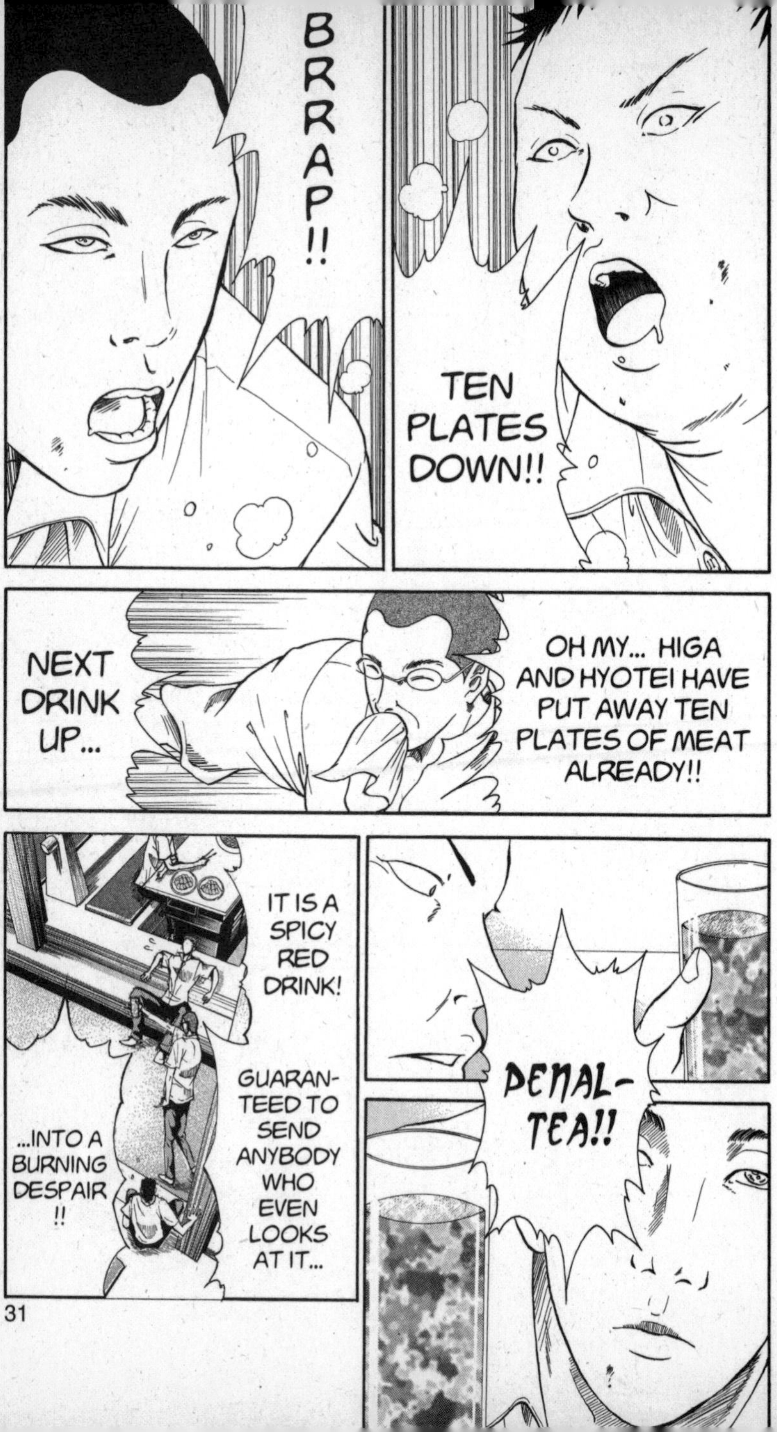
TEN PLATES DOWN!!
BRRRAP!!
OH MY... HIGA AND HYOTEI HAVE PUT AWAY TEN PLATES OF MEAT ALREADY!!
NEXT DRINK UP...
PENAL-TEA!!
IT IS A SPICY RED DRINK!
GUARAN-TEED TO SEND ANYBODY WHO EVEN LOOKS AT IT...
...INTO A BURNING DESPAIR!!

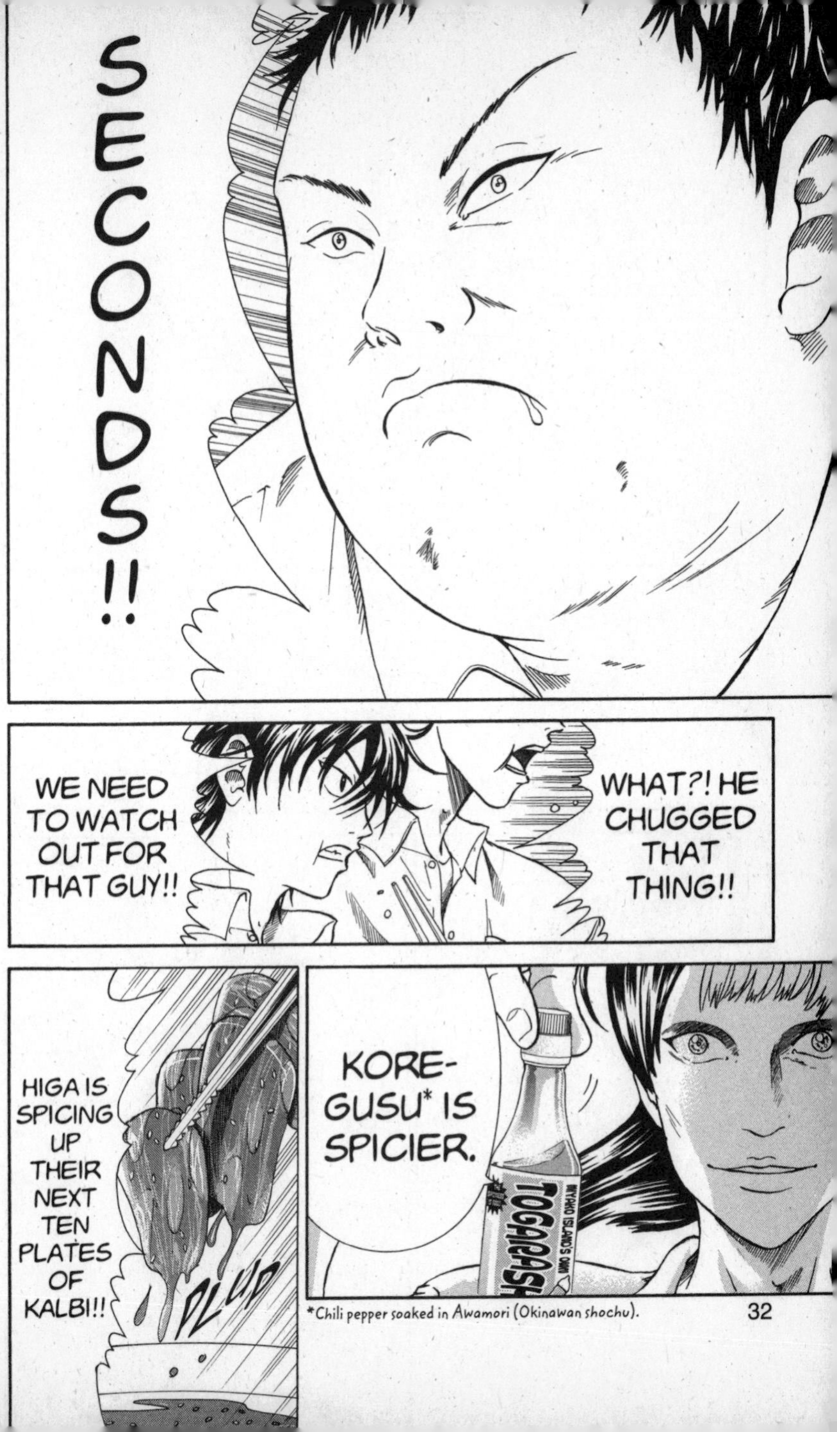
SECONDS!!
WHAT?! HE CHUGGED THAT THING!!
WE NEED TO WATCH OUT FOR THAT GUY!!
KORE-GUSU* IS SPICIER.
MIYAKO ISLAND'S OWN
TOGARASH
HIGA IS SPICING UP THEIR NEXT TEN PLATES OF KALBI!!
PLUP

*Chili pepper soaked in Awamori (Okinawan shochu).

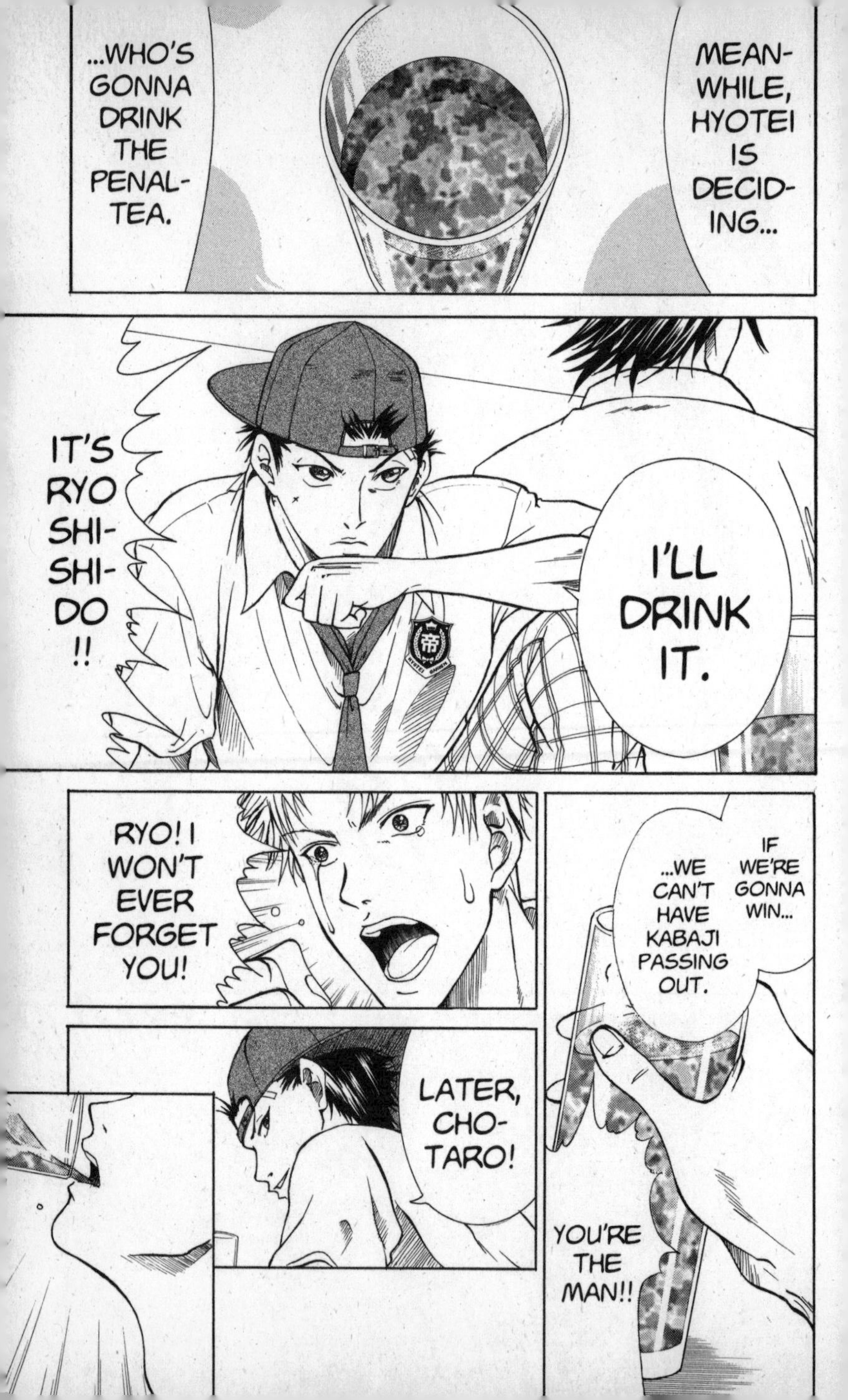
MEANWHILE, HYOTEI IS DECIDING...
...WHO'S GONNA DRINK THE PENAL-TEA.
I'LL DRINK IT.
IT'S RYO SHISHIDO!!
IF WE'RE GONNA WIN...
...WE CAN'T HAVE KABAJI PASSING OUT.
YOU'RE THE MAN!!
RYO! I WON'T EVER FORGET YOU!
LATER, CHOTARO!

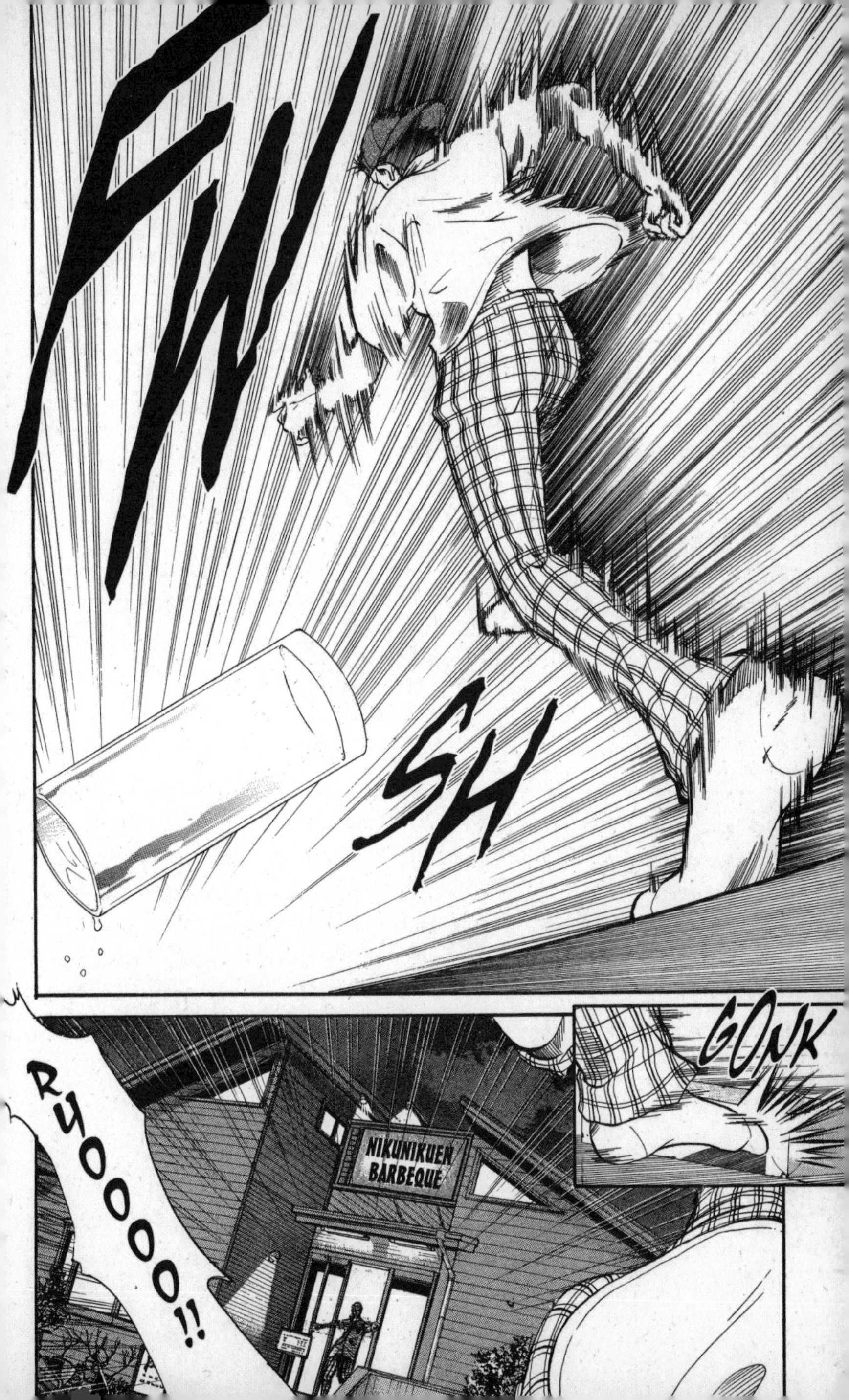
FW
SH
GONK
RUOOOOO!!
NIKUNIKUEN
BARBEQUE

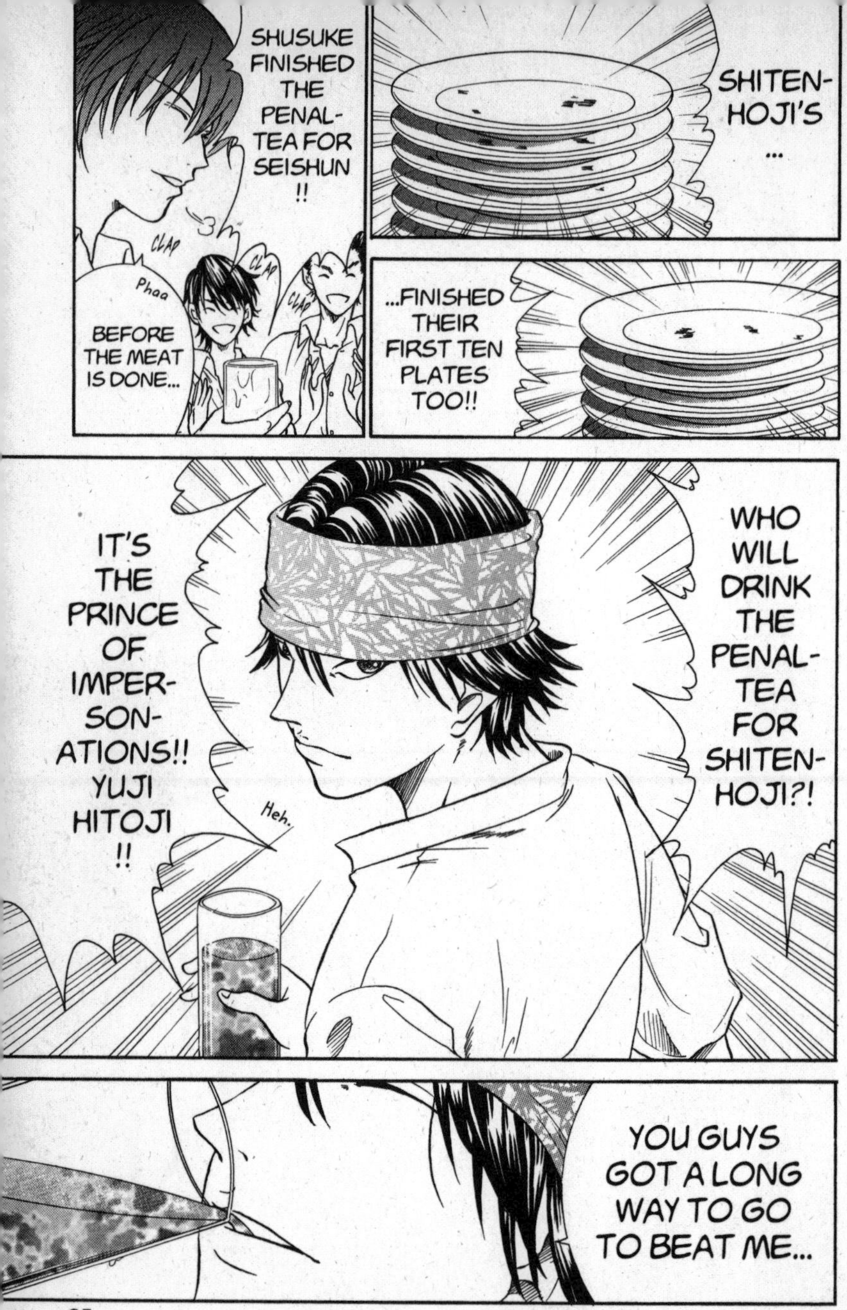
SHITEN-HOJI'S ...
...FINISHED THEIR FIRST TEN PLATES TOO!!
SHUSUKE FINISHED THE PENAL-TEA FOR SEISHUN !!
CLAP
CLAP
CLAP
Phaa
BEFORE THE MEAT IS DONE...
WHO WILL DRINK THE PENAL-TEA FOR SHITEN-HOJI?!
IT'S THE PRINCE OF IMPERSONATIONS!! YUJI HITOJI !!
Heh.
YOU GUYS GOT A LONG WAY TO GO TO BEAT ME...

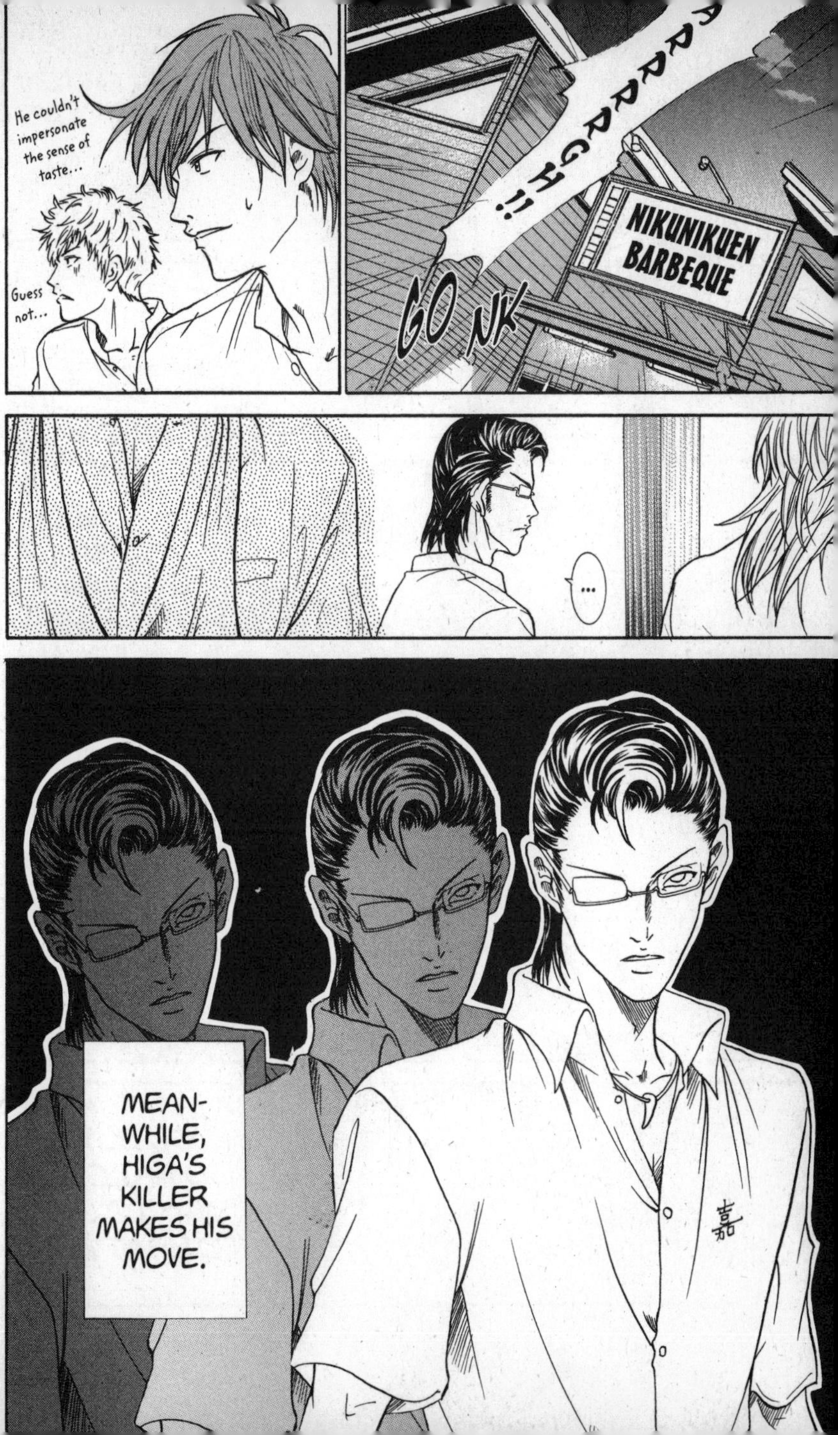
ARRRRGH!!
NIKUNIKUEN BARBEQUE
GONK
He couldn't impersonate the sense of taste...
Guess not...
...
MEAN-WHILE, HIGA'S KILLER MAKES HIS MOVE.

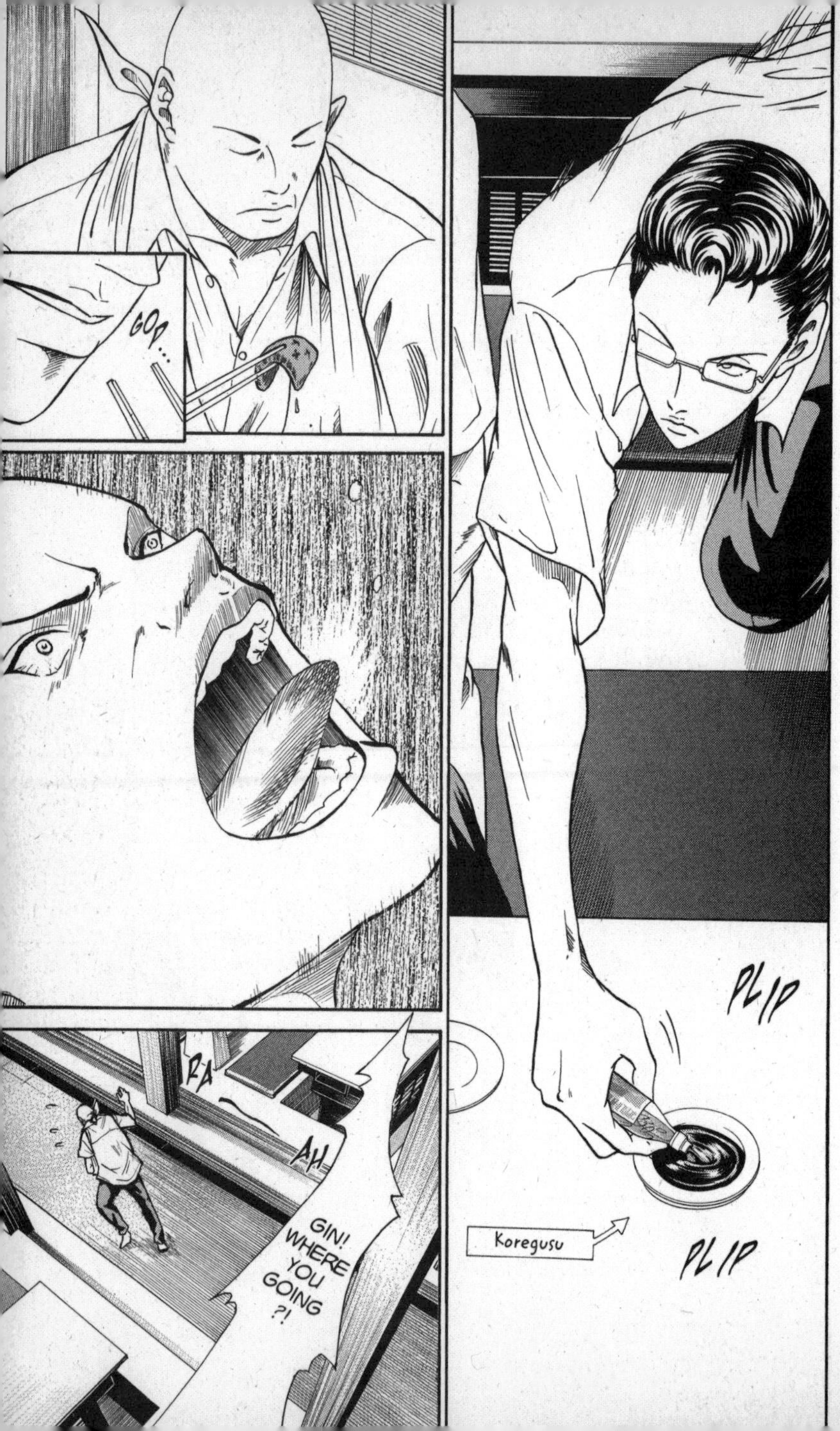
PLIP
Koregusu
PLIP
GOP...
RA
AH
GIN! WHERE YOU GOING ?!

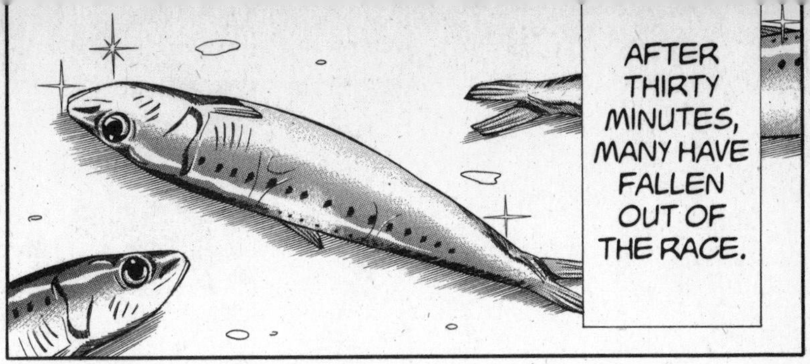
AFTER THIRTY MINUTES, MANY HAVE FALLEN OUT OF THE RACE.

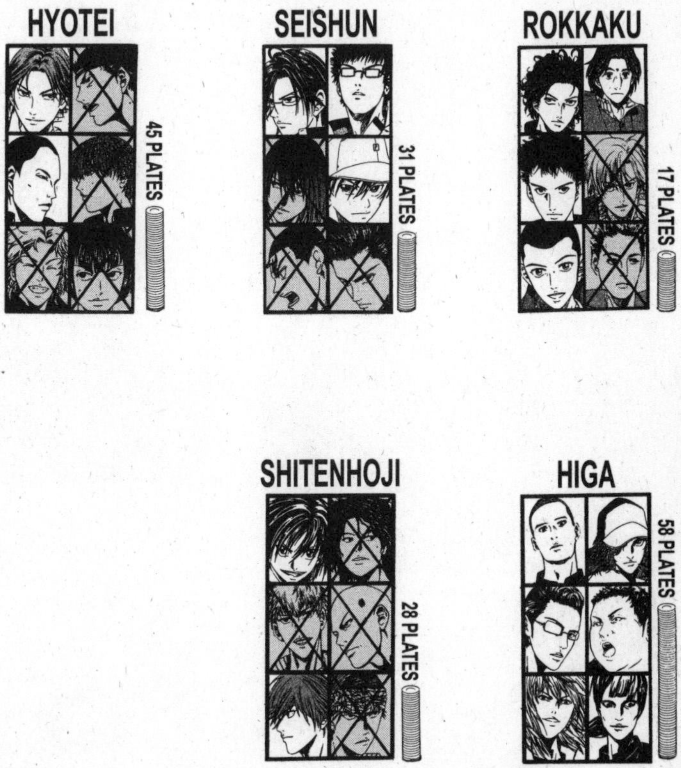
ROKKAKU
17 PLATES
SEISHUN
31 PLATES
HYOTEI
45 PLATES
HIGA
58 PLATES
SHITENHOJI
28 PLATES

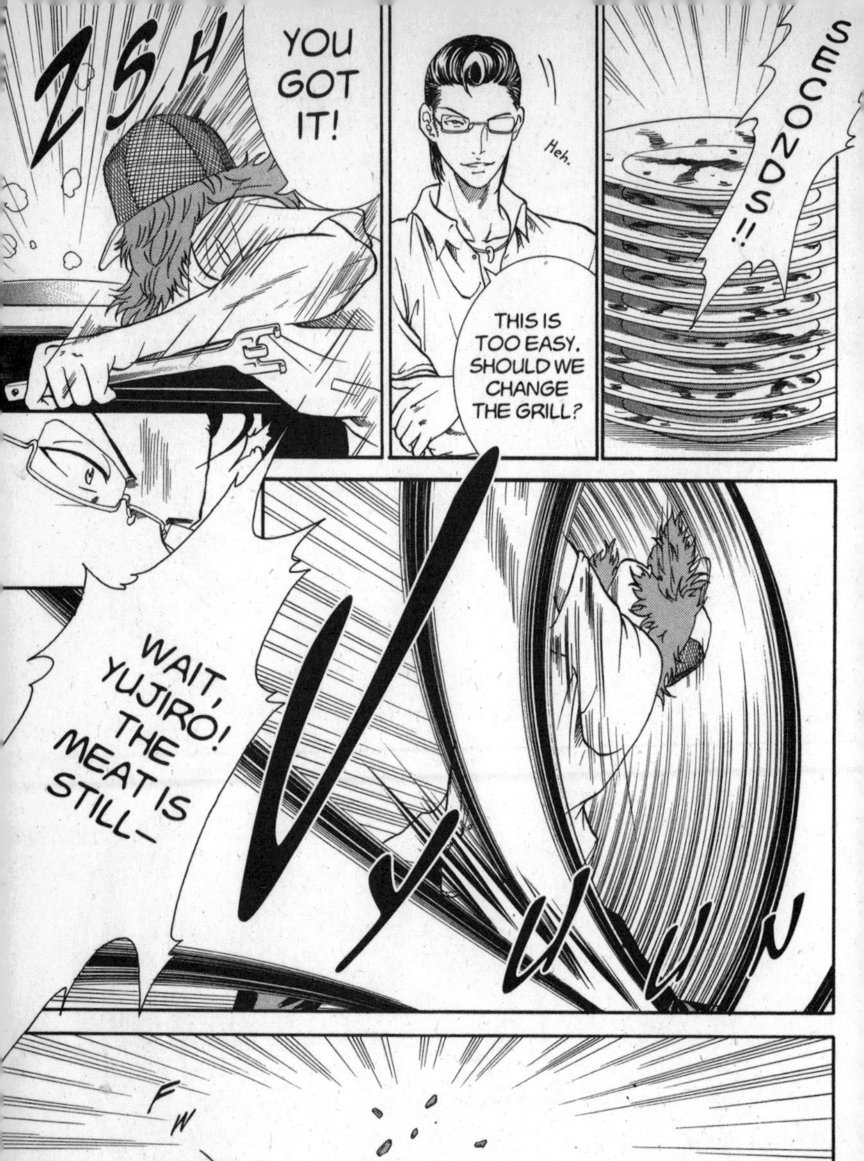
SECONDS!!
Heh.
THIS IS TOO EASY. SHOULD WE CHANGE THE GRILL?
ZSH
YOU GOT IT!
VVUUN
WAIT, YUJIRO! THE MEAT IS STILL—
FWIP

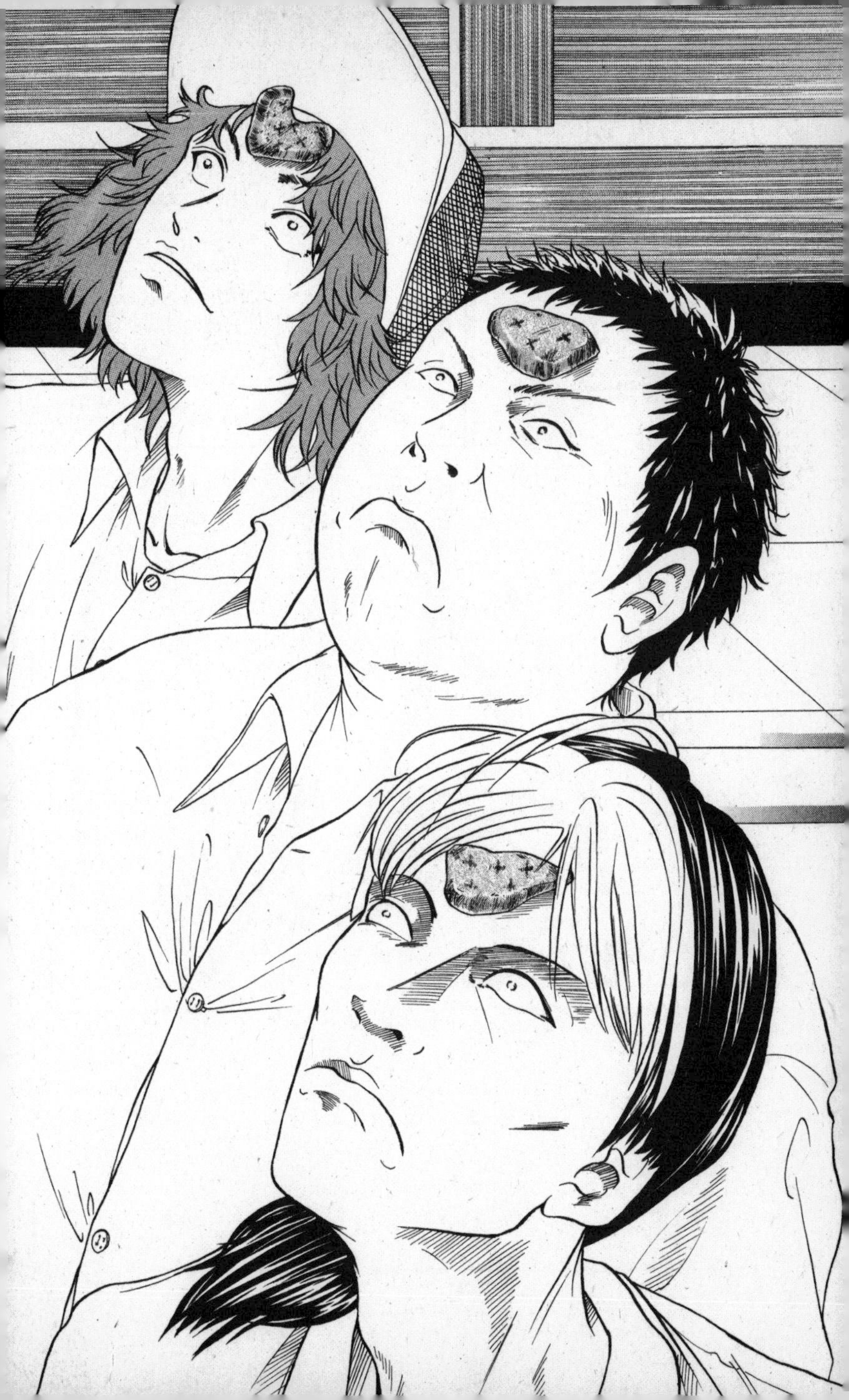

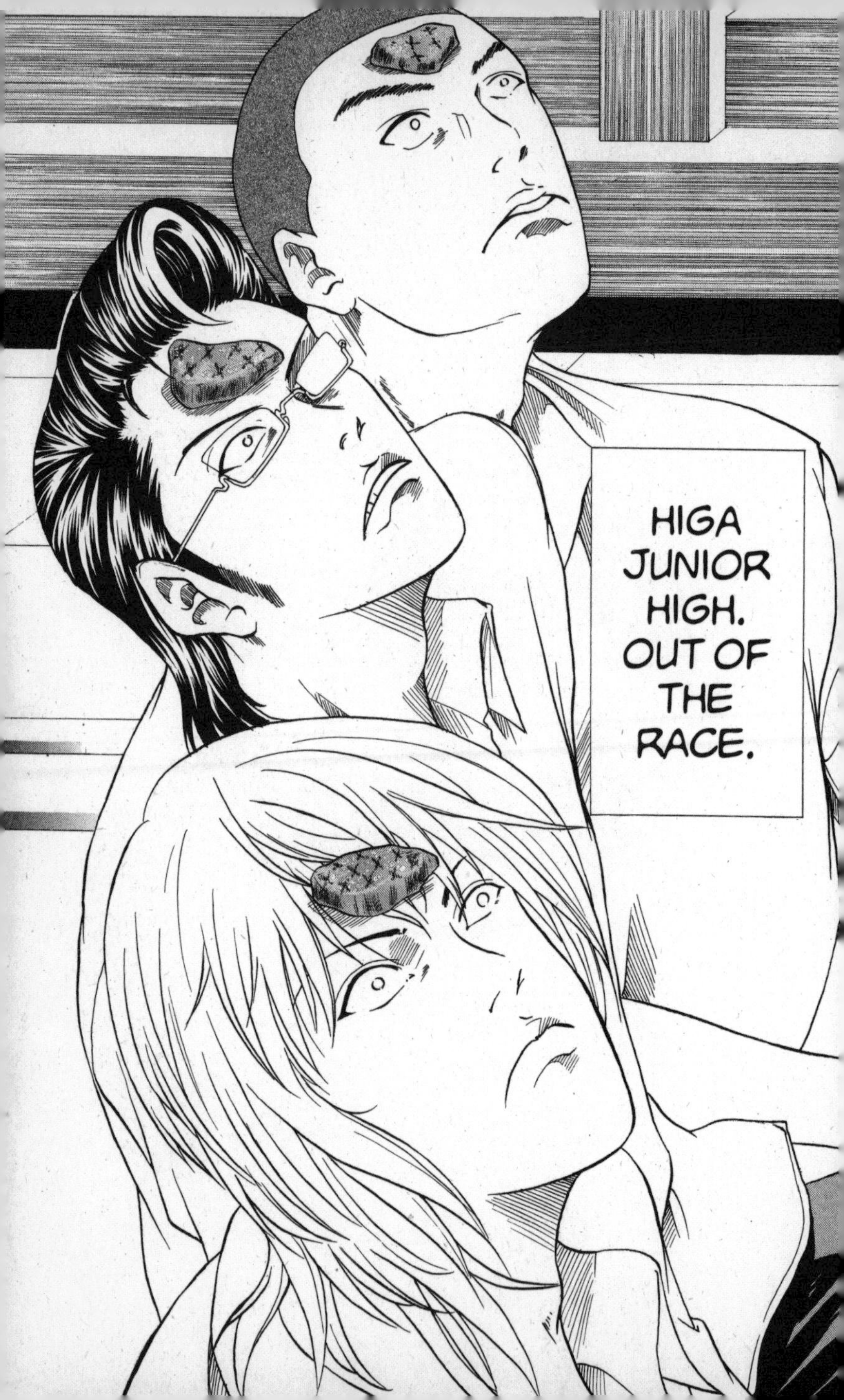
HIGA JUNIOR HIGH. OUT OF THE RACE.

テニスの王子様

THE PRINCE OF TENNIS

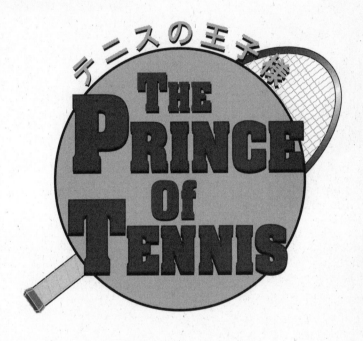

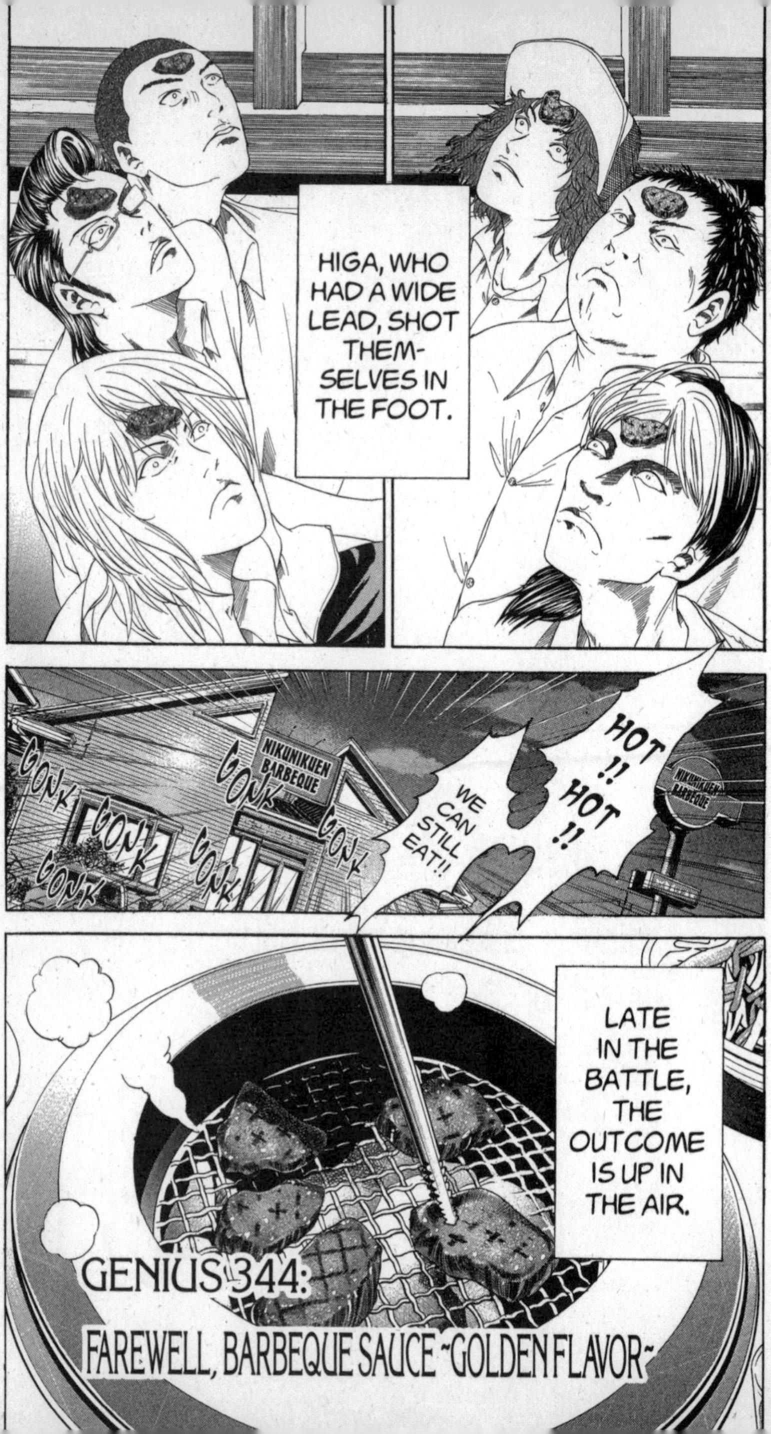
HIGA, WHO HAD A WIDE LEAD, SHOT THEM-SELVES IN THE FOOT.
NIKUNIKUEN BARBEQUE
HOT!! HOT!!
WE CAN STILL EAT!!
NIKUNIKUEN BARBEQUE
GONK GONK GONK GONK GONK GONK GONK
LATE IN THE BATTLE, THE OUTCOME IS UP IN THE AIR.
GENIUS 344:
FAREWELL, BARBEQUE SAUCE ~GOLDEN FLAVOR~

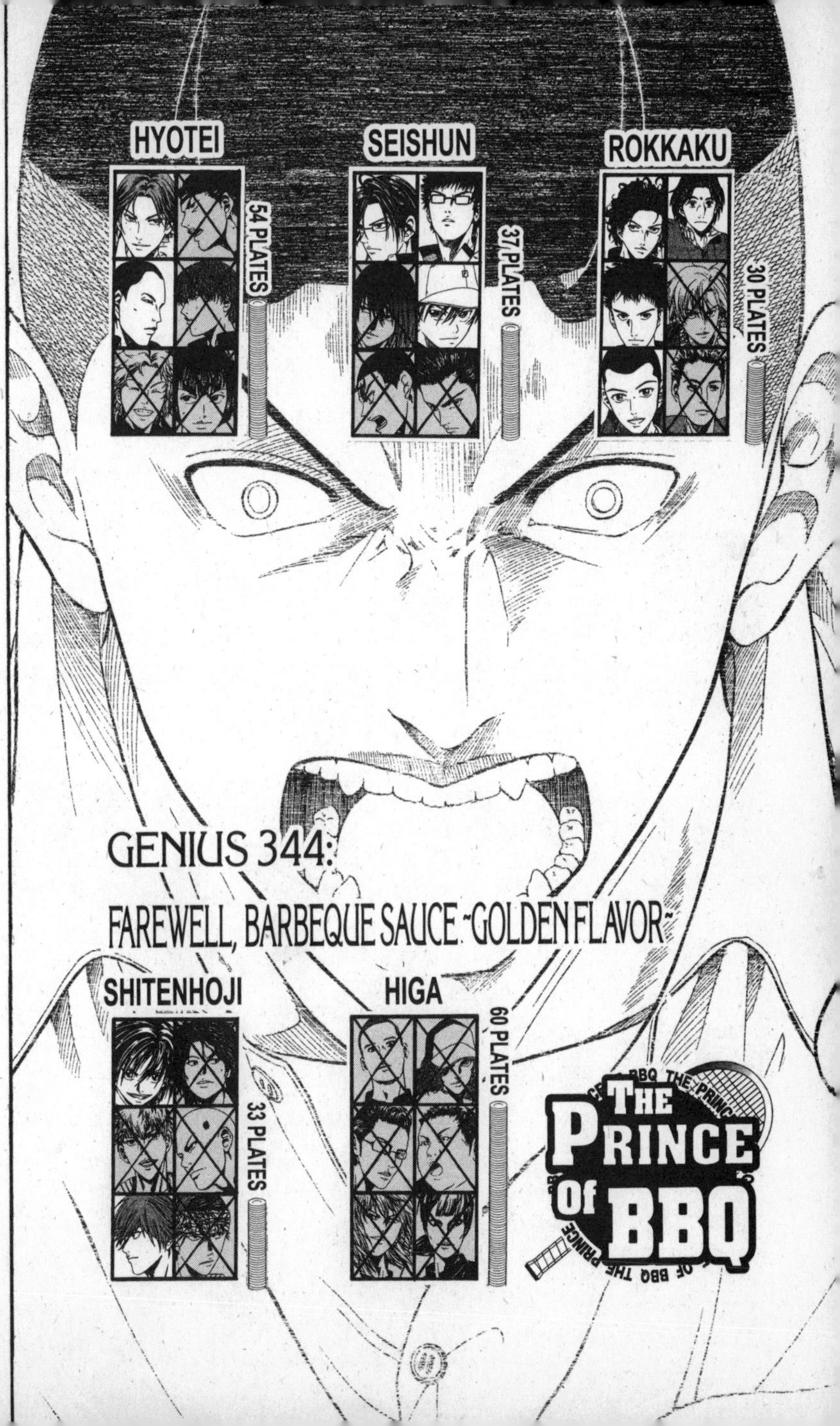
HYOTEI
54 PLATES
SEISHUN
37 PLATES
ROKKAKU
30 PLATES
GENIUS 344:
FAREWELL, BARBEQUE SAUCE ~GOLDEN FLAVOR~
SHITENHOJI
33 PLATES
HIGA
60 PLATES
THE PRINCE of BBQ
BBQ THE PRINCE OF BBQ THE PRINCE

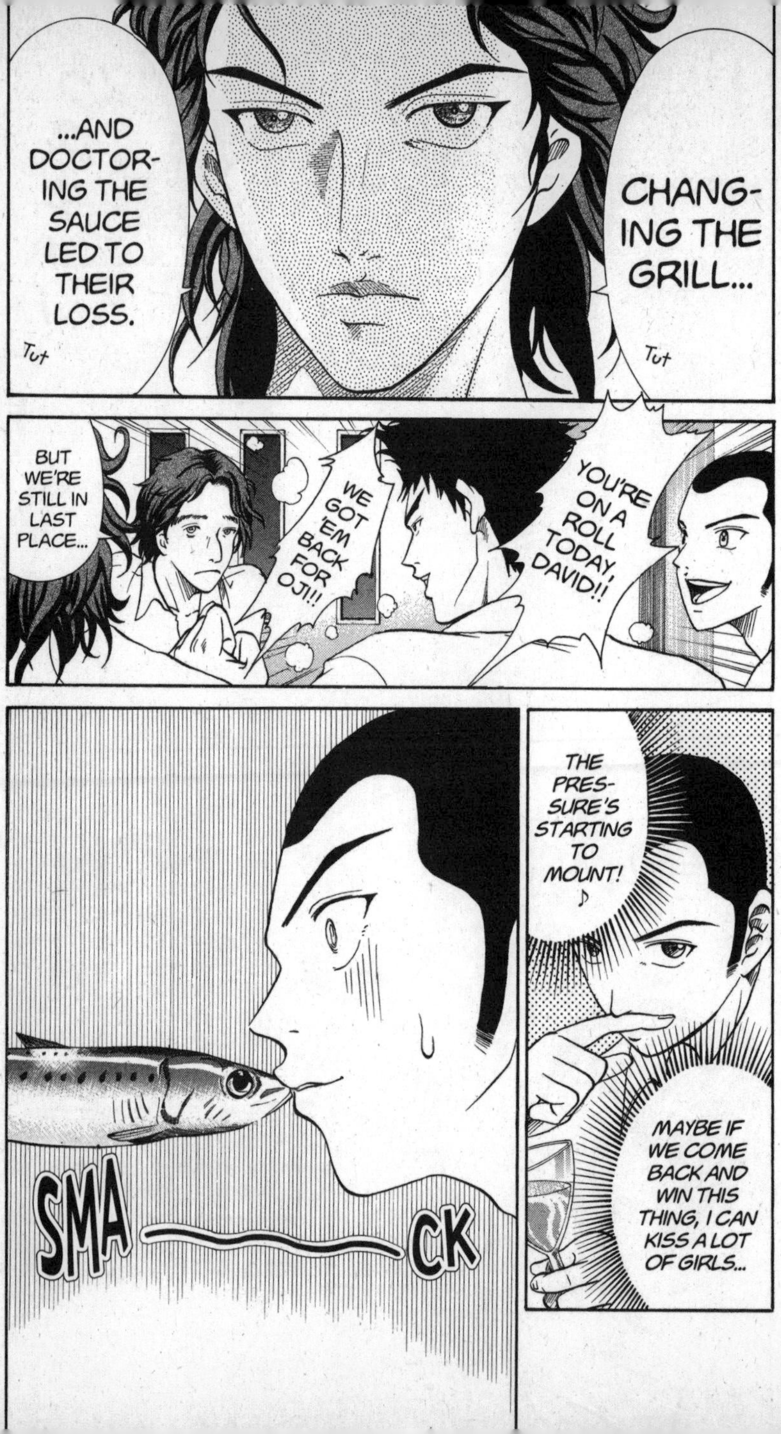
CHANG-ING THE GRILL...
Tut
...AND DOCTOR-ING THE SAUCE LED TO THEIR LOSS.
Tut
YOU'RE ON A ROLL TODAY, DAVID!!
WE GOT 'EM BACK FOR OJI!!
BUT WE'RE STILL IN LAST PLACE...
THE PRES-SURE'S STARTING TO MOUNT! ♪
MAYBE IF WE COME BACK AND WIN THIS THING, I CAN KISS A LOT OF GIRLS...
SMA———CK

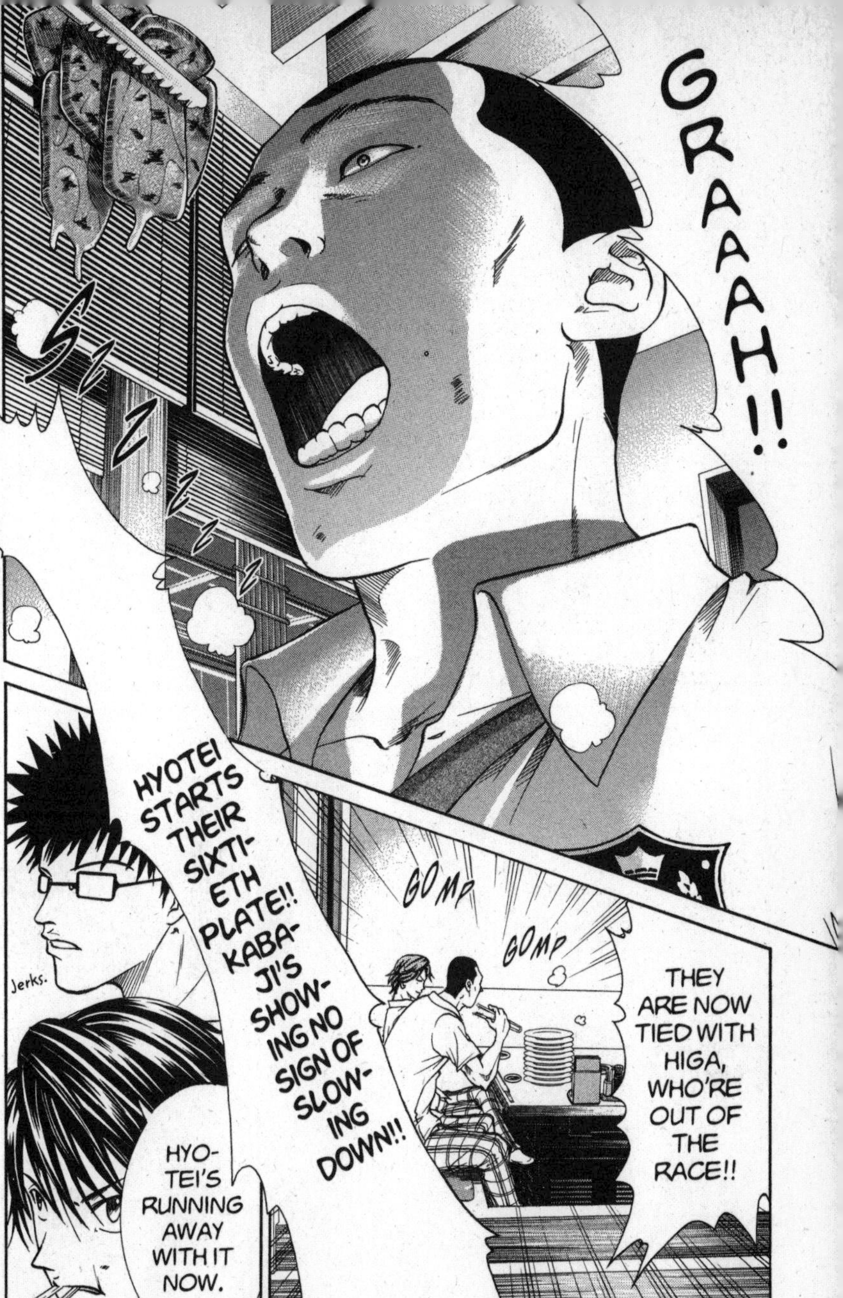
GRAAAH!!
SIZZZZZ
HYOTEI STARTS THEIR SIXTIETH PLATE!! KABAJI'S SHOWING NO SIGN OF SLOWING DOWN!!
GOMP
GOMP
THEY ARE NOW TIED WITH HIGA, WHO'RE OUT OF THE RACE!!
Jerks.
HYOTEI'S RUNNING AWAY WITH IT NOW.

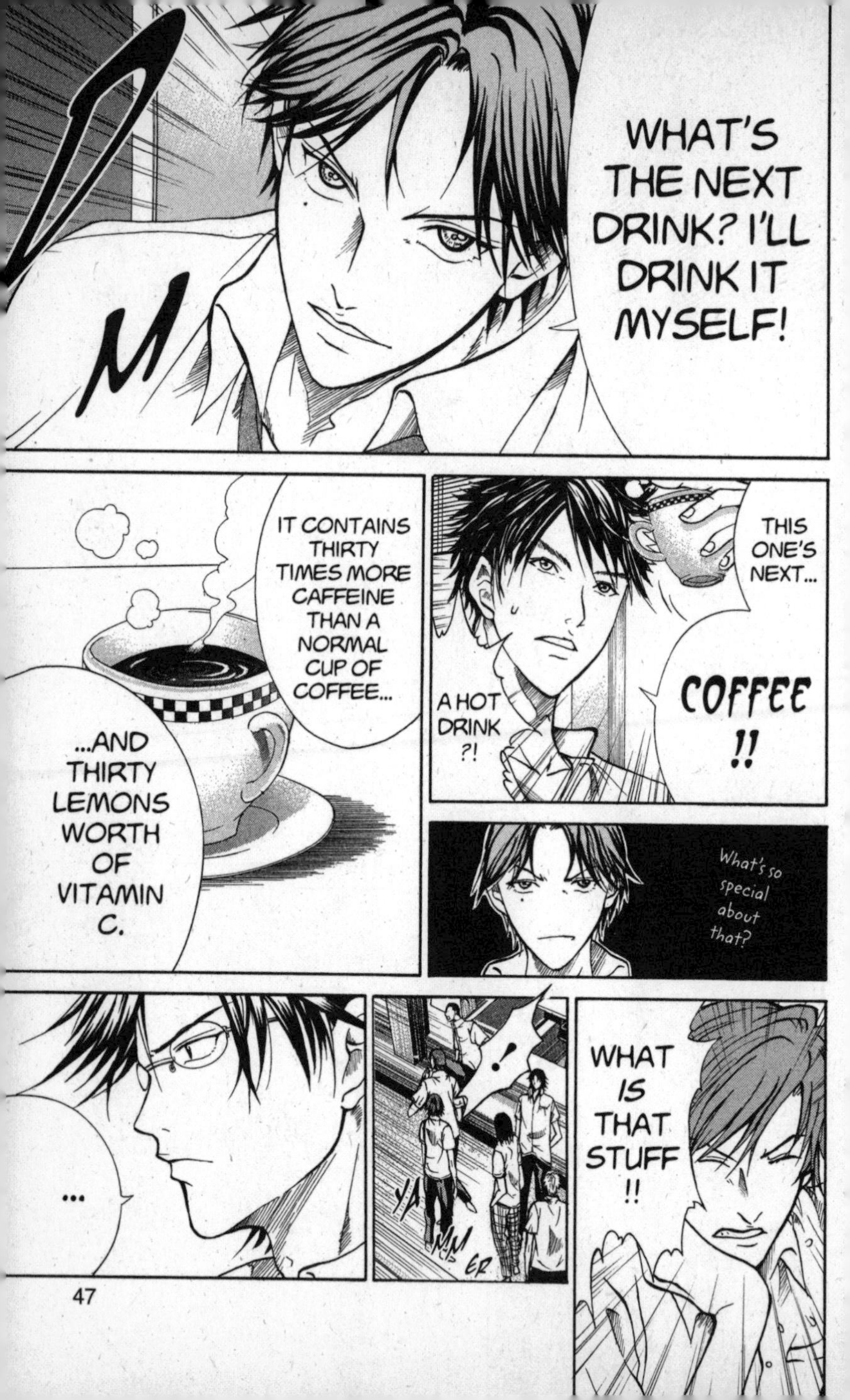
WHAT'S THE NEXT DRINK? I'LL DRINK IT MYSELF!
THIS ONE'S NEXT...
COFFEE !!
A HOT DRINK ?!
What's so special about that?
IT CONTAINS THIRTY TIMES MORE CAFFEINE THAN A NORMAL CUP OF COFFEE...
...AND THIRTY LEMONS WORTH OF VITAMIN C.
WHAT IS THAT STUFF !!
!
...

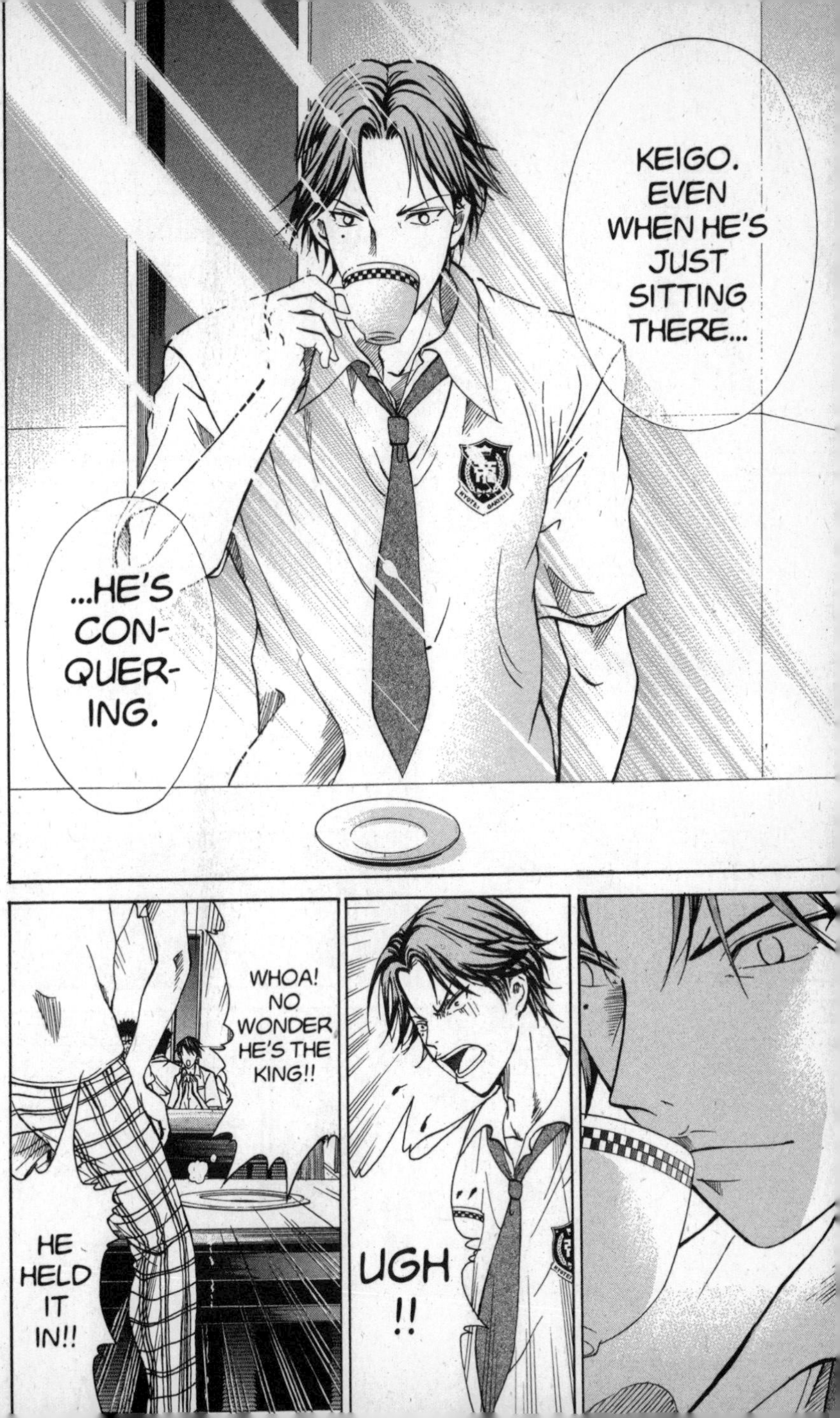
KEIGO. EVEN WHEN HE'S JUST SITTING THERE...
...HE'S CON-QUER-ING.
UGH !!
WHOA! NO WONDER HE'S THE KING!!
HE HELD IT IN!!

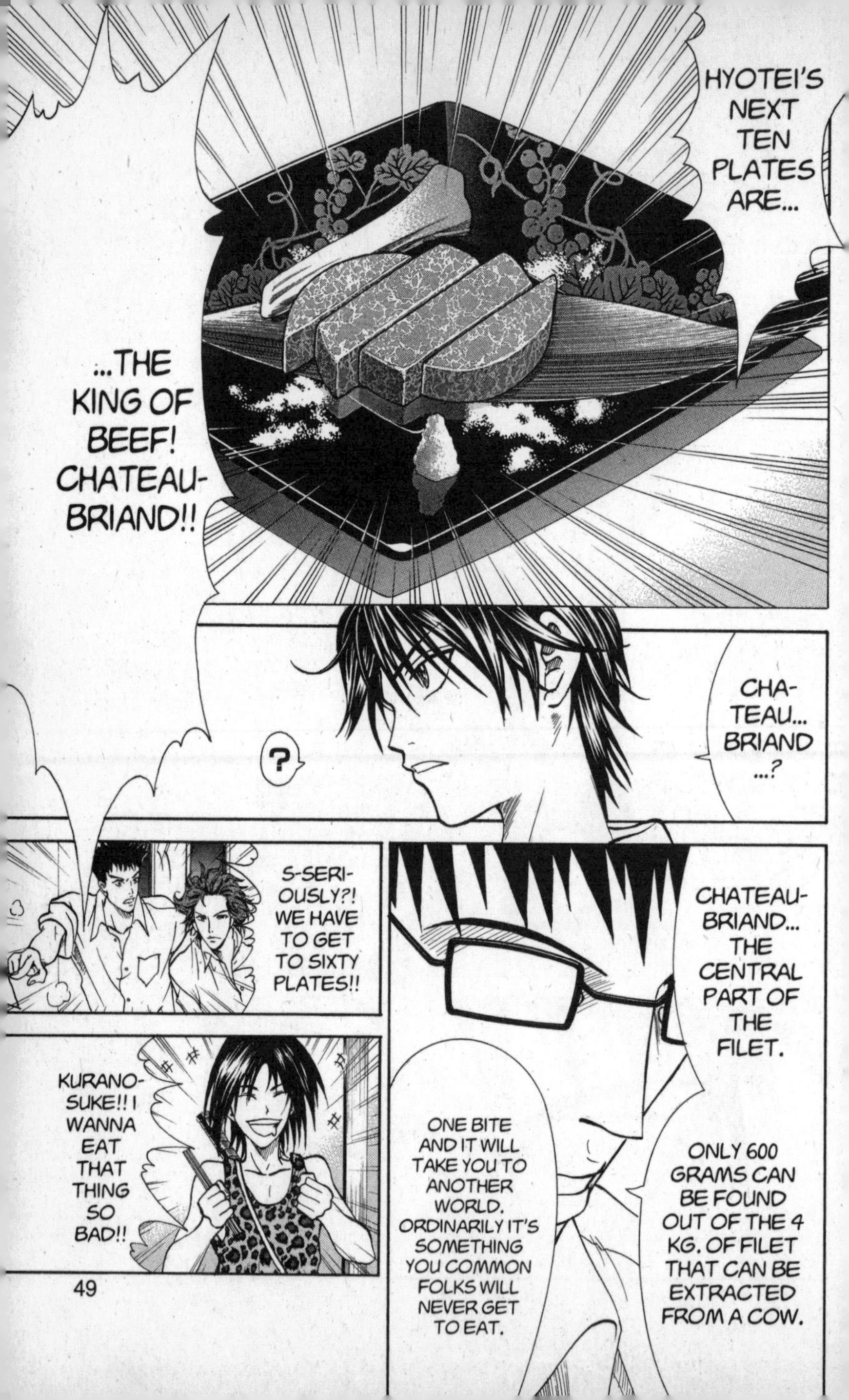
HYOTEI'S NEXT TEN PLATES ARE...
...THE KING OF BEEF! CHATEAU-BRIAND!!
CHA-TEAU... BRIAND ...?
?
CHATEAU-BRIAND... THE CENTRAL PART OF THE FILET.
ONLY 600 GRAMS CAN BE FOUND OUT OF THE 4 KG. OF FILET THAT CAN BE EXTRACTED FROM A COW.
ONE BITE AND IT WILL TAKE YOU TO ANOTHER WORLD. ORDINARILY IT'S SOMETHING YOU COMMON FOLKS WILL NEVER GET TO EAT.
S-SERI-OUSLY?! WE HAVE TO GET TO SIXTY PLATES!!
KURANO-SUKE!! I WANNA EAT THAT THING SO BAD!!

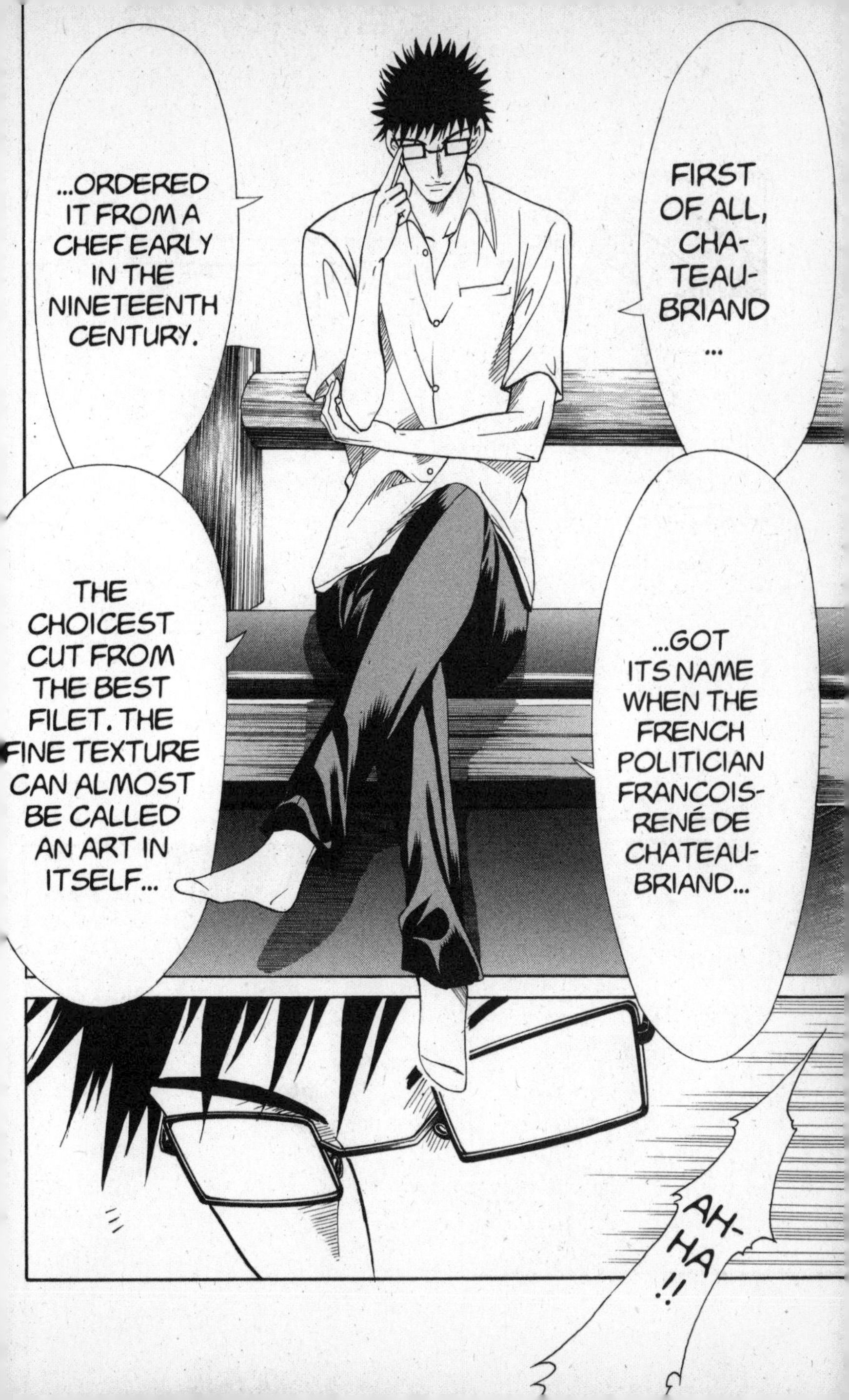
FIRST OF ALL, CHATEAUBRIAND ...
...GOT ITS NAME WHEN THE FRENCH POLITICIAN FRANCOIS-RENÉ DE CHATEAUBRIAND...
...ORDERED IT FROM A CHEF EARLY IN THE NINETEENTH CENTURY.
THE CHOICEST CUT FROM THE BEST FILET. THE FINE TEXTURE CAN ALMOST BE CALLED AN ART IN ITSELF...
AH-HA!!

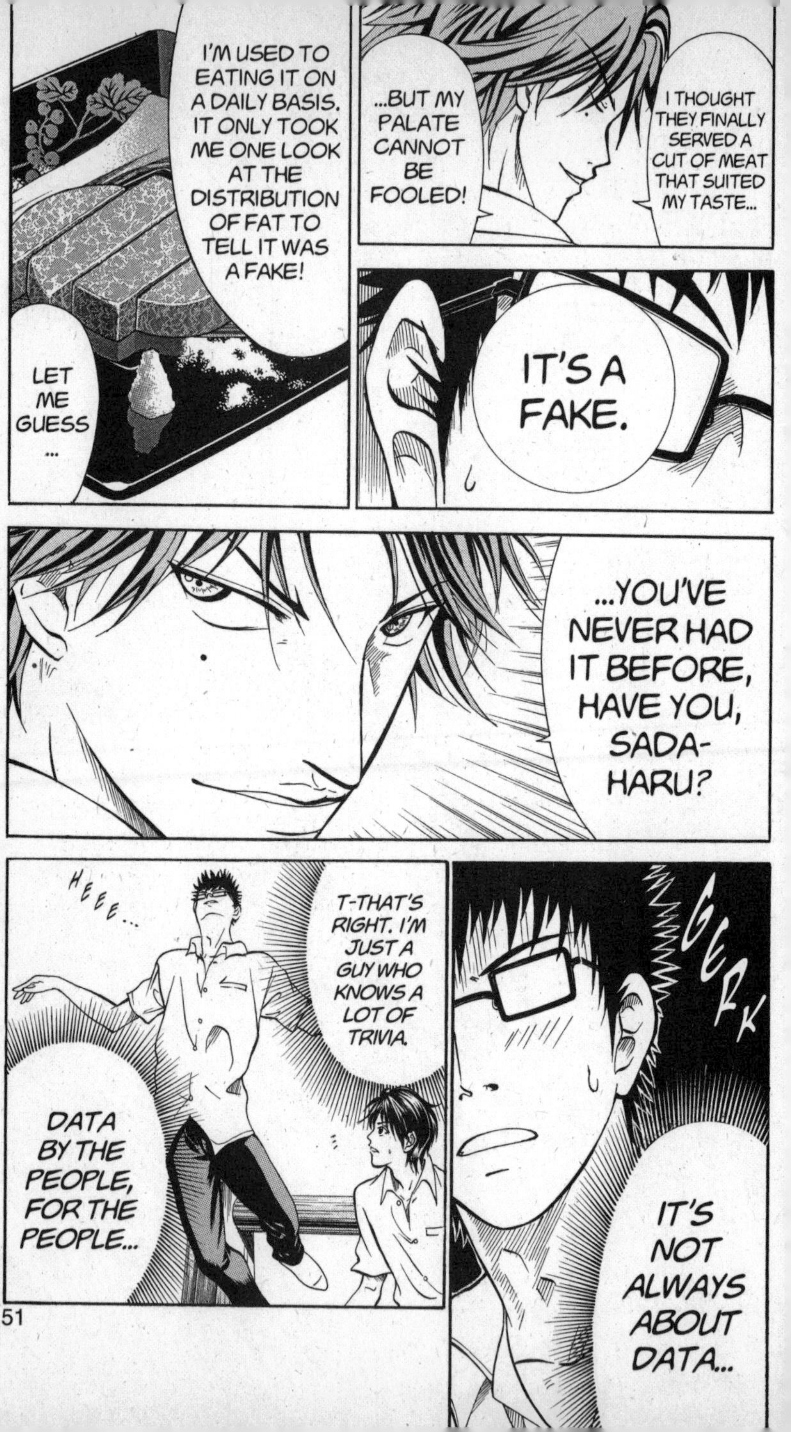
I THOUGHT THEY FINALLY SERVED A CUT OF MEAT THAT SUITED MY TASTE...
...BUT MY PALATE CANNOT BE FOOLED!
IT'S A FAKE.
I'M USED TO EATING IT ON A DAILY BASIS. IT ONLY TOOK ME ONE LOOK AT THE DISTRIBUTION OF FAT TO TELL IT WAS A FAKE!
LET ME GUESS ...
...YOU'VE NEVER HAD IT BEFORE, HAVE YOU, SADA-HARU?
GERK
IT'S NOT ALWAYS ABOUT DATA...
T-THAT'S RIGHT. I'M JUST A GUY WHO KNOWS A LOT OF TRIVIA.
HEEE...
DATA BY THE PEOPLE, FOR THE PEOPLE...

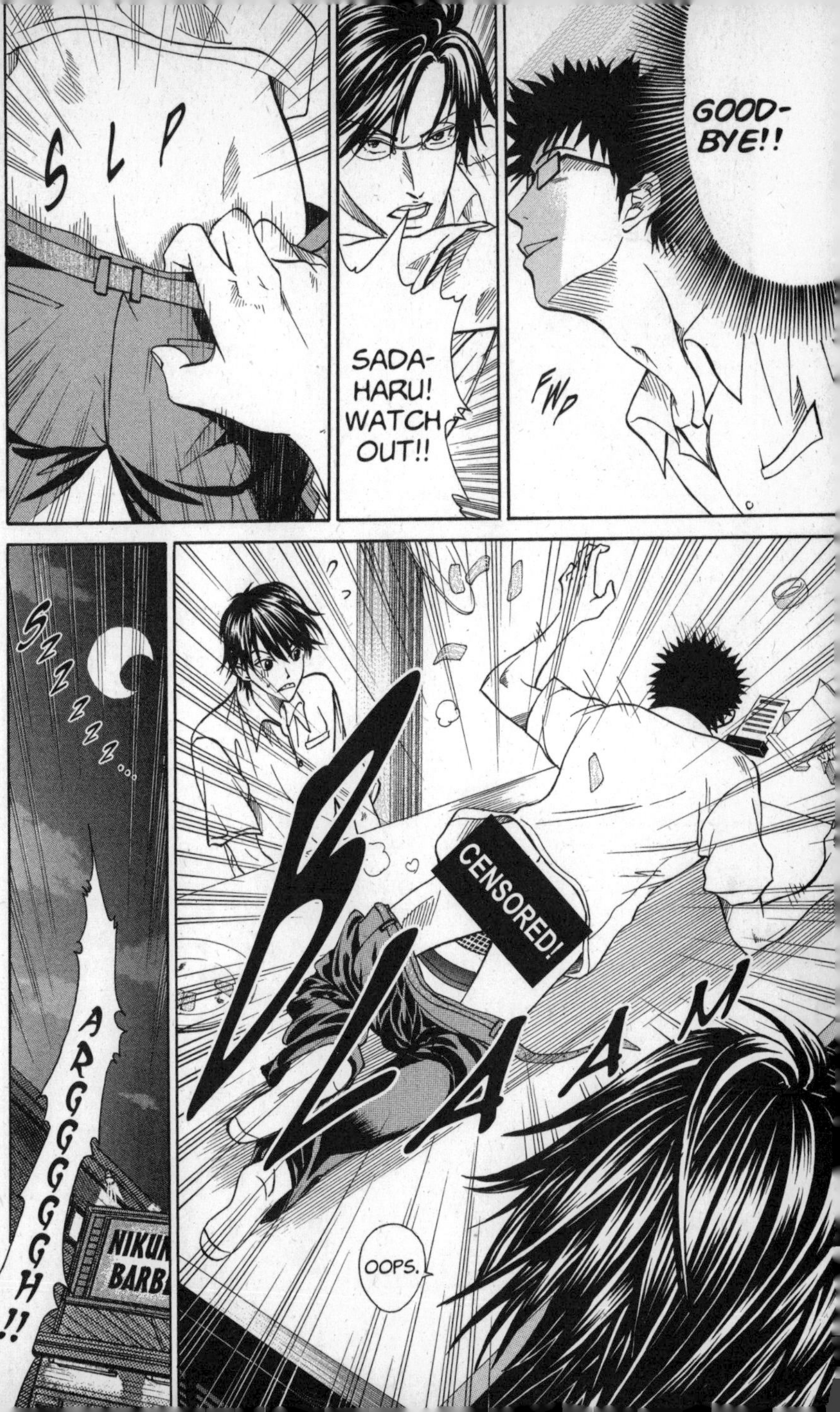
GOOD-BYE!!
FWP
SADA-HARU! WATCH OUT!!
SLP
WHAAM
CENSORED!
OOPS.
SZZZZZZ...
ARGGGGGGH!!
NIKUN
BARBE

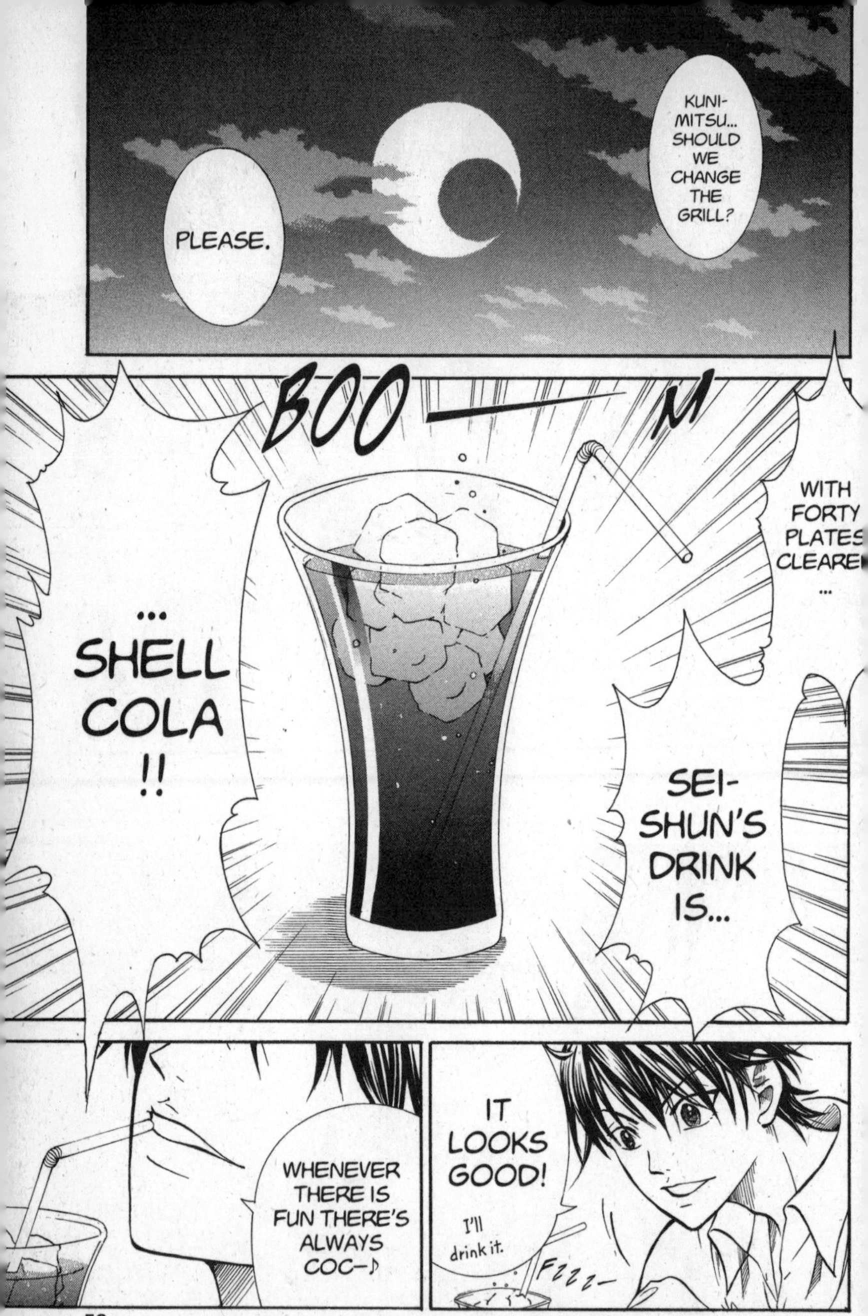
KUNI-MITSU... SHOULD WE CHANGE THE GRILL?
PLEASE.
BOO—M
WITH FORTY PLATES CLEARE ...
SEI-SHUN'S DRINK IS...
... SHELL COLA !!
IT LOOKS GOOD!
I'll drink it.
FZZZ—
WHENEVER THERE IS FUN THERE'S ALWAYS COC—♪

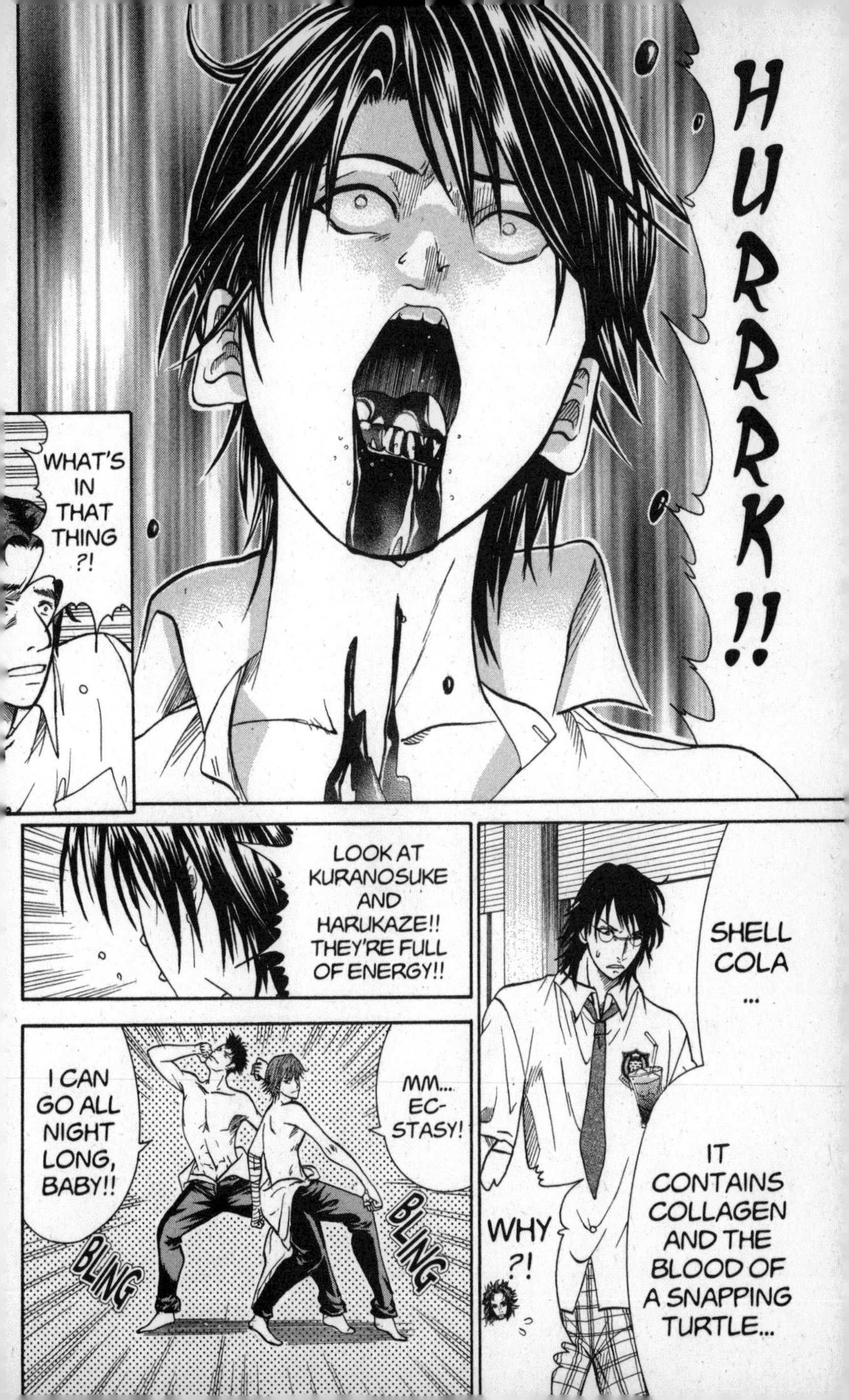
HURRRK!!
WHAT'S IN THAT THING?!
SHELL COLA...
IT CONTAINS COLLAGEN AND THE BLOOD OF A SNAPPING TURTLE...
WHY?!
LOOK AT KURANOSUKE AND HARUKAZE!! THEY'RE FULL OF ENERGY!!
MM... EC-STASY!
BLING
I CAN GO ALL NIGHT LONG, BABY!!
BLING

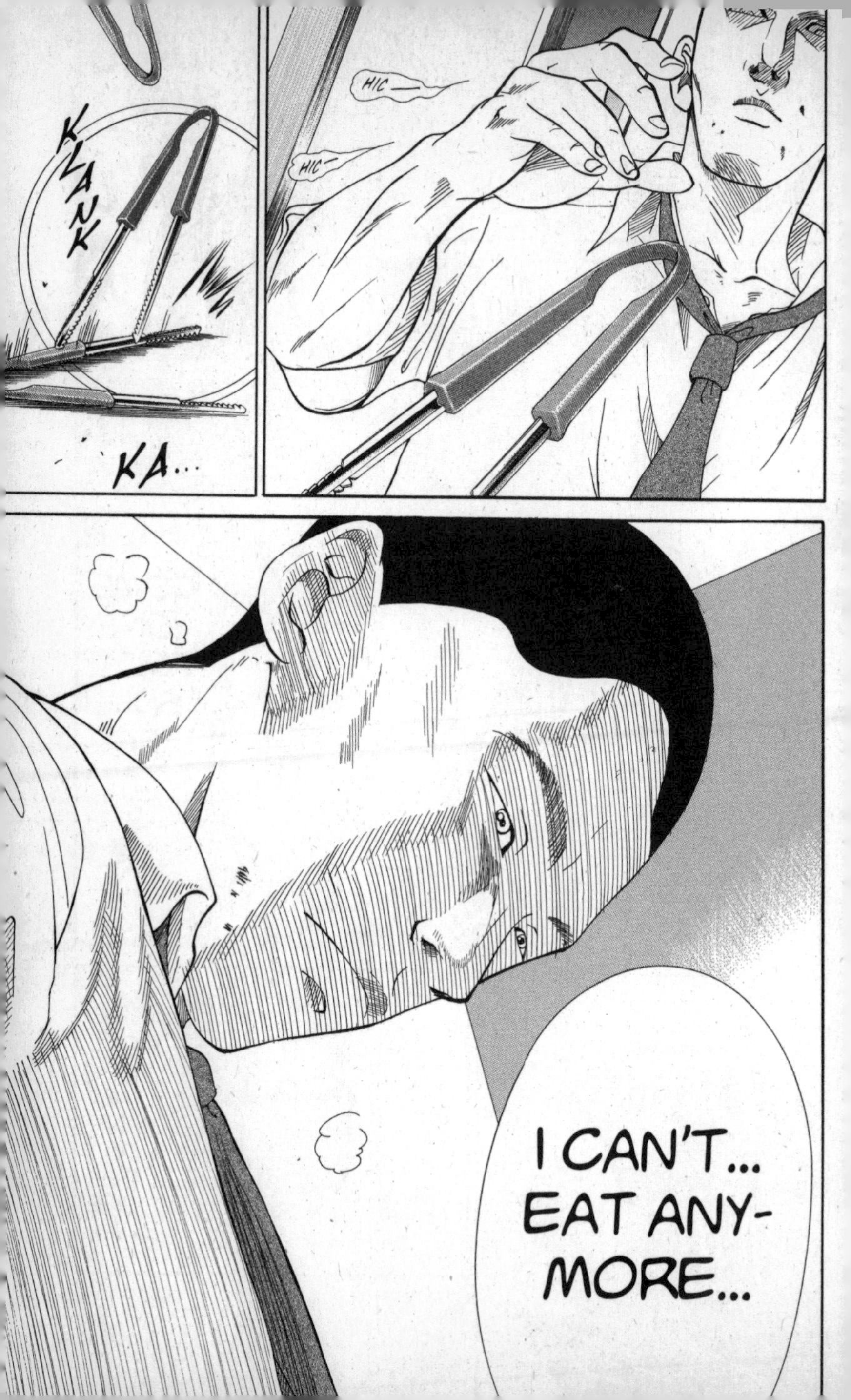
HIC
HIC
KLANK
KA...
I CAN'T... EAT ANY-MORE...

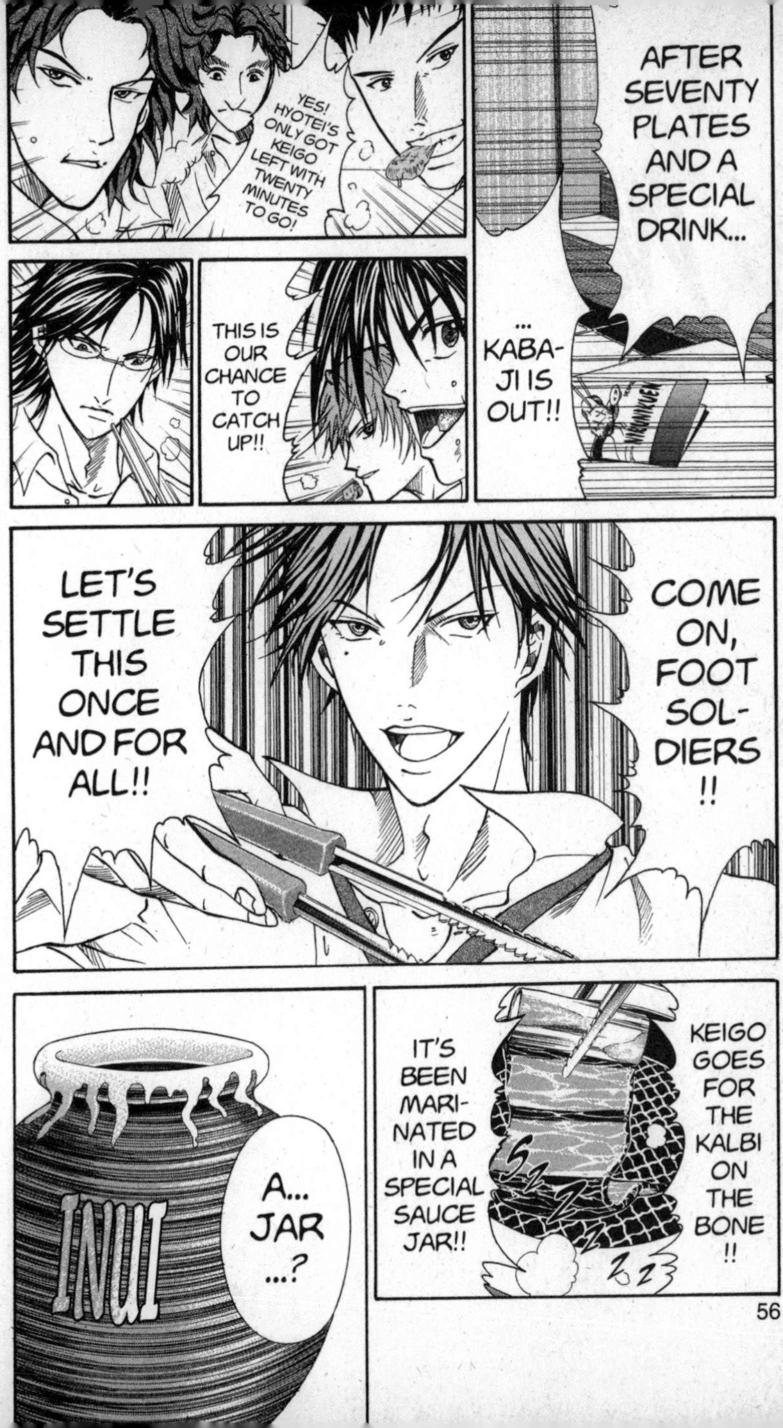
AFTER SEVENTY PLATES AND A SPECIAL DRINK...
...KABA-JI IS OUT!!
YES! HYOTEI'S ONLY GOT KEIGO LEFT WITH TWENTY MINUTES TO GO!
THIS IS OUR CHANCE TO CATCH UP!!
COME ON, FOOT SOL-DIERS!!
LET'S SETTLE THIS ONCE AND FOR ALL!!
KEIGO GOES FOR THE KALBI ON THE BONE!!
IT'S BEEN MARI-NATED IN A SPECIAL SAUCE JAR!!
A... JAR...?
INUI

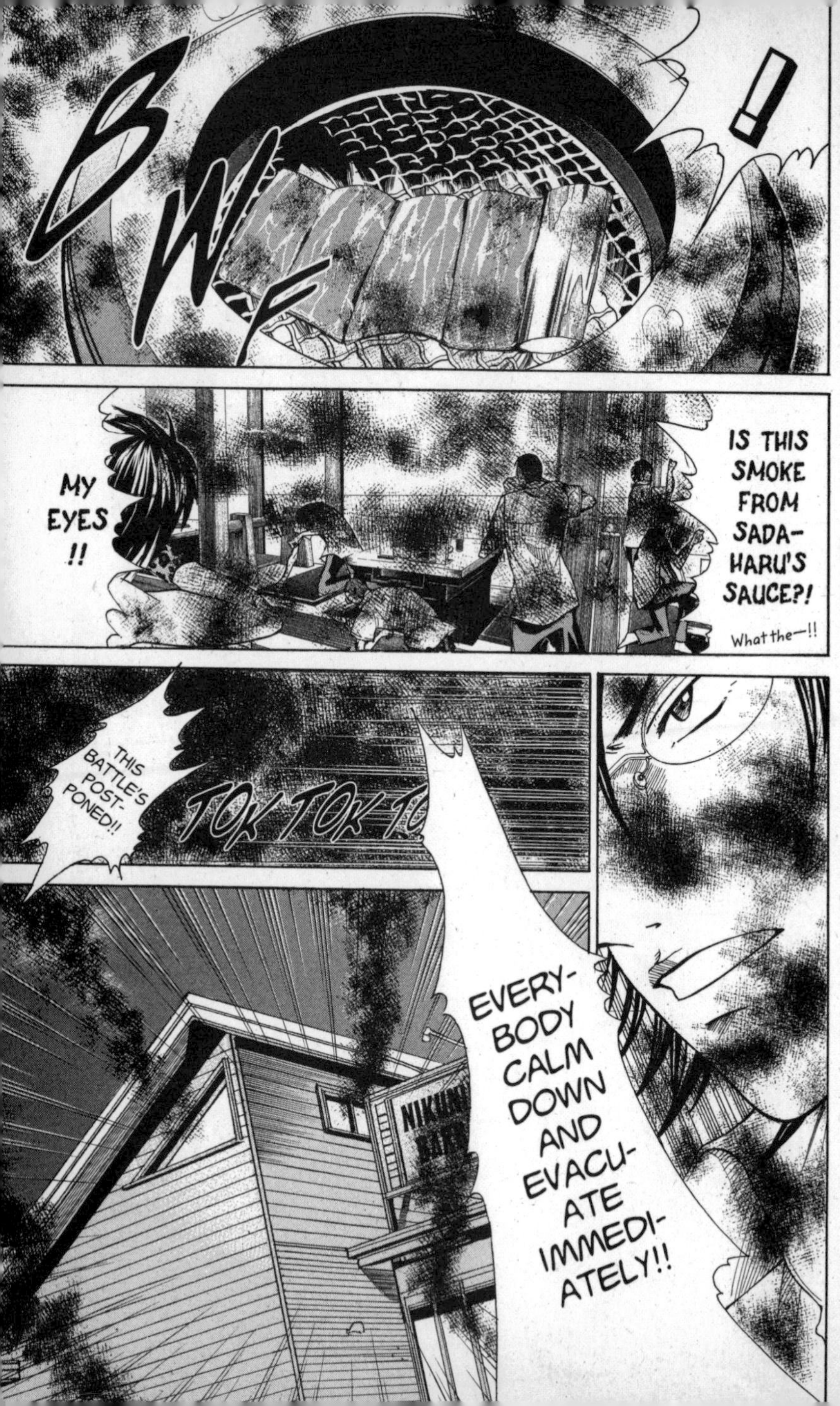
BWF
!
IS THIS SMOKE FROM SADAHARU'S SAUCE?!
What the—!!
MY EYES!!
EVERYBODY CALM DOWN AND EVACUATE IMMEDIATELY!!
THIS BATTLE'S POSTPONED!!
TOK TOK TO

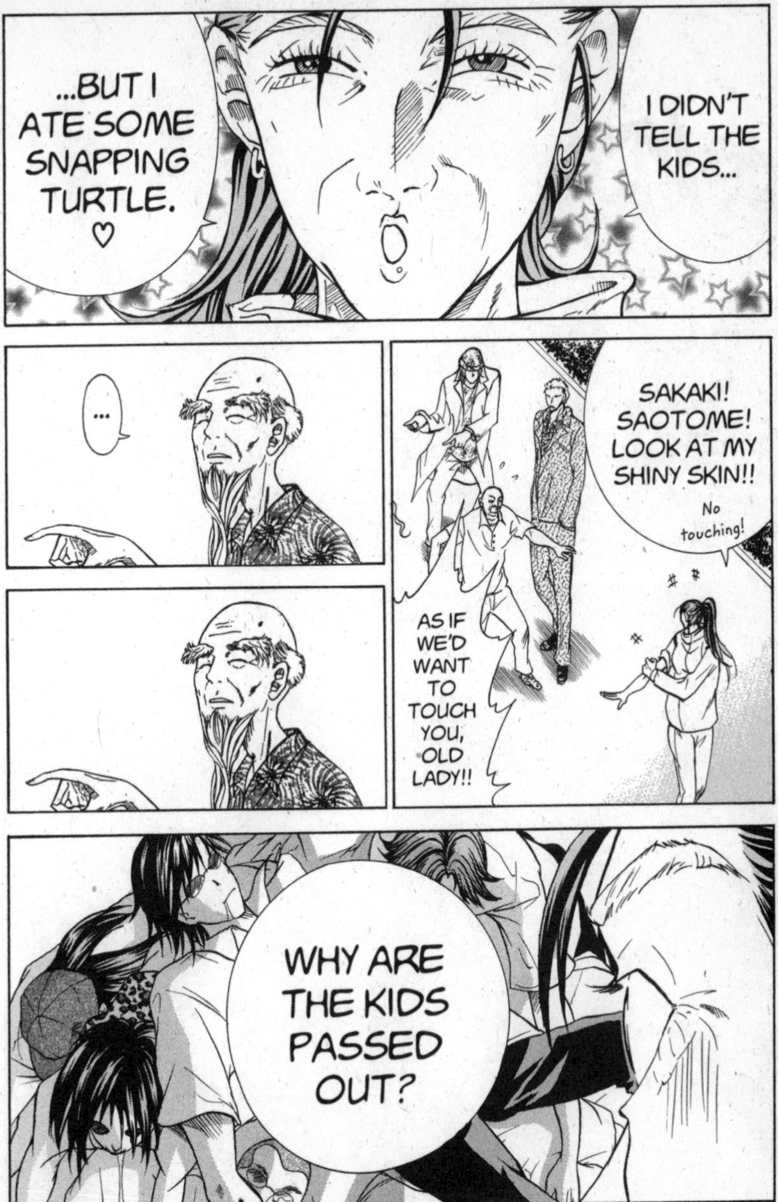
I DIDN'T TELL THE KIDS...
...BUT I ATE SOME SNAPPING TURTLE. ♡
SAKAKI! SAOTOME! LOOK AT MY SHINY SKIN!!
No touching!
AS IF WE'D WANT TO TOUCH YOU, OLD LADY!!
...
WHY ARE THE KIDS PASSED OUT?

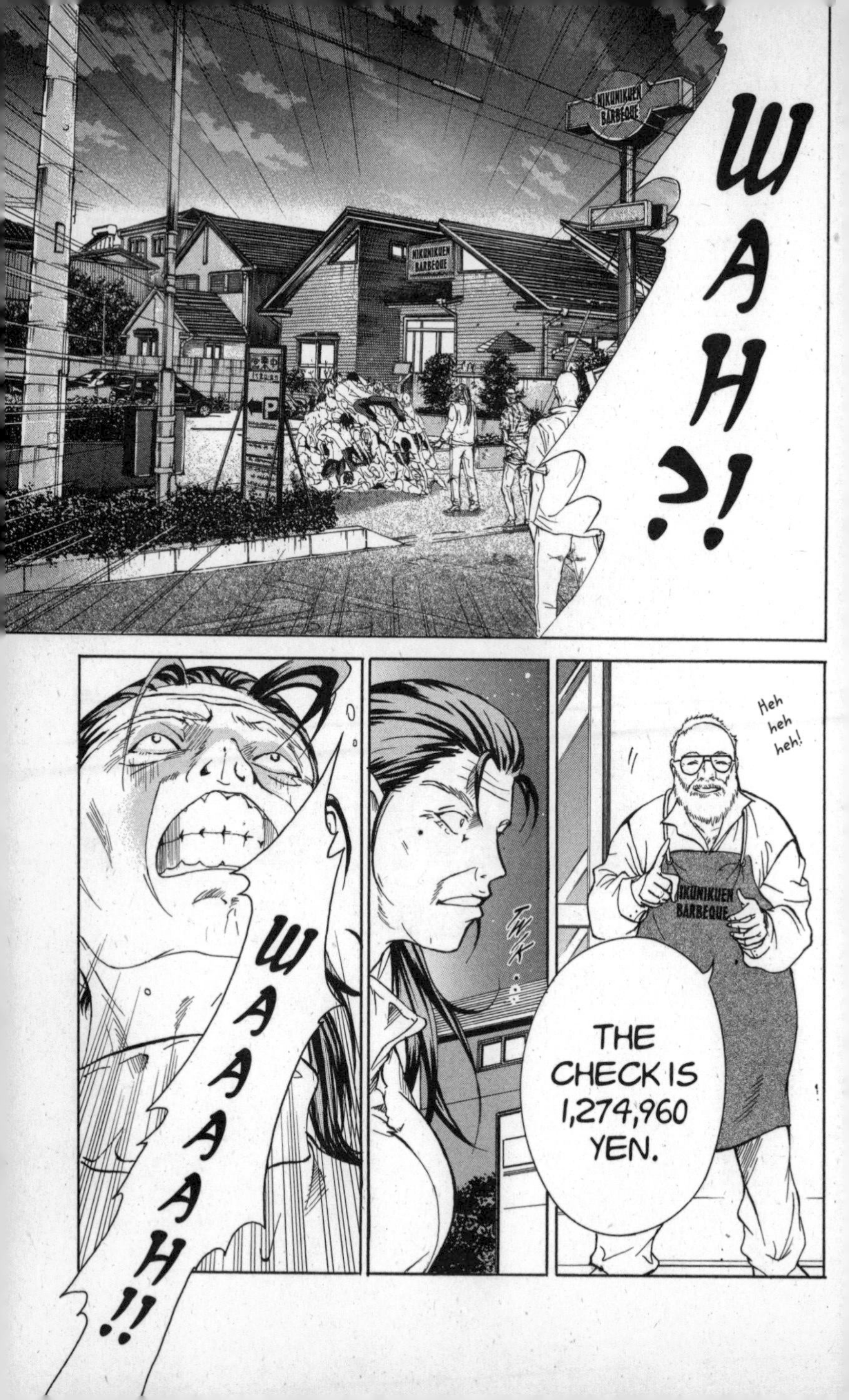
NIKUNIKUEN BARBEQUE
NIKUNIKUEN BARBEQUE
WAH?!
Heh heh heh!
NIKUNIKUEN BARBEQUE
THE CHECK IS 1,274,960 YEN.
TWK...
WAAAAAAH!!

テニスの王子様

THE PRINCE OF TENNIS

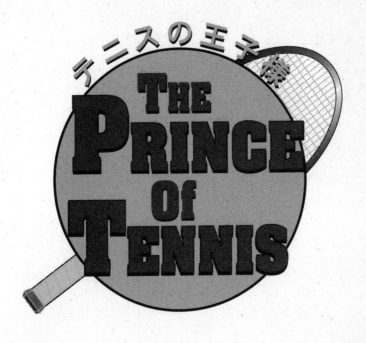

GENIUS 345: WHERE IS RYOMA?

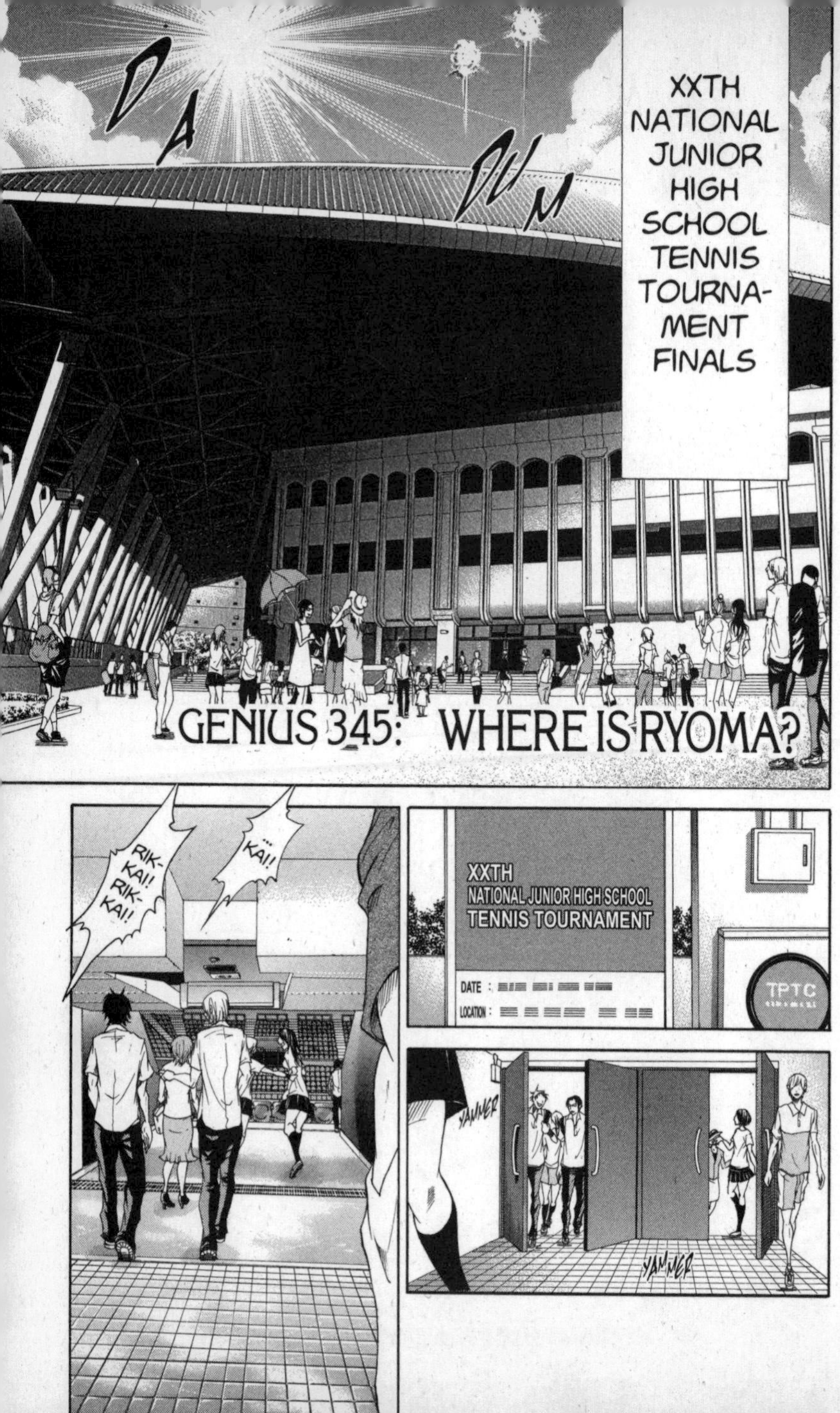
DA
DUM
XXTH NATIONAL JUNIOR HIGH SCHOOL TENNIS TOURNAMENT FINALS
XXTH
NATIONAL JUNIOR HIGH SCHOOL
TENNIS TOURNAMENT
DATE :
LOCATION :
TPTC
YAMMER
YAMMER
...KAI!!
RIK-KAI!! RIK-KAI!!

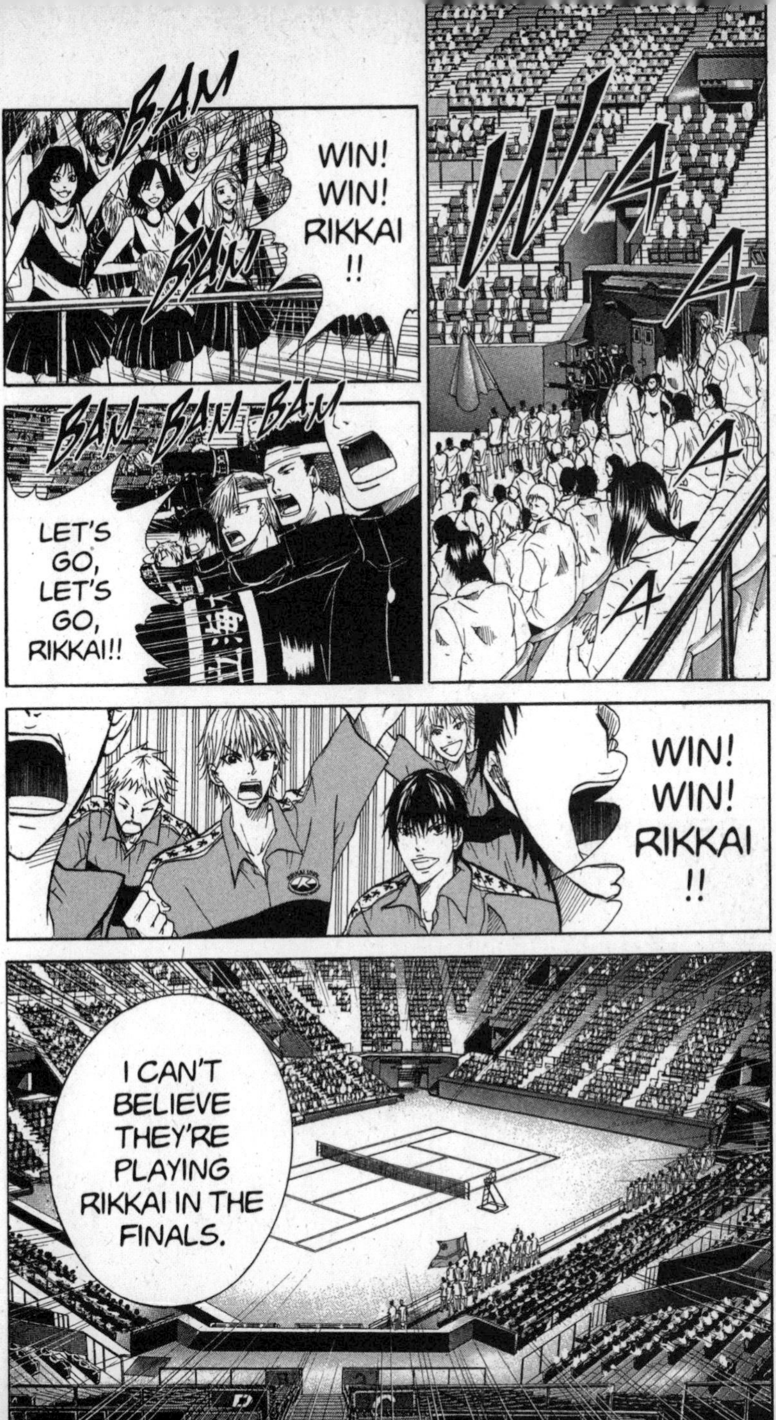
WAAA
BAM
BAM
WIN! WIN! RIKKAI!!
BAM BAM BAM
LET'S GO, LET'S GO, RIKKAI!!
WIN! WIN! RIKKAI!!
I CAN'T BELIEVE THEY'RE PLAYING RIKKAI IN THE FINALS.

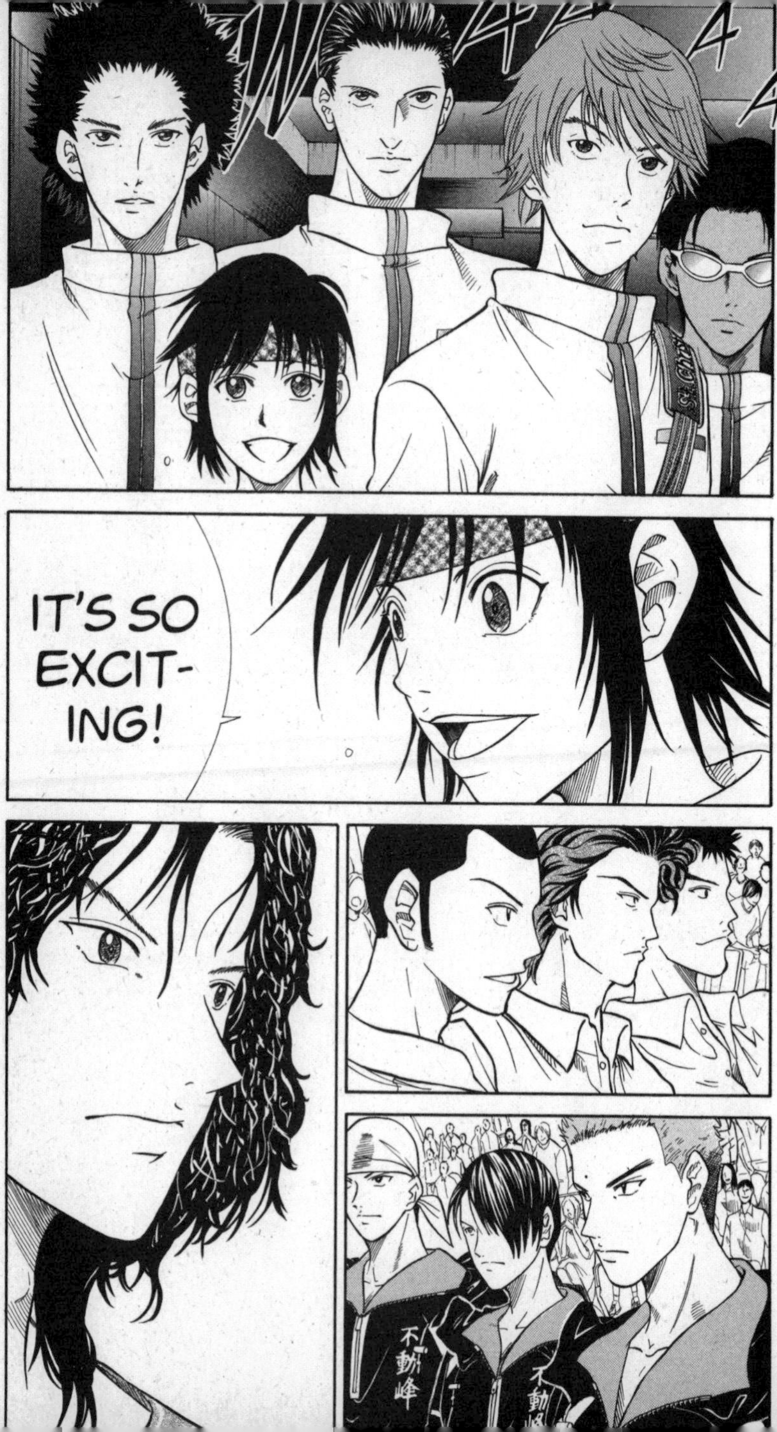
IT'S SO EXCIT-ING!

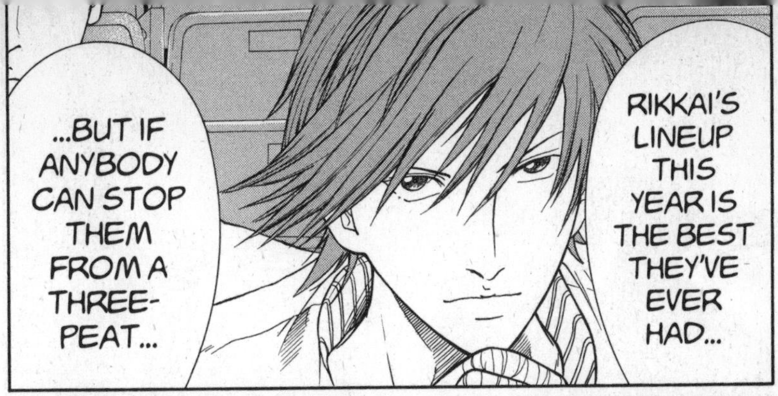
RIKKAI'S LINEUP THIS YEAR IS THE BEST THEY'VE EVER HAD...
...BUT IF ANYBODY CAN STOP THEM FROM A THREE-PEAT...
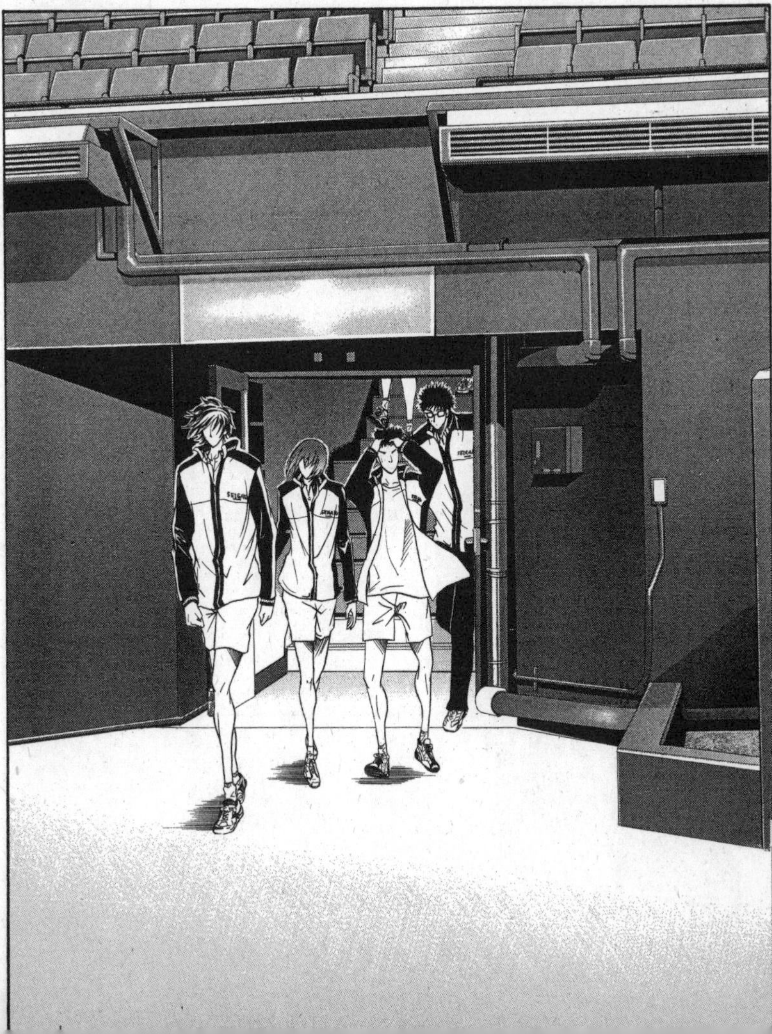

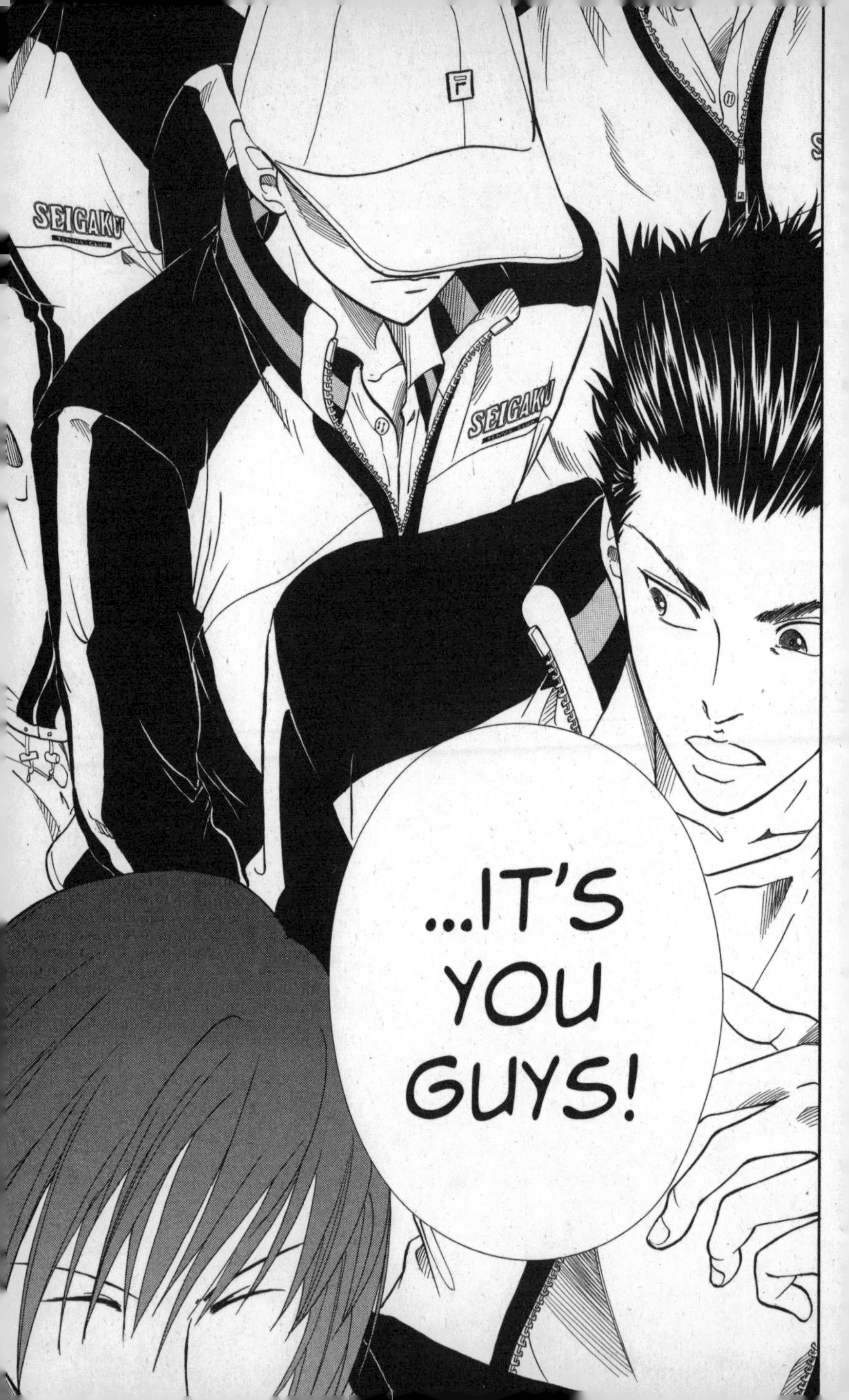
SEIGAKU TENNIS CLUB
SEIGAKU TENNIS CLUB
...IT'S YOU GUYS!

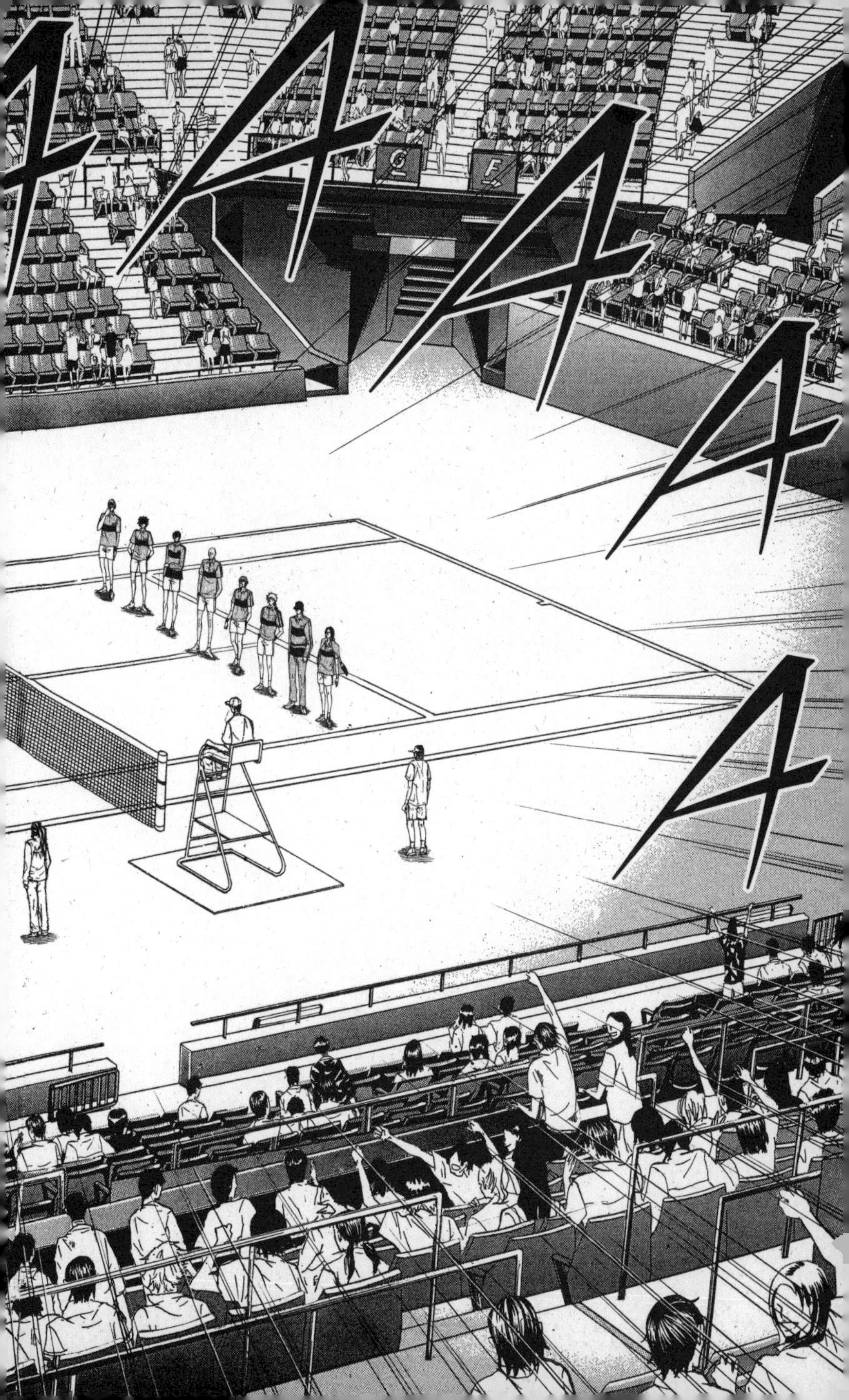
AAAAAA

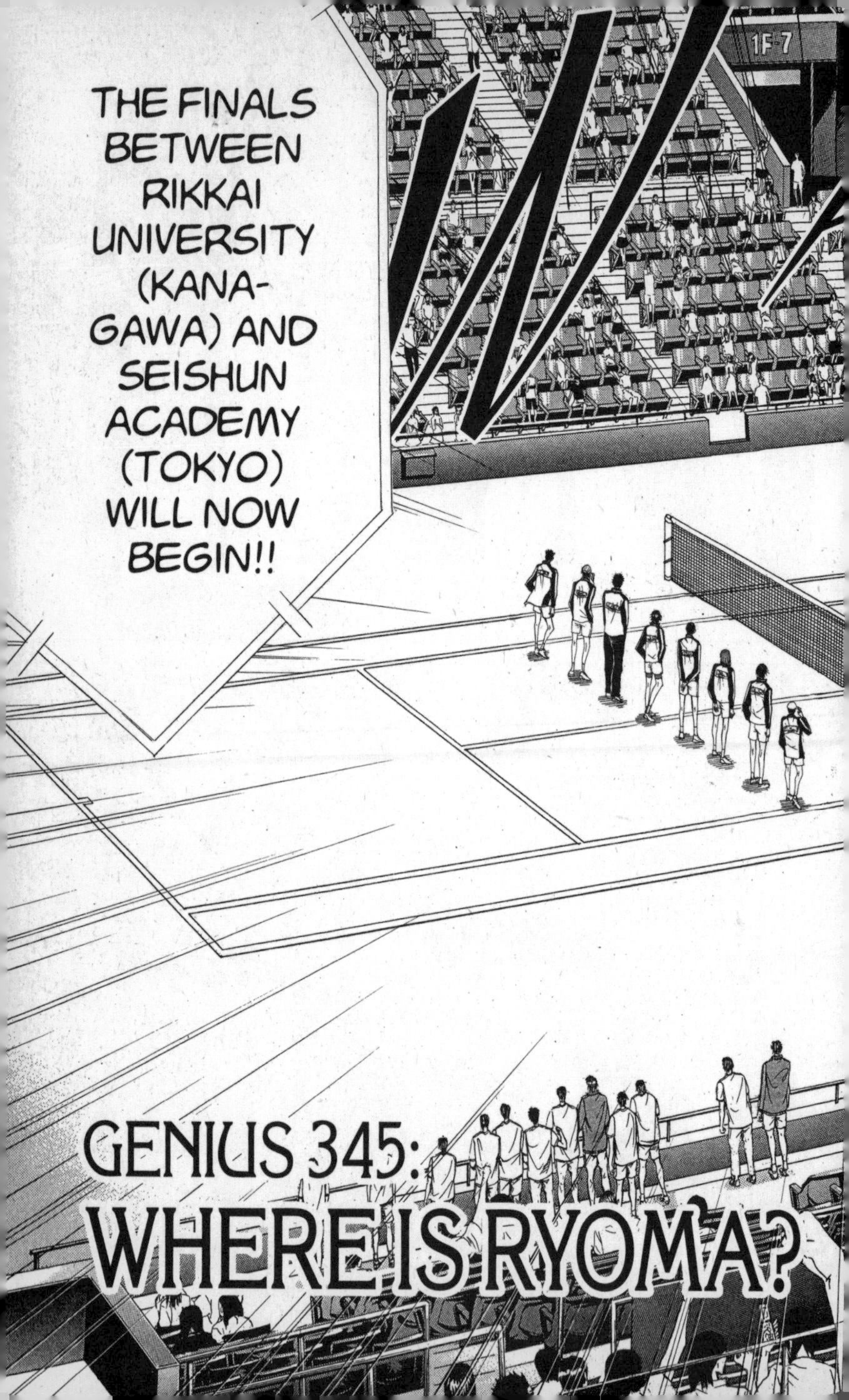

THE FINALS BETWEEN RIKKAI UNIVERSITY (KANAGAWA) AND SEISHUN ACADEMY (TOKYO) WILL NOW BEGIN!!
1F-7
GENIUS 345:
WHERE IS RYOMA?

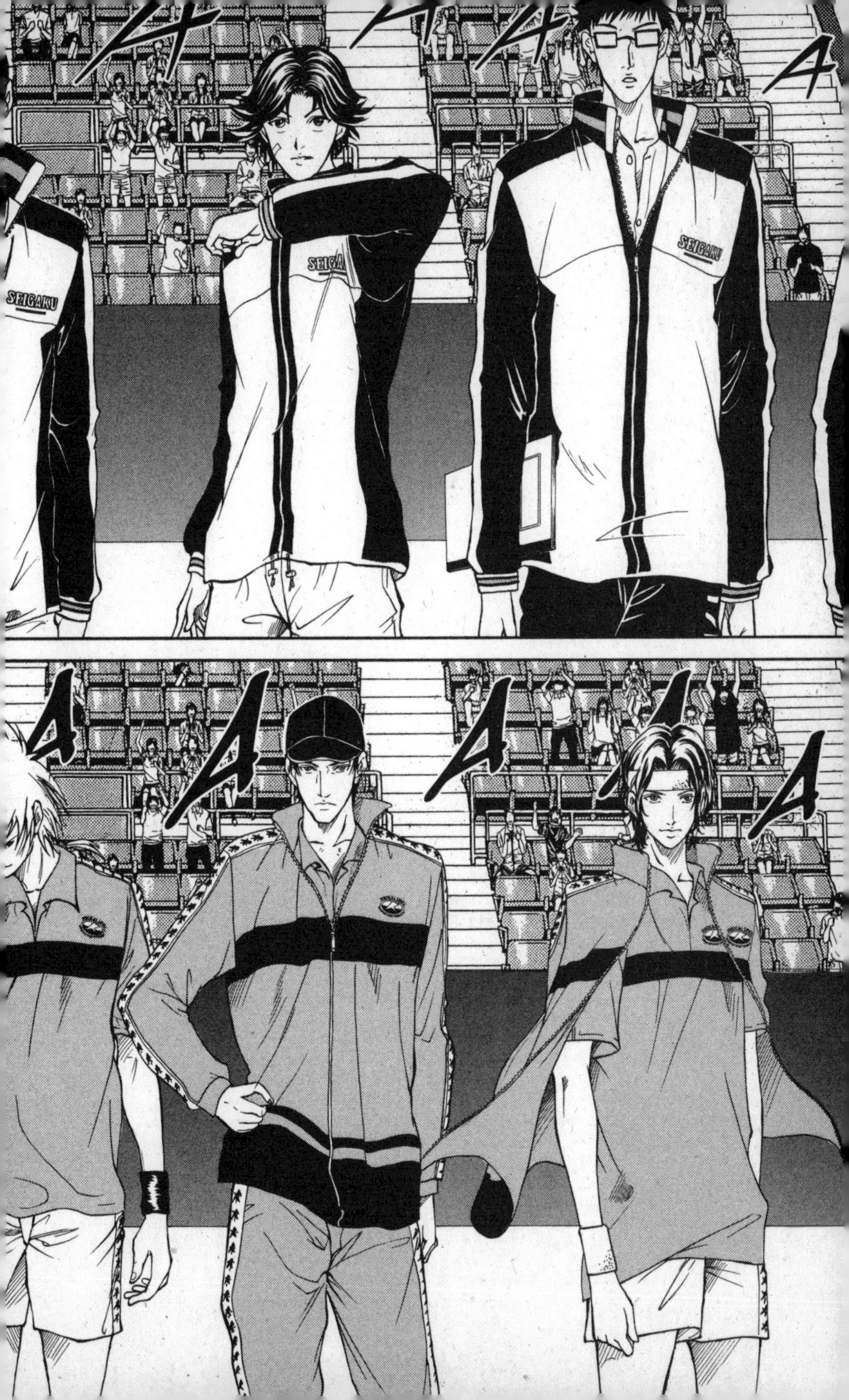
SEIGAKU
SEIGAKU
SEIGAKU

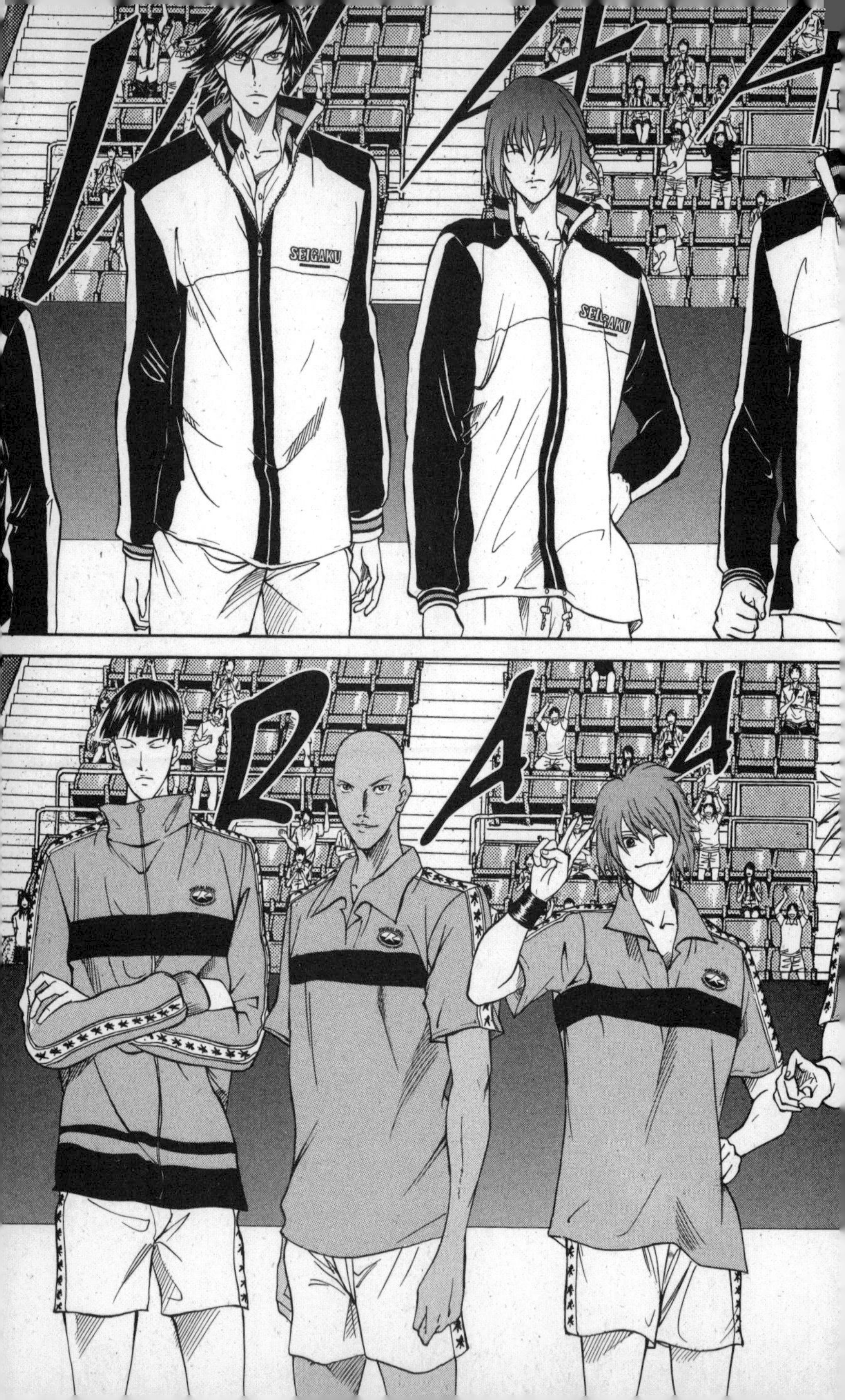
SEIGAKU
SEIGAKU

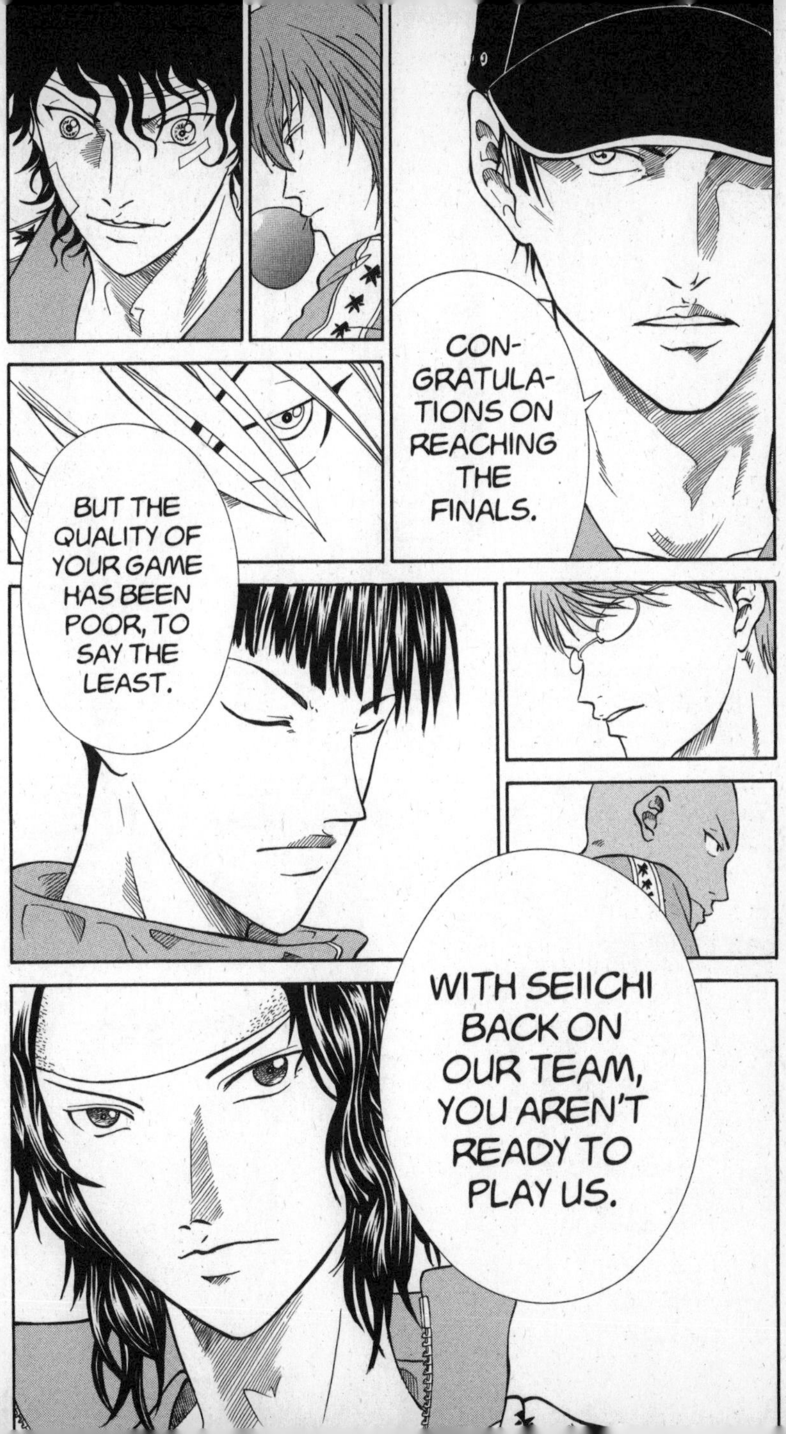
CON-GRATULA-TIONS ON REACHING THE FINALS.
BUT THE QUALITY OF YOUR GAME HAS BEEN POOR, TO SAY THE LEAST.
WITH SEIICHI BACK ON OUR TEAM, YOU AREN'T READY TO PLAY US.

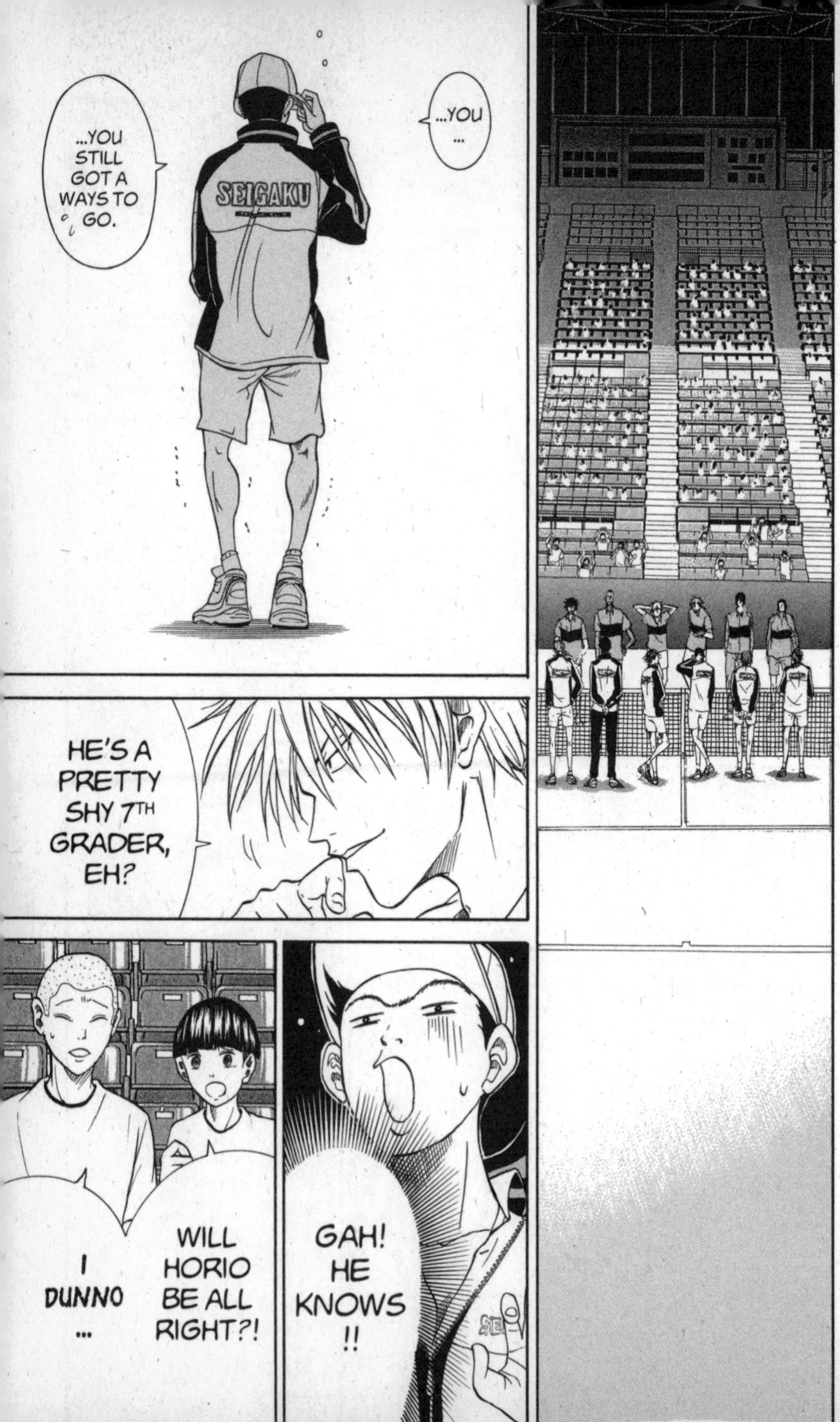
...YOU ...
...YOU STILL GOT A WAYS TO GO.
HE'S A PRETTY SHY 7TH GRADER, EH?
GAH! HE KNOWS!!
WILL HORIO BE ALL RIGHT?!
I DUNNO ...

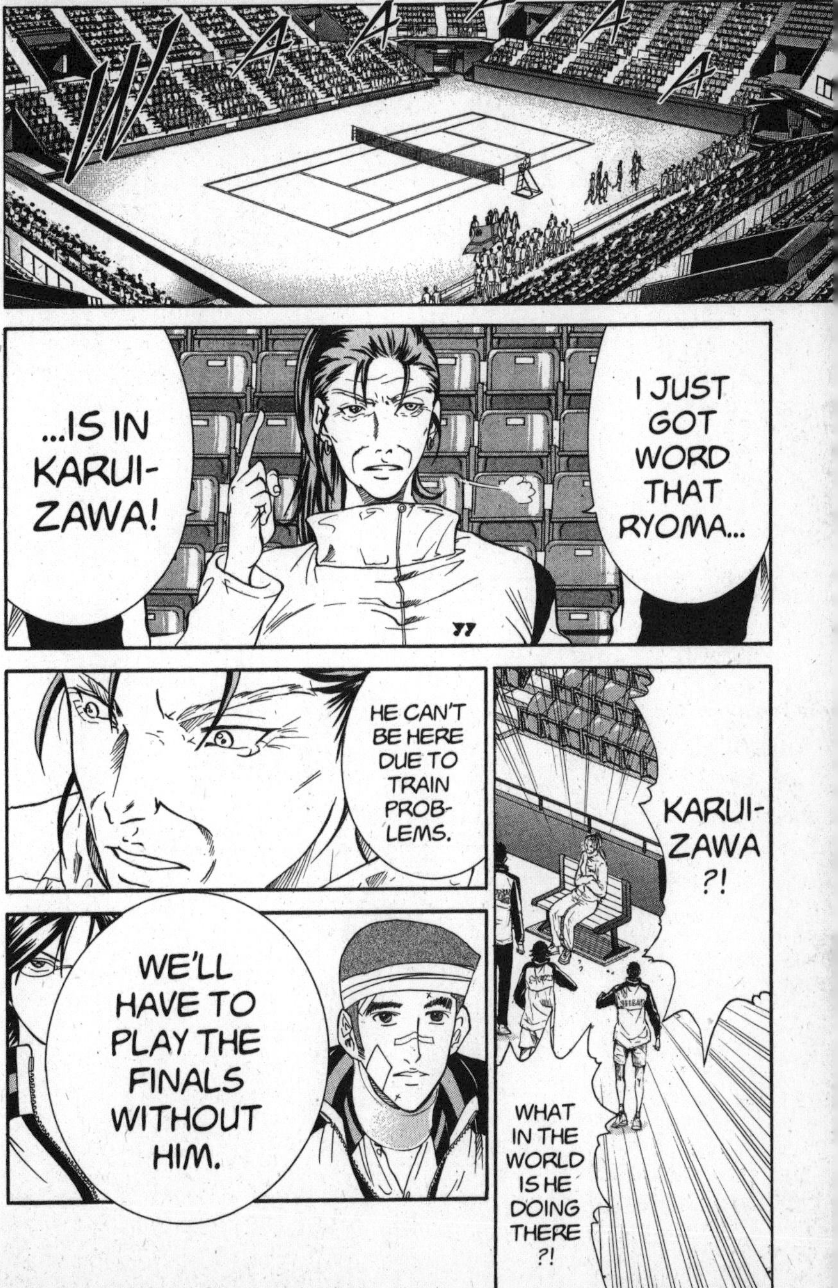
WAAAA
I JUST GOT WORD THAT RYOMA...
...IS IN KARUI-ZAWA!
KARUI-ZAWA ?!
WHAT IN THE WORLD IS HE DOING THERE ?!
HE CAN'T BE HERE DUE TO TRAIN PROB-LEMS.
WE'LL HAVE TO PLAY THE FINALS WITHOUT HIM.

READ THIS WAY

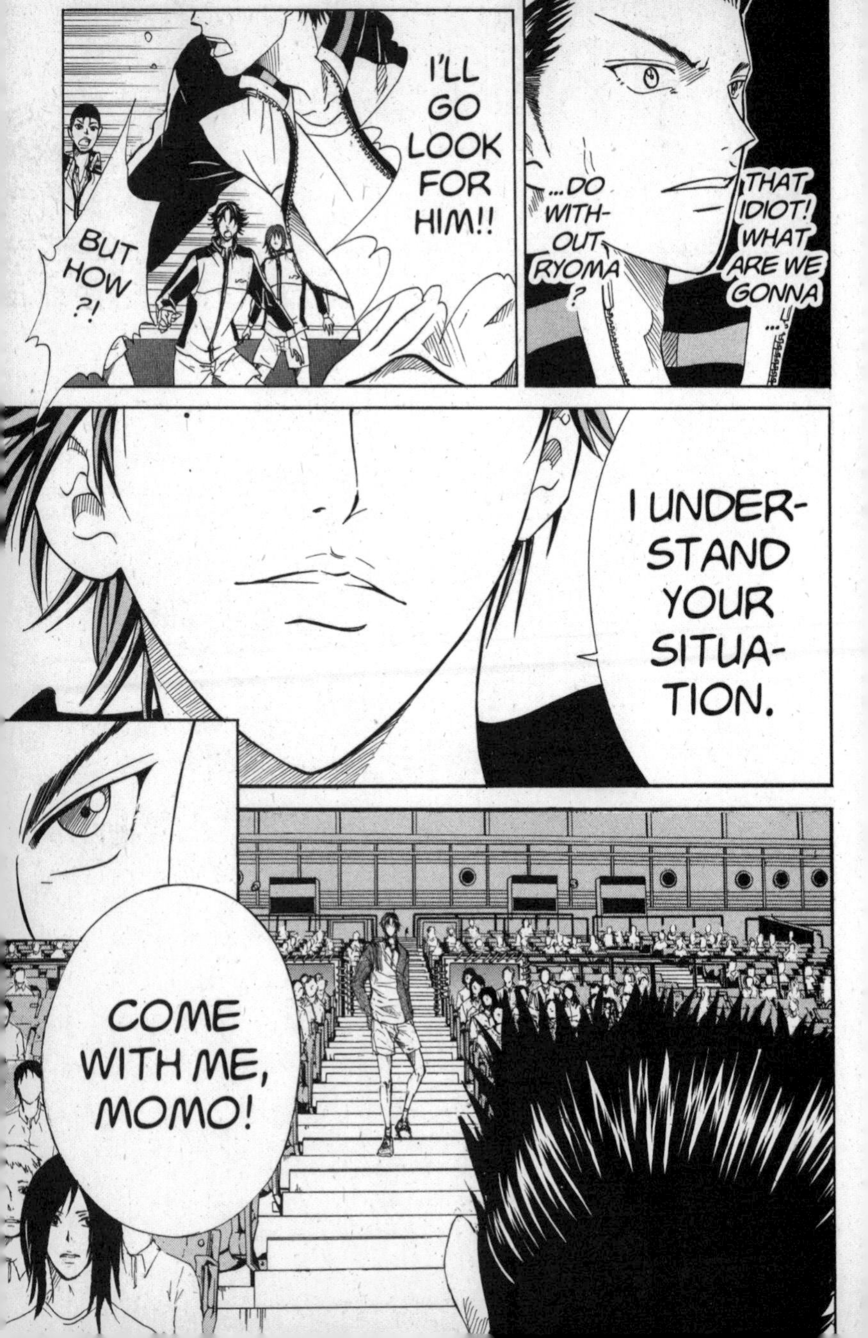
THAT IDIOT! WHAT ARE WE GONNA ...
...DO WITHOUT RYOMA?
I'LL GO LOOK FOR HIM!!
BUT HOW?!
I UNDERSTAND YOUR SITUATION.
COME WITH ME, MOMO!

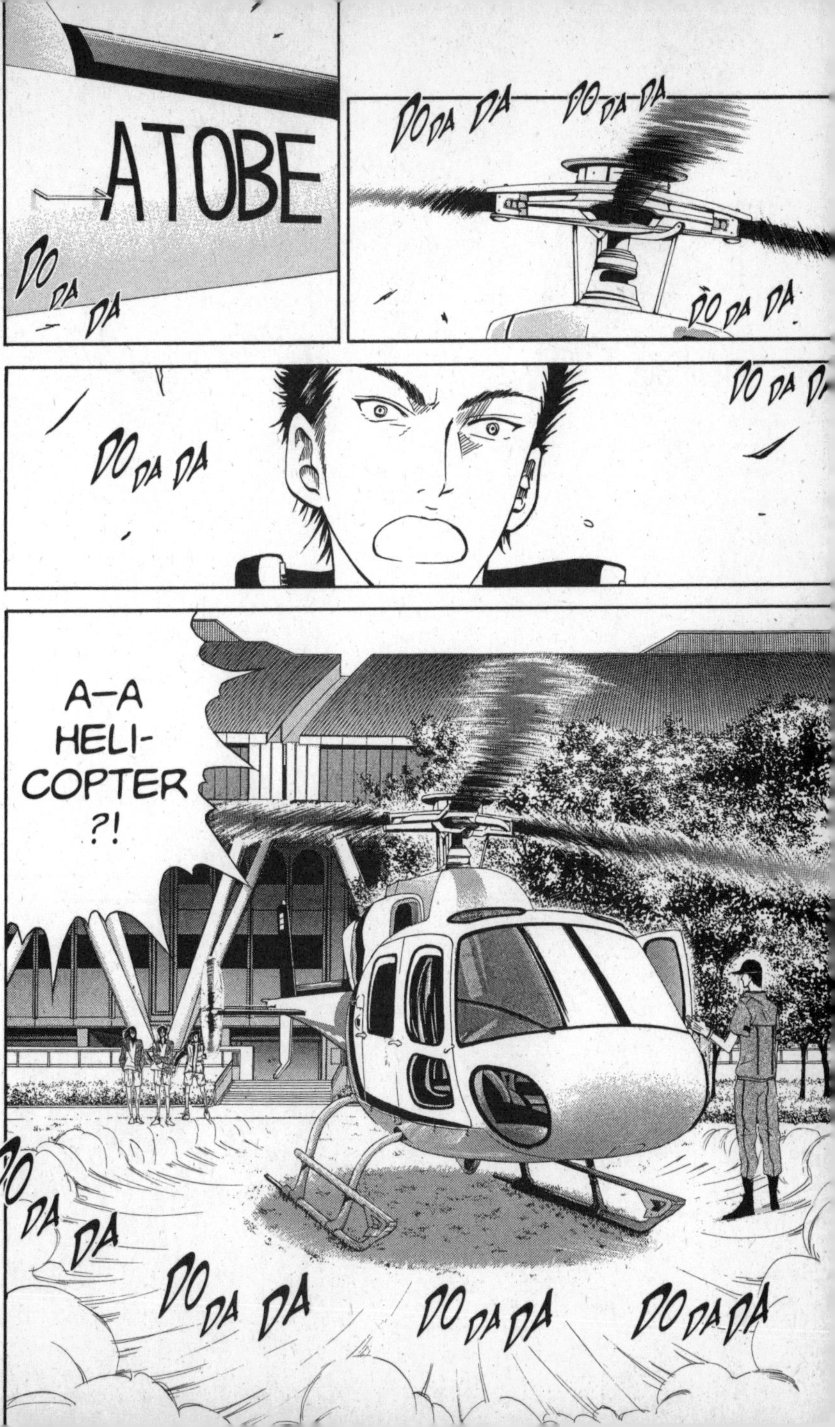
DO DA DA
DO DA DA
DO DA DA
ATOBE
DO DA DA
DO DA DA
DO DA DA
A—A HELI-COPTER?!
DO DA DA
DO DA DA
DO DA DA
DO DA DA

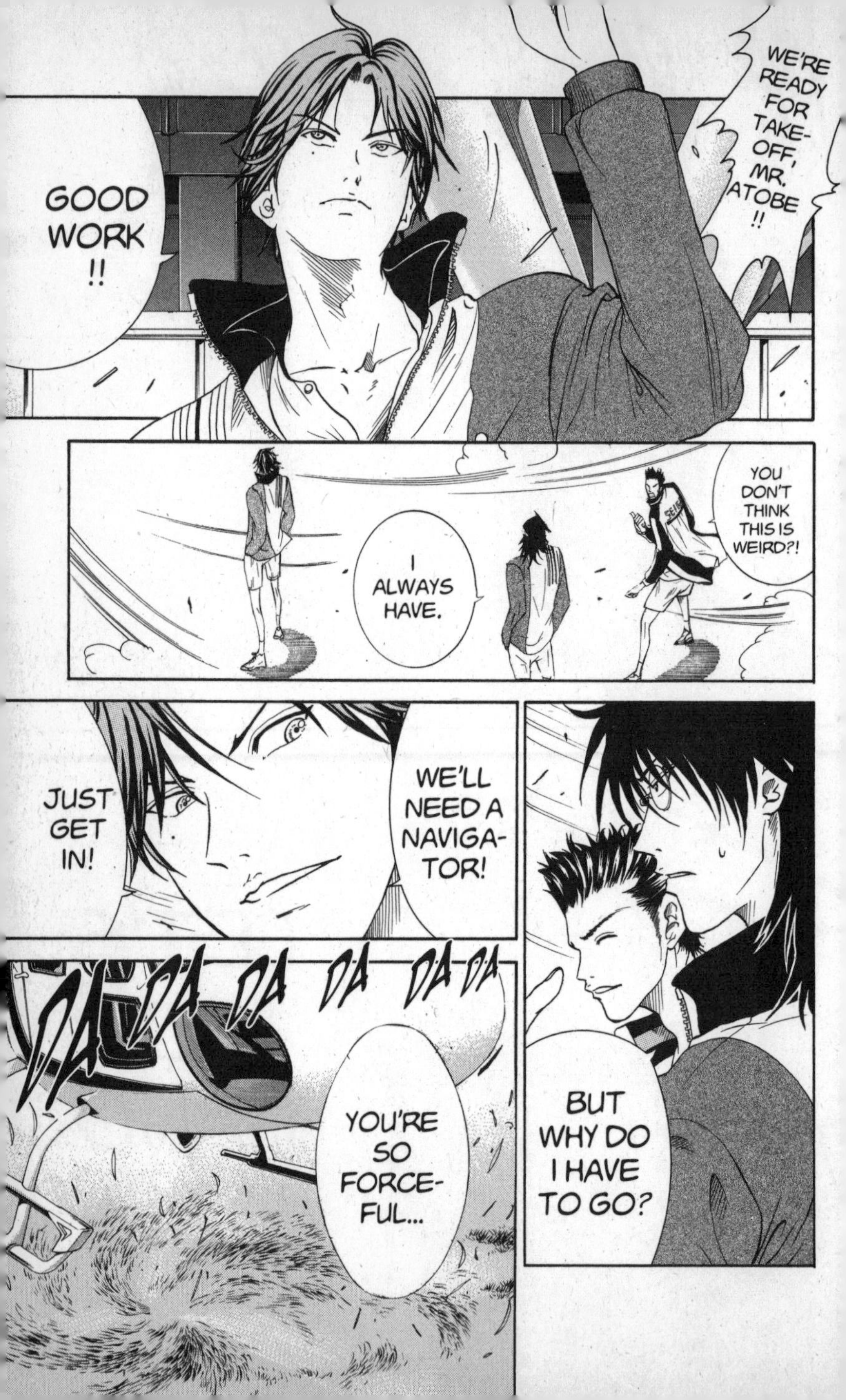
WE'RE READY FOR TAKE-OFF, MR. ATOBE!!
GOOD WORK!!
YOU DON'T THINK THIS IS WEIRD?!
I ALWAYS HAVE.
BUT WHY DO I HAVE TO GO?
WE'LL NEED A NAVIGATOR!
JUST GET IN!
DA DA DA DA DA DA
YOU'RE SO FORCEFUL...

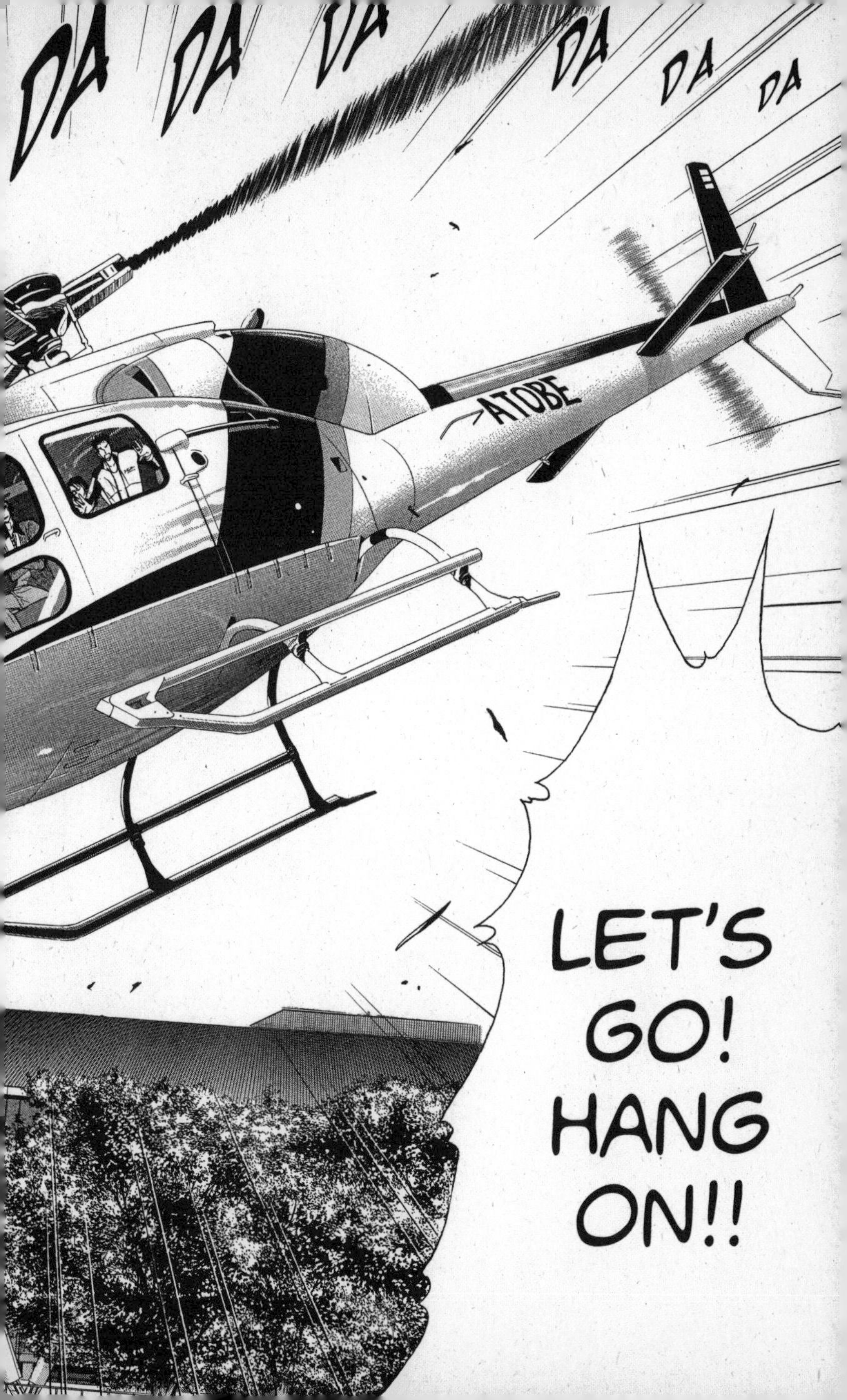
DA DA DA DA DA DA
ATOBE
LET'S GO! HANG ON!!

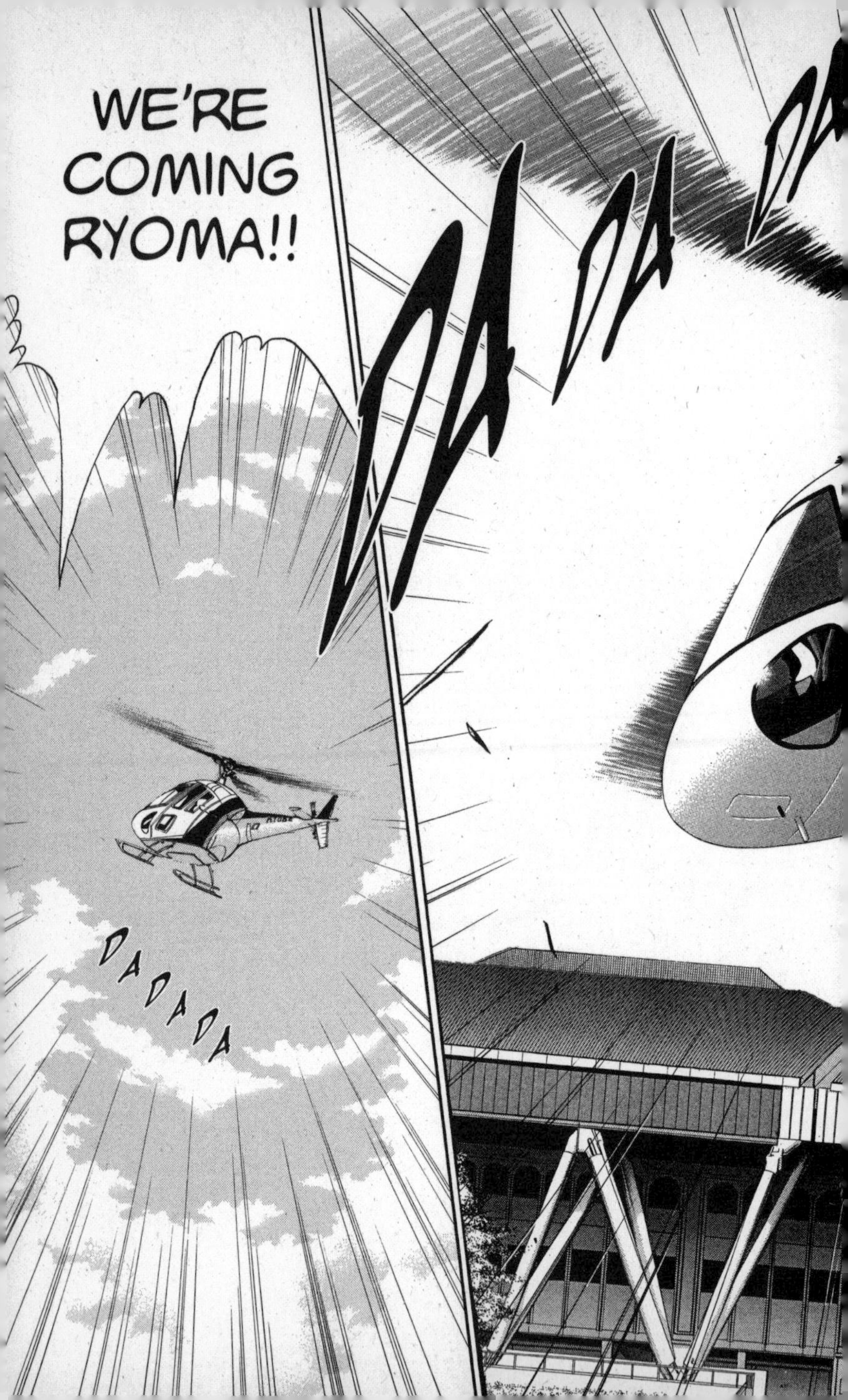
DA DA DA DA
WE'RE COMING RYOMA!!
DADADA

テニスの王子様

THE PRINCE OF TENNIS

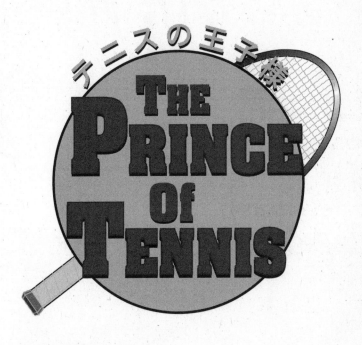

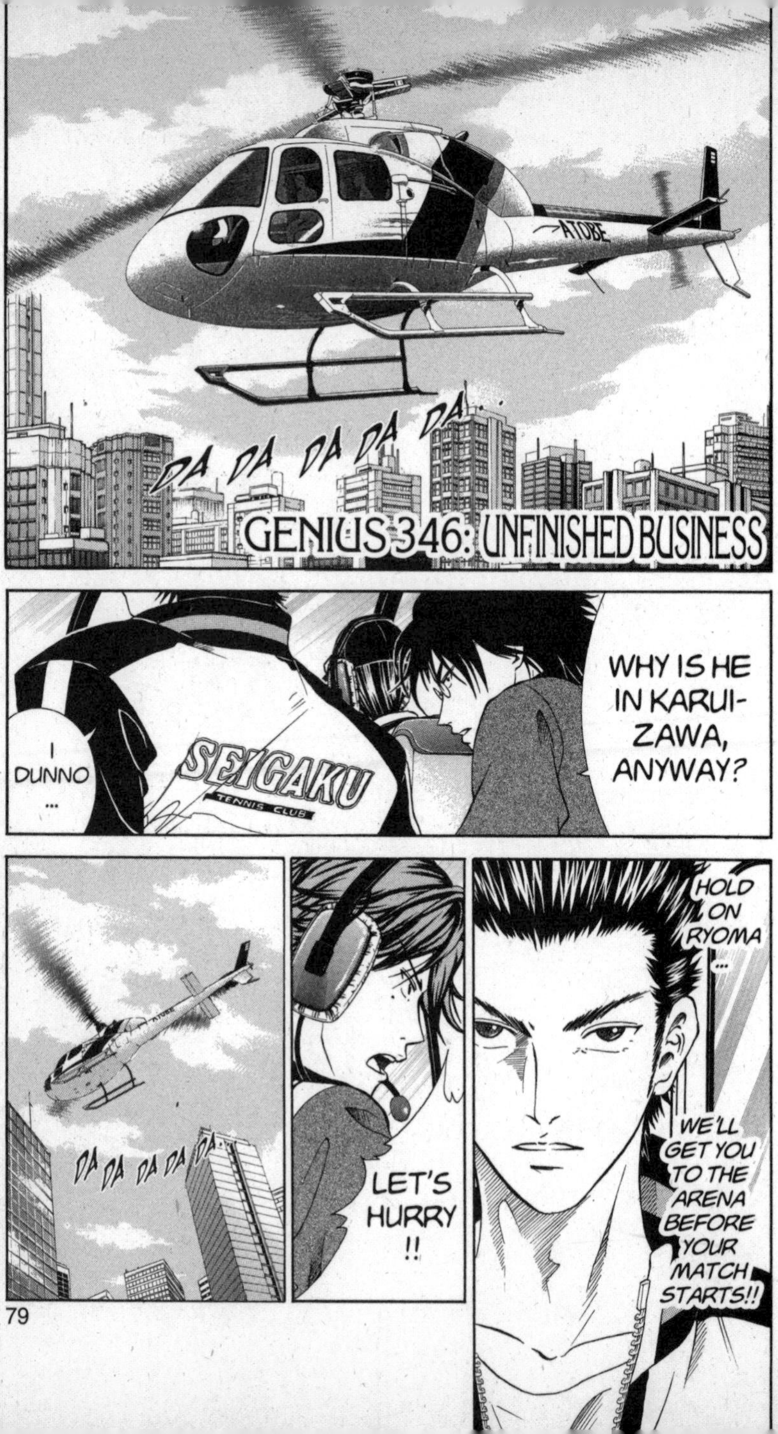
DA DA DA DA DA
GENIUS 346: UNFINISHED BUSINESS
WHY IS HE IN KARUI-ZAWA, ANYWAY?
I DUNNO ...
HOLD ON RYOMA ...
WE'LL GET YOU TO THE ARENA BEFORE YOUR MATCH STARTS!!
LET'S HURRY !!
DA DA DA DA DA

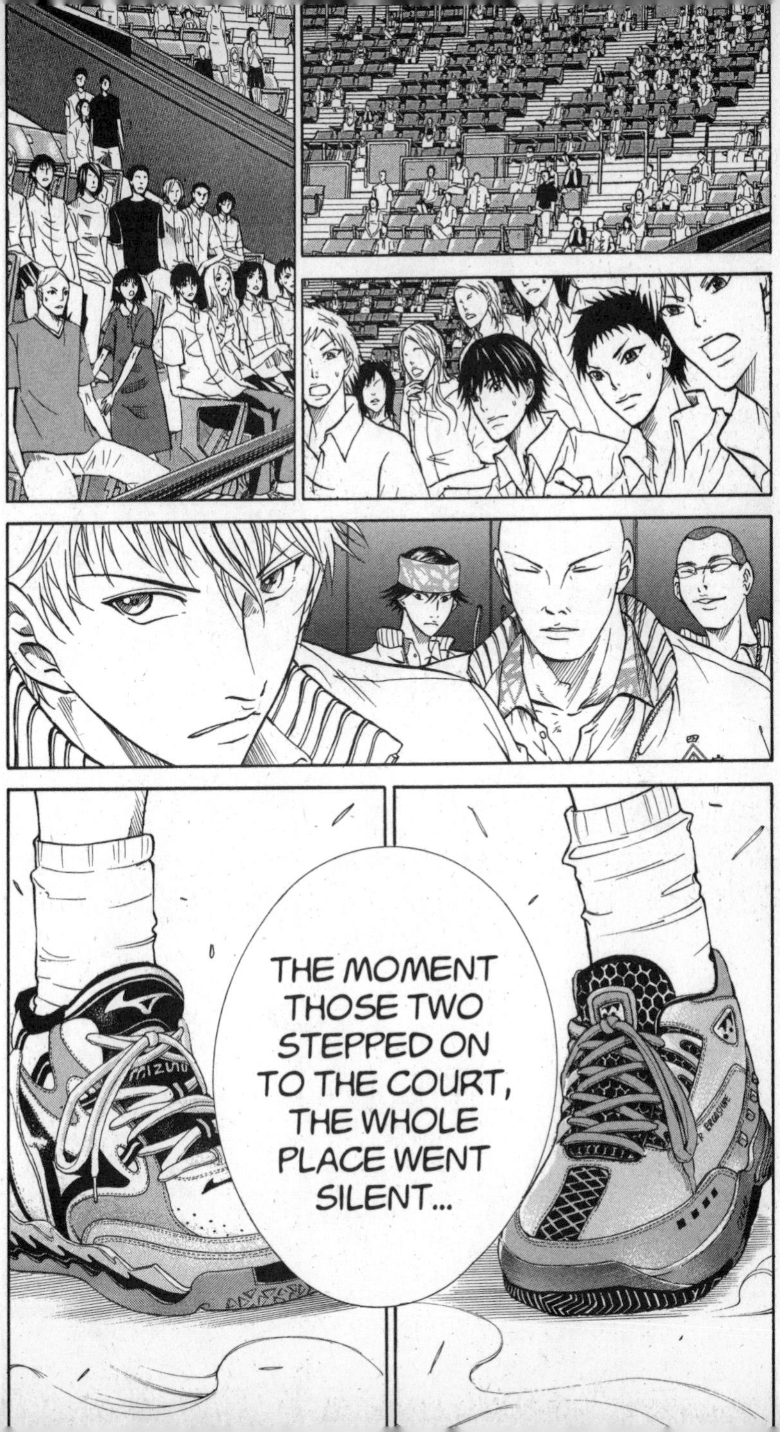
THE MOMENT THOSE TWO STEPPED ON TO THE COURT, THE WHOLE PLACE WENT SILENT...

READ THIS WAY

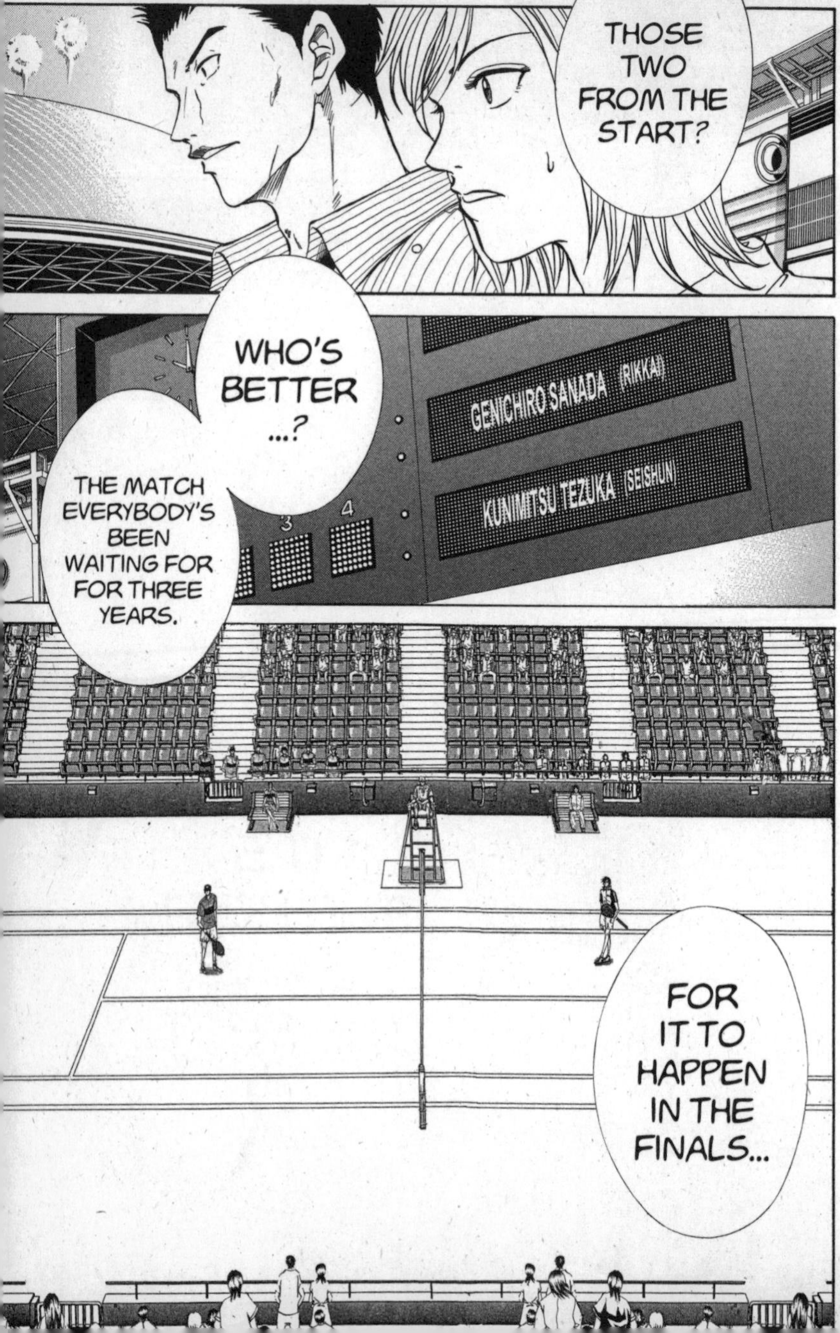
THOSE TWO FROM THE START?
GENICHIRO SANADA (RIKKAI)
KUNIMITSU TEZUKA (SEISHUN)
WHO'S BETTER ...?
THE MATCH EVERYBODY'S BEEN WAITING FOR FOR THREE YEARS.
FOR IT TO HAPPEN IN THE FINALS...

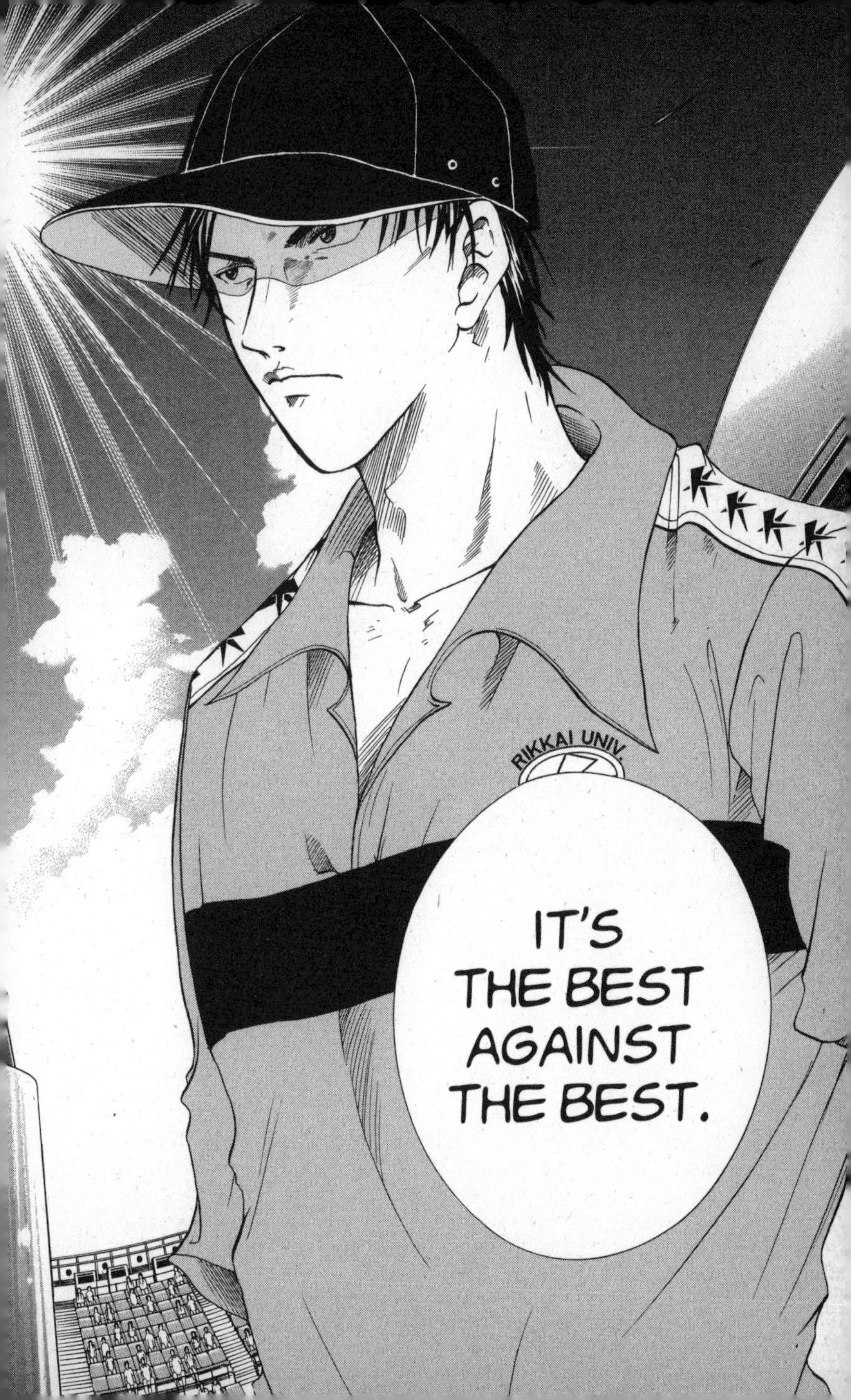
RIKKAI UNIV.
IT'S THE BEST AGAINST THE BEST.

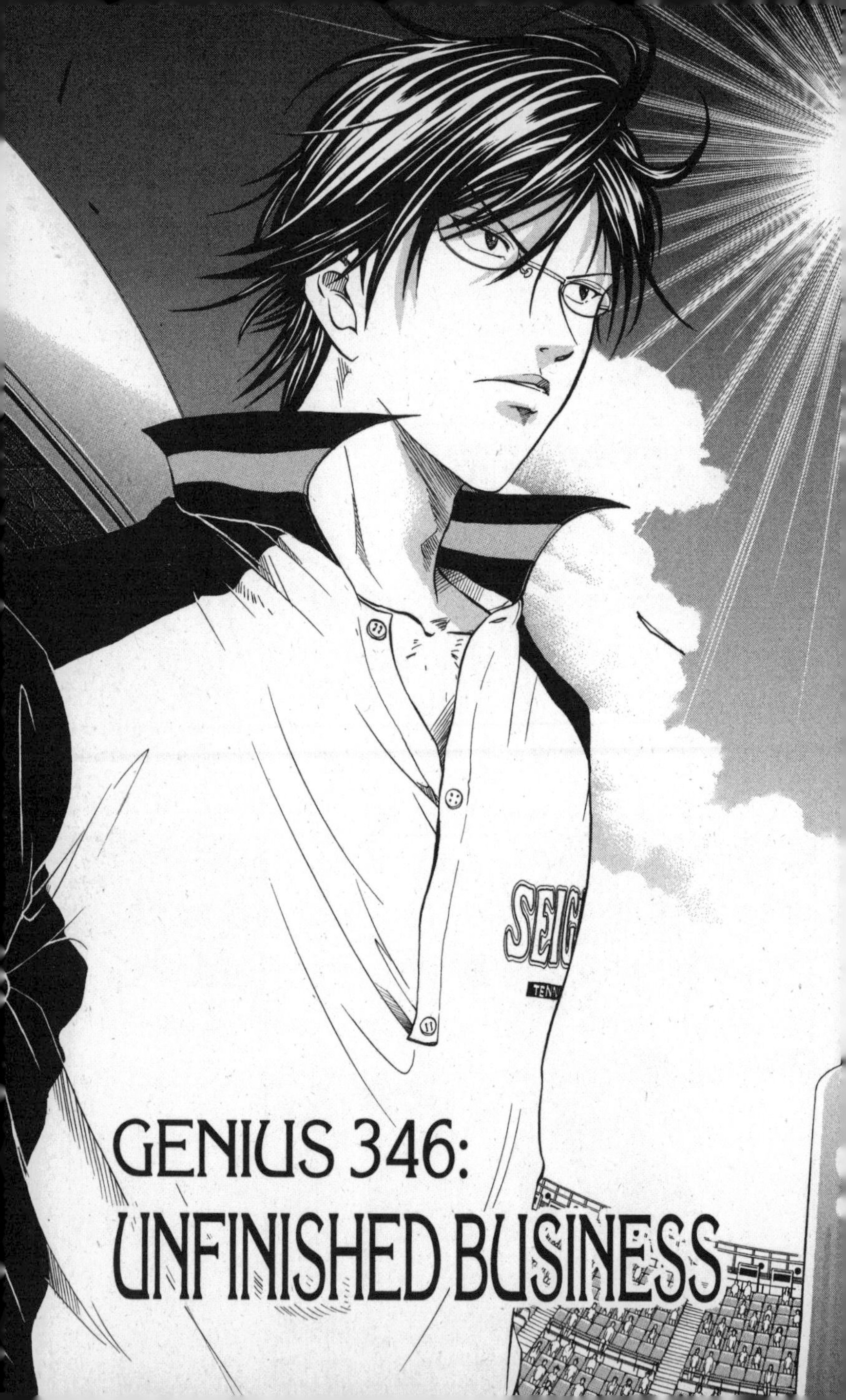

GENIUS 346: UNFINISHED BUSINESS

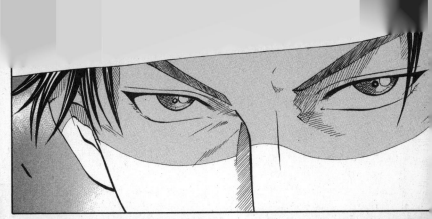

YOU'RE NOT LEAVING UN-SCATHED.

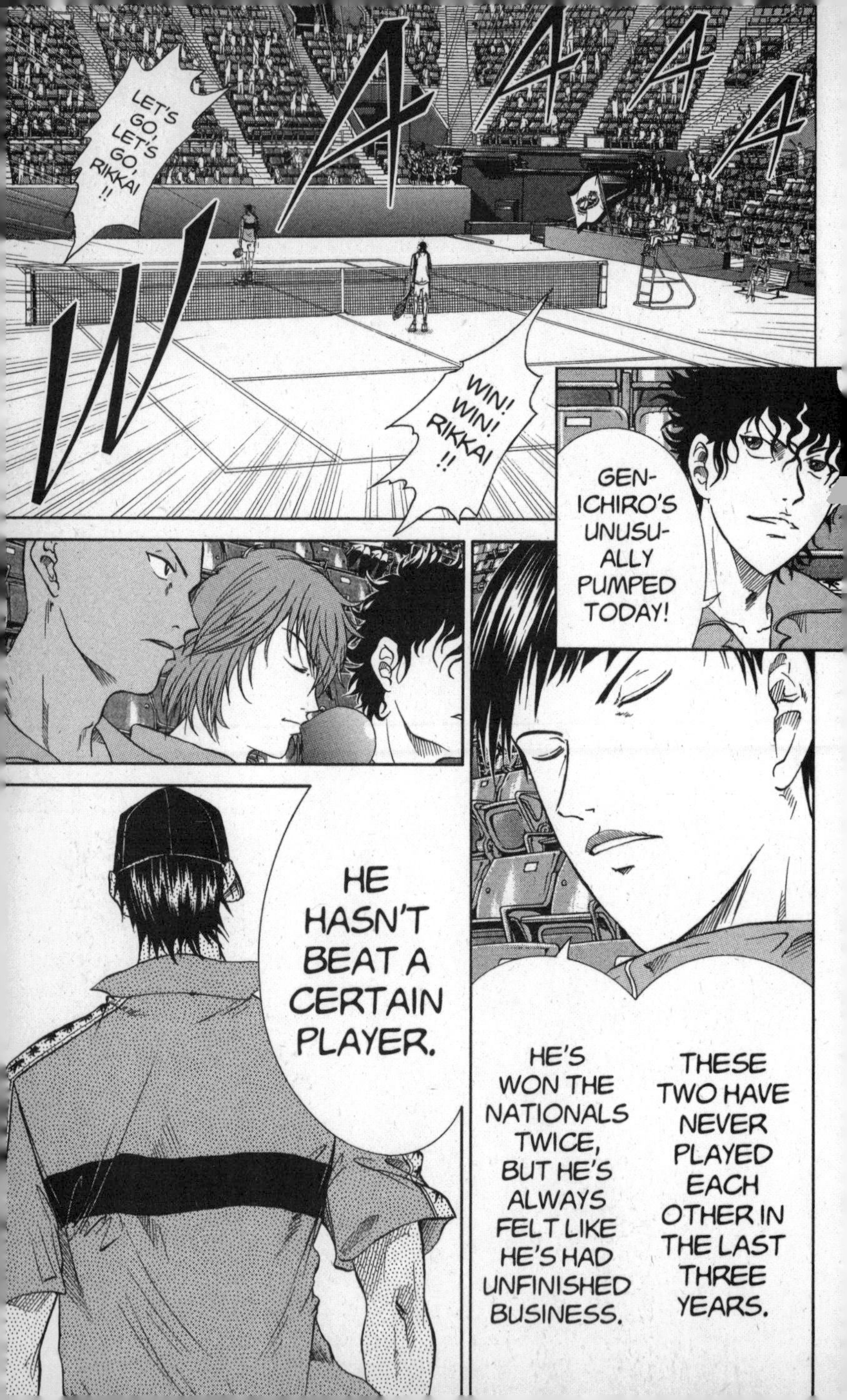
WAAAA
LET'S GO, LET'S GO, RIKKAI!!
WIN! WIN! RIKKAI!!
GEN-ICHIRO'S UNUSU-ALLY PUMPED TODAY!
THESE TWO HAVE NEVER PLAYED EACH OTHER IN THE LAST THREE YEARS.
HE'S WON THE NATIONALS TWICE, BUT HE'S ALWAYS FELT LIKE HE'S HAD UNFINISHED BUSINESS.
HE HASN'T BEAT A CERTAIN PLAYER.

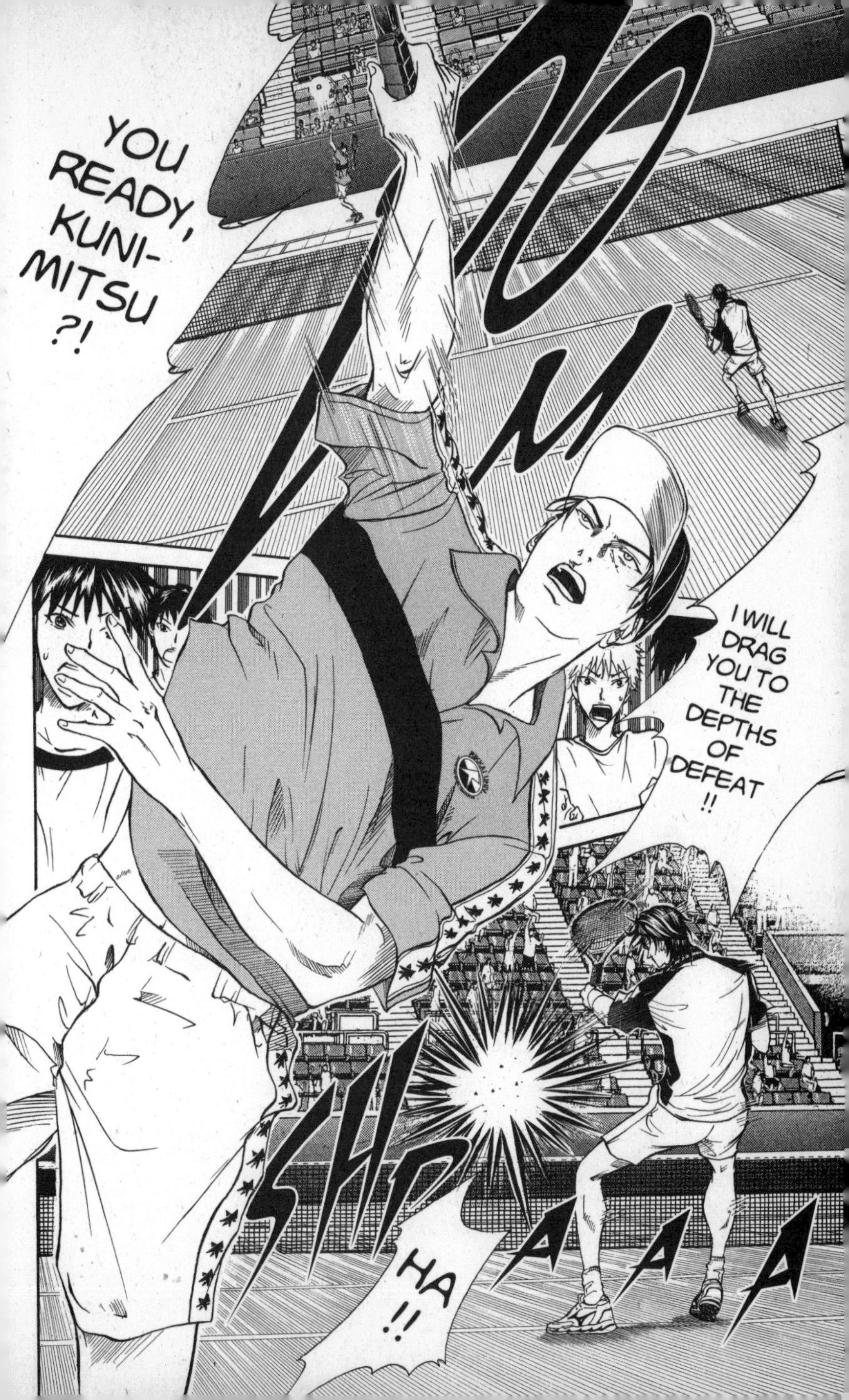
YOU READY, KUNI-MITSU?!
I WILL DRAG YOU TO THE DEPTHS OF DEFEAT!!
SHPAAA
HA!!

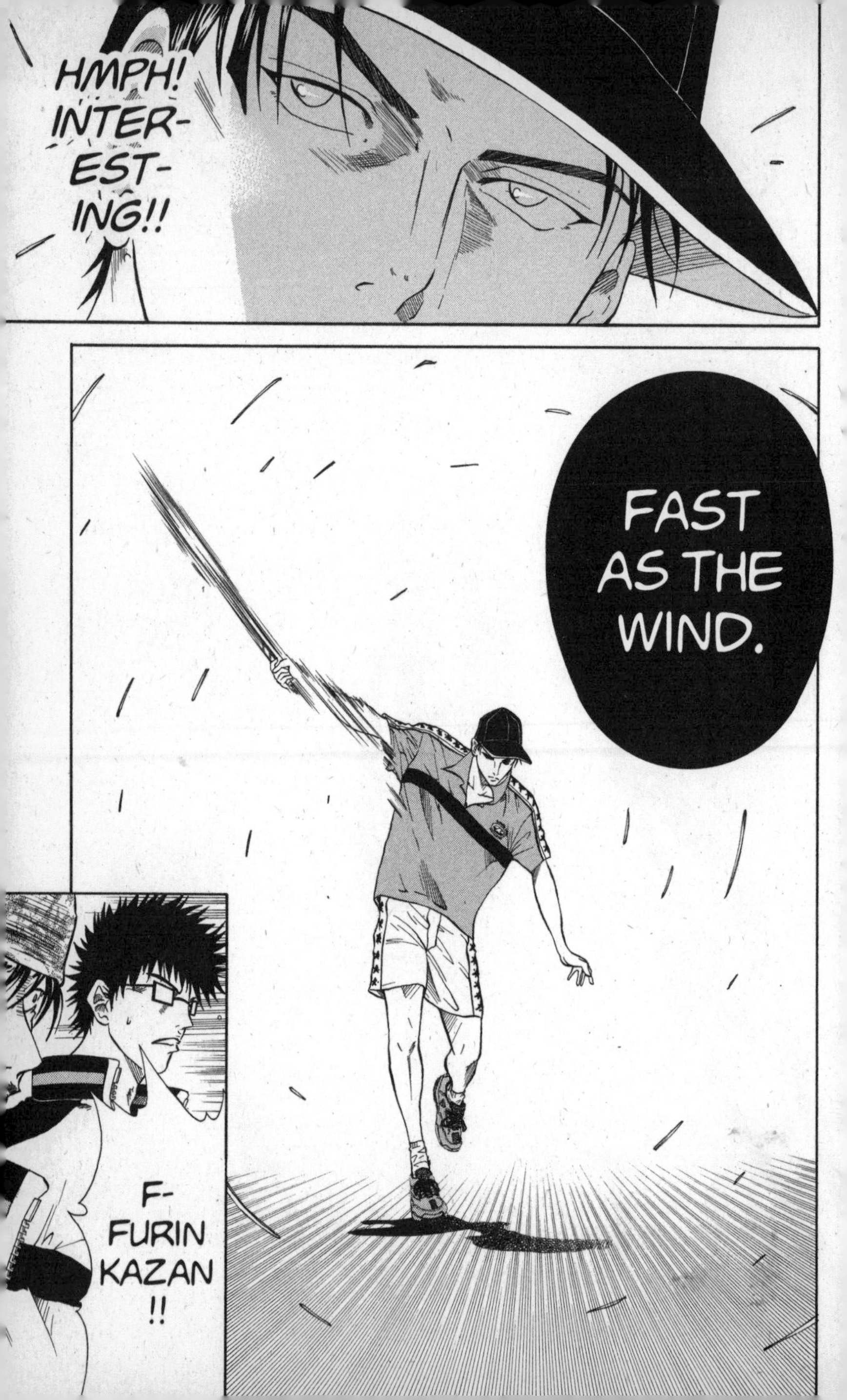
HMPH! INTER-EST-ING!!
FAST AS THE WIND.
F-FURIN KAZAN!!

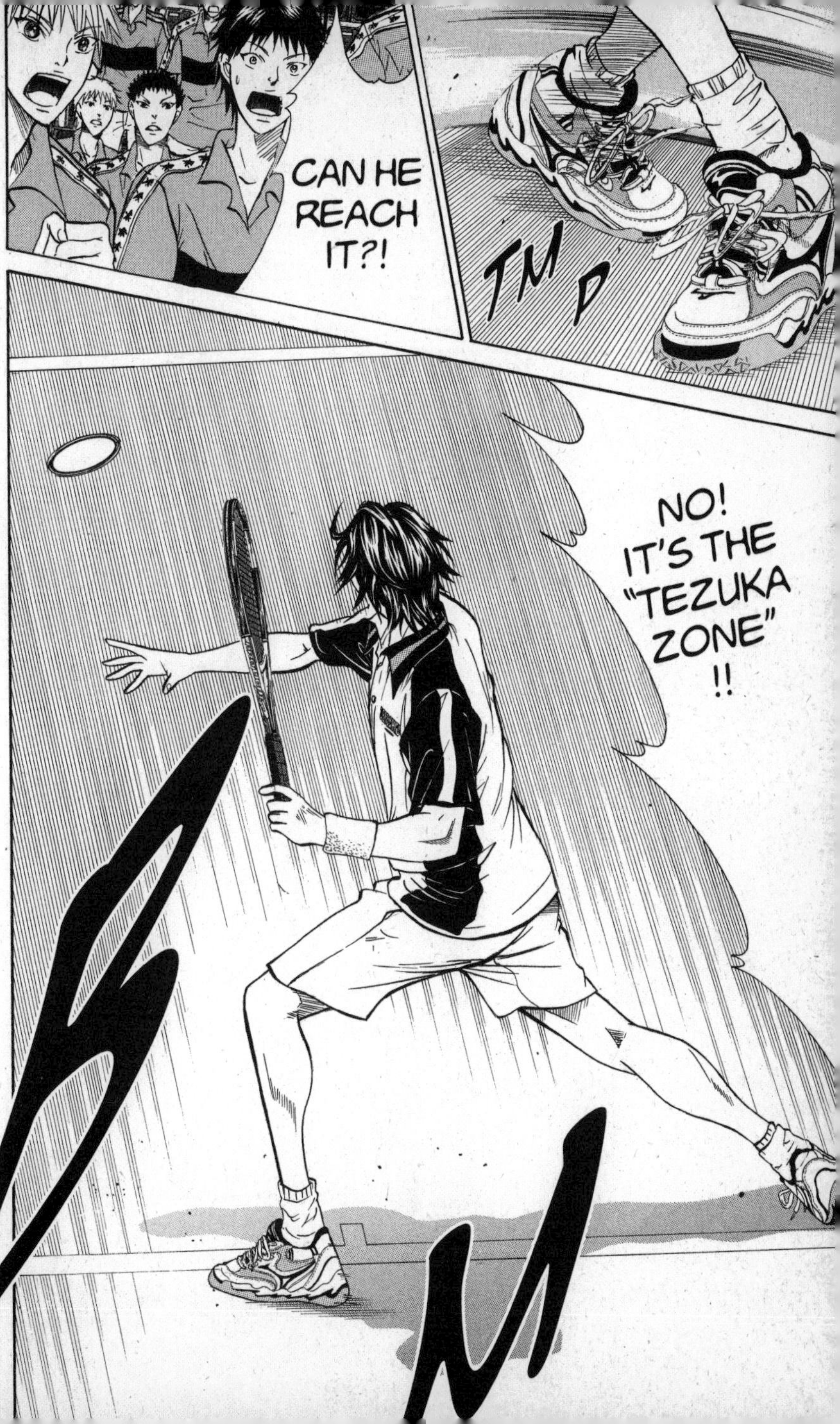
TMP
CAN HE REACH IT?!
NO! IT'S THE "TEZUKA ZONE" !!

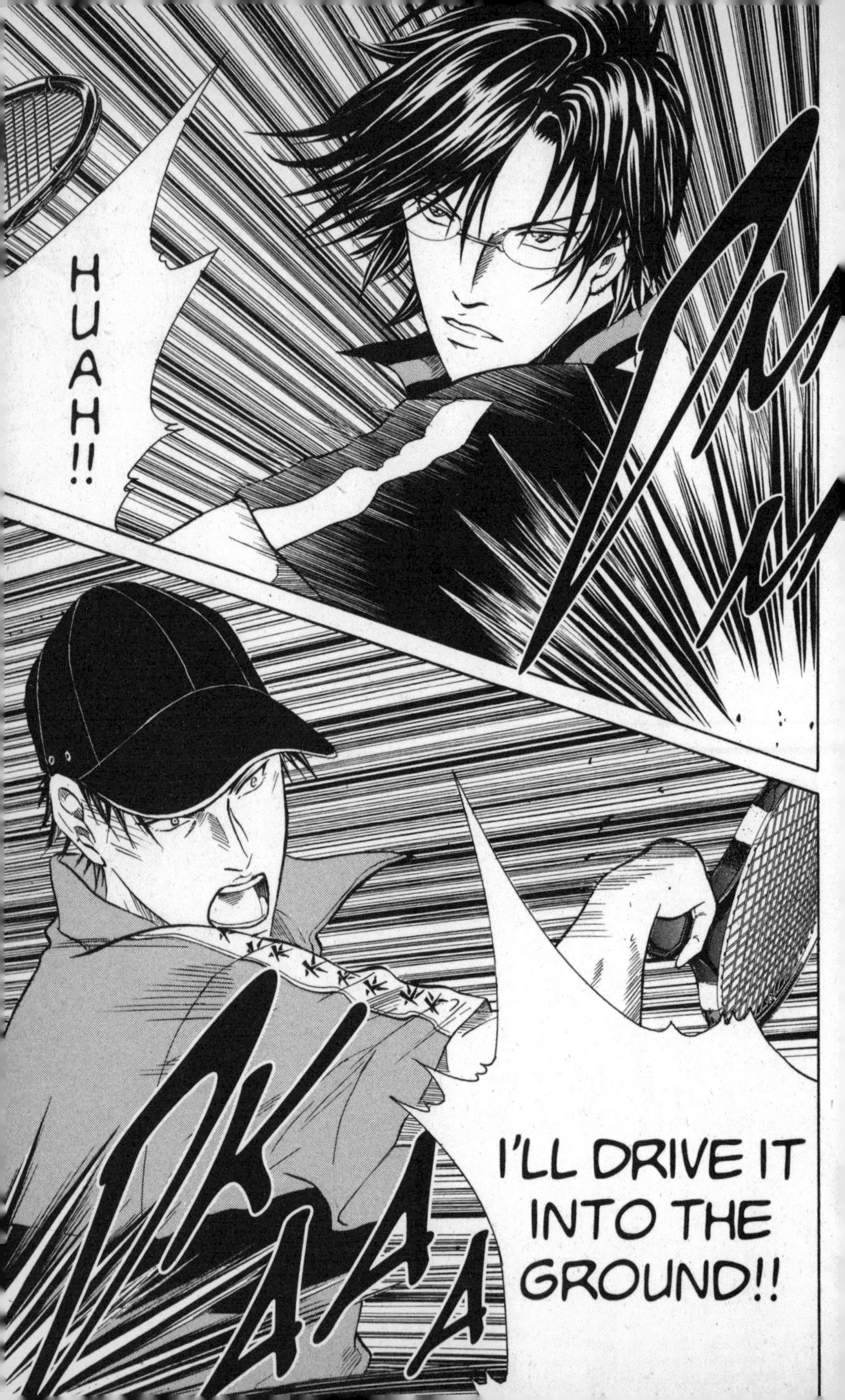
HUAH!!
I'LL DRIVE IT INTO THE GROUND!!

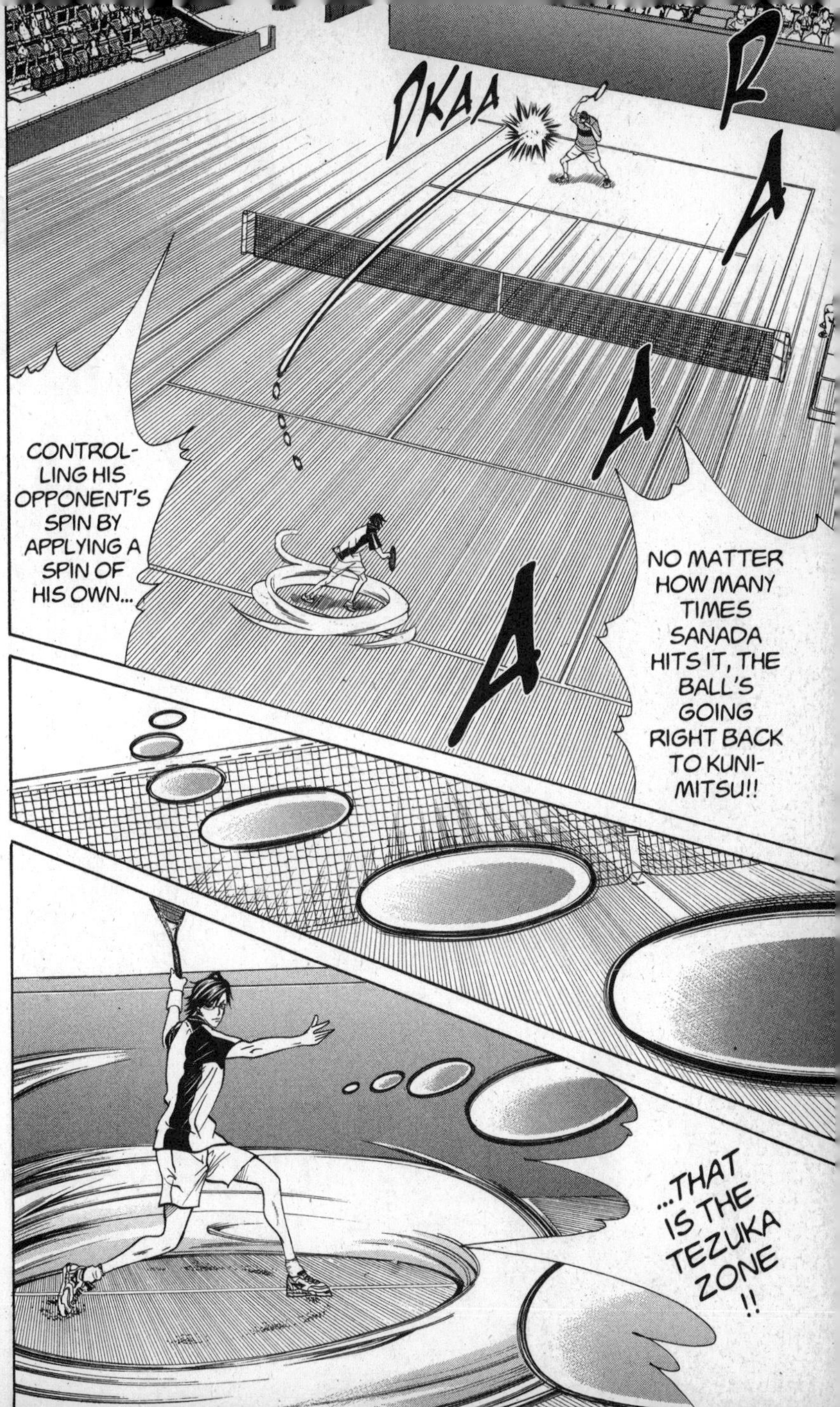
DKAA
RAAAA
CONTROLLING HIS OPPONENT'S SPIN BY APPLYING A SPIN OF HIS OWN...
NO MATTER HOW MANY TIMES SANADA HITS IT, THE BALL'S GOING RIGHT BACK TO KUNIMITSU!!
...THAT IS THE TEZUKA ZONE!!

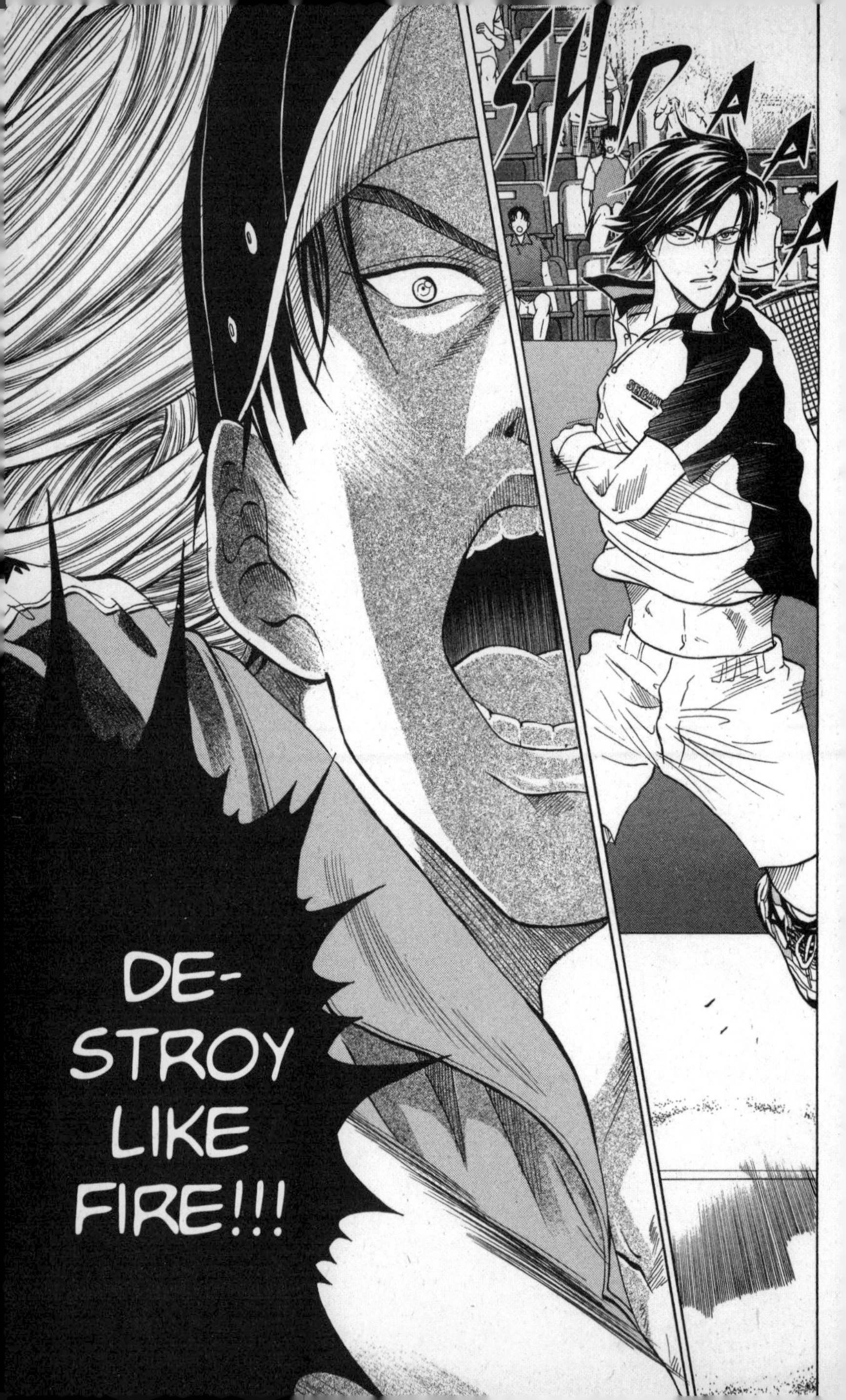
SHPAAAA
DE-STROY LIKE FIRE!!!

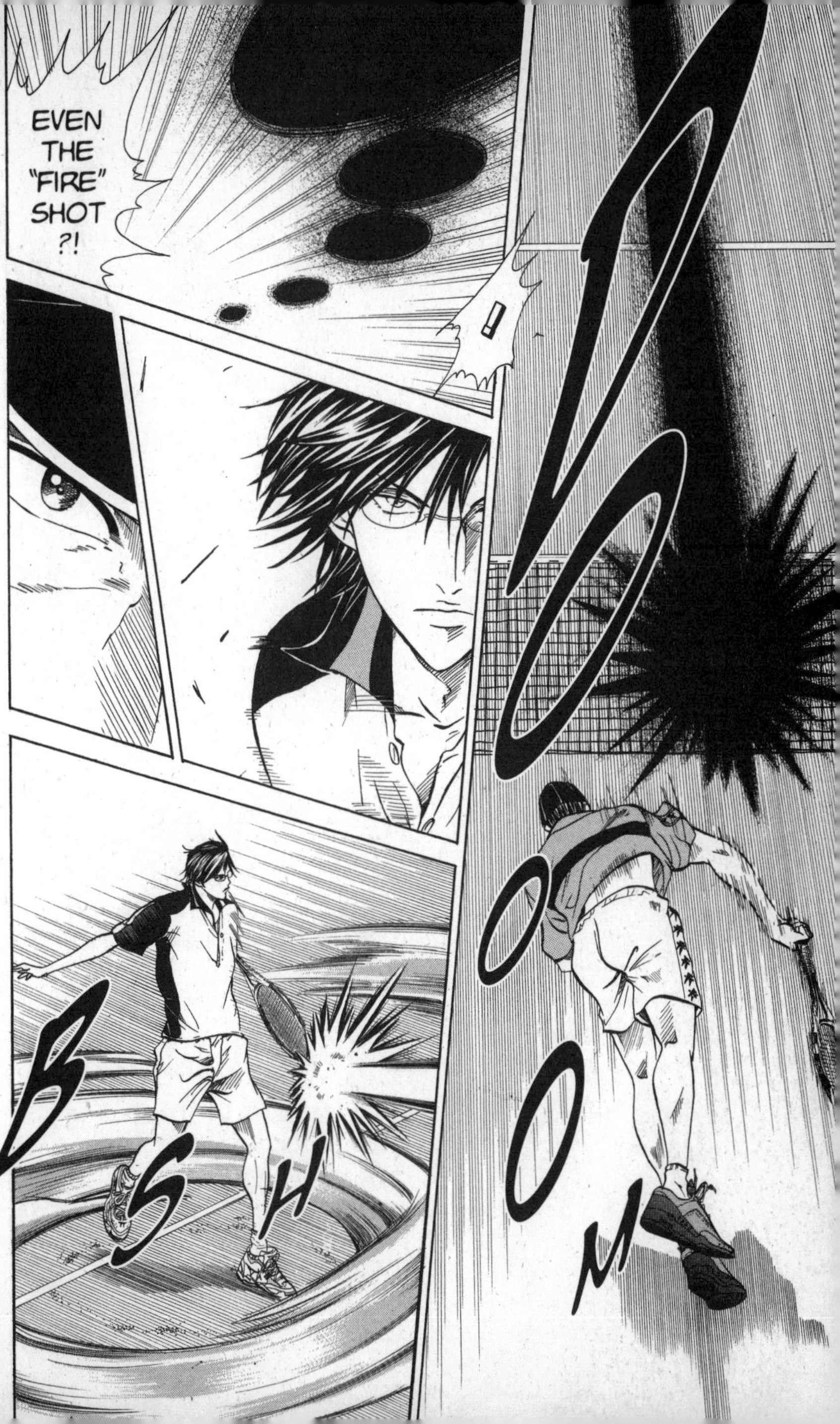
EVEN THE "FIRE" SHOT ?!
!
BSH

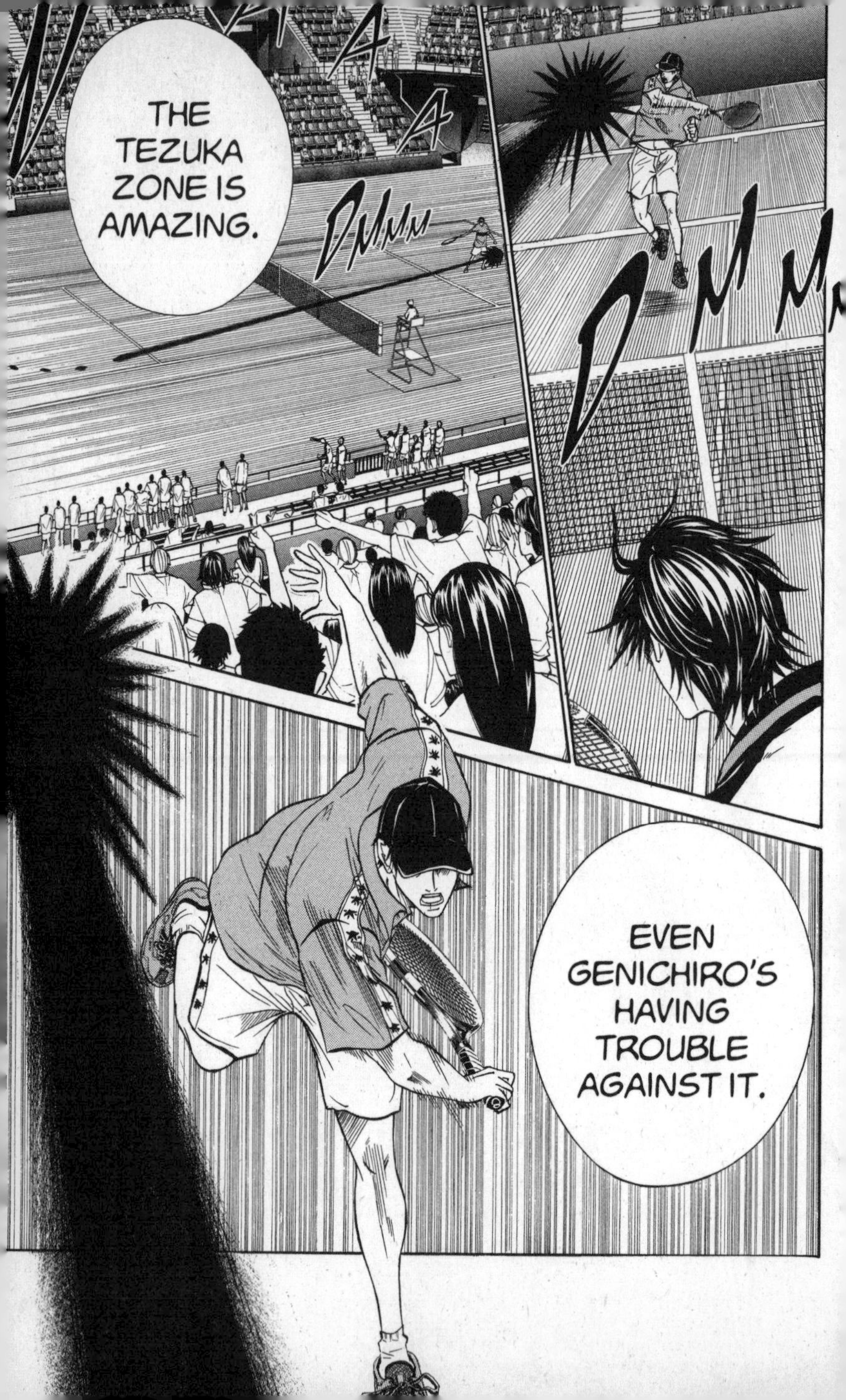
DMMM
THE TEZUKA ZONE IS AMAZING.
DMMM
EVEN GENICHIRO'S HAVING TROUBLE AGAINST IT.

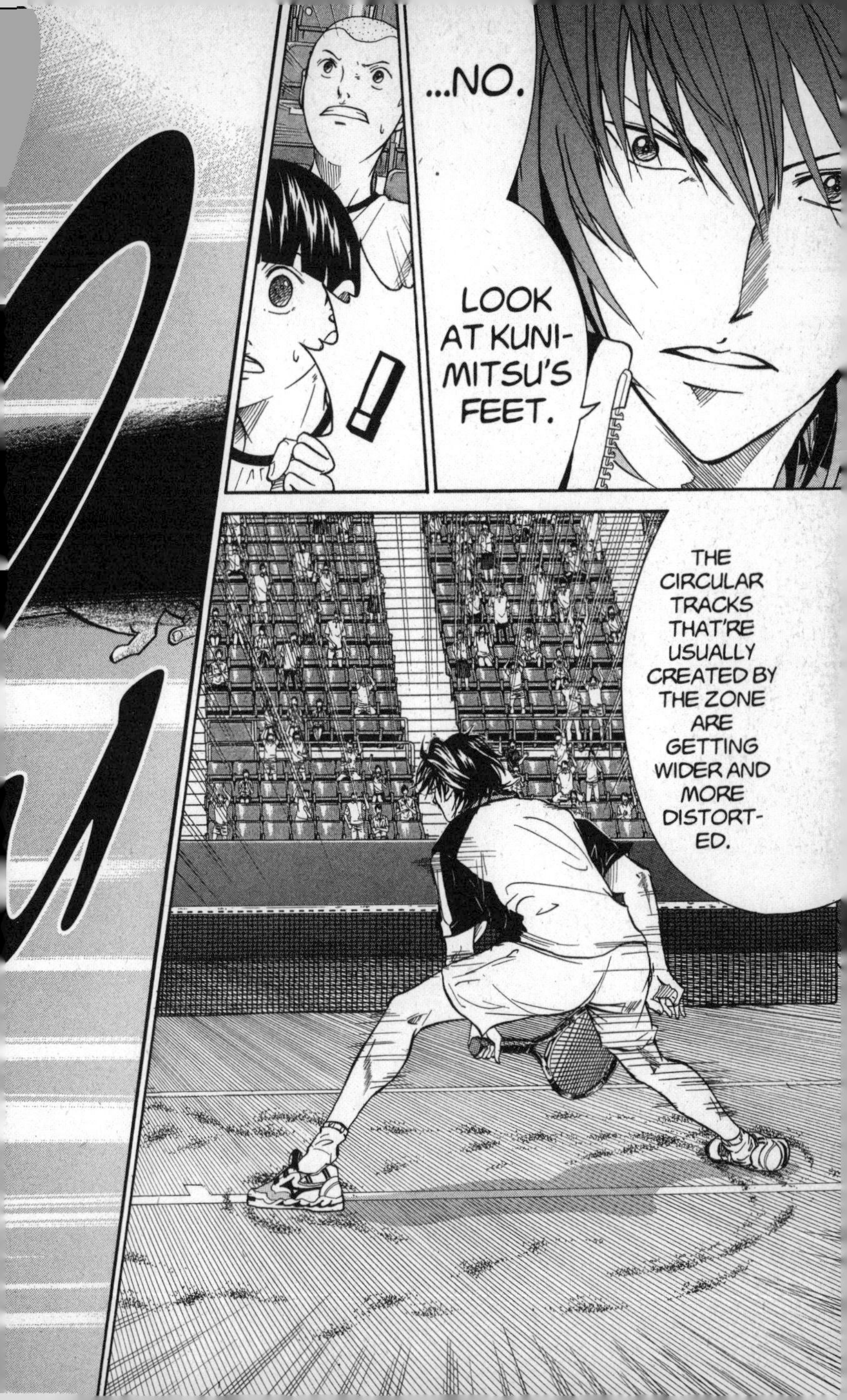
...NO.
LOOK AT KUNI-MITSU'S FEET.
!
THE CIRCULAR TRACKS THAT'RE USUALLY CREATED BY THE ZONE ARE GETTING WIDER AND MORE DISTORT-ED.

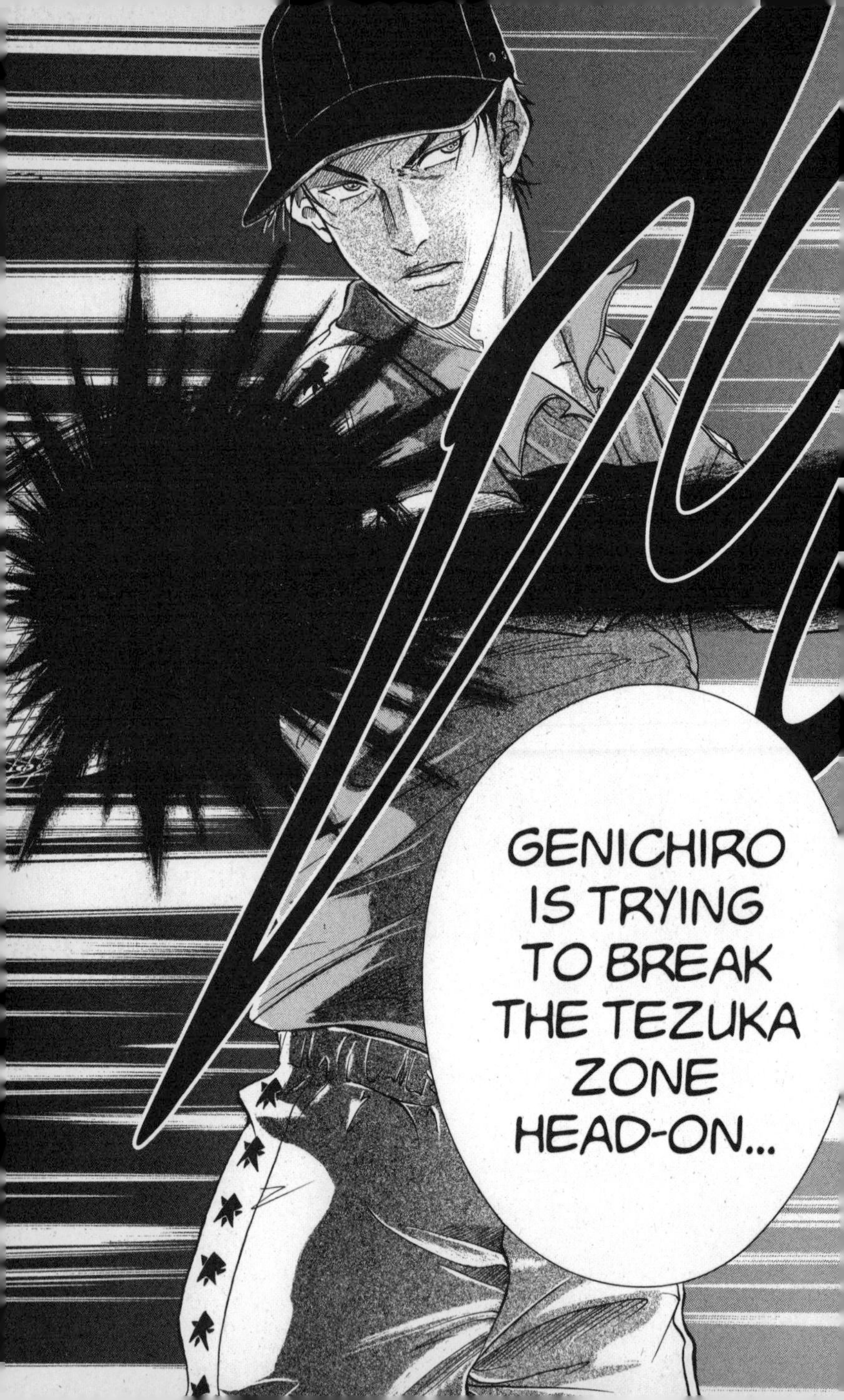
GENICHIRO IS TRYING TO BREAK THE TEZUKA ZONE HEAD-ON...

テニスの王子様

THE PRINCE OF TENNIS

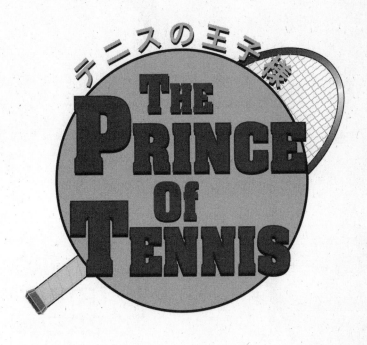

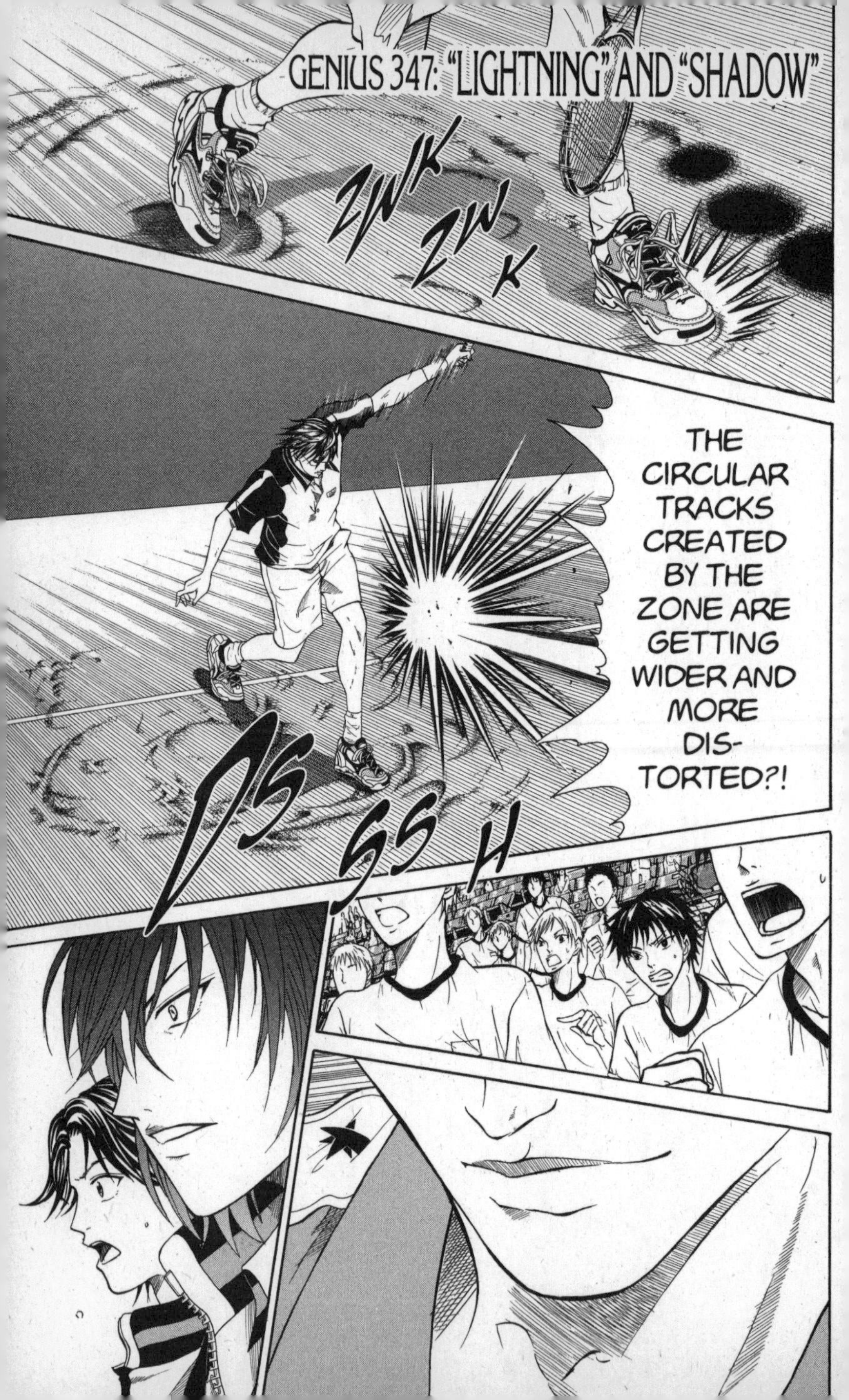
GENIUS 347: "LIGHTNING" AND "SHADOW"
ZWK ZWK
THE CIRCULAR TRACKS CREATED BY THE ZONE ARE GETTING WIDER AND MORE DIS-TORTED?!
DSSSH

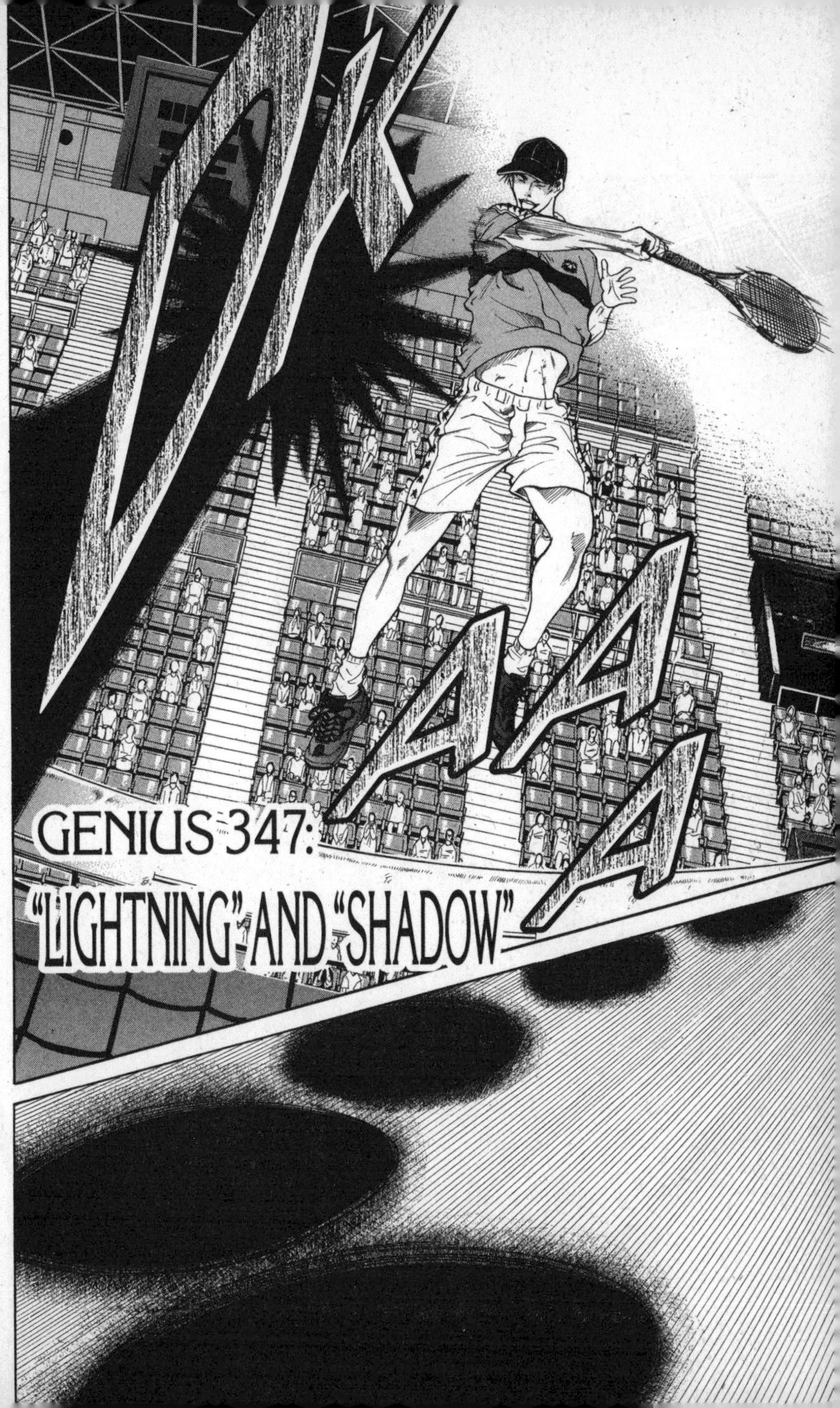
GENIUS 347:
"LIGHTNING" AND "SHADOW"

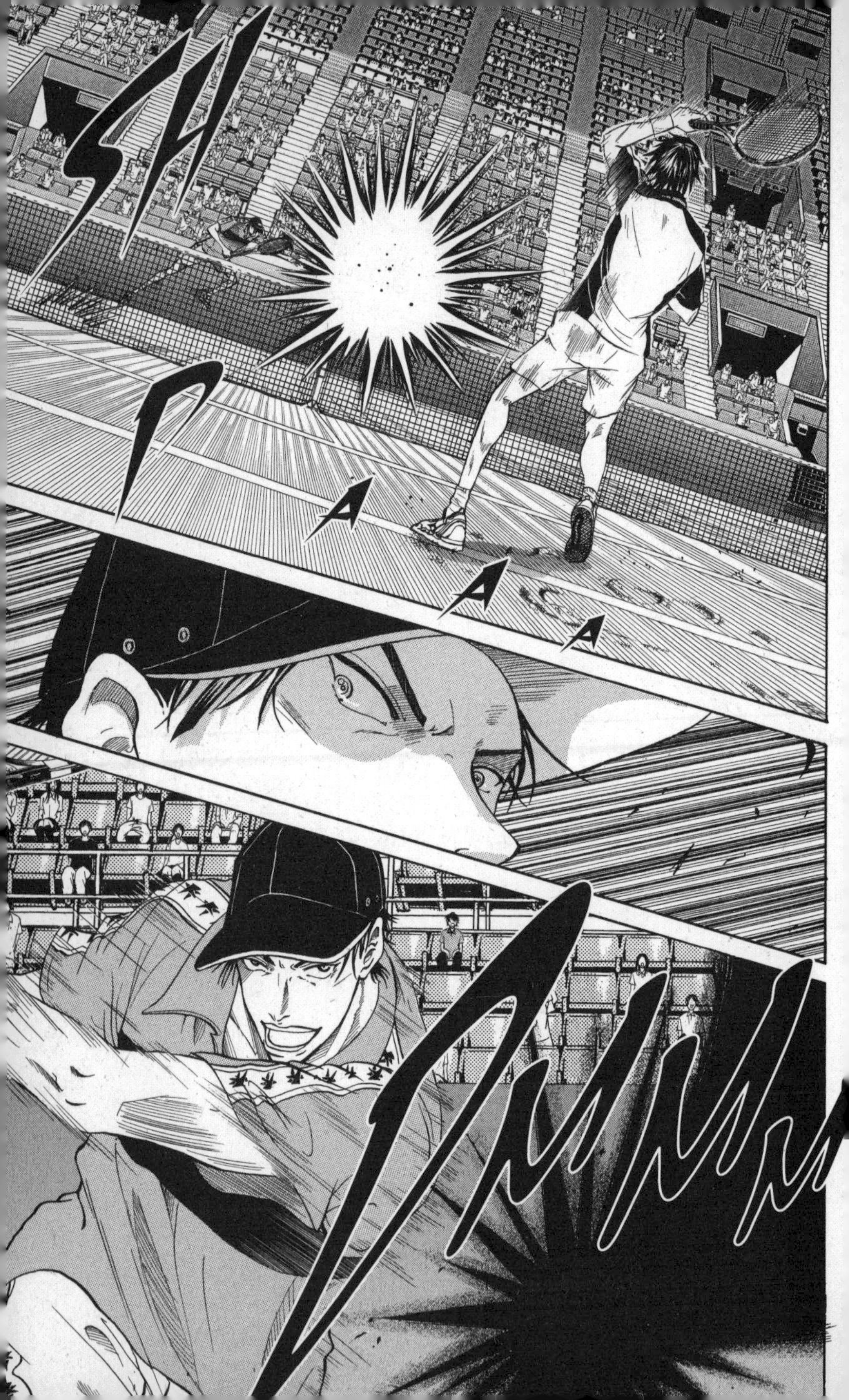

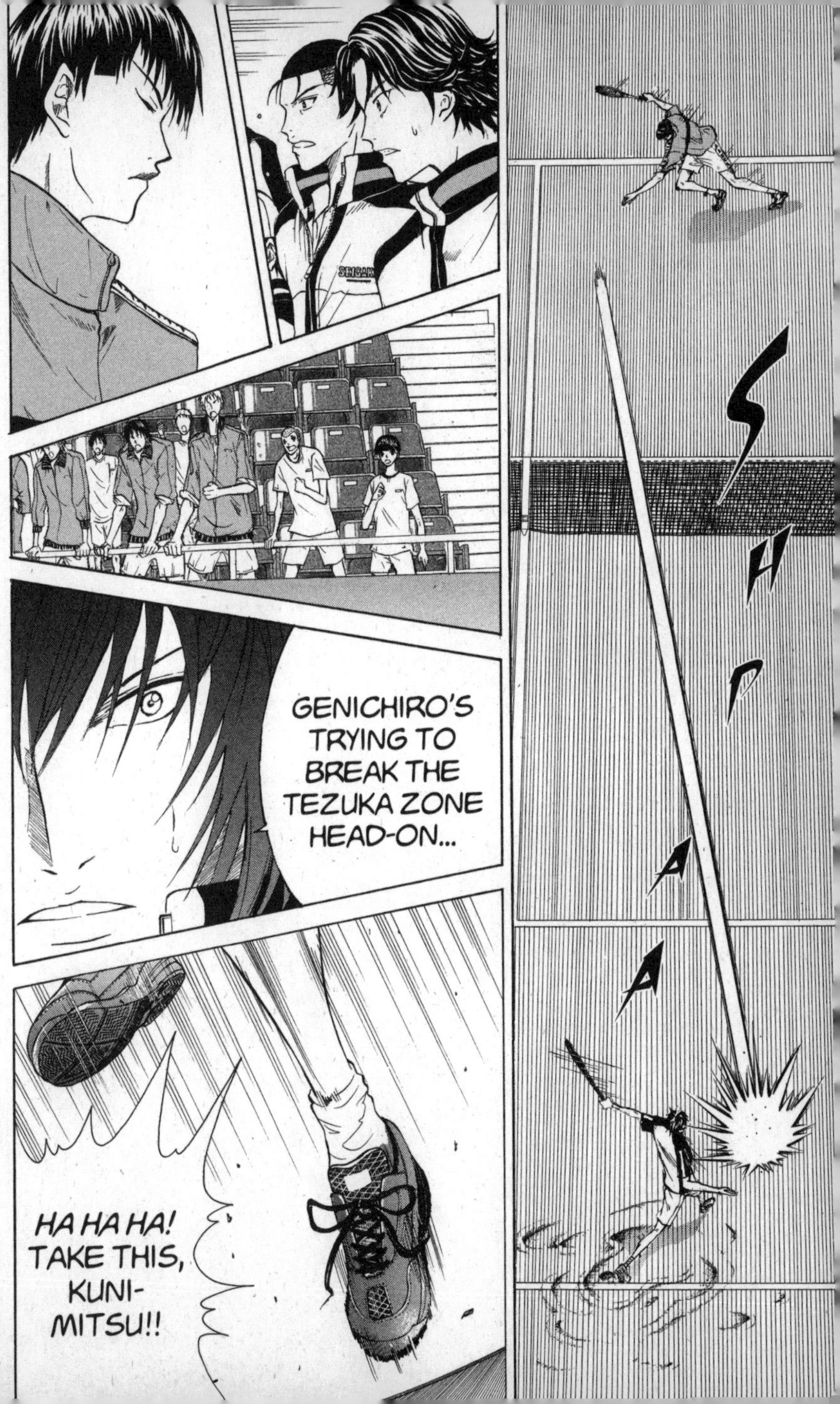
SHPAAA
GENICHIRO'S TRYING TO BREAK THE TEZUKA ZONE HEAD-ON...
HA HA HA! TAKE THIS, KUNI-MITSU!!

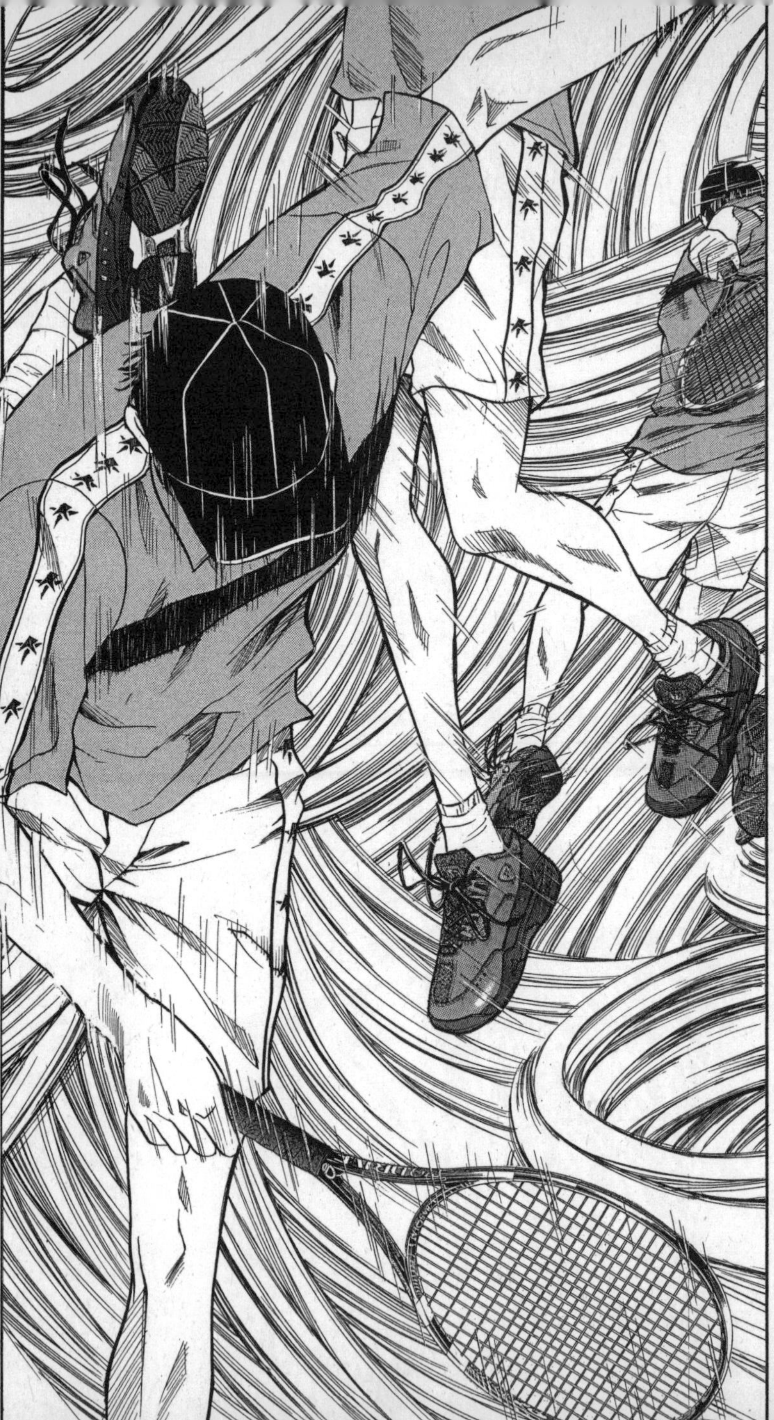

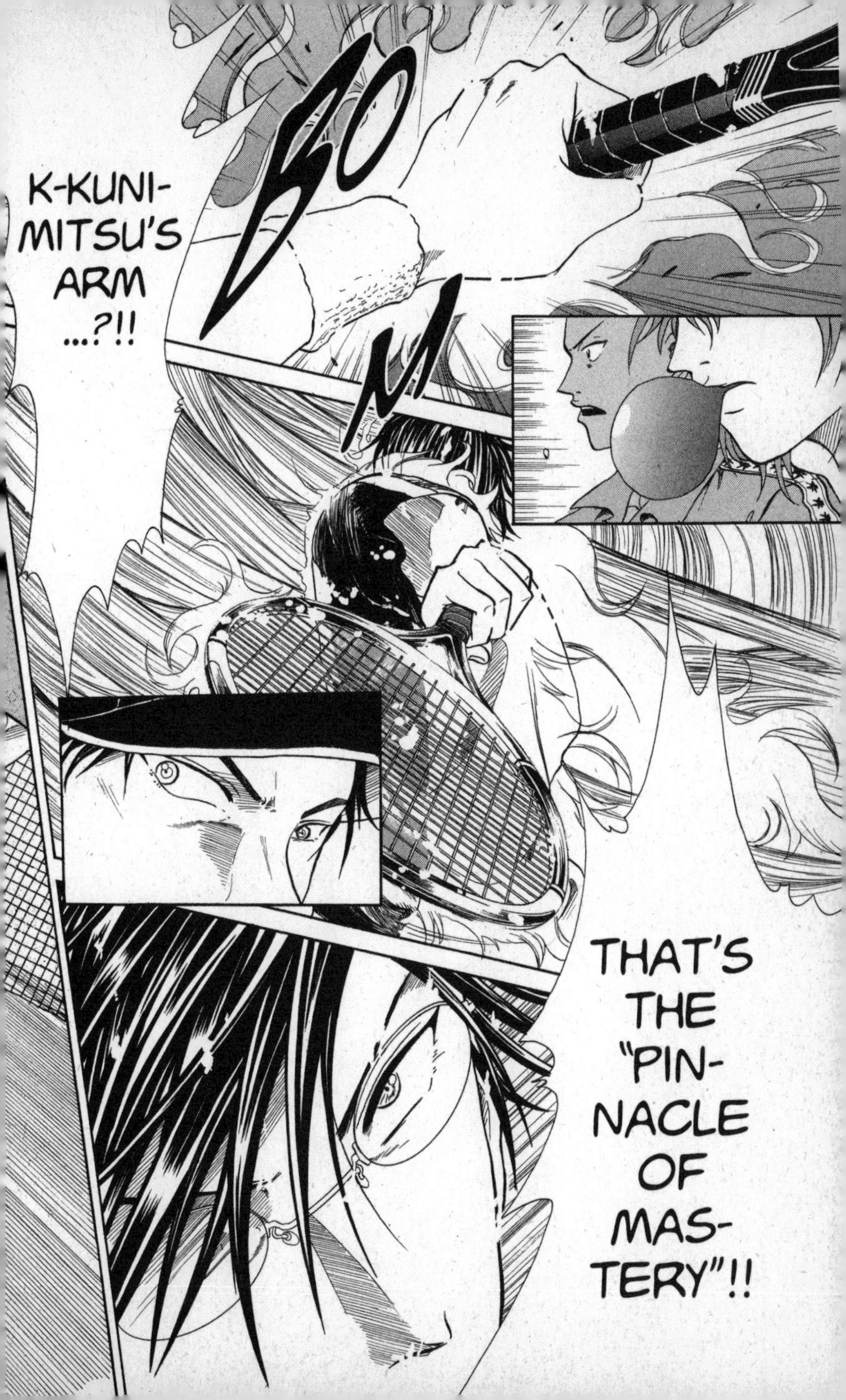
BOOM
K-KUNI-MITSU'S ARM ...?!!
THAT'S THE "PIN-NACLE OF MAS-TERY"!!

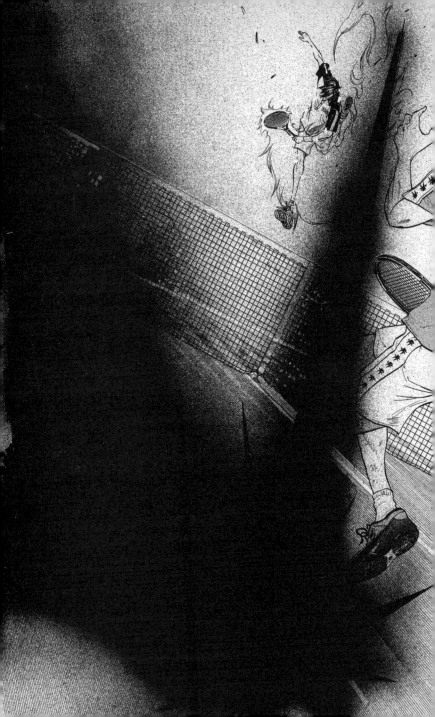

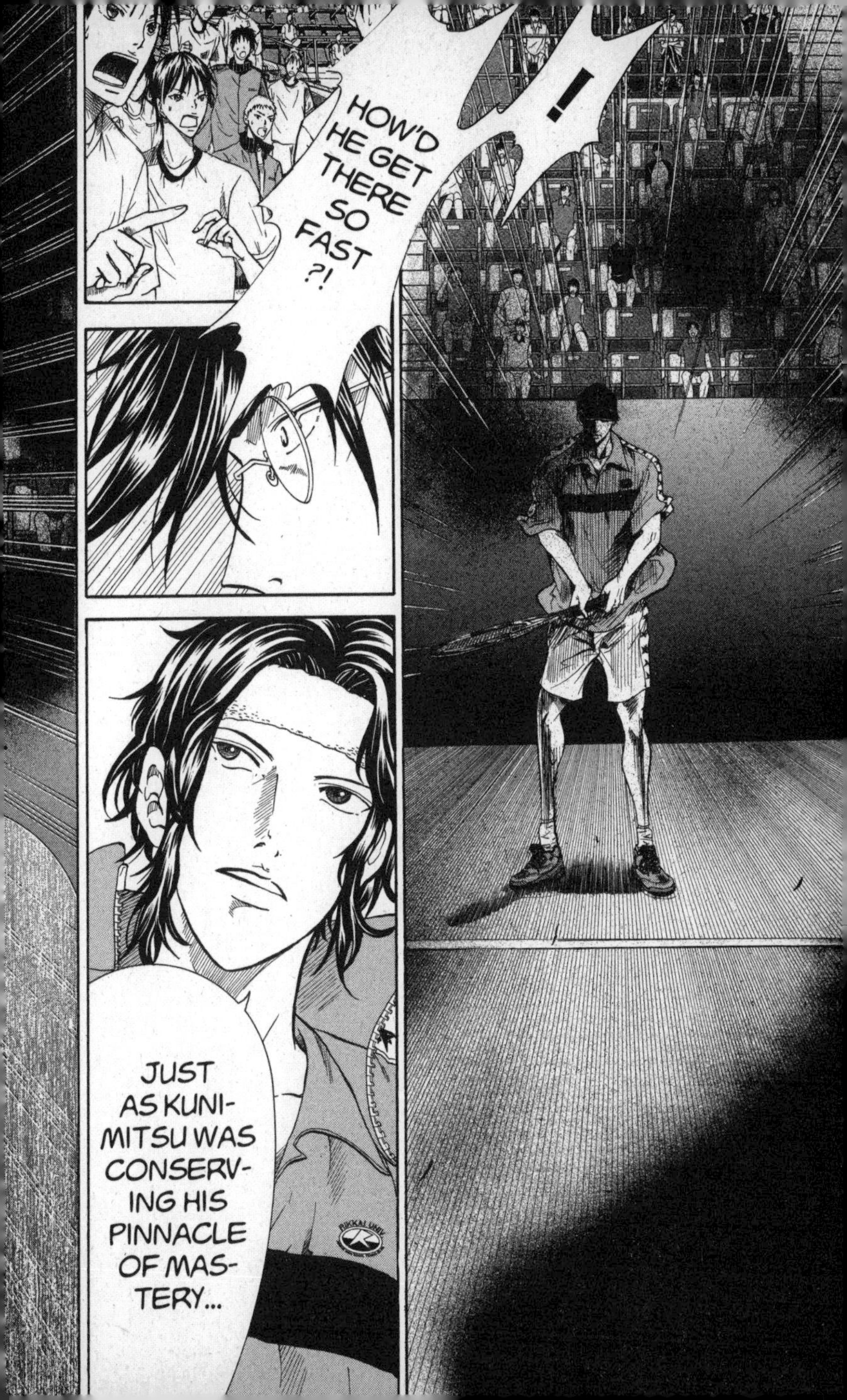
!
HOW'D HE GET THERE SO FAST ?!
JUST AS KUNI-MITSU WAS CONSERV-ING HIS PINNACLE OF MAS-TERY...

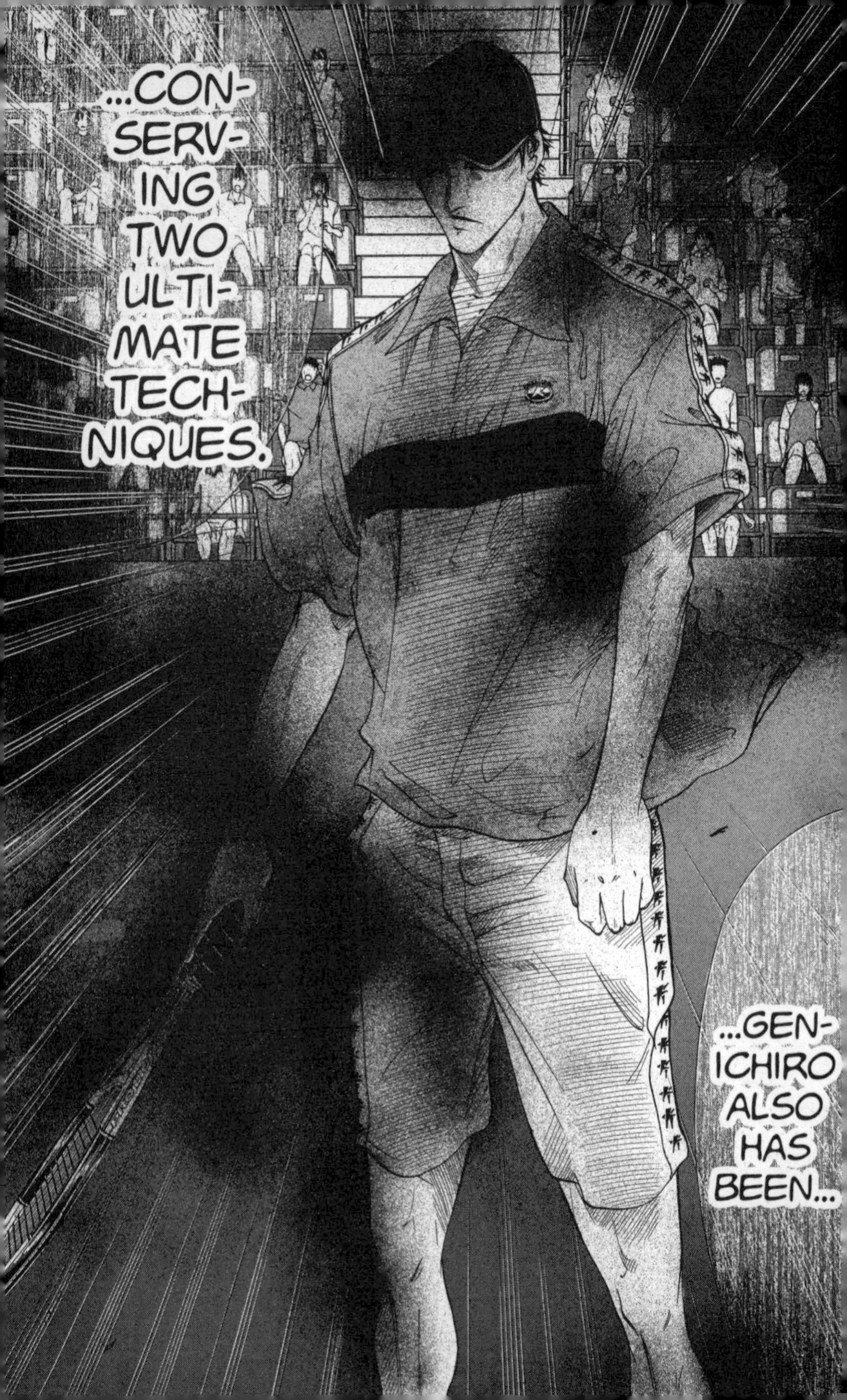
...GEN-ICHIRO ALSO HAS BEEN...
...CON-SERV-ING TWO ULTI-MATE TECH-NIQUES.

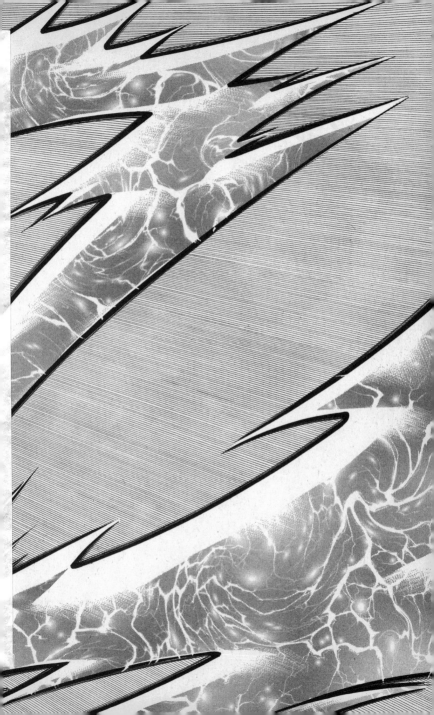

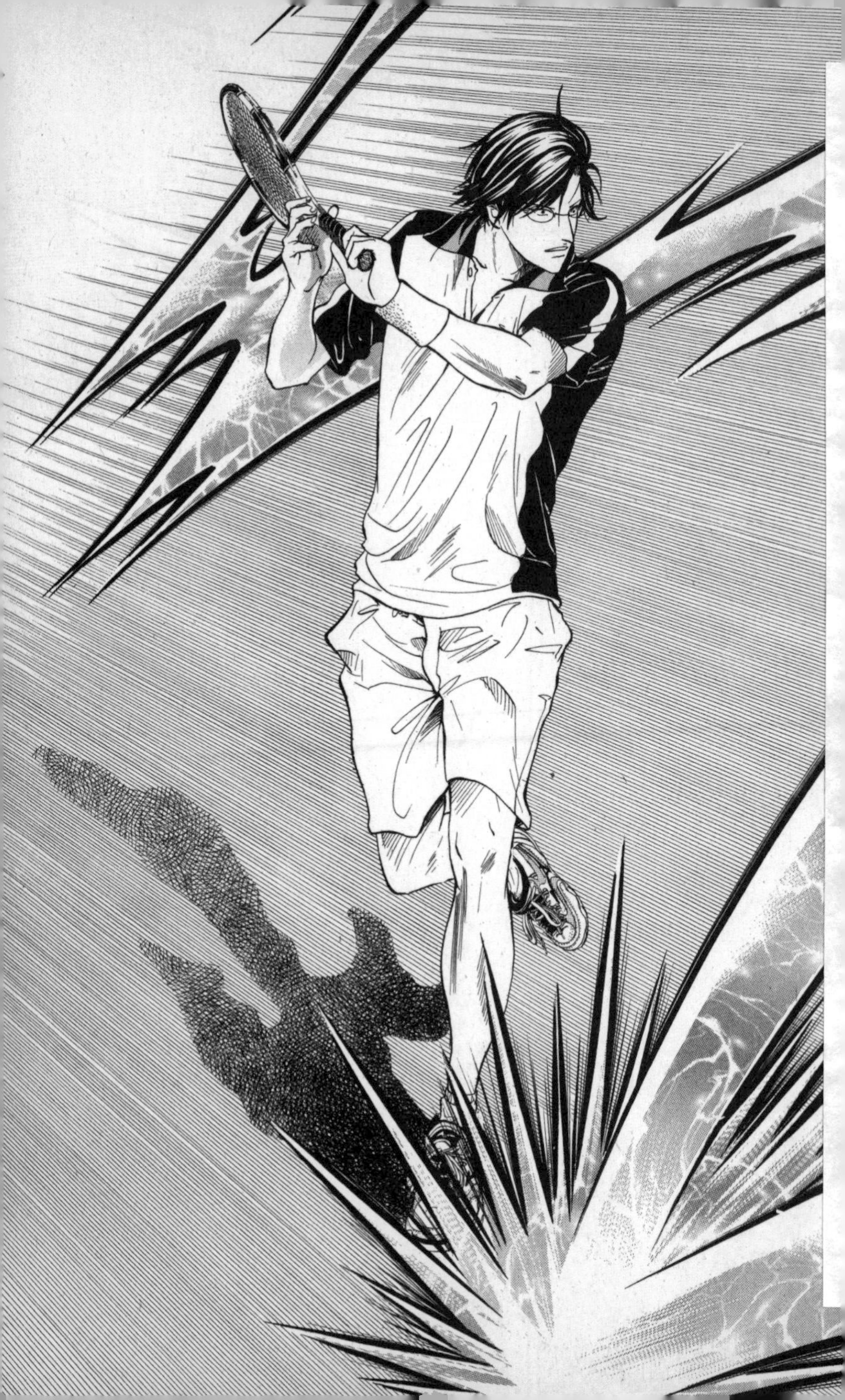

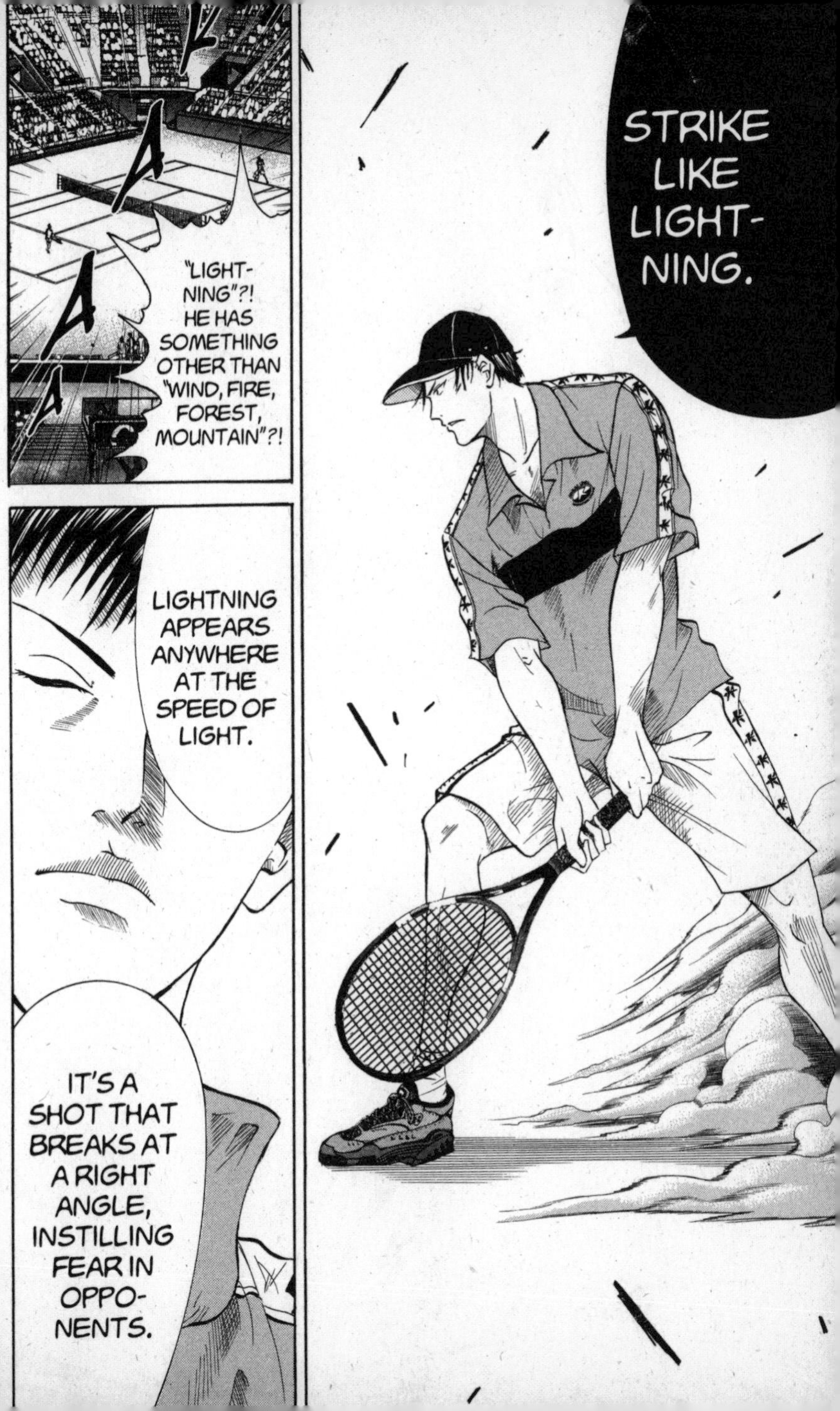
STRIKE LIKE LIGHT-NING.
"LIGHT-NING"?! HE HAS SOMETHING OTHER THAN "WIND, FIRE, FOREST, MOUNTAIN"?!
LIGHTNING APPEARS ANYWHERE AT THE SPEED OF LIGHT.
IT'S A SHOT THAT BREAKS AT A RIGHT ANGLE, INSTILLING FEAR IN OPPO-NENTS.

READ THIS WAY

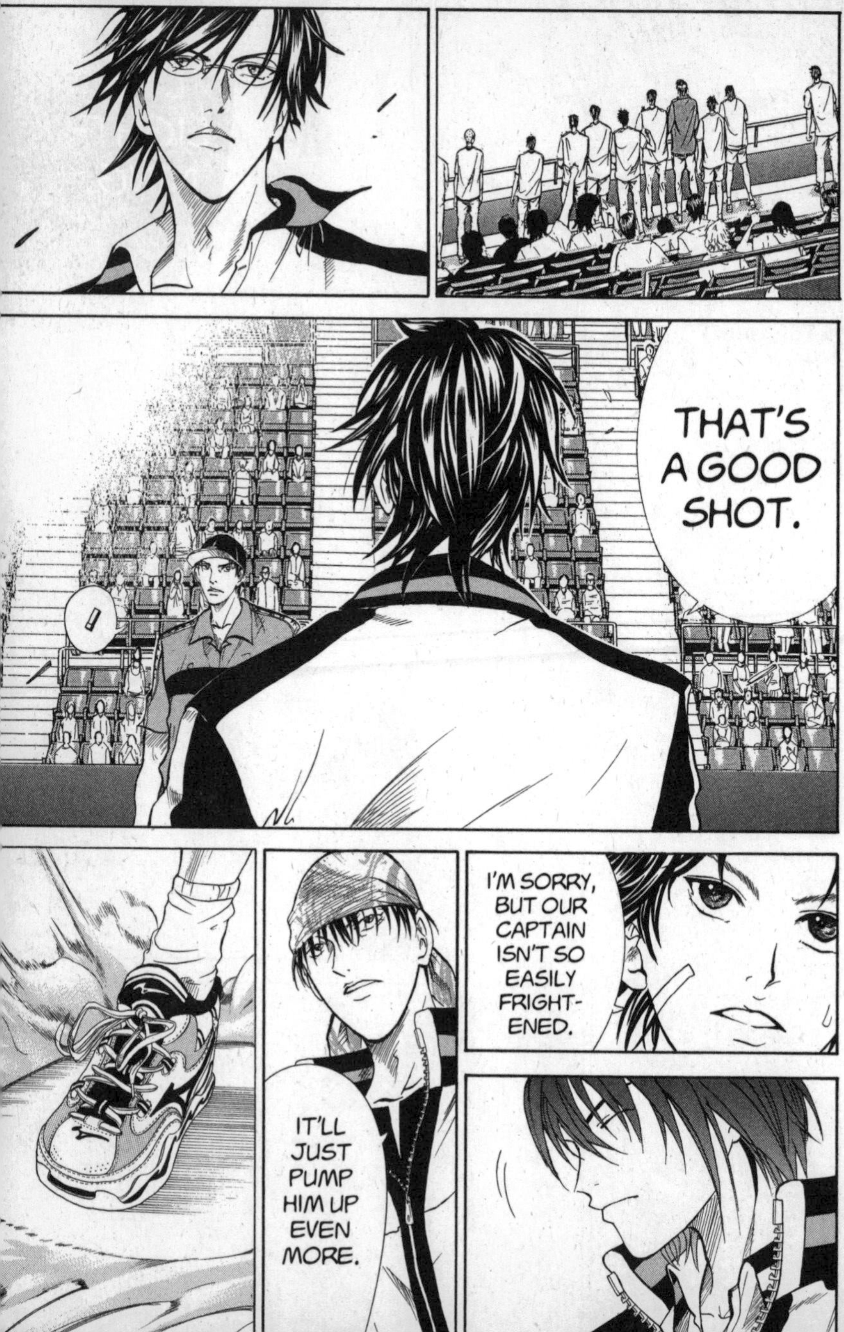
THAT'S A GOOD SHOT.
I'M SORRY, BUT OUR CAPTAIN ISN'T SO EASILY FRIGHT-ENED.
IT'LL JUST PUMP HIM UP EVEN MORE.

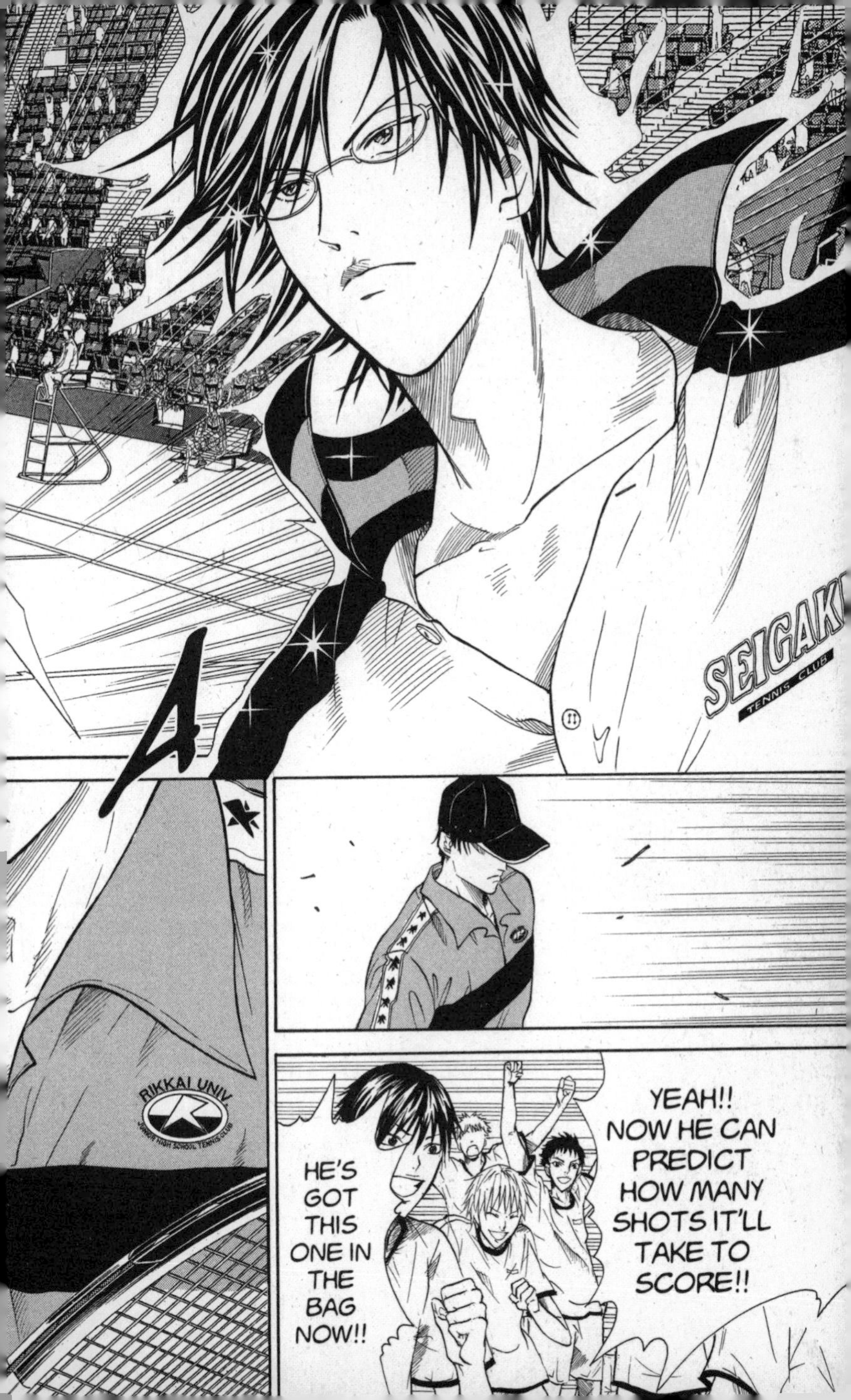
YEAH!! NOW HE CAN PREDICT HOW MANY SHOTS IT'LL TAKE TO SCORE!!
HE'S GOT THIS ONE IN THE BAG NOW!!

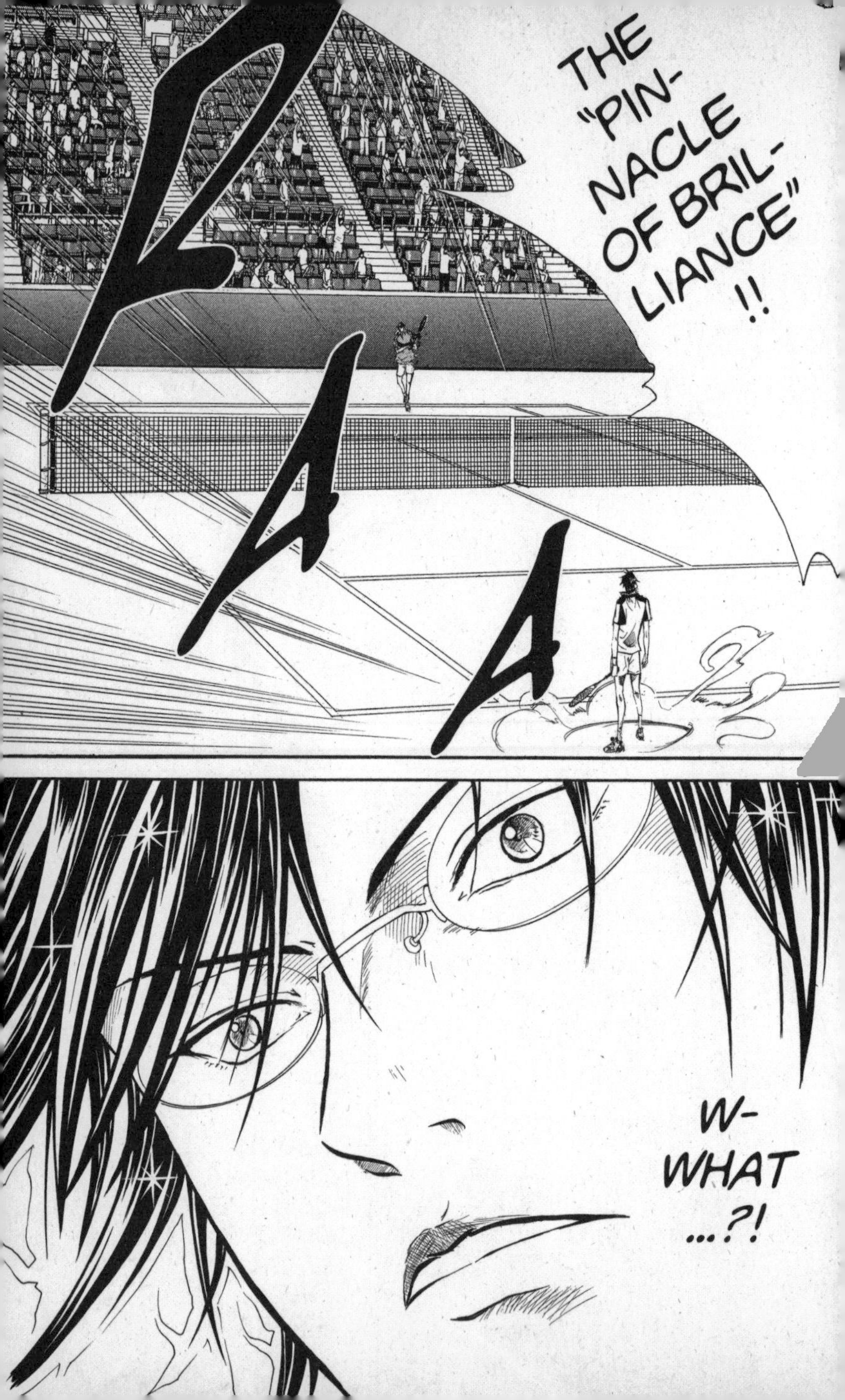
THE "PIN-NACLE OF BRIL-LIANCE" !!
W-WHAT ...?!

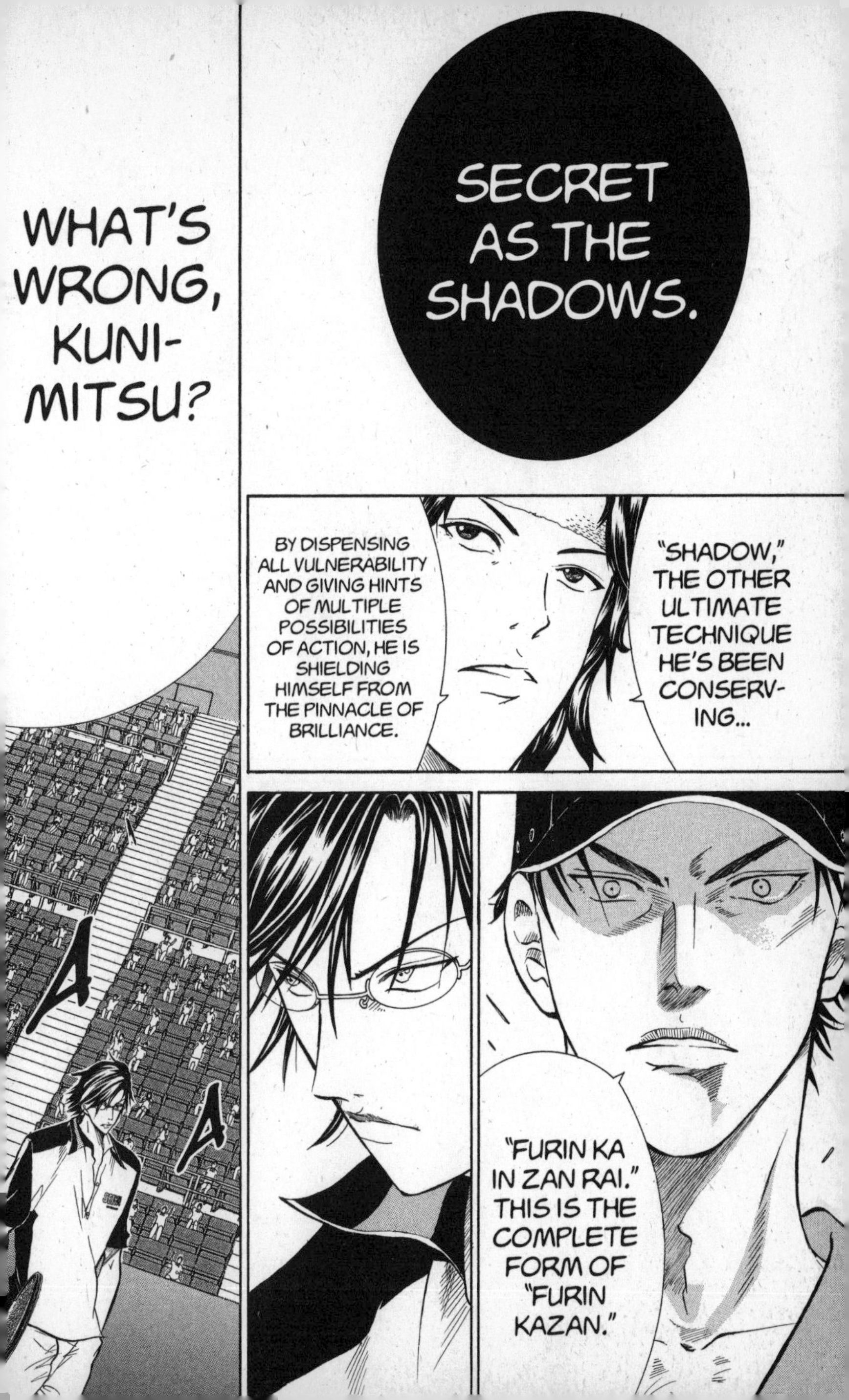

SECRET AS THE SHADOWS.
"SHADOW," THE OTHER ULTIMATE TECHNIQUE HE'S BEEN CONSERV-ING...
BY DISPENSING ALL VULNERABILITY AND GIVING HINTS OF MULTIPLE POSSIBILITIES OF ACTION, HE IS SHIELDING HIMSELF FROM THE PINNACLE OF BRILLIANCE.
"FURIN KA IN ZAN RAI." THIS IS THE COMPLETE FORM OF "FURIN KAZAN."
WHAT'S WRONG, KUNI-MITSU?

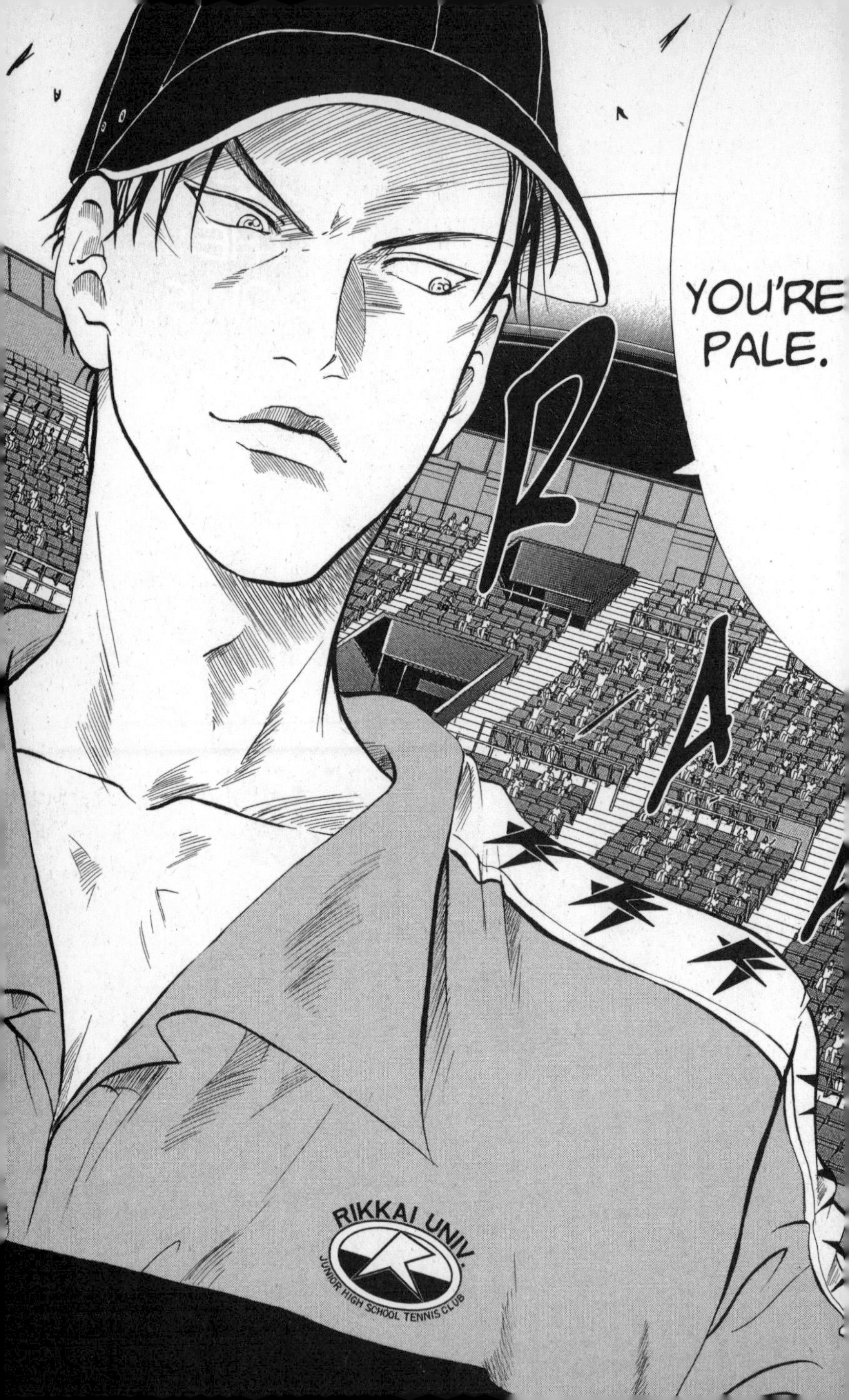
YOU'RE PALE.
RIKKAI UNIV.
JUNIOR HIGH SCHOOL TENNIS CLUB

テニスの王子様

THE PRINCE OF TENNIS

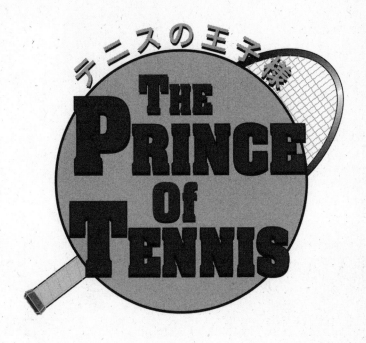

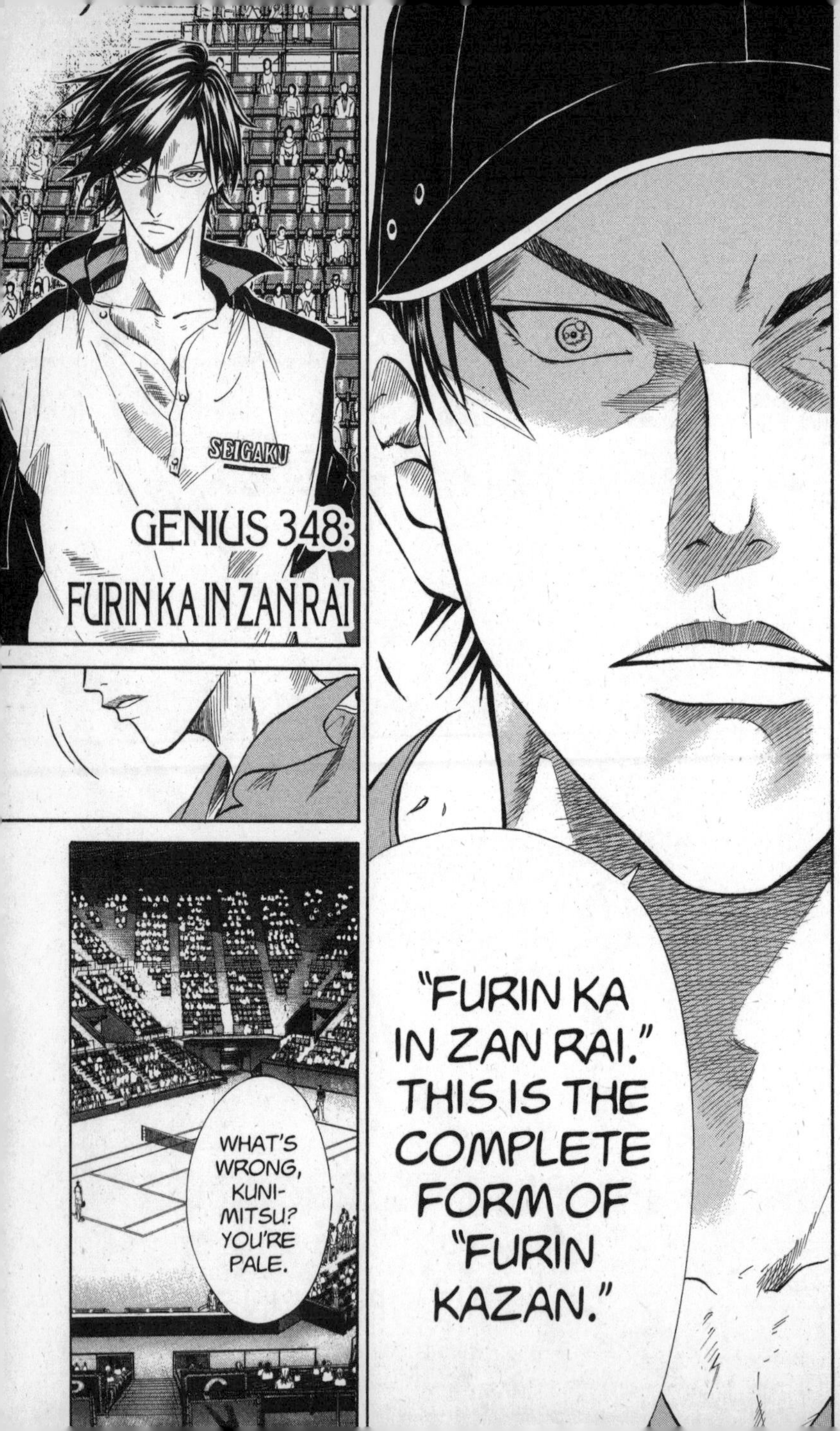
"FURIN KA IN ZAN RAI." THIS IS THE COMPLETE FORM OF "FURIN KAZAN."
GENIUS 348: FURIN KA IN ZAN RAI
SEIGAKU
WHAT'S WRONG, KUNI-MITSU? YOU'RE PALE.

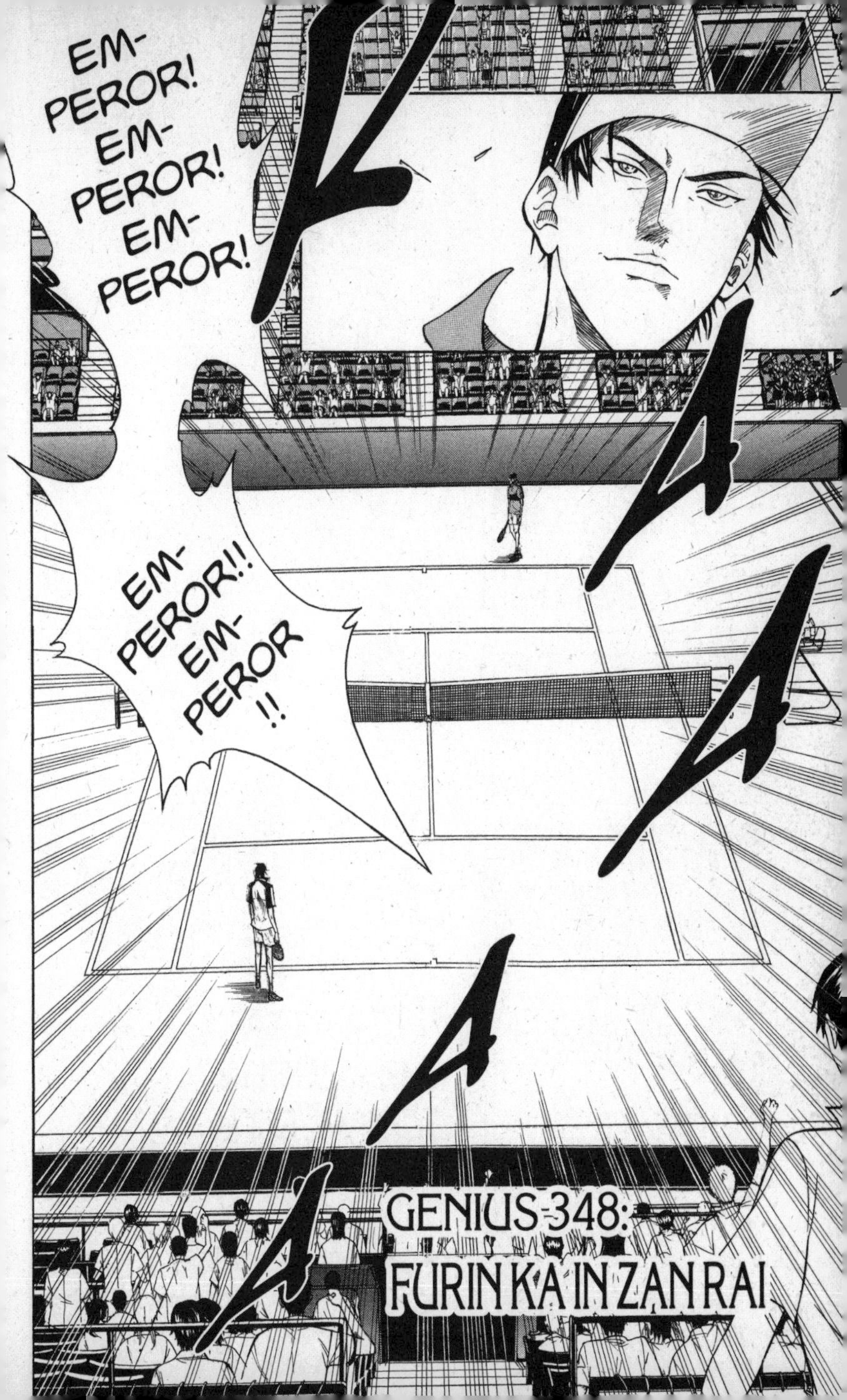
EM-PEROR! EM-PEROR! EM-PEROR!
EM-PEROR!! EM-PEROR!!
GENIUS 348:
FURIN KA IN ZAN RAI

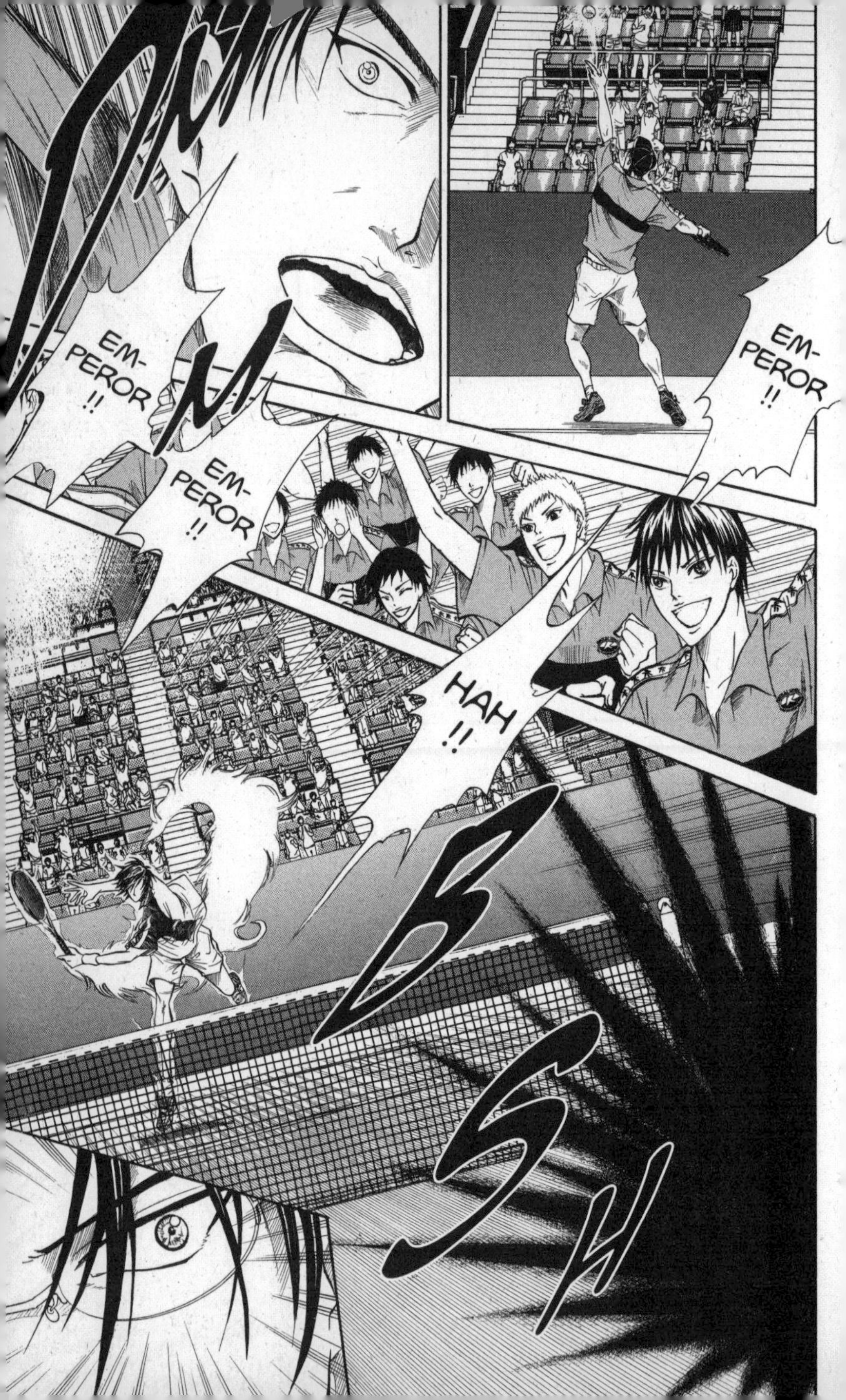
EM-PEROR!!
EM-PEROR!!
EM-PEROR!!
HAH!!

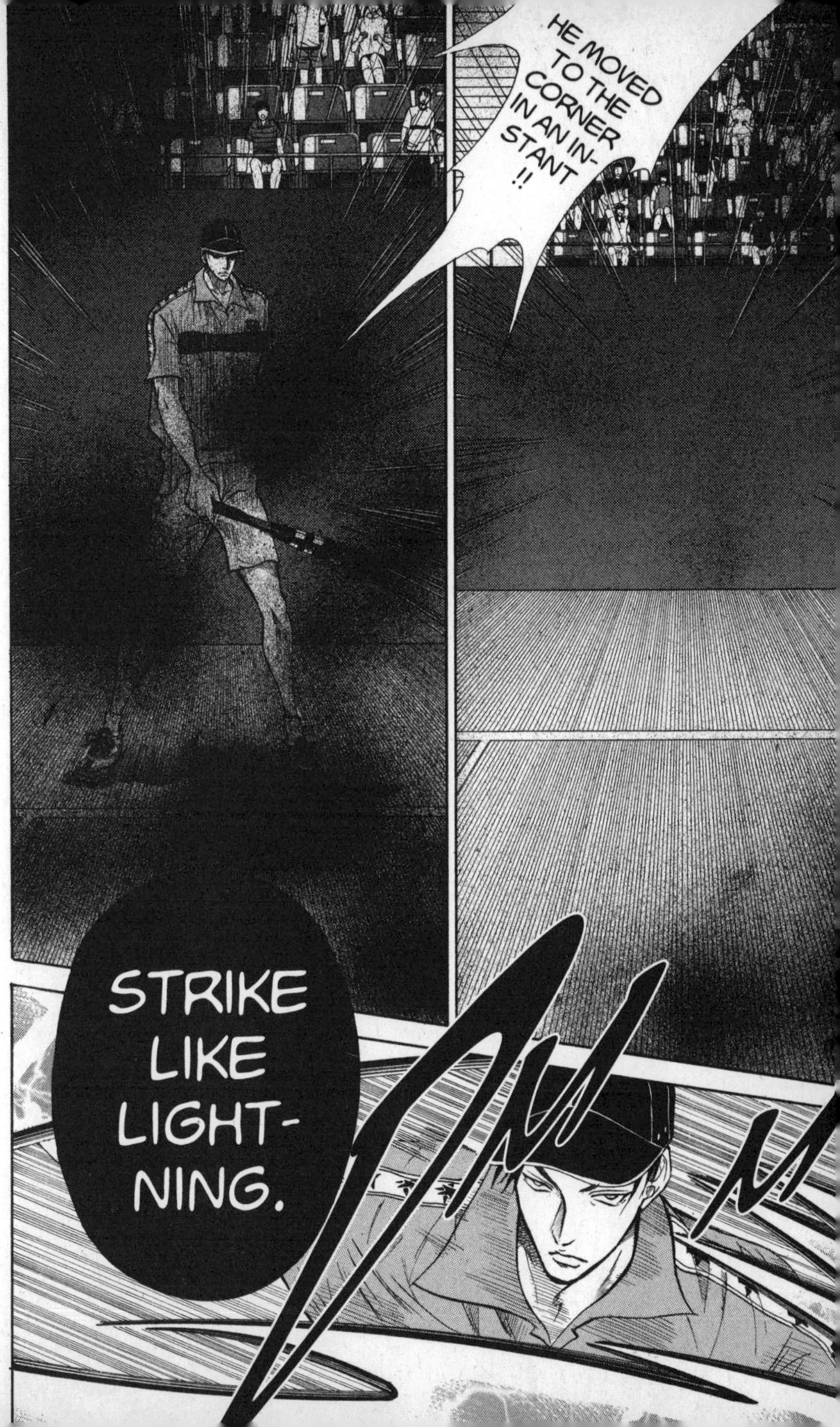
HE MOVED TO THE CORNER IN AN IN-STANT !!
STRIKE LIKE LIGHT-NING.

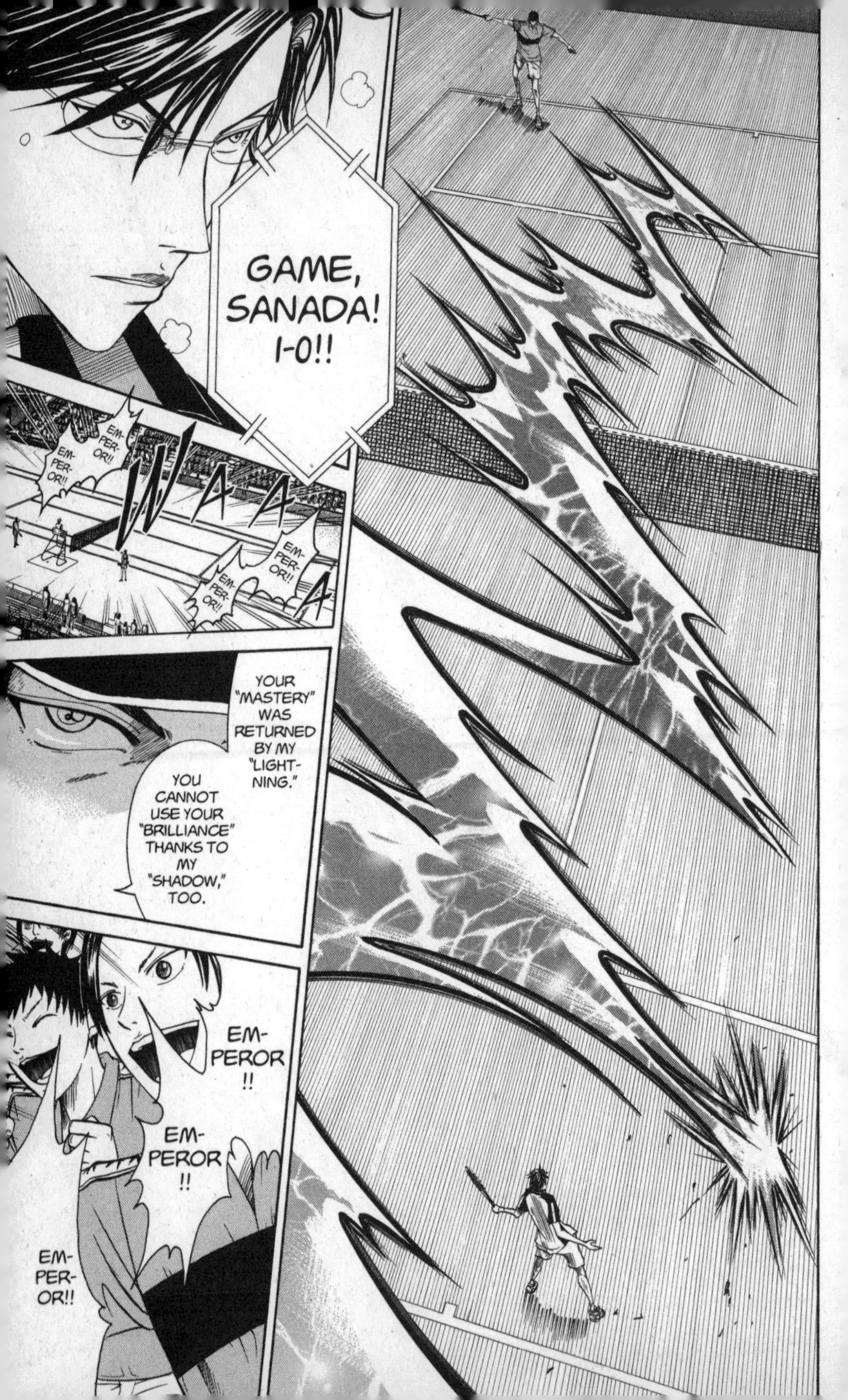
GAME, SANADA! 1-0!!
WAAA
EMPEROR!!
EMPEROR!!
EMPEROR!!
EMPEROR!!
YOUR "MASTERY" WAS RETURNED BY MY "LIGHTNING."
YOU CANNOT USE YOUR "BRILLIANCE" THANKS TO MY "SHADOW," TOO.
EMPEROR!!
EMPEROR!!
EMPEROR!!

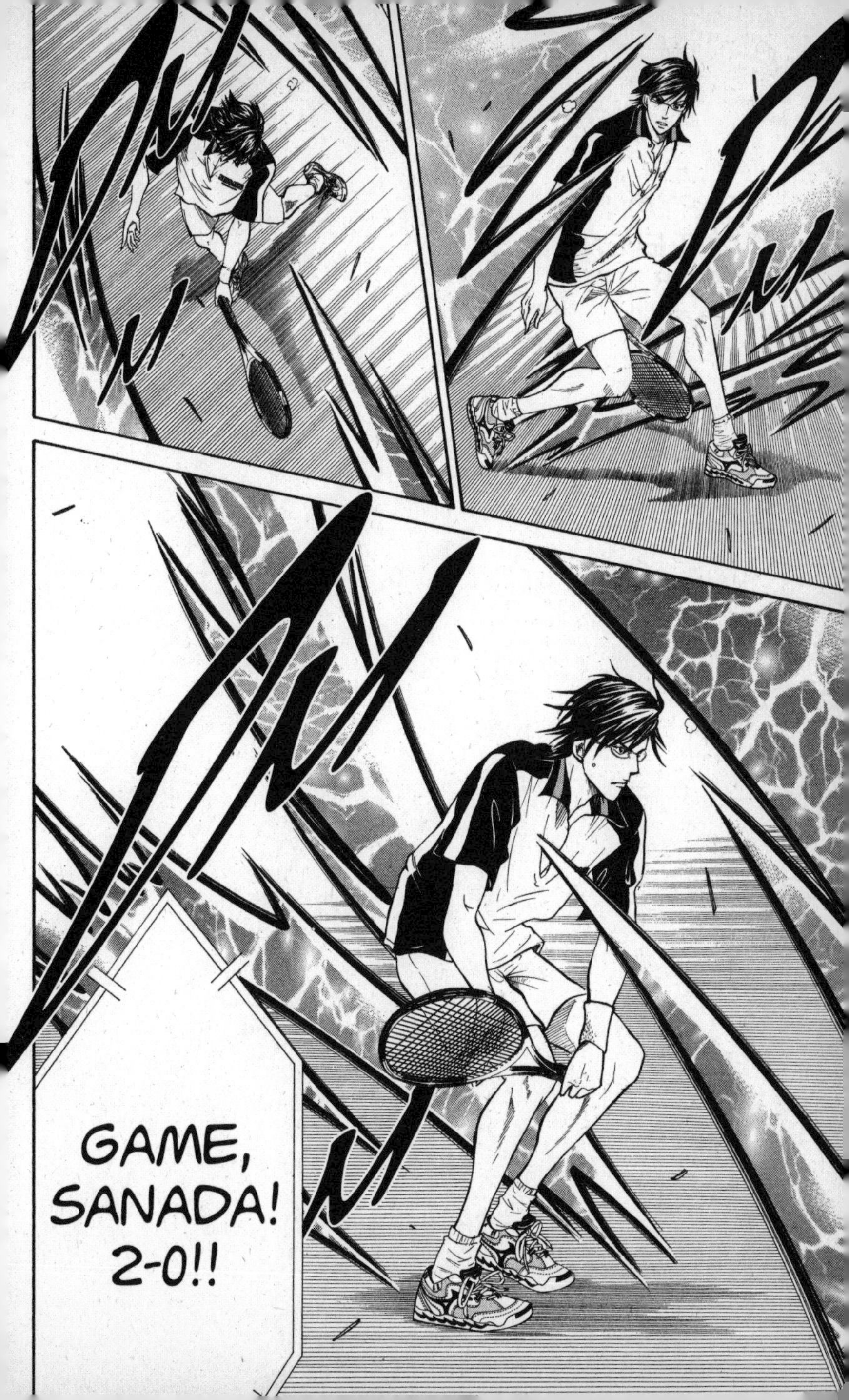
GAME, SANADA! 2-0!!

READ THIS WAY

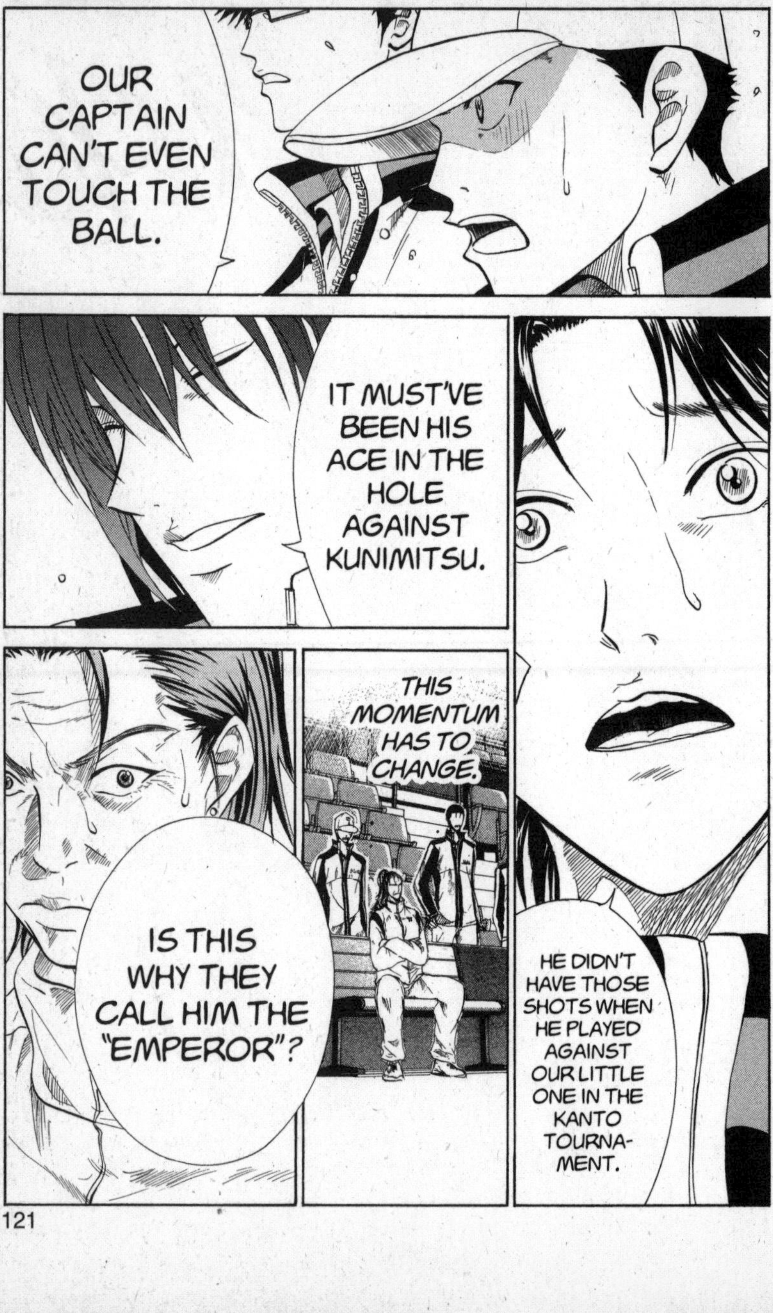
OUR CAPTAIN CAN'T EVEN TOUCH THE BALL.
HE DIDN'T HAVE THOSE SHOTS WHEN HE PLAYED AGAINST OUR LITTLE ONE IN THE KANTO TOURNA-MENT.
IT MUST'VE BEEN HIS ACE IN THE HOLE AGAINST KUNIMITSU.
THIS MOMENTUM HAS TO CHANGE.
IS THIS WHY THEY CALL HIM THE "EMPEROR"?

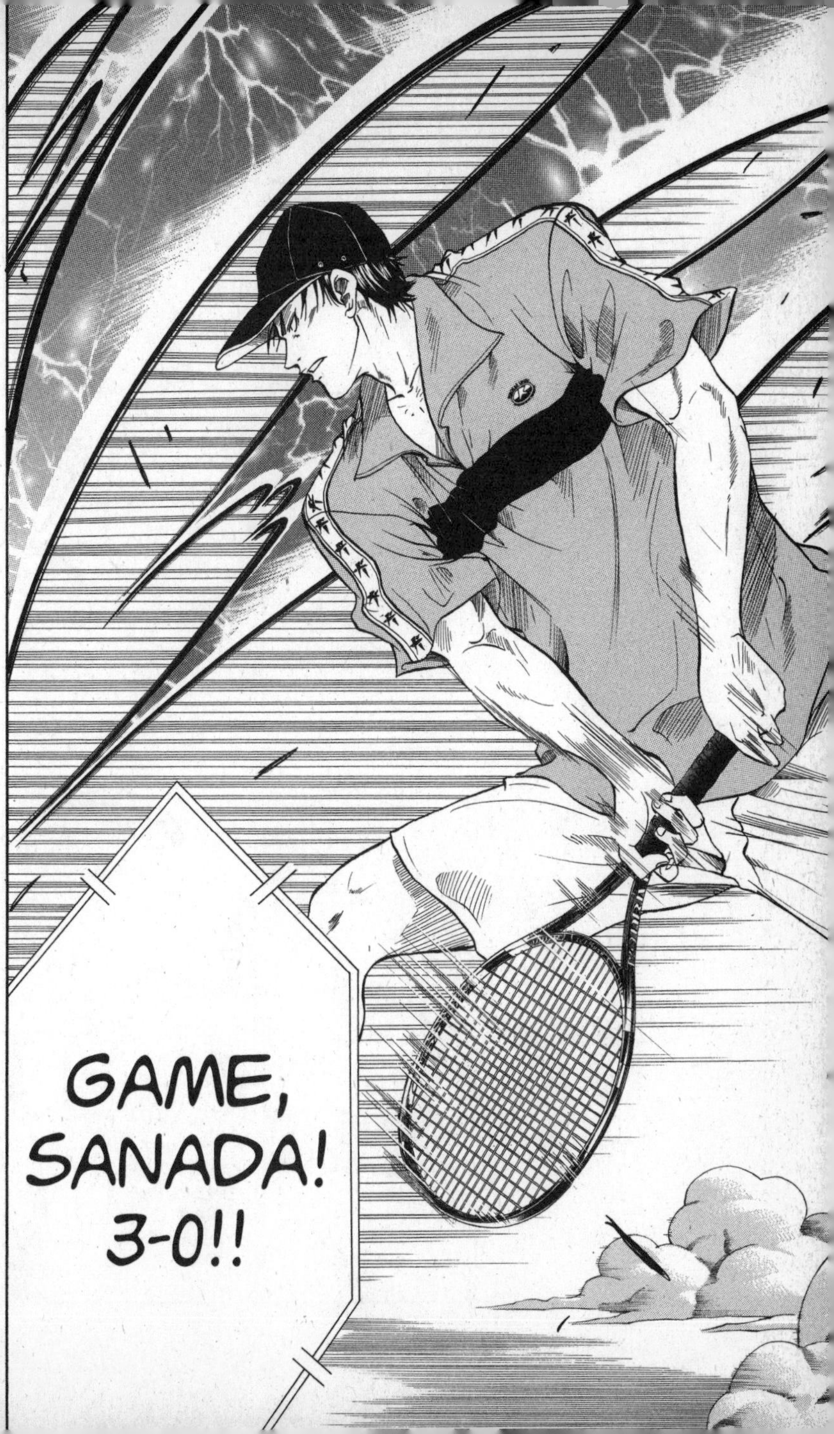
GAME, SANADA! 3-0!!

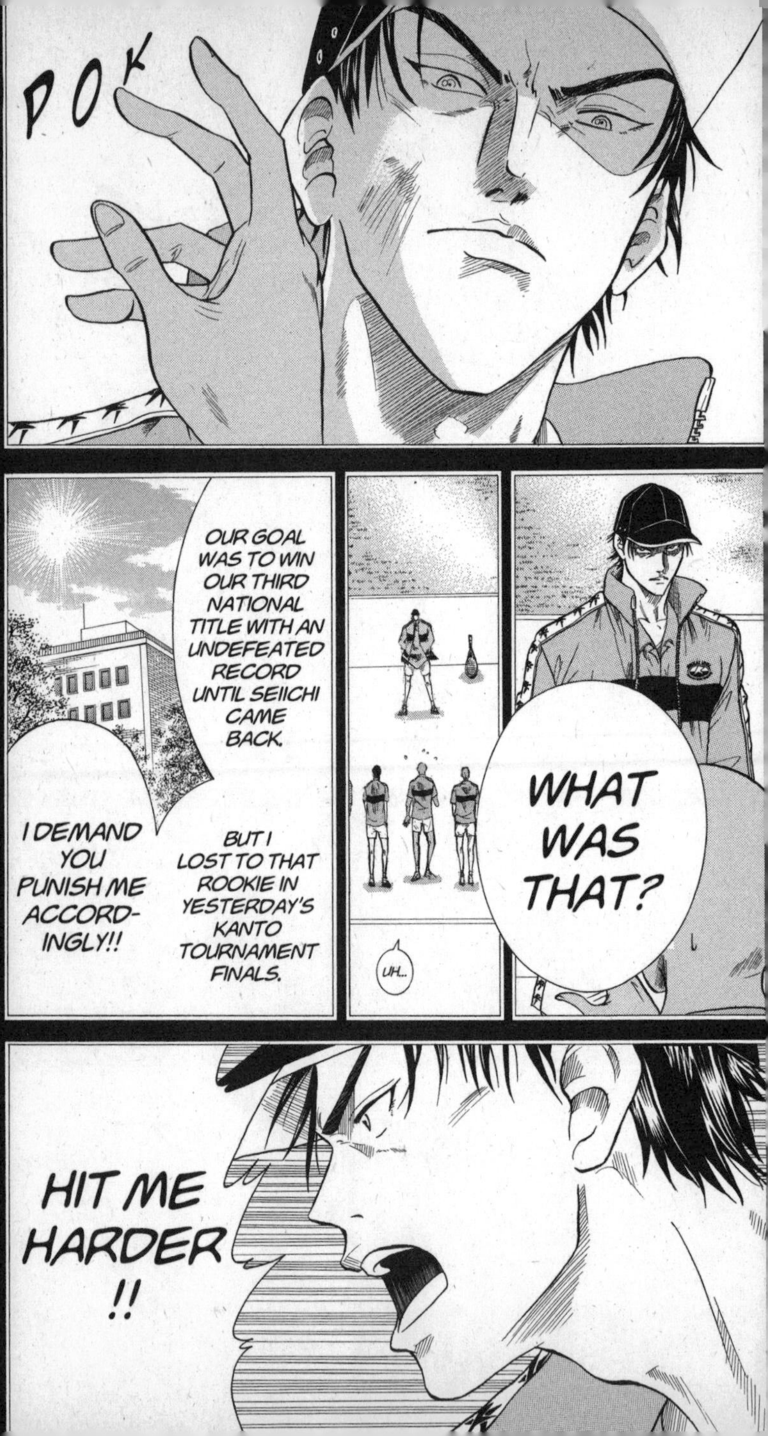
POK
WHAT WAS THAT?
UH...
OUR GOAL WAS TO WIN OUR THIRD NATIONAL TITLE WITH AN UNDEFEATED RECORD UNTIL SEIICHI CAME BACK.
BUT I LOST TO THAT ROOKIE IN YESTERDAY'S KANTO TOURNAMENT FINALS.
I DEMAND YOU PUNISH ME ACCORD-INGLY!!
HIT ME HARDER !!

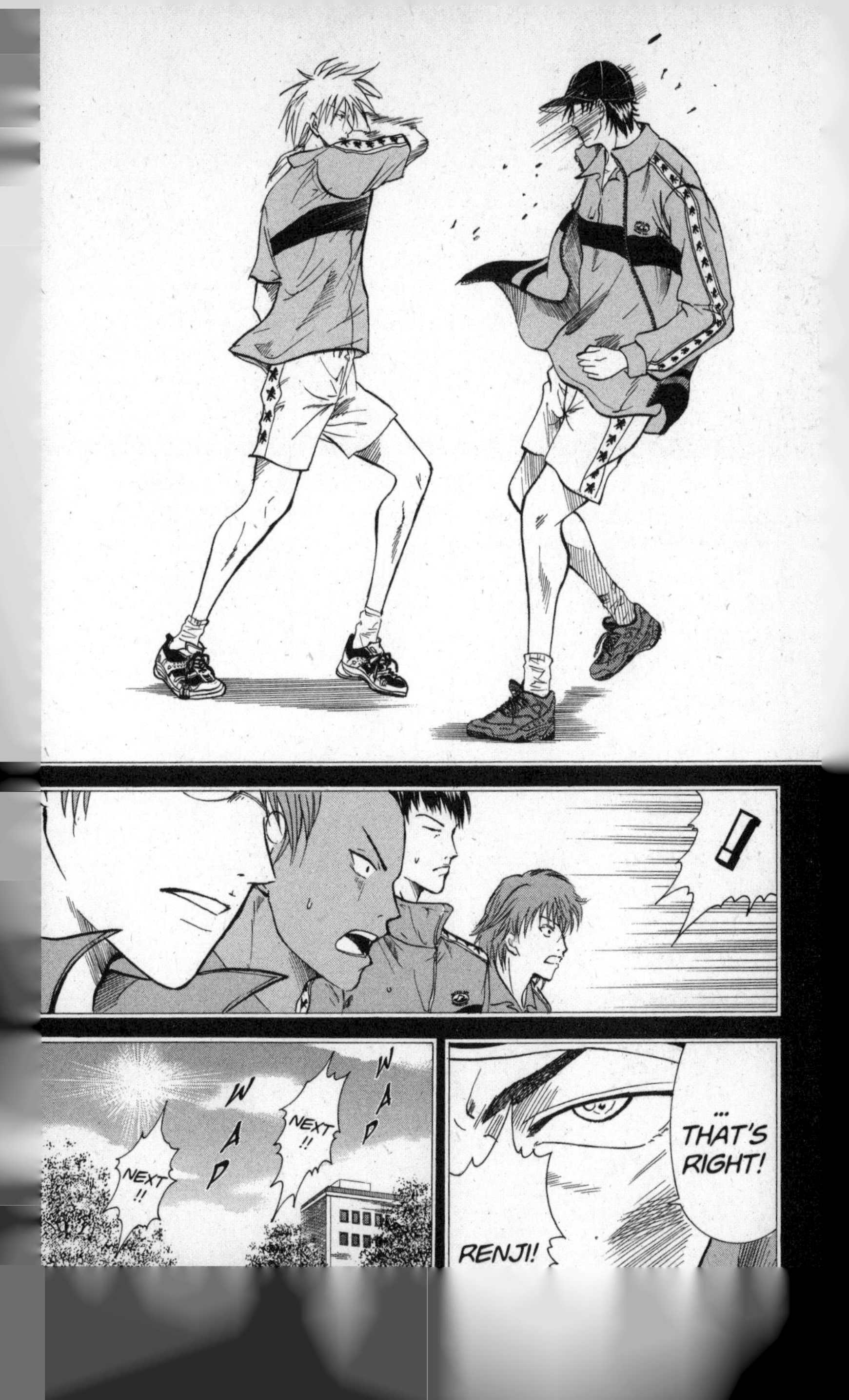
!
...THAT'S RIGHT!
RENJI!
WAP
NEXT!!
WAP
NEXT!!

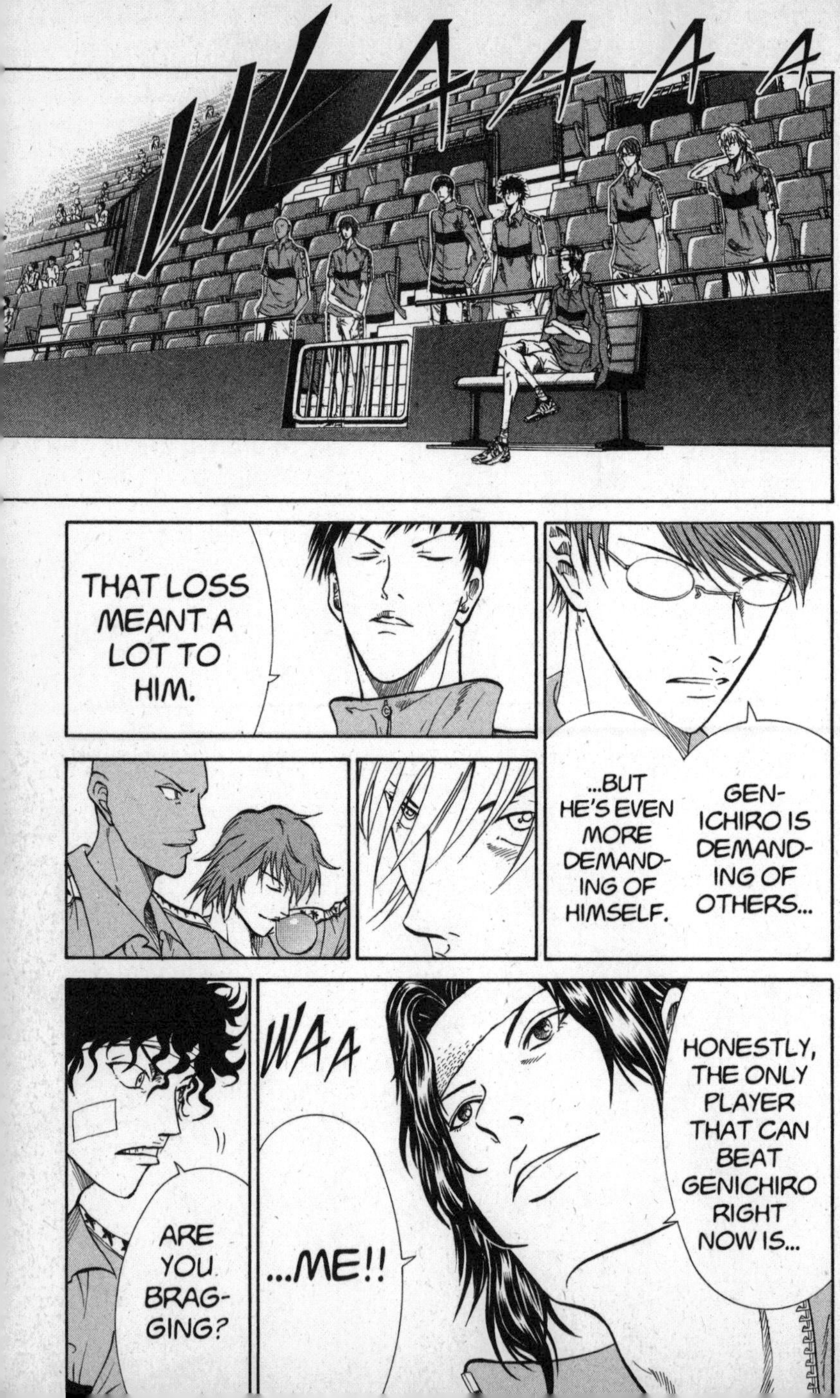
WAAAAA
GEN-ICHIRO IS DEMAND-ING OF OTHERS...
...BUT HE'S EVEN MORE DEMAND-ING OF HIMSELF.
THAT LOSS MEANT A LOT TO HIM.
HONESTLY, THE ONLY PLAYER THAT CAN BEAT GENICHIRO RIGHT NOW IS...
WAA
...ME!!
ARE YOU BRAG-GING?

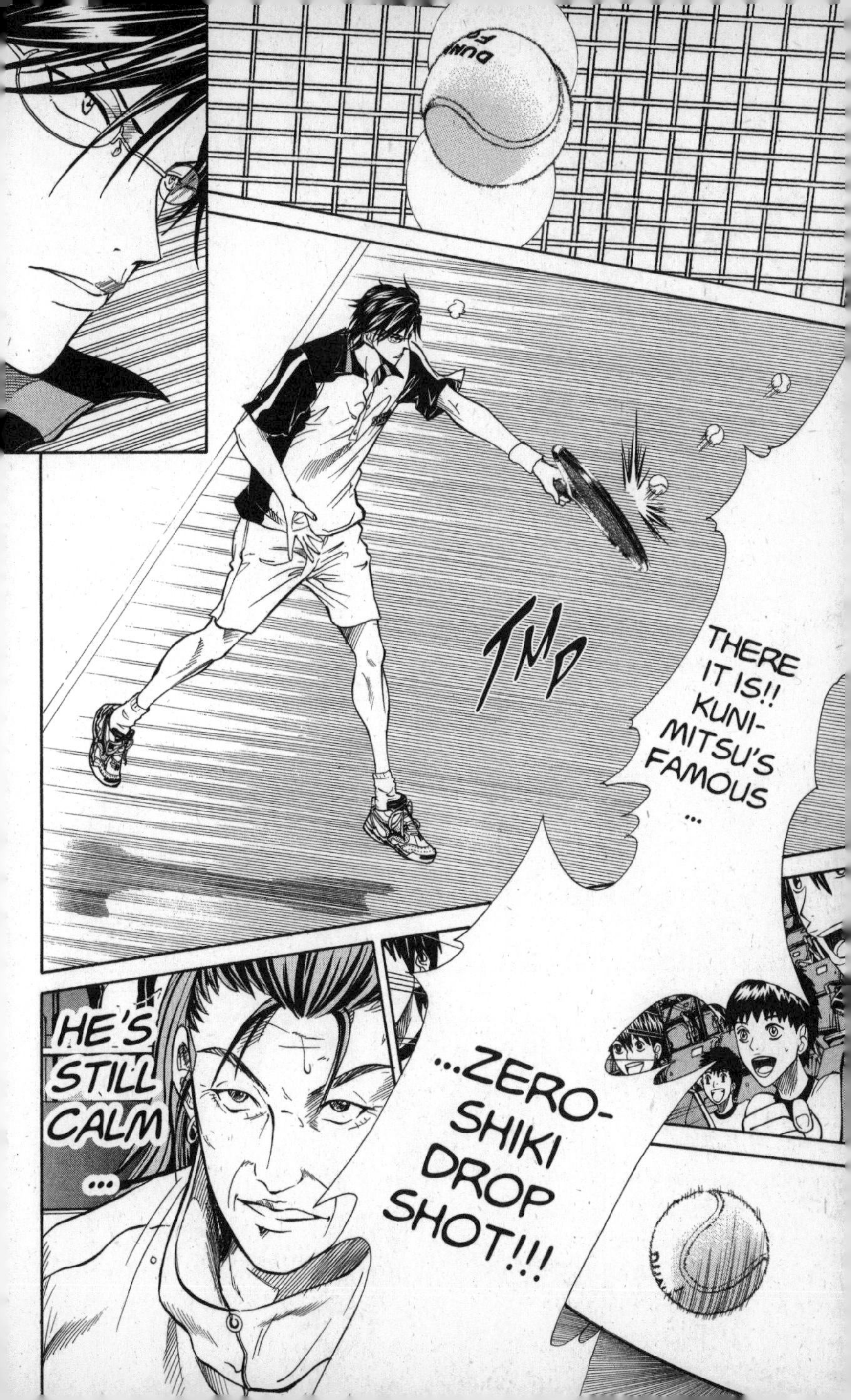
TMD
THERE IT IS!! KUNI-MITSU'S FAMOUS ...
...ZERO-SHIKI DROP SHOT!!!
HE'S STILL CALM ...

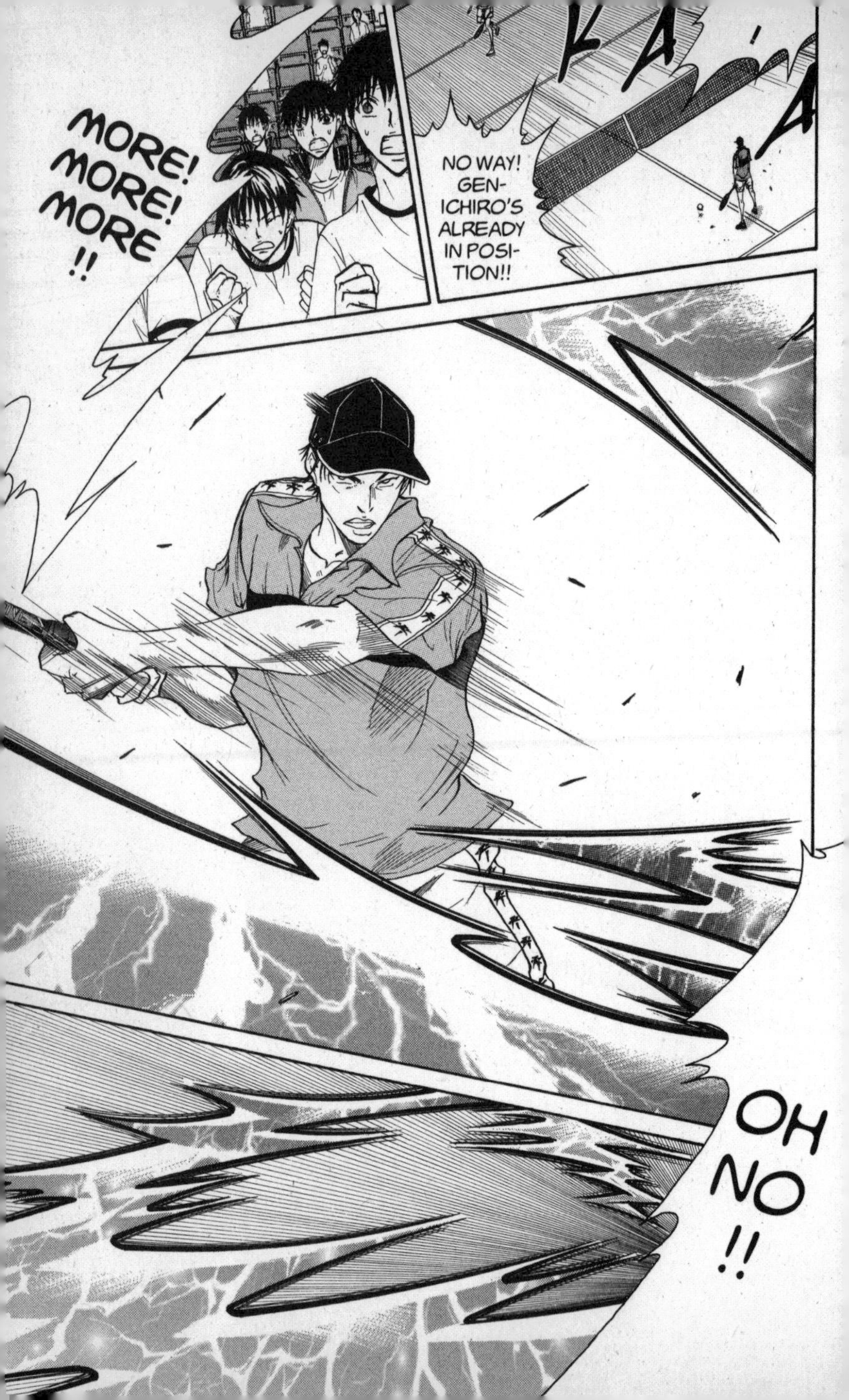
NO WAY! GEN-ICHIRO'S ALREADY IN POSITION!!
MORE! MORE! MORE!!
OH NO!!

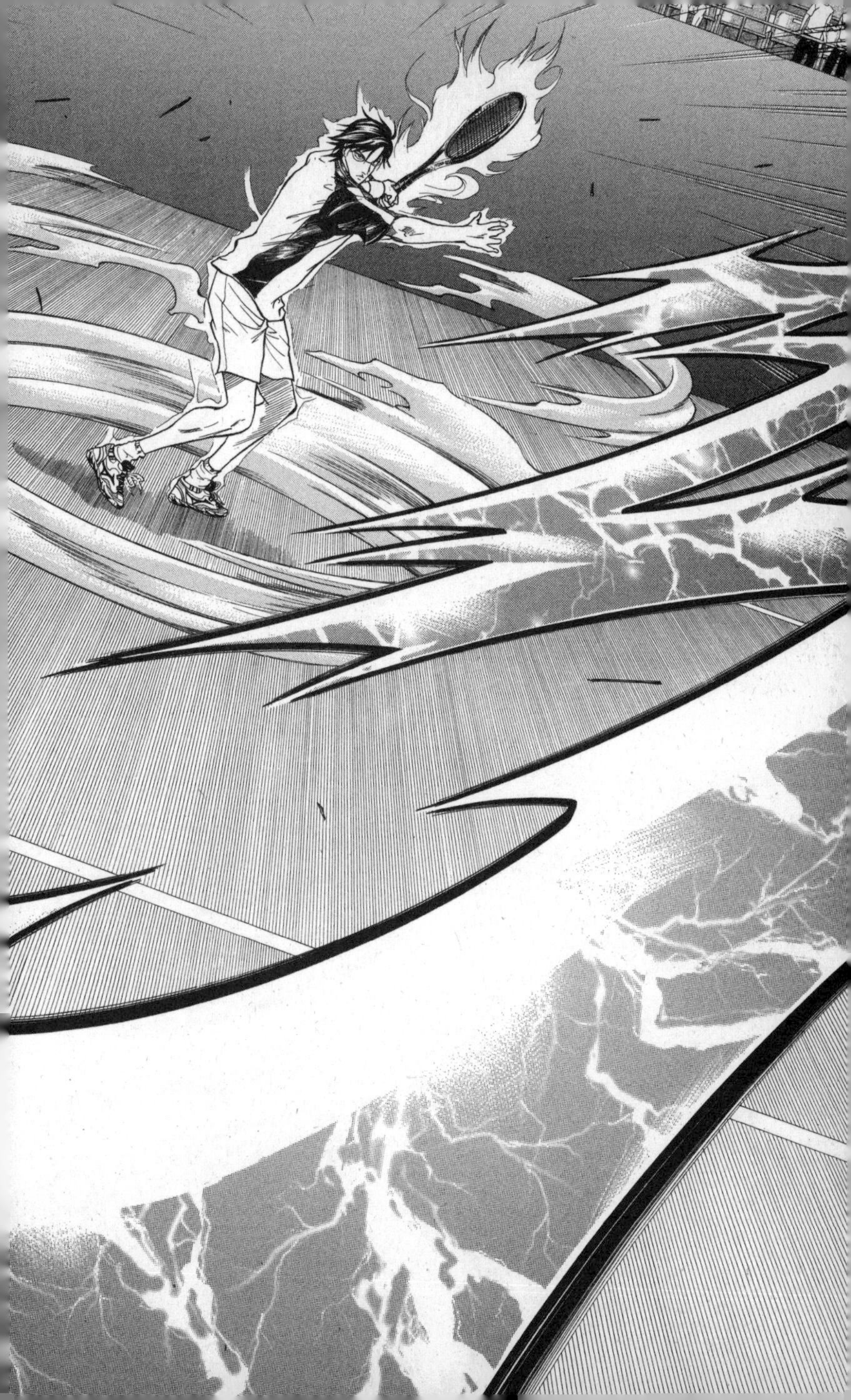

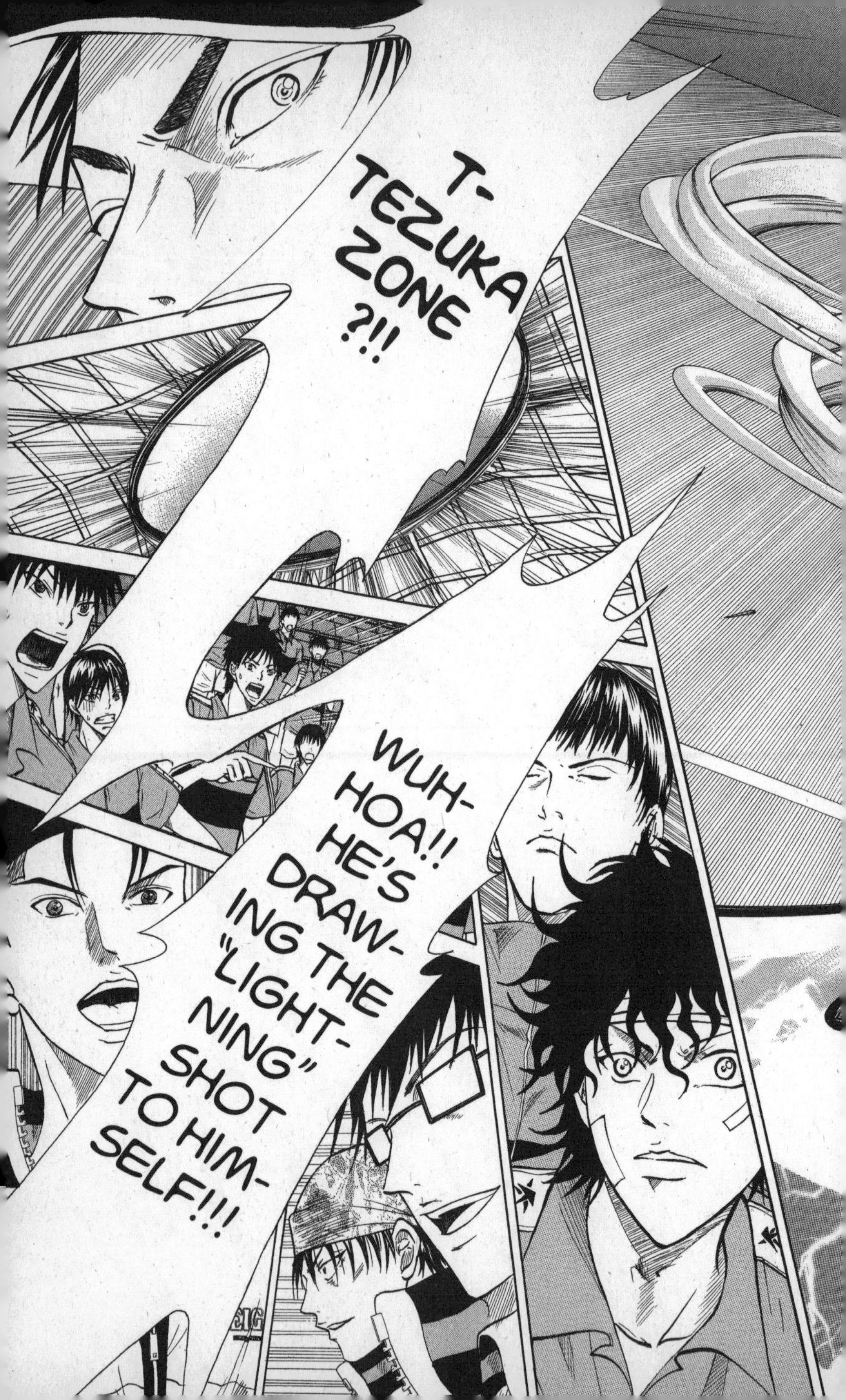
T-TEZUKA ZONE ?!!
WUH-HOA!! HE'S DRAW-ING THE "LIGHT-NING" SHOT TO HIM-SELF!!!

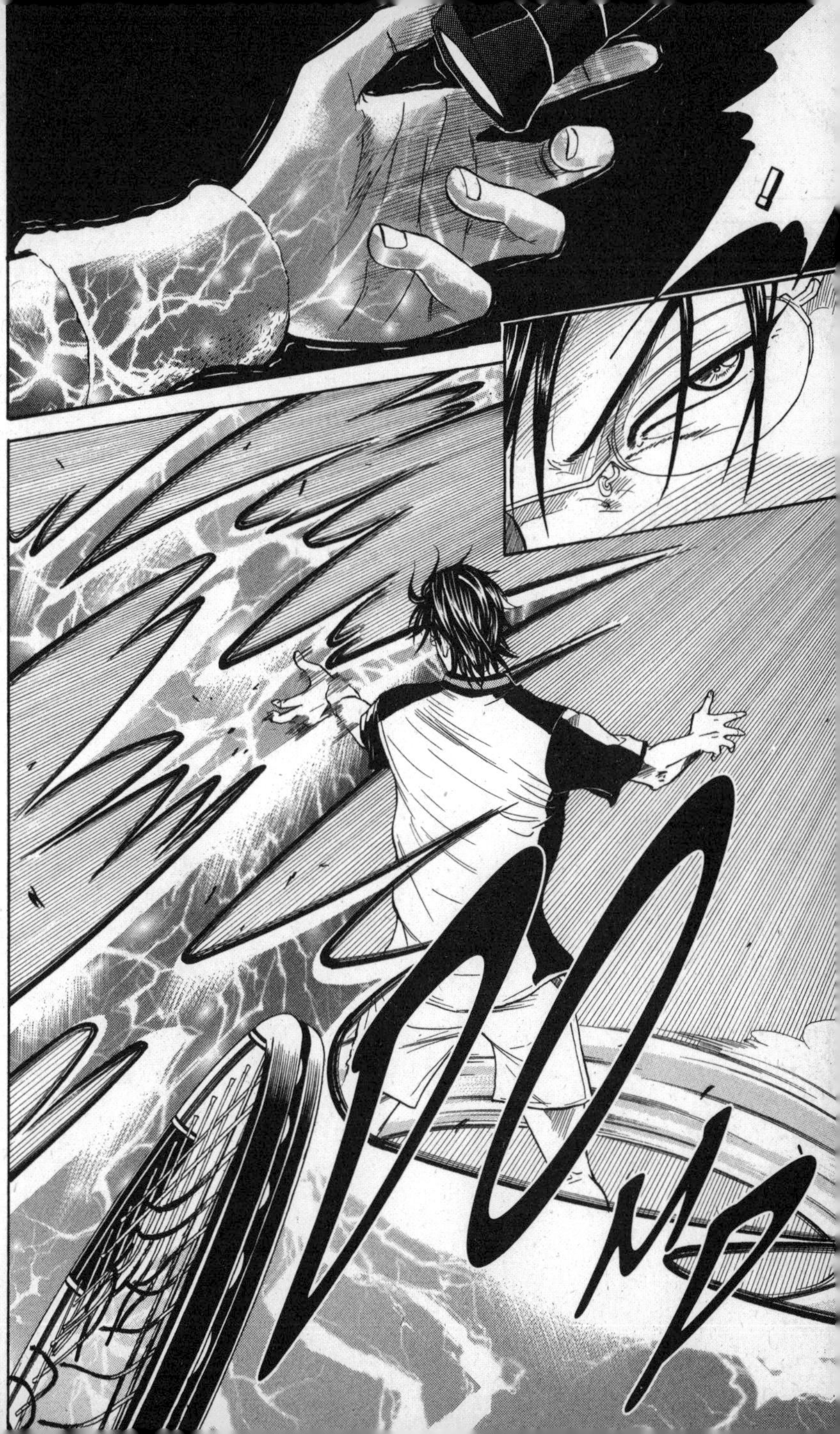
!

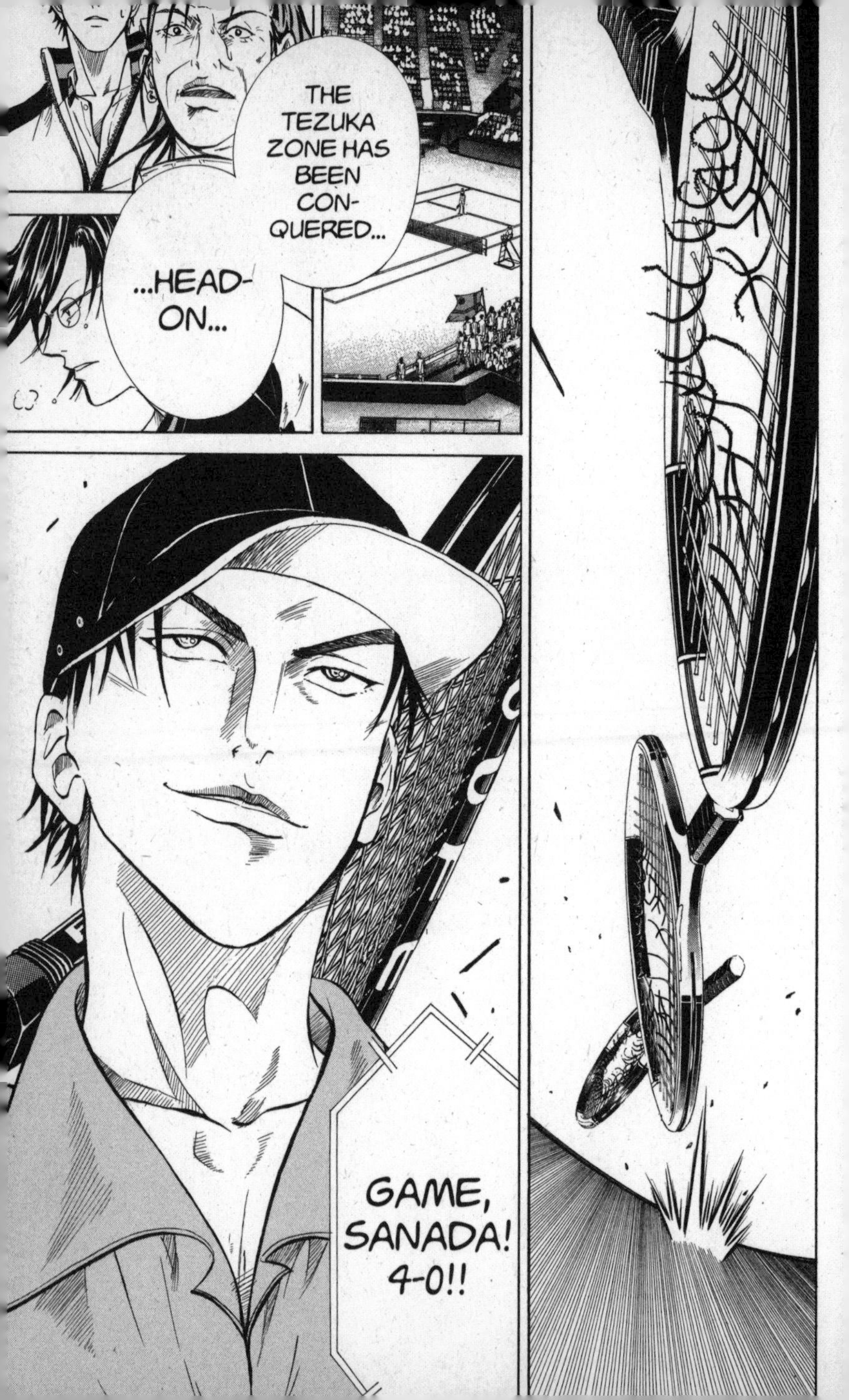
THE TEZUKA ZONE HAS BEEN CON-QUERED...
...HEAD-ON...
GAME, SANADA! 4-0!!

テニスの王子様

THE PRINCE OF TENNIS

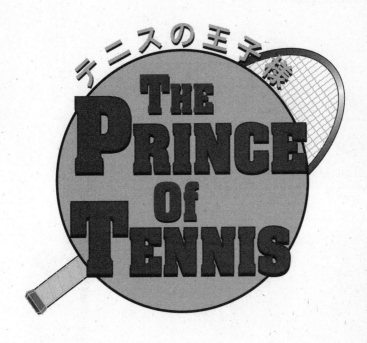

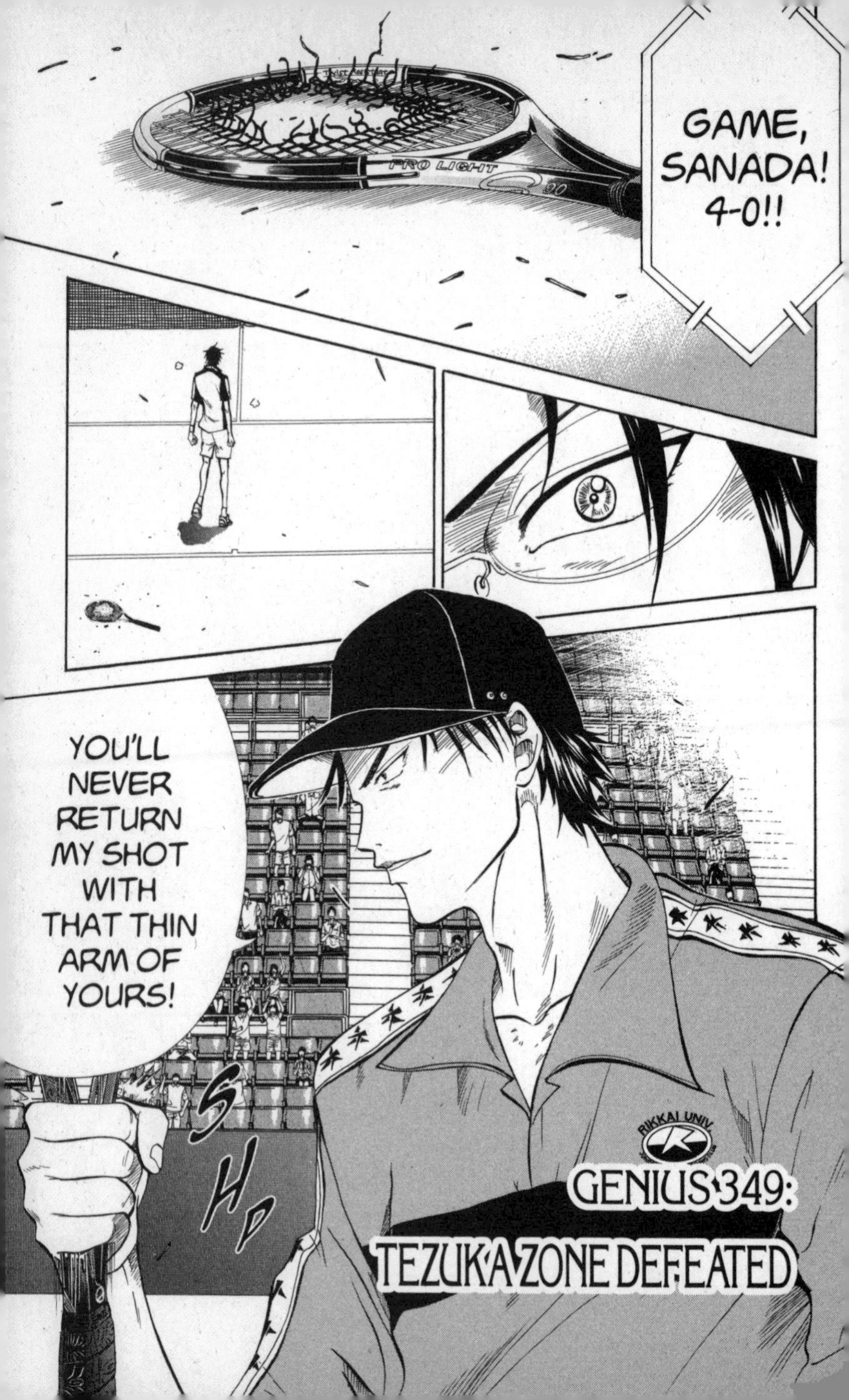
GAME, SANADA! 4-0!!
PRO LIGHT
YOU'LL NEVER RETURN MY SHOT WITH THAT THIN ARM OF YOURS!
SHP
RIKKAI UNIV
GENIUS 349:
TEZUKA ZONE DEFEATED

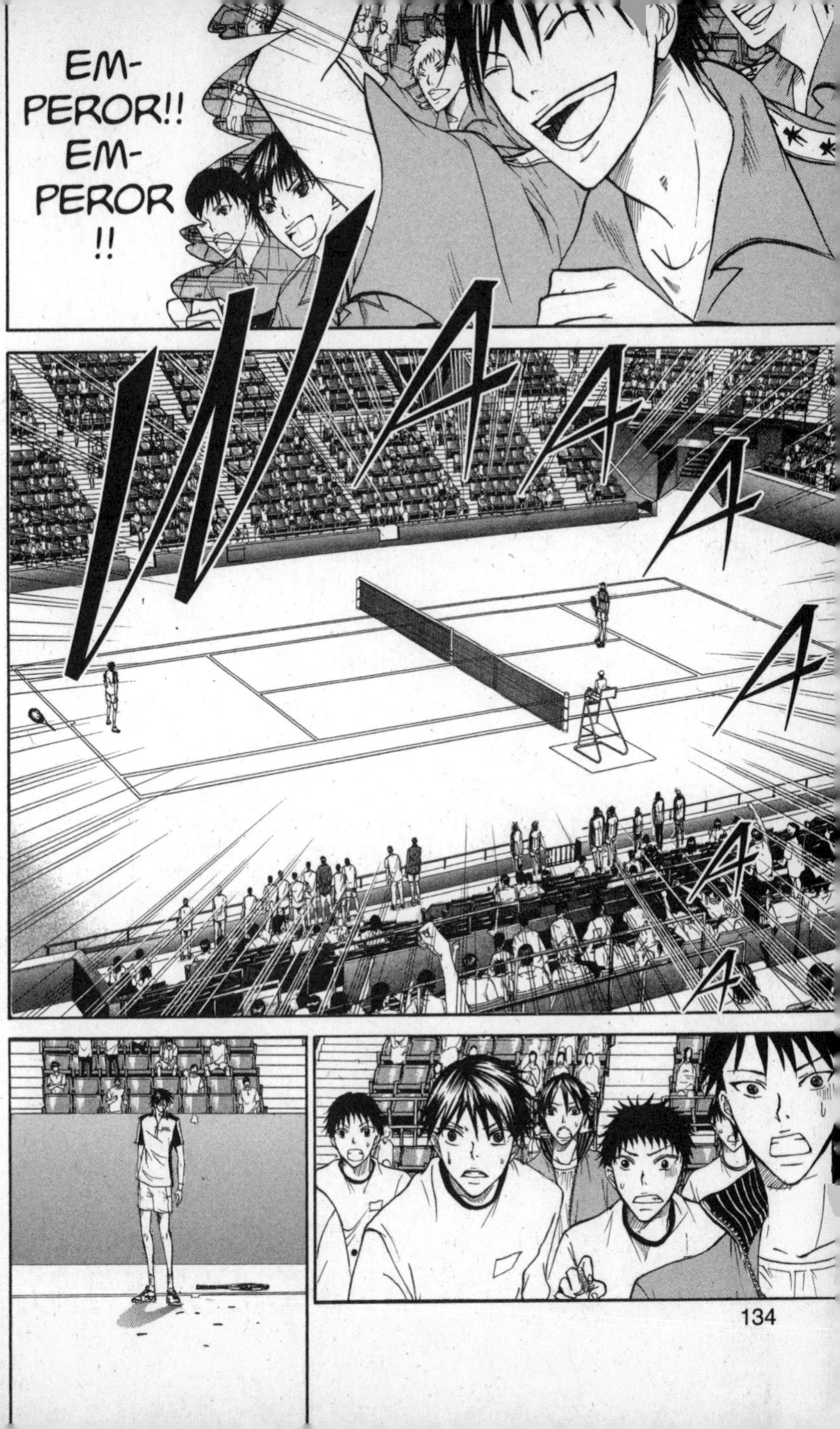
EM-
PEROR!!
EM-
PEROR
!!
WAAAAAA

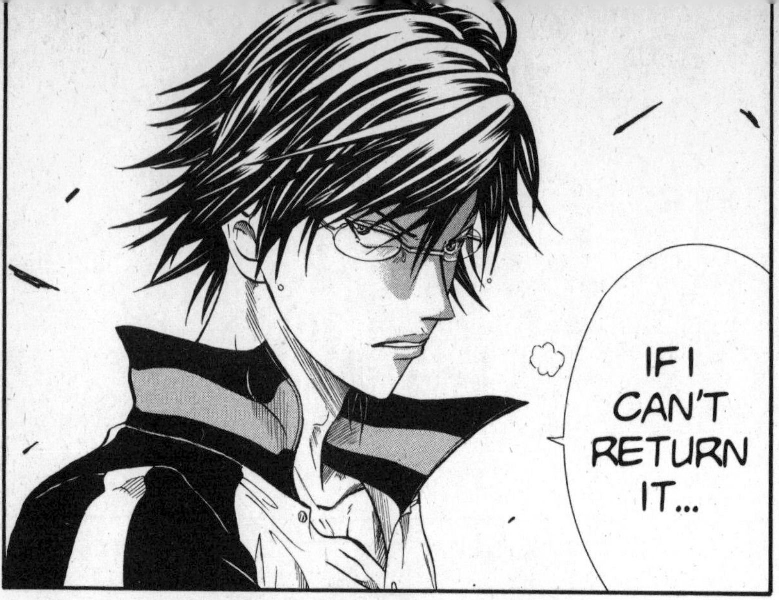
IF I CAN'T RETURN IT...

GENIUS 349: TEZUKA ZONE DEFEATED

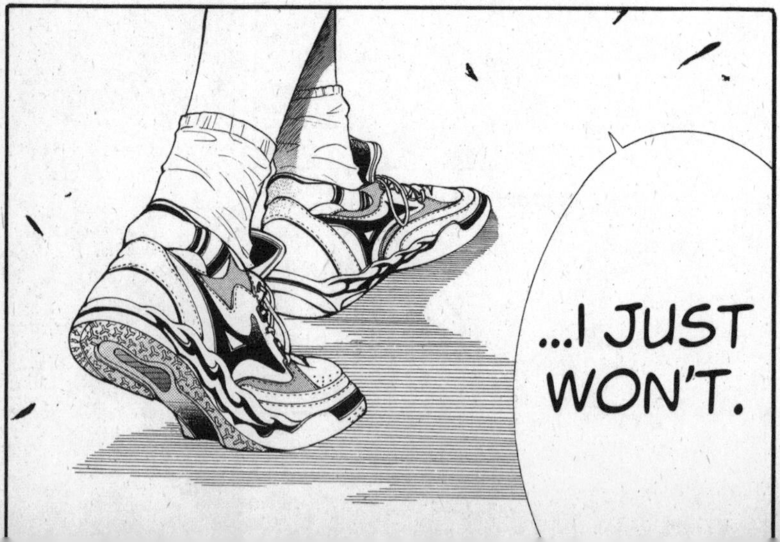
...I JUST WON'T.

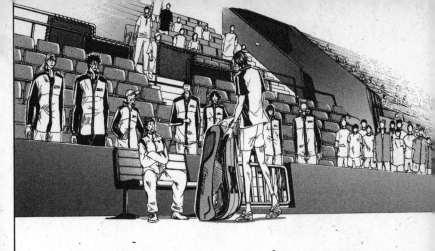

HAVE YOU LOST YOUR MIND?

HMPH...

K-KUNI-MITSU...

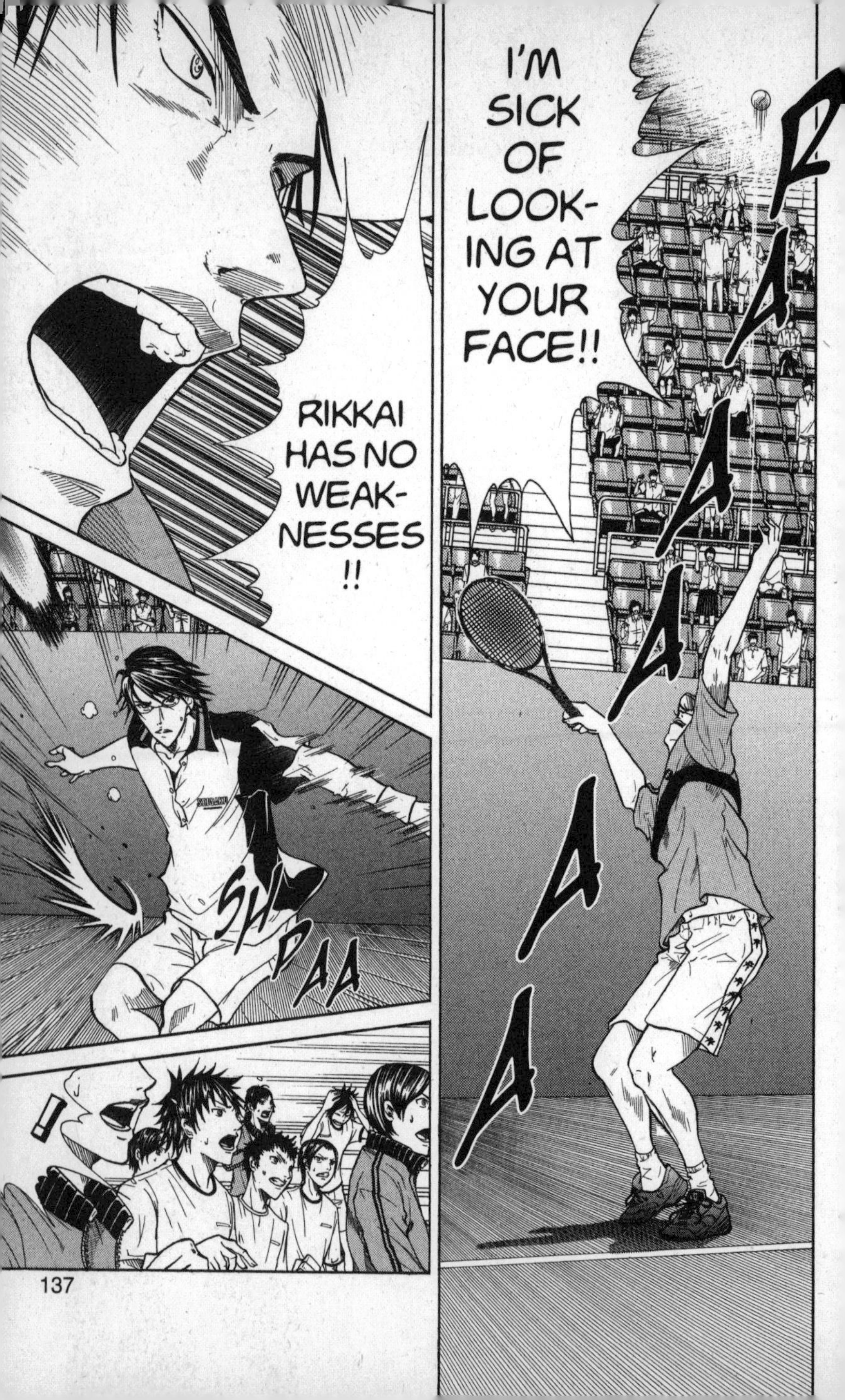
I'M SICK OF LOOKING AT YOUR FACE!!
PAAAAA
RIKKAI HAS NO WEAKNESSES!!
SHPAA
!

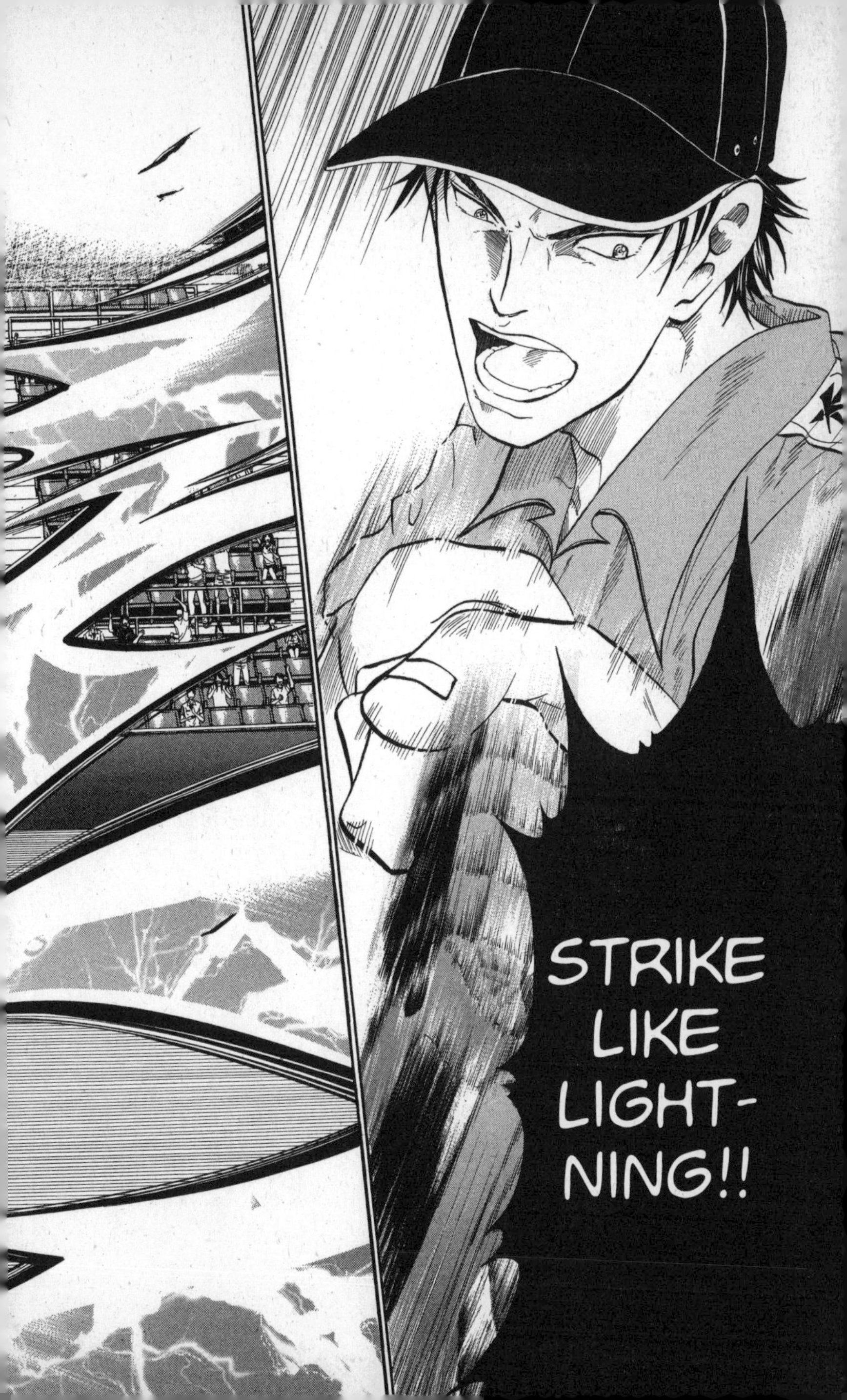
STRIKE LIKE LIGHT-NING!!

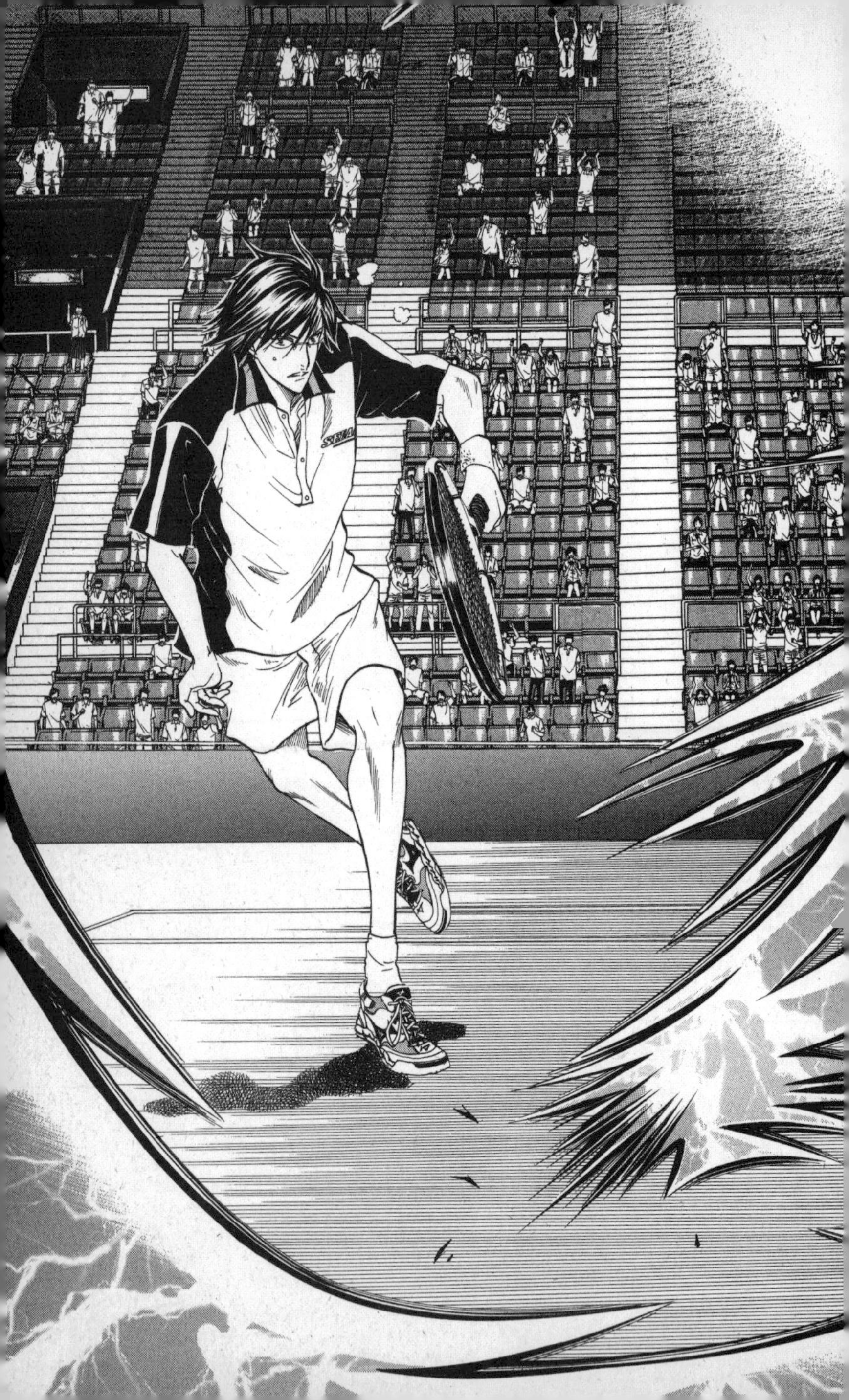

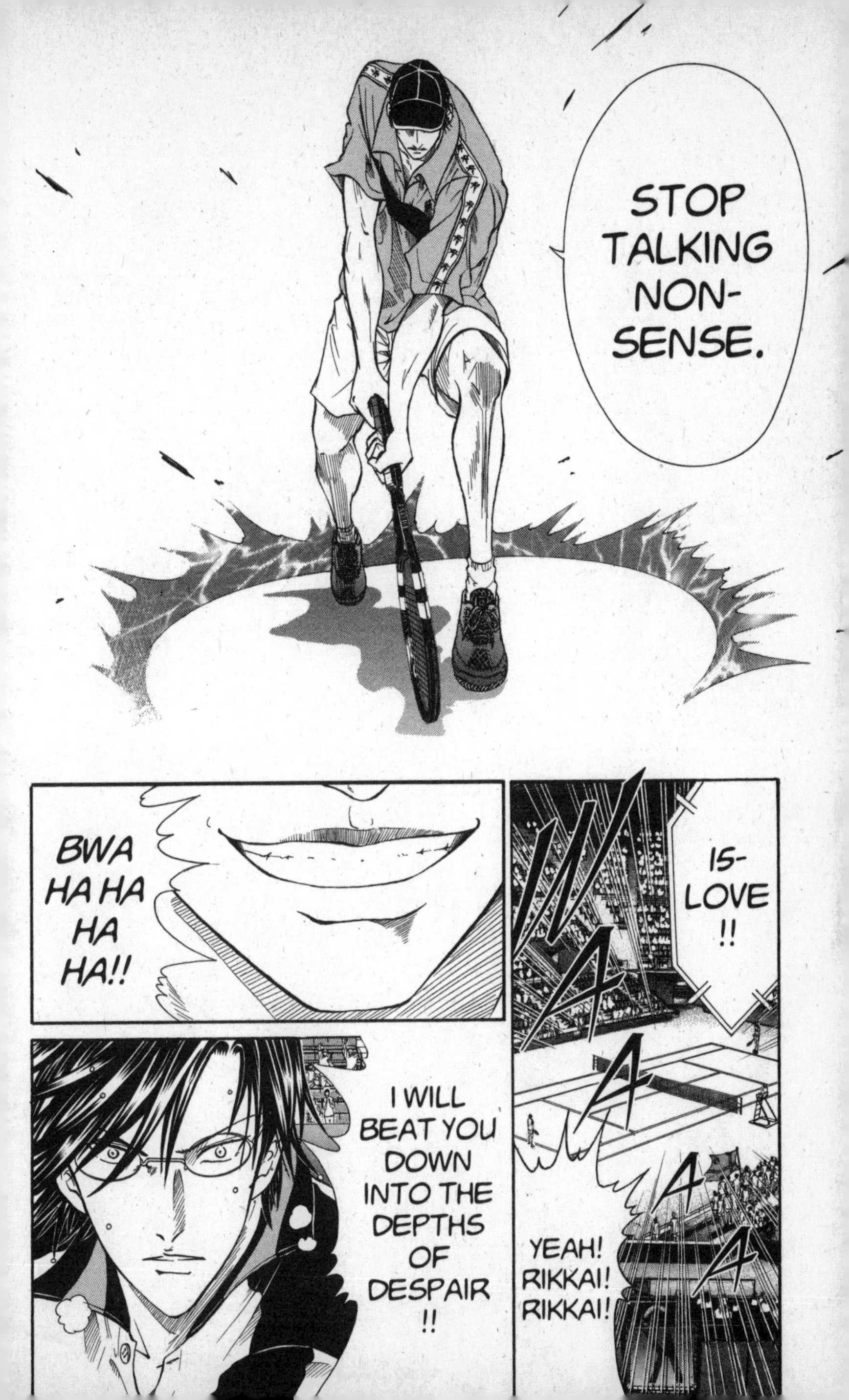
STOP TALKING NON-SENSE.
15-LOVE !!
WAAAA
YEAH! RIKKAI! RIKKAI!
BWA HA HA HA HA!!
I WILL BEAT YOU DOWN INTO THE DEPTHS OF DESPAIR !!

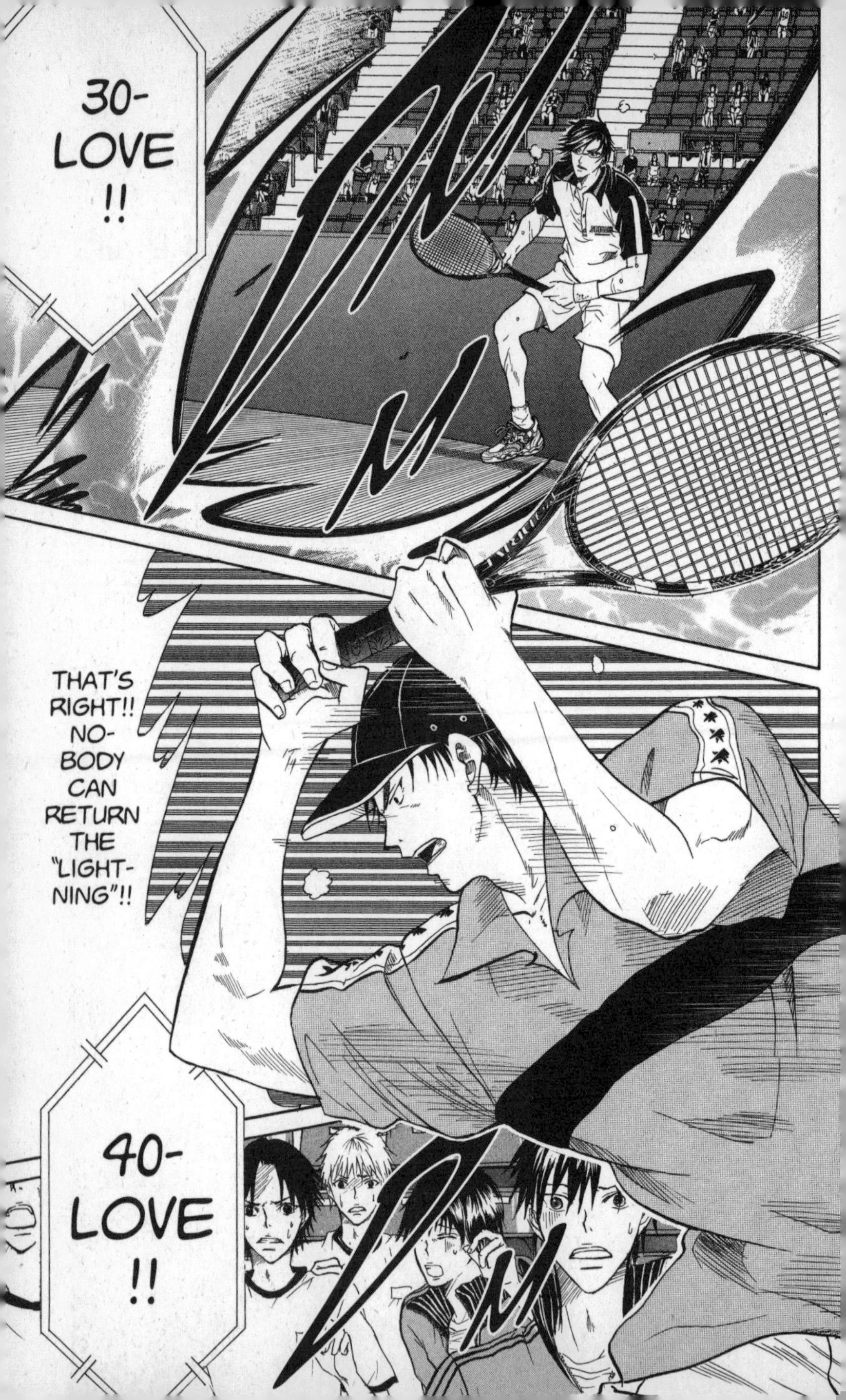
30-LOVE!!
THAT'S RIGHT!! NOBODY CAN RETURN THE "LIGHTNING"!!
40-LOVE!!

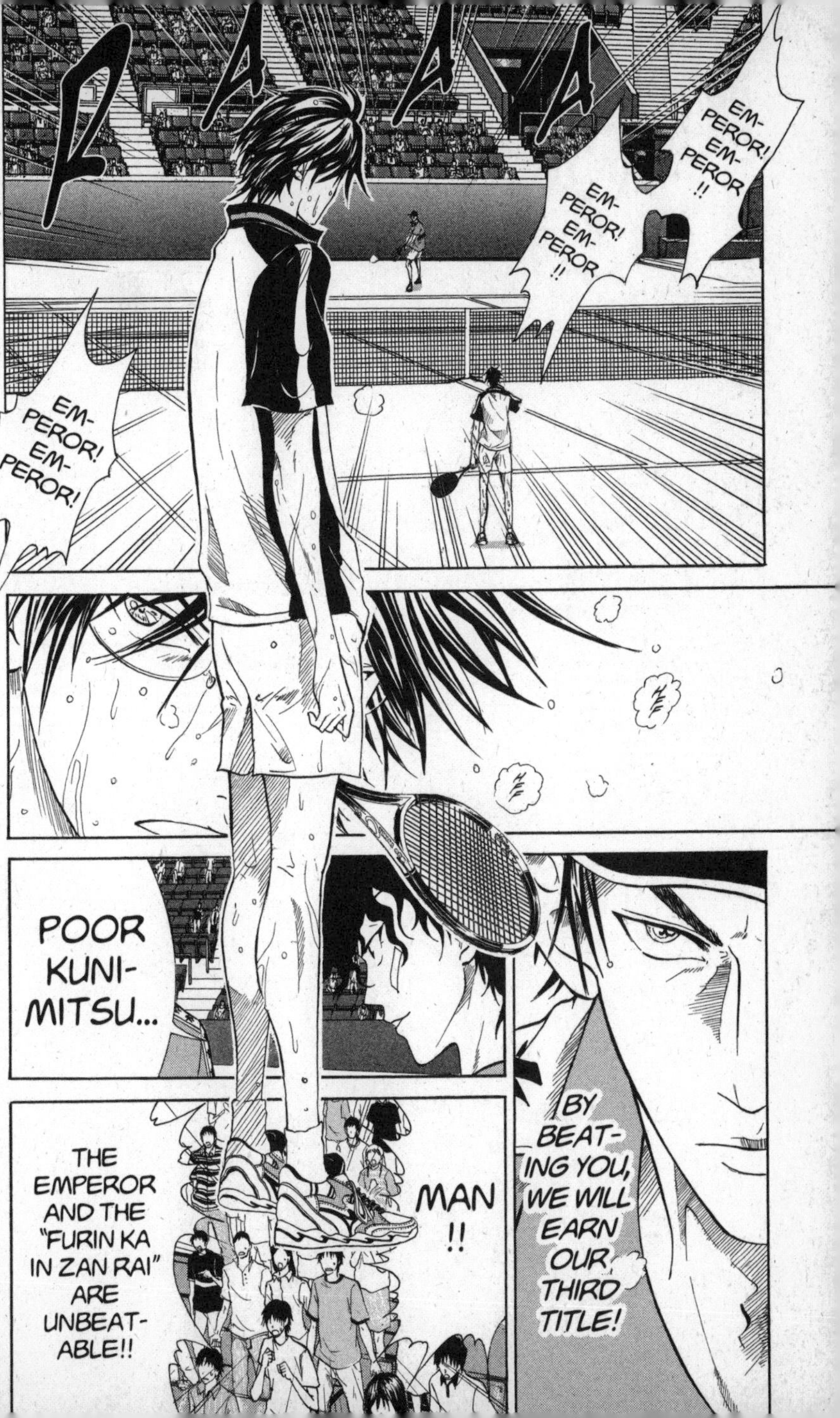
EMPEROR! EMPEROR!!
EMPEROR! EMPEROR!!
EMPEROR! EMPEROR!
BY BEATING YOU, WE WILL EARN OUR THIRD TITLE!
POOR KUNIMITSU...
MAN!!
THE EMPEROR AND THE "FURIN KA IN ZAN RAI" ARE UNBEATABLE!!

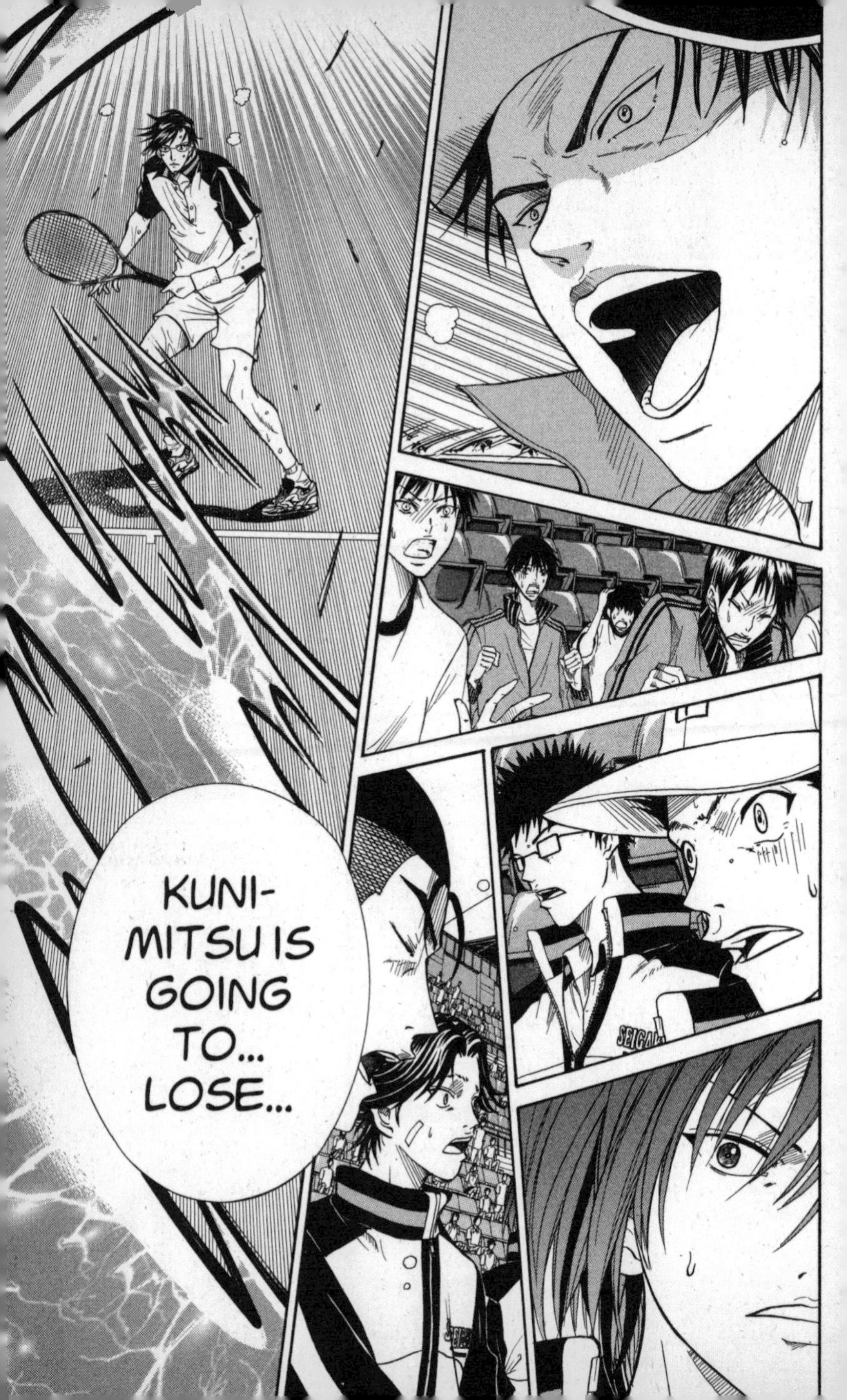
KUNI-MITSU IS GOING TO... LOSE...

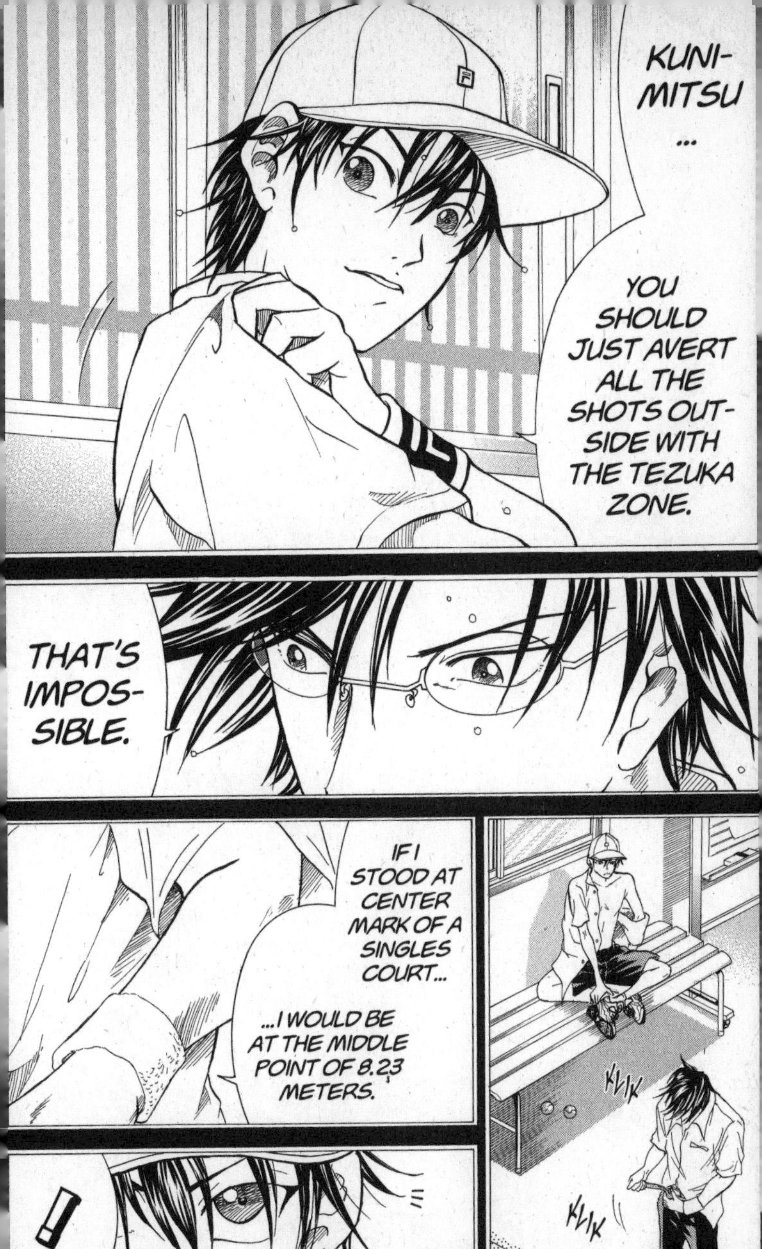
KUNI-MITSU ...
YOU SHOULD JUST AVERT ALL THE SHOTS OUT-SIDE WITH THE TEZUKA ZONE.
THAT'S IMPOS-SIBLE.
KLIK
KLIK
IF I STOOD AT CENTER MARK OF A SINGLES COURT...
...I WOULD BE AT THE MIDDLE POINT OF 8.23 METERS.
!

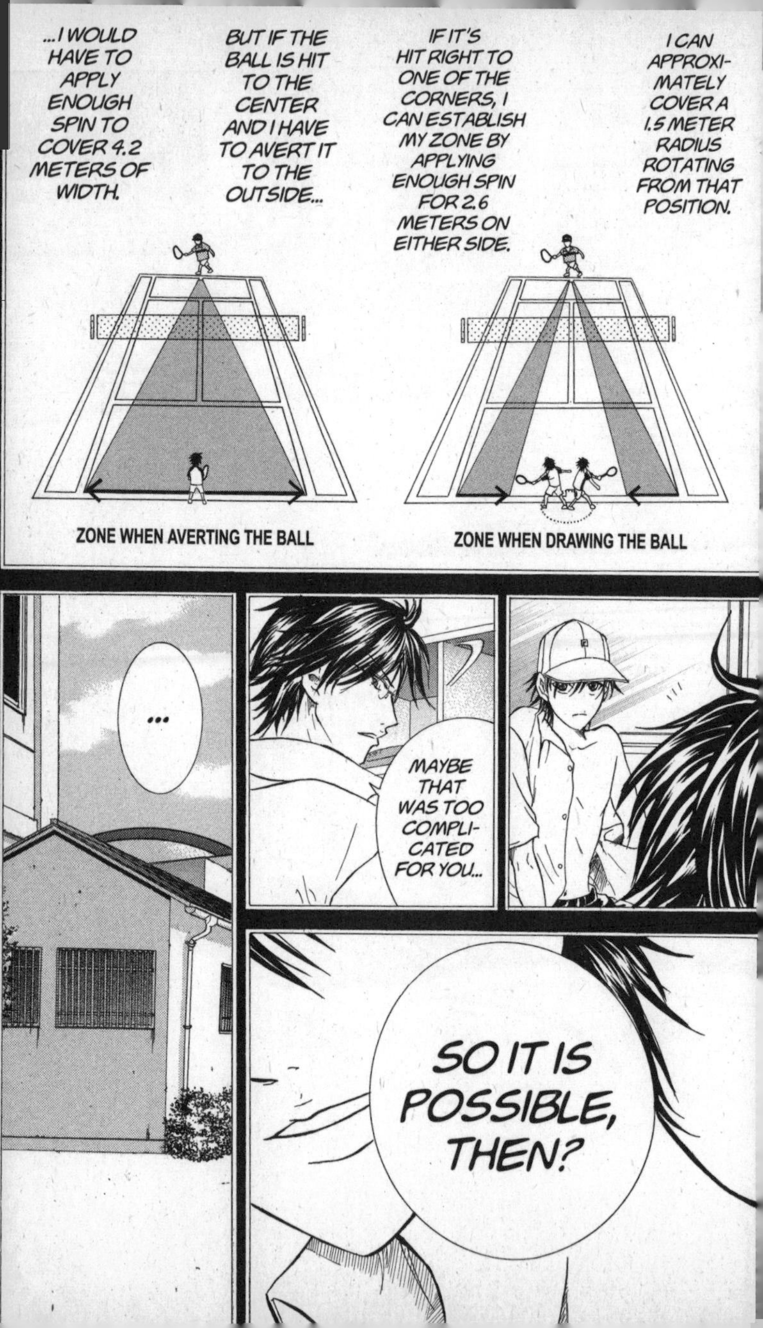
I CAN APPROXI-MATELY COVER A 1.5 METER RADIUS ROTATING FROM THAT POSITION.
IF IT'S HIT RIGHT TO ONE OF THE CORNERS, I CAN ESTABLISH MY ZONE BY APPLYING ENOUGH SPIN FOR 2.6 METERS ON EITHER SIDE.
BUT IF THE BALL IS HIT TO THE CENTER AND I HAVE TO AVERT IT TO THE OUTSIDE...
...I WOULD HAVE TO APPLY ENOUGH SPIN TO COVER 4.2 METERS OF WIDTH.
ZONE WHEN DRAWING THE BALL
ZONE WHEN AVERTING THE BALL
MAYBE THAT WAS TOO COMPLI-CATED FOR YOU...
SO IT IS POSSIBLE, THEN?
...

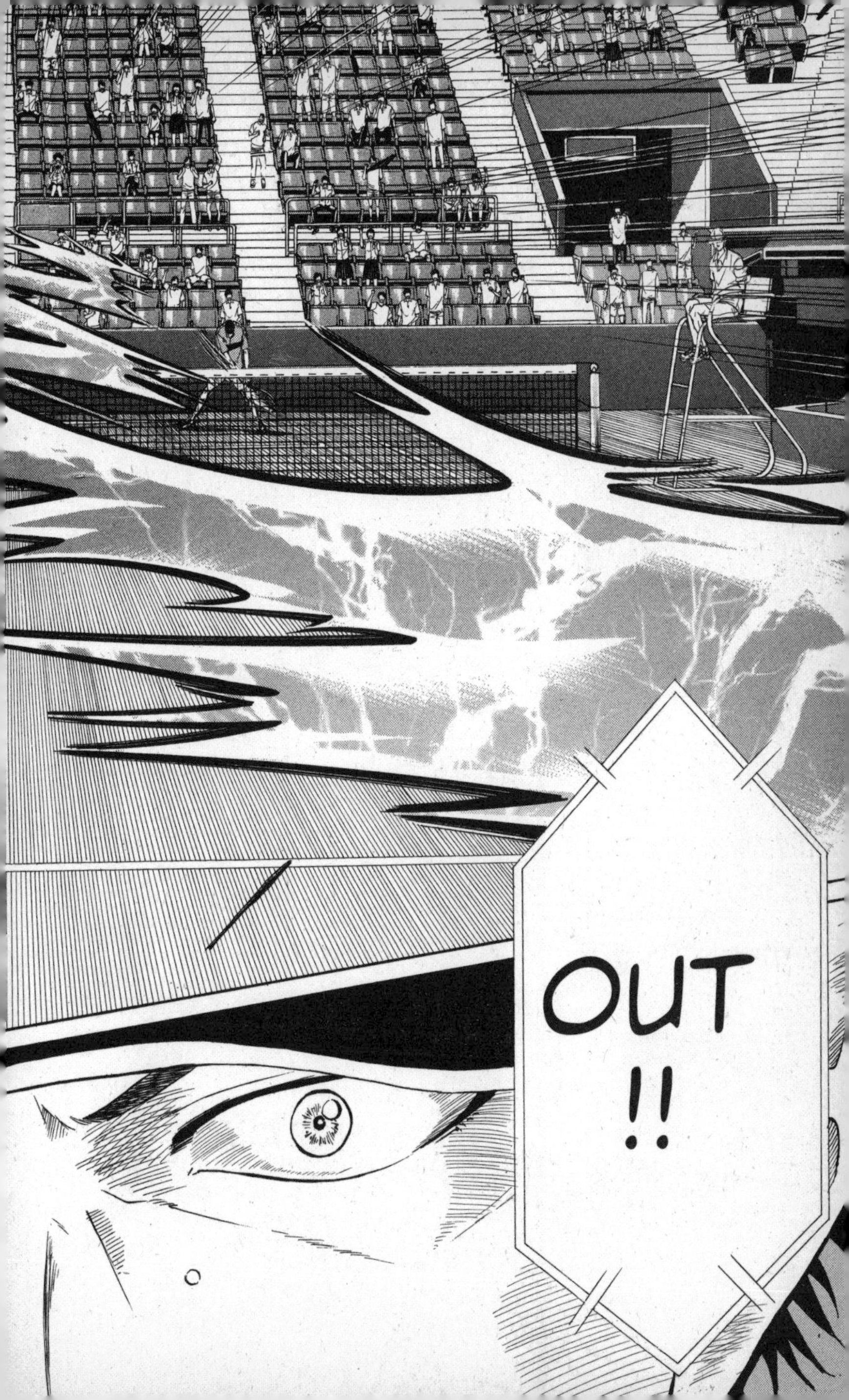
OUT !!

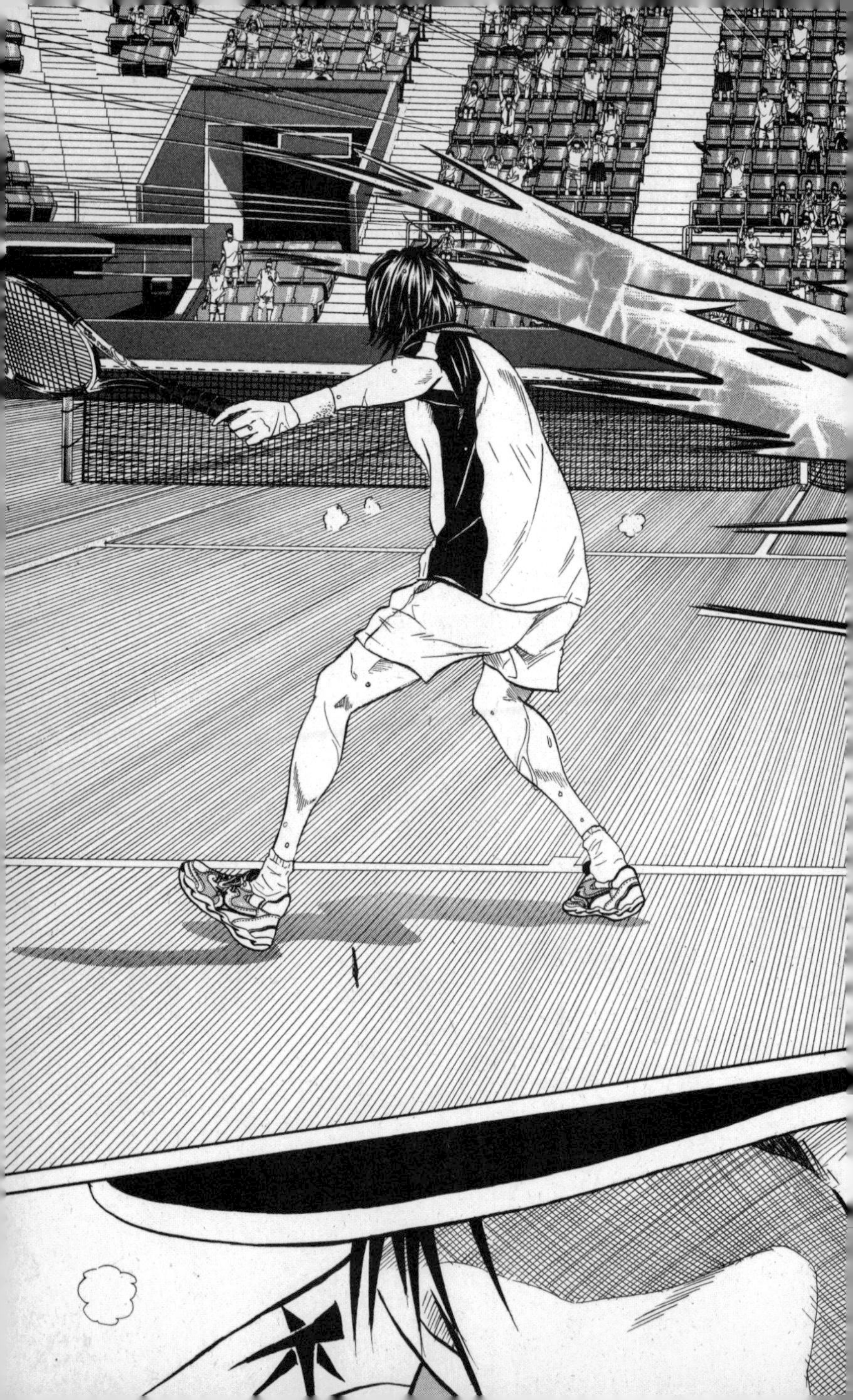

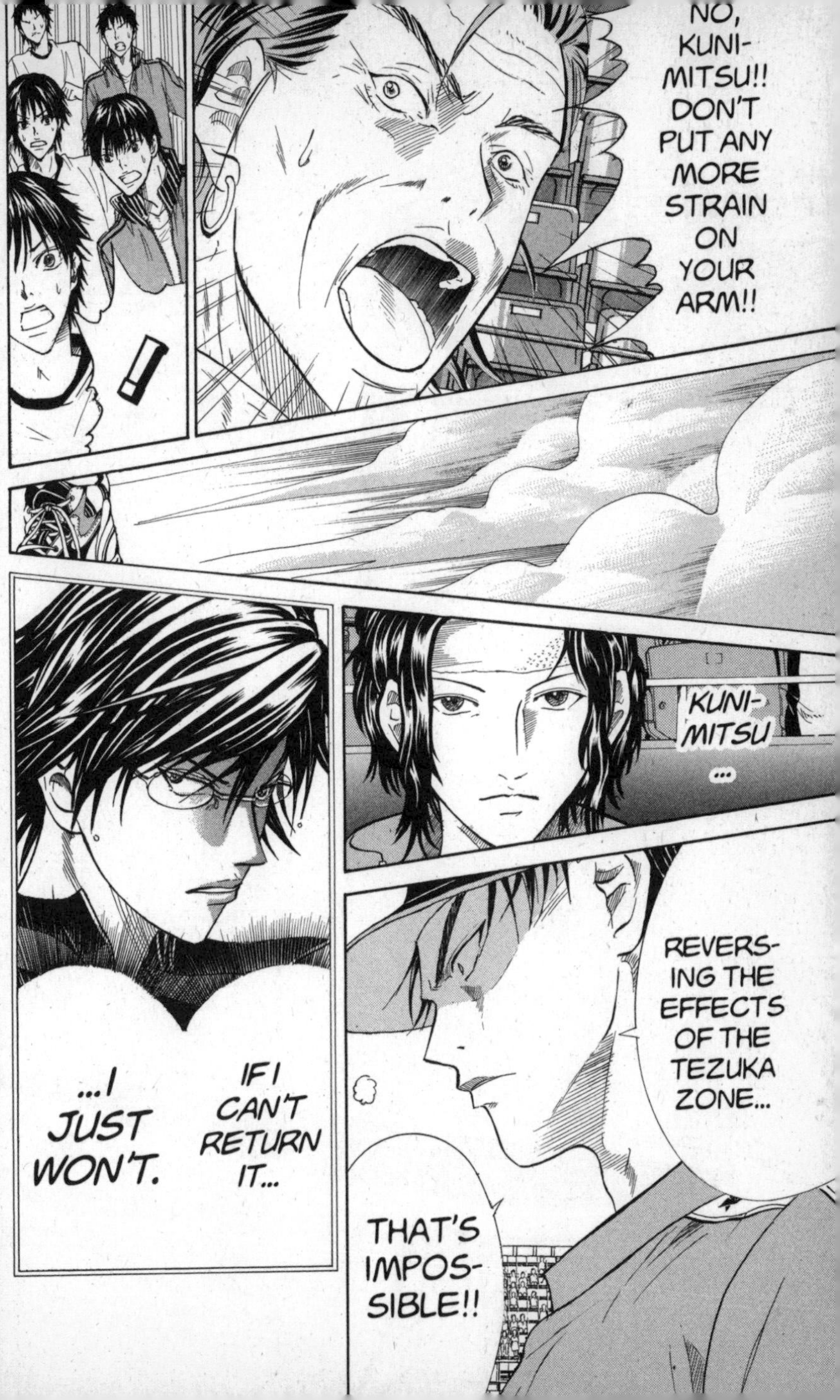
NO, KUNI-MITSU!! DON'T PUT ANY MORE STRAIN ON YOUR ARM!!
KUNI-MITSU ...
REVERS-ING THE EFFECTS OF THE TEZUKA ZONE...
THAT'S IMPOS-SIBLE!!
IF I CAN'T RETURN IT...
...I JUST WON'T.

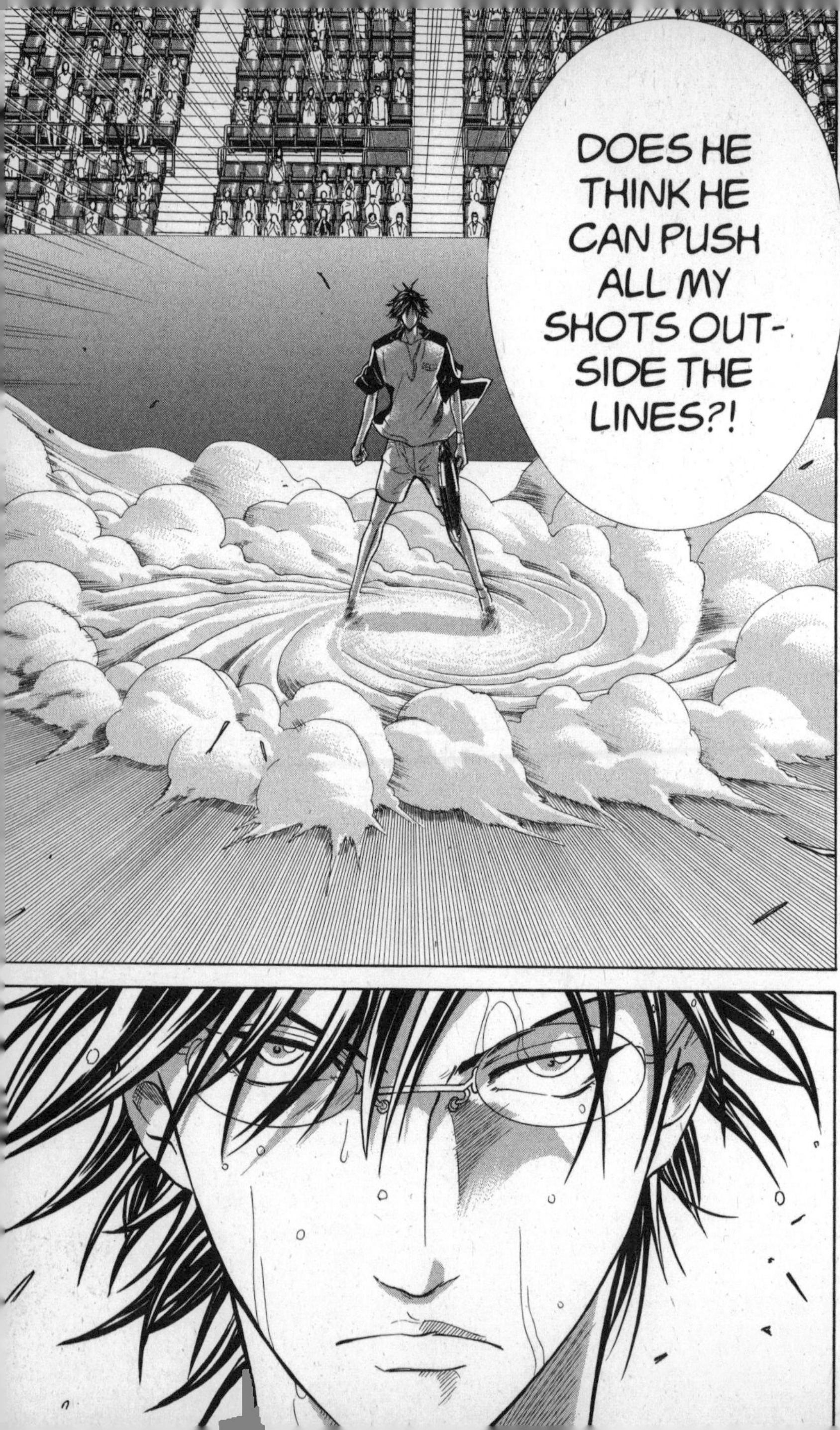
DOES HE THINK HE CAN PUSH ALL MY SHOTS OUT-SIDE THE LINES?!

テニスの王子様

THE PRINCE OF TENNIS

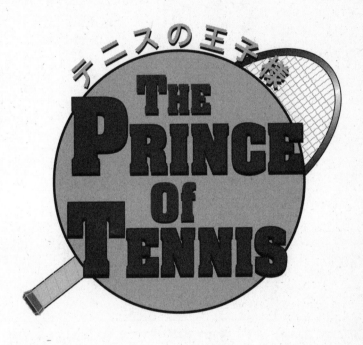

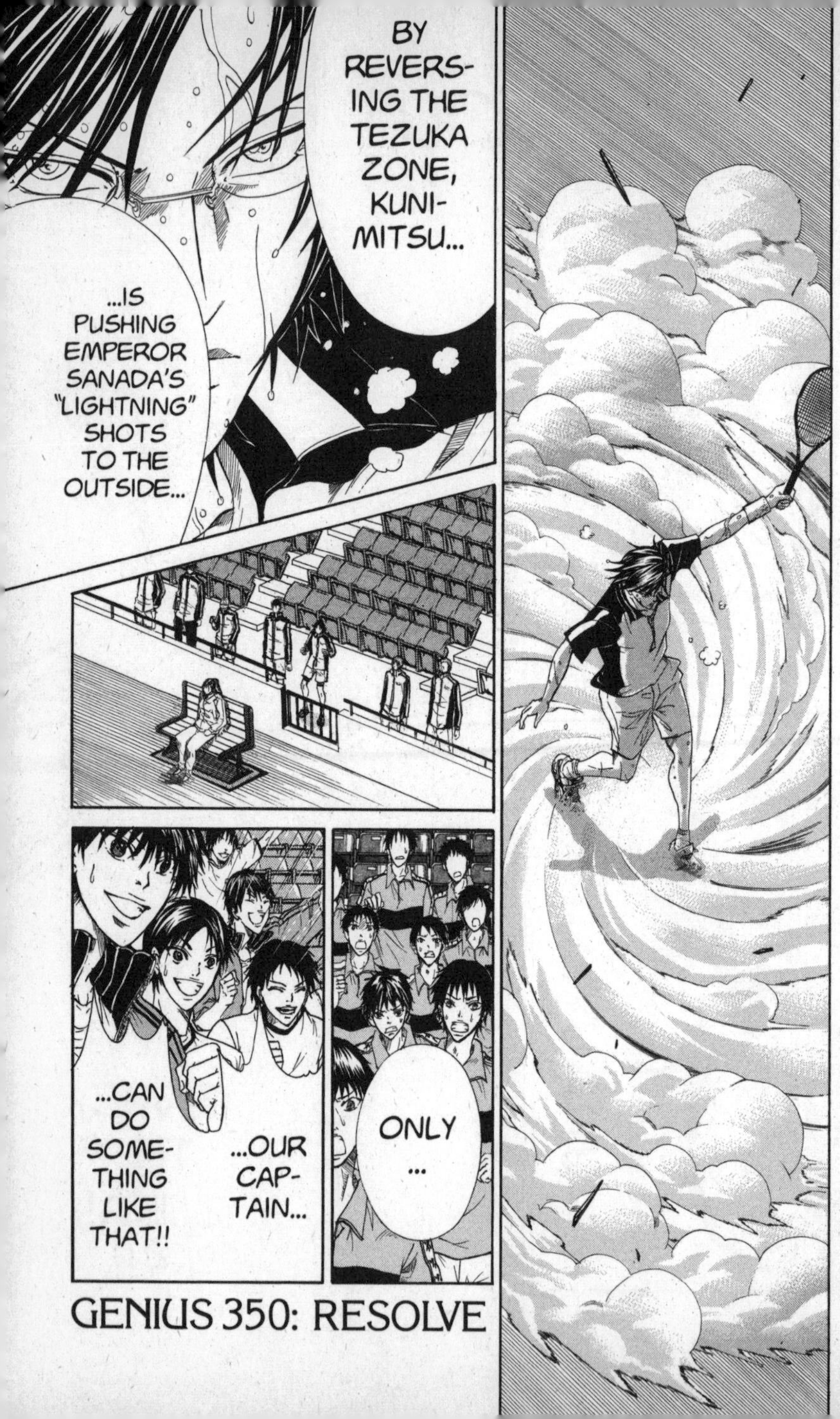
BY REVERSING THE TEZUKA ZONE, KUNIMITSU...
...IS PUSHING EMPEROR SANADA'S "LIGHTNING" SHOTS TO THE OUTSIDE...
ONLY ...
...OUR CAPTAIN...
...CAN DO SOMETHING LIKE THAT!!

GENIUS 350: RESOLVE

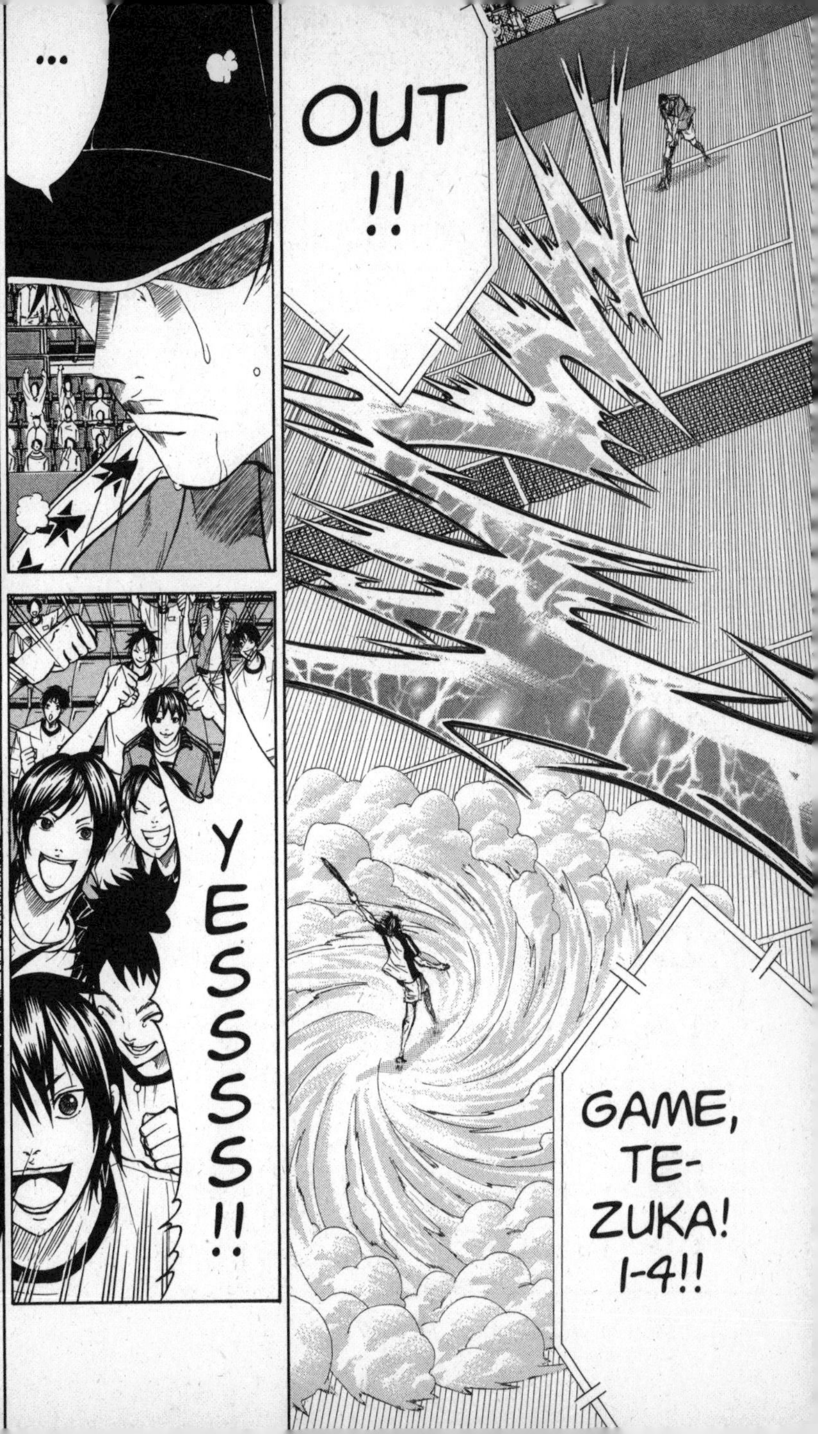
OUT !!
GAME, TE-ZUKA! 1-4!!
...
YESSS!!

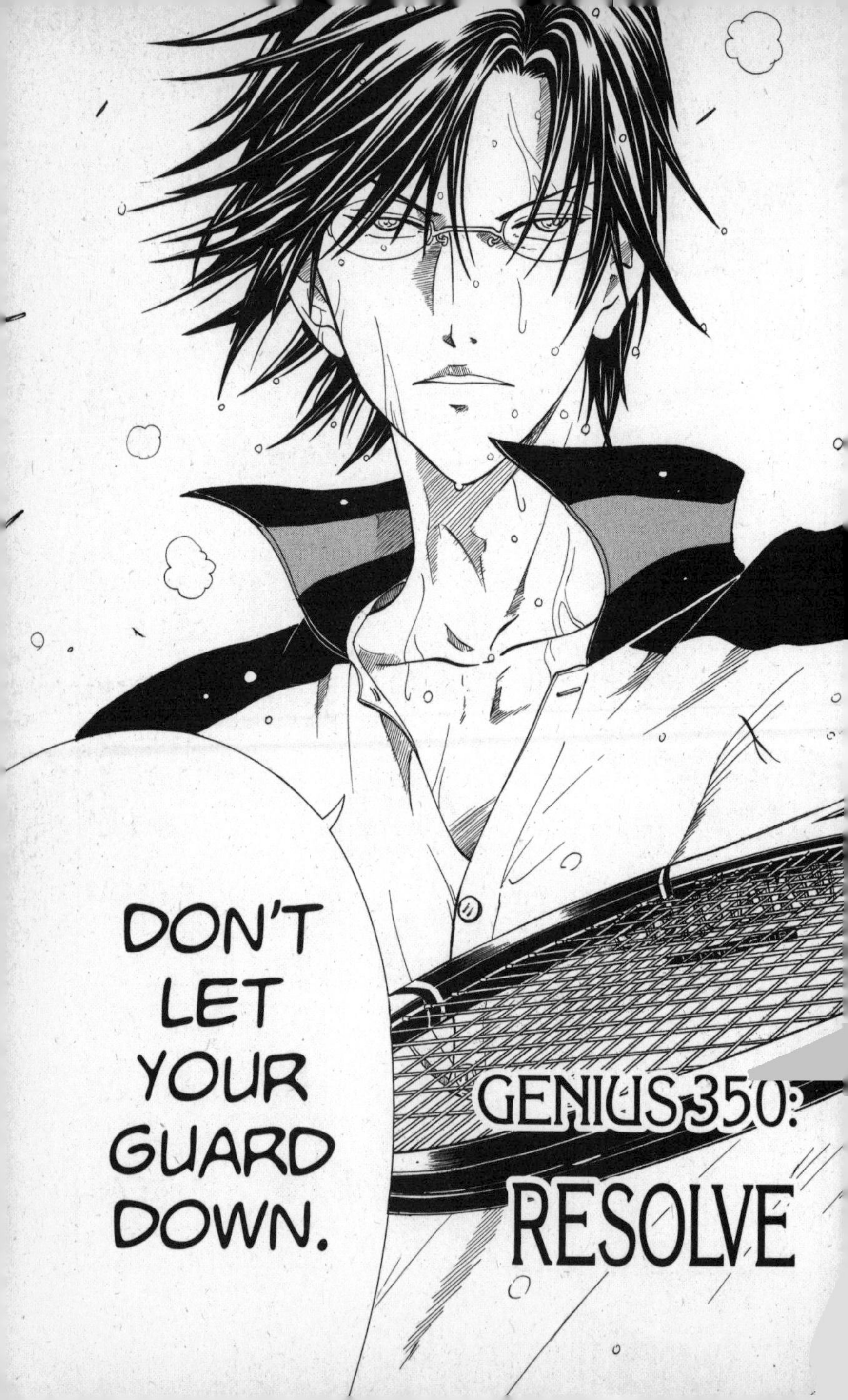
GENIUS 350:
RESOLVE
DON'T LET YOUR GUARD DOWN.

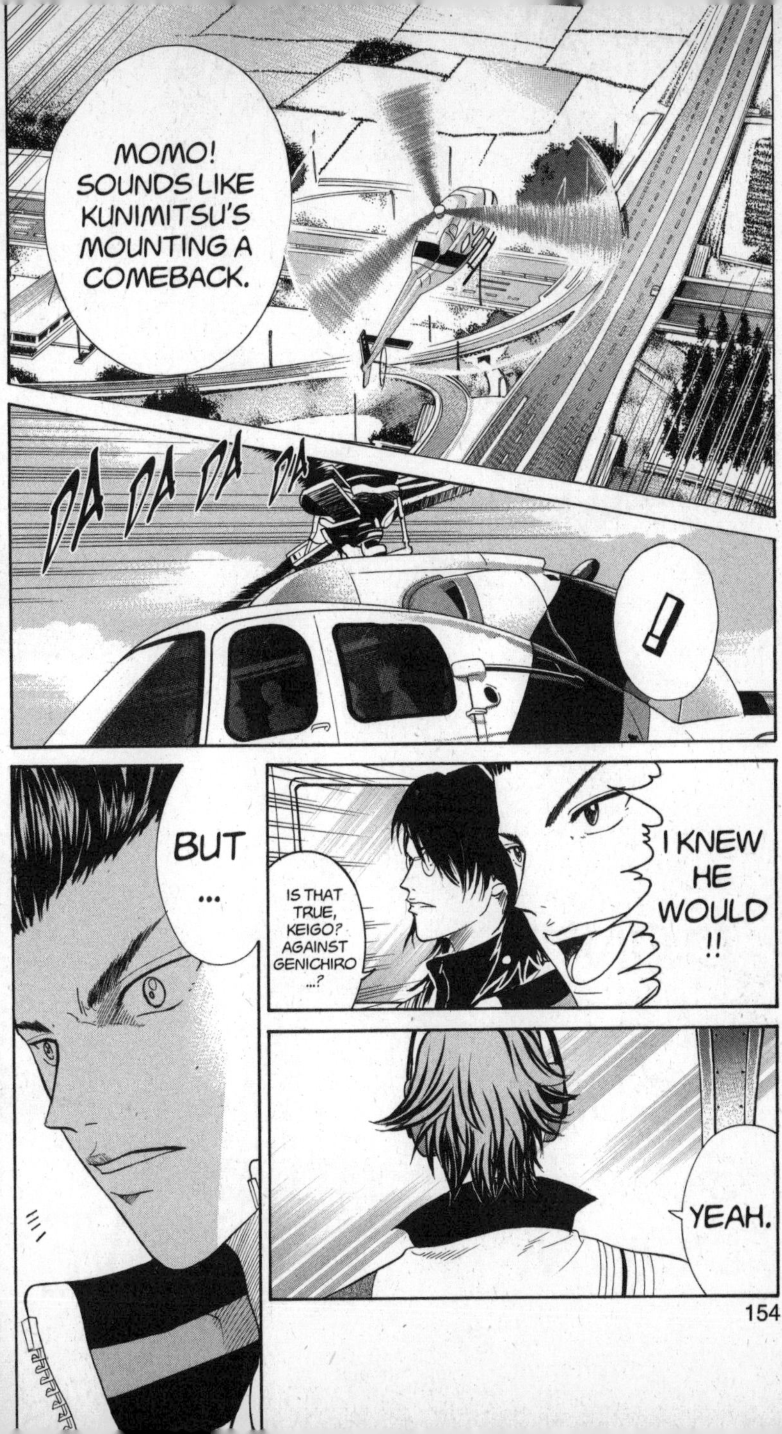

MOMO! SOUNDS LIKE KUNIMITSU'S MOUNTING A COMEBACK.
DA DA DA DA
!
I KNEW HE WOULD !!
IS THAT TRUE, KEIGO? AGAINST GENICHIRO ...?
YEAH.
BUT ...

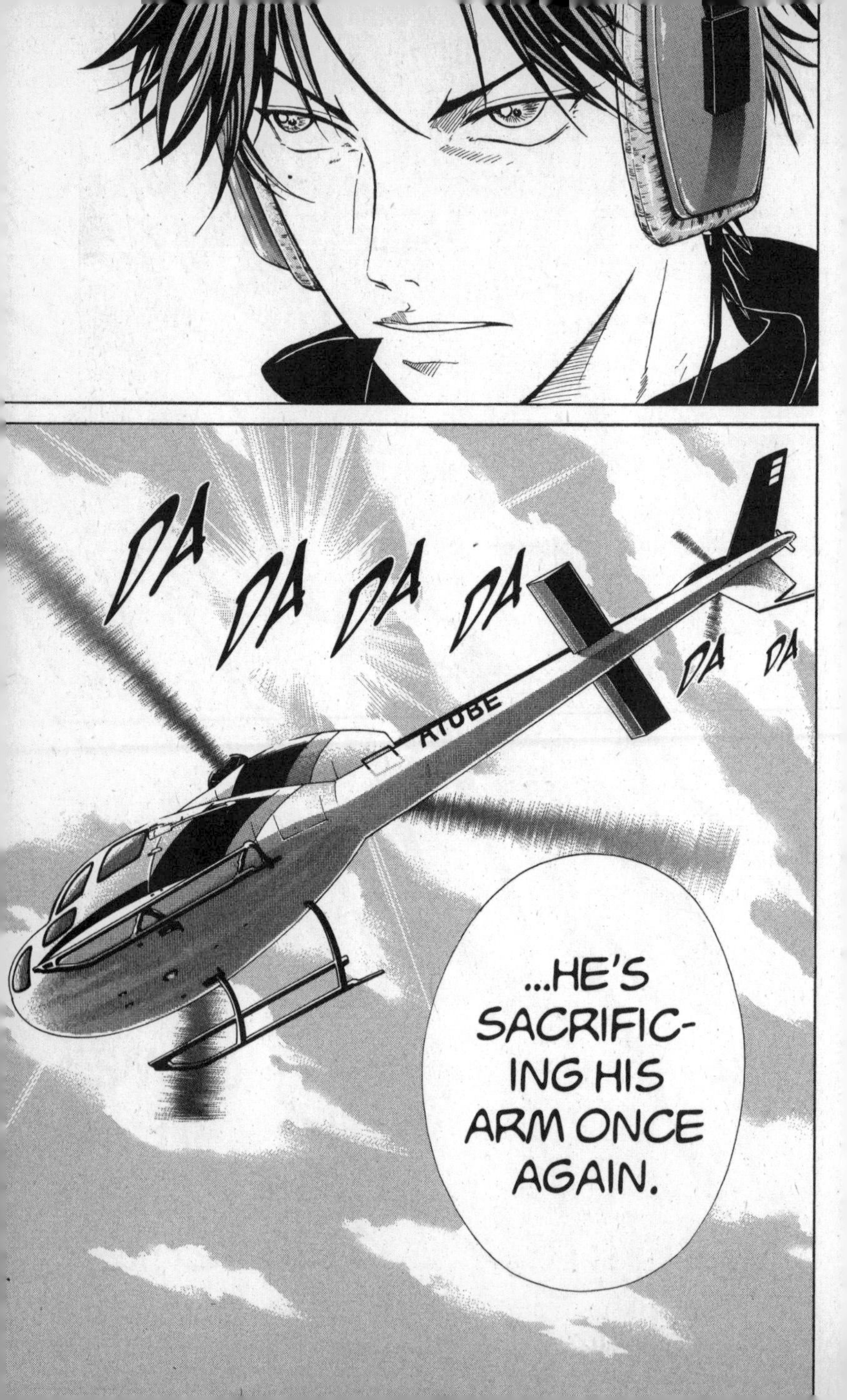
DA DA DA DA DA DA
ATOBE
...HE'S SACRIFICING HIS ARM ONCE AGAIN.

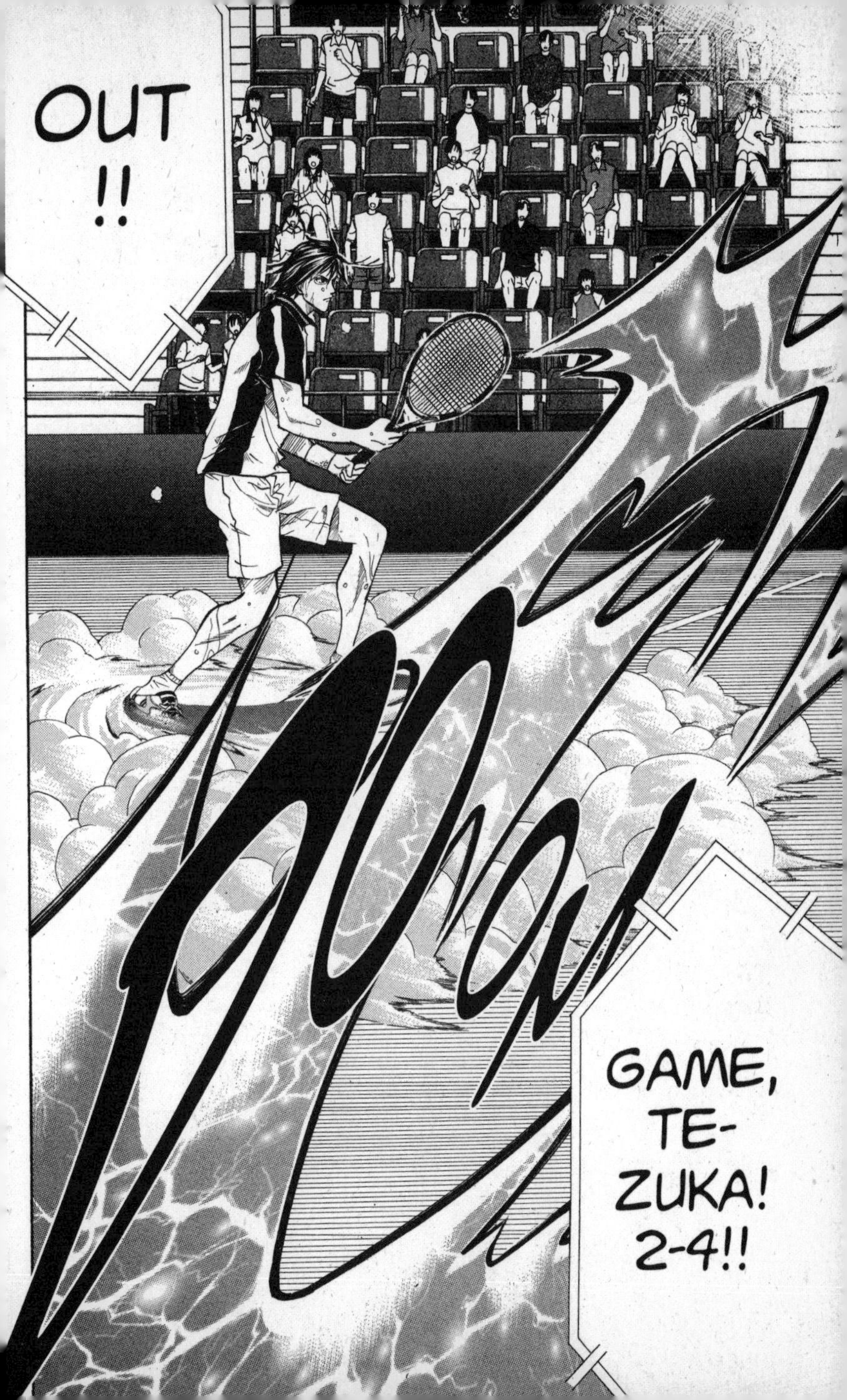
OUT !!
GAME, TE-ZUKA! 2-4!!

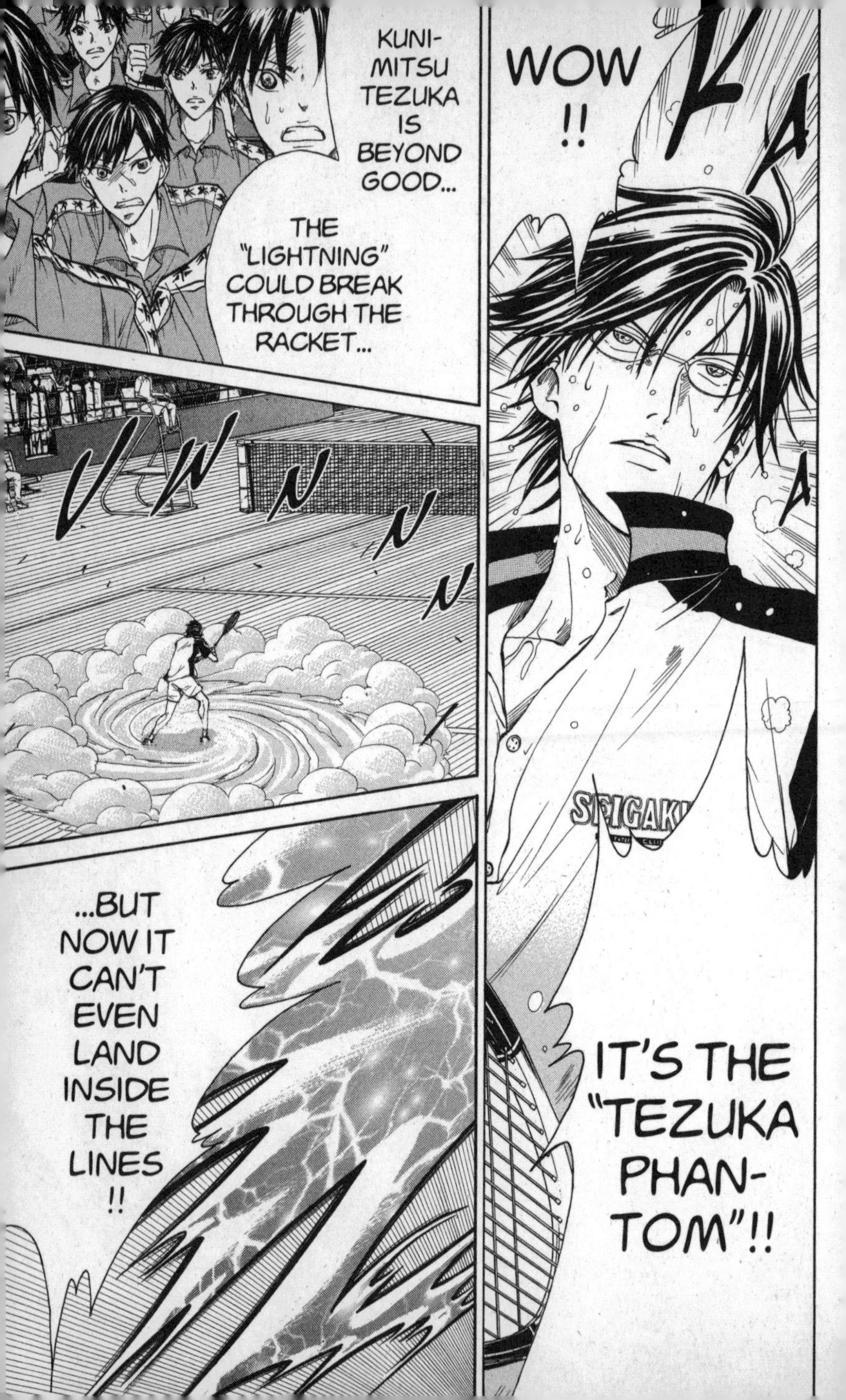
WOW!!
IT'S THE "TEZUKA PHANTOM"!!
KUNIMITSU TEZUKA IS BEYOND GOOD...
THE "LIGHTNING" COULD BREAK THROUGH THE RACKET...
...BUT NOW IT CAN'T EVEN LAND INSIDE THE LINES!!

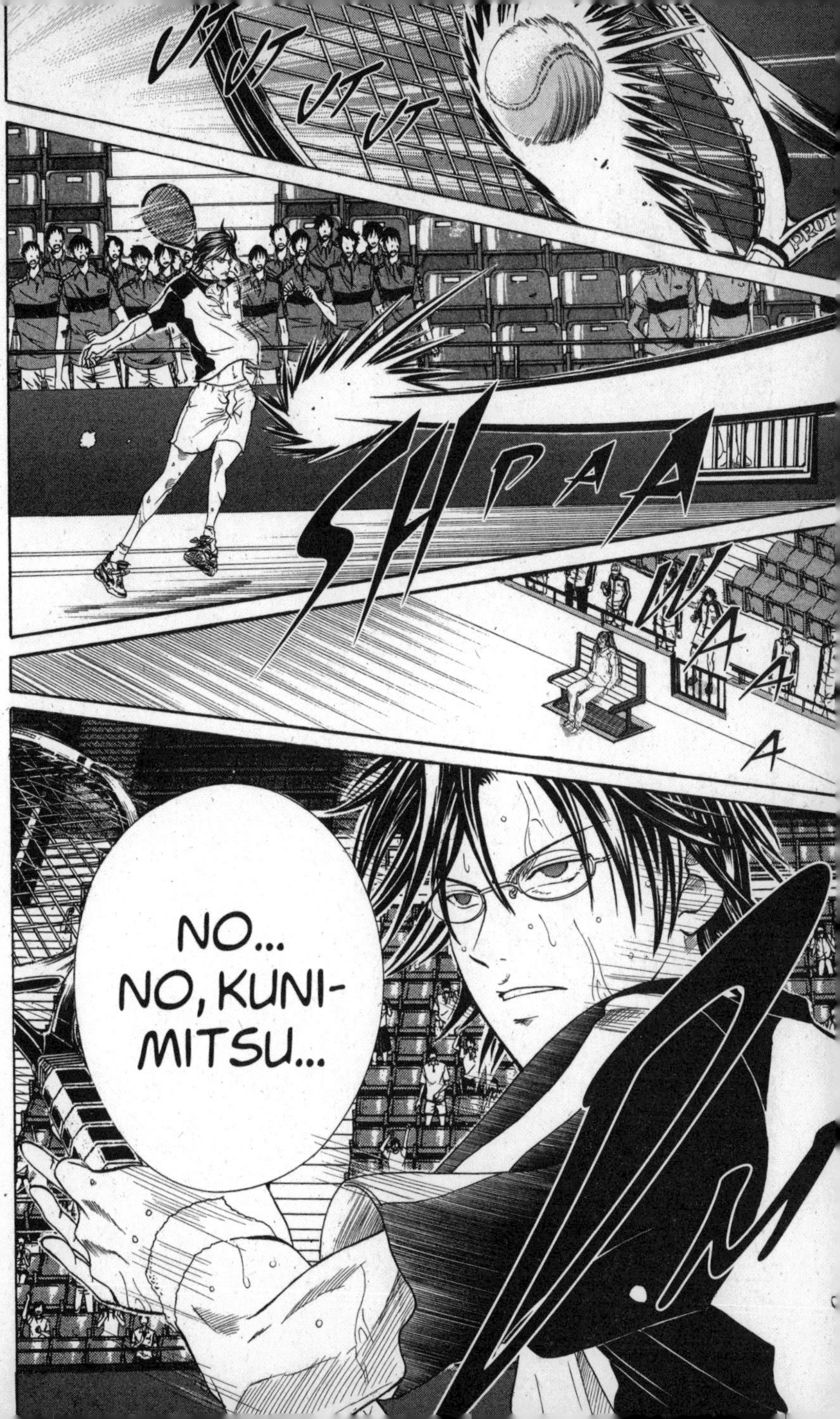
JYUT JYUT JYUT
SHPAAA
WAAAA
NO... NO, KUNI-MITSU...
VMM

READ THIS WAY

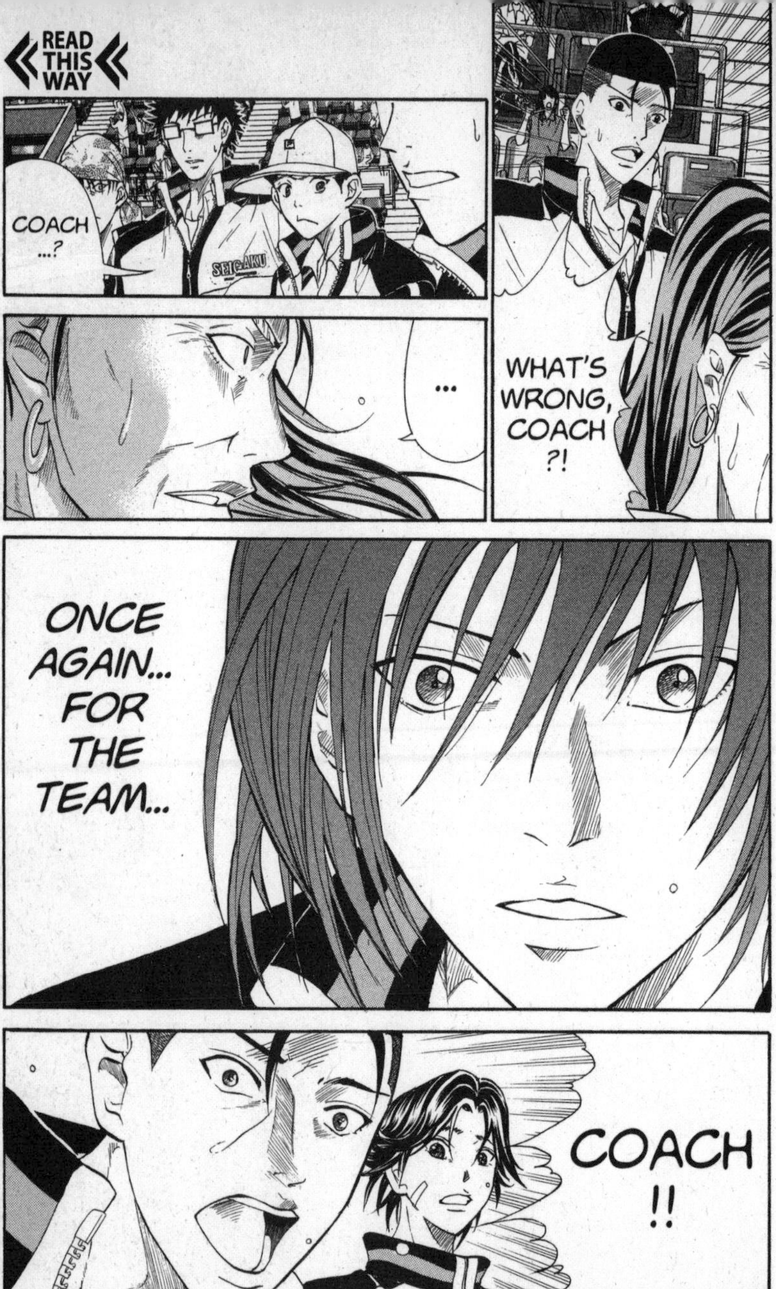
WHAT'S WRONG, COACH ?!
COACH ...?
...
ONCE AGAIN... FOR THE TEAM...
COACH !!

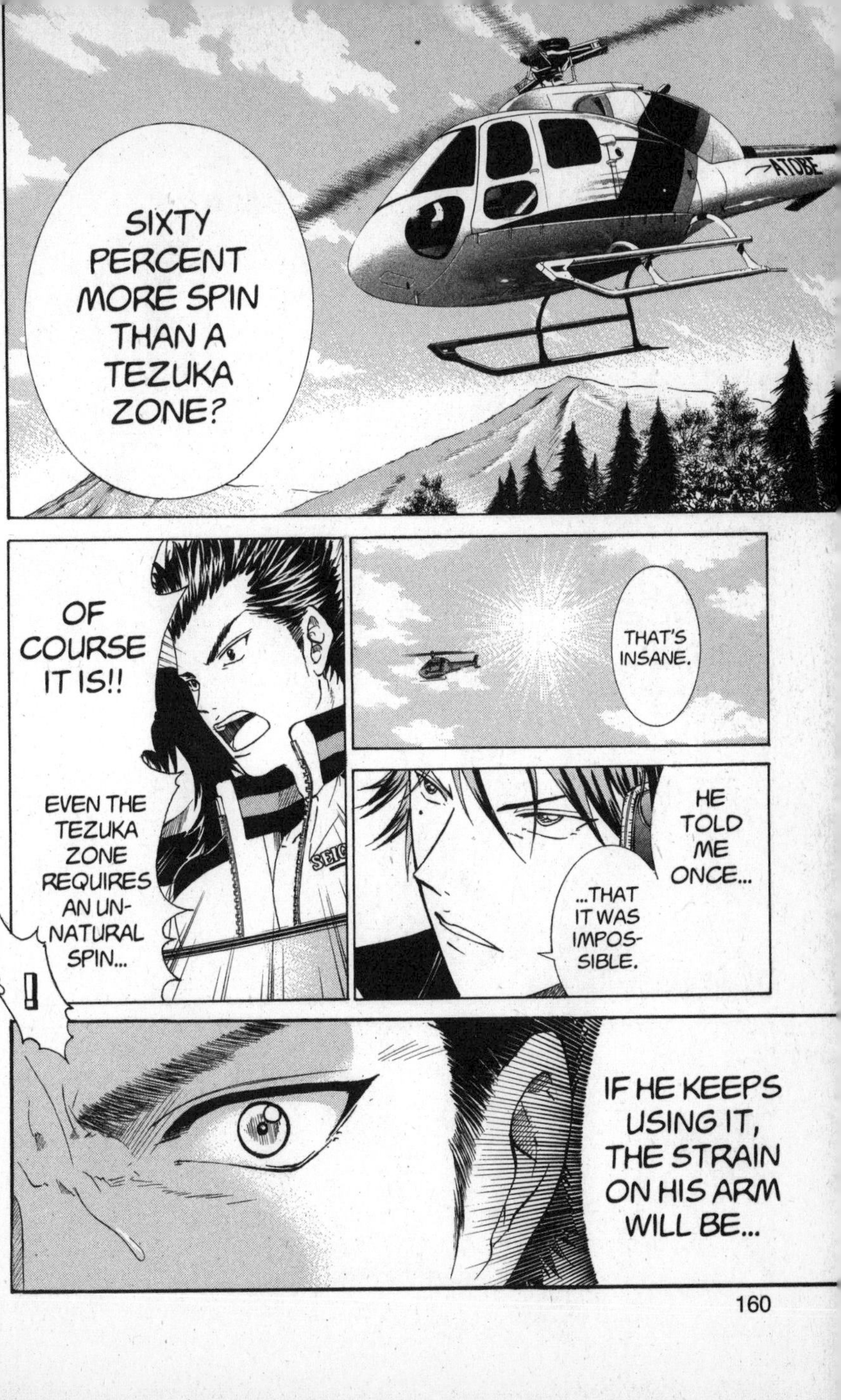
ATOBE
SIXTY PERCENT MORE SPIN THAN A TEZUKA ZONE?
THAT'S INSANE.
HE TOLD ME ONCE...
...THAT IT WAS IMPOSSIBLE.
OF COURSE IT IS!!
EVEN THE TEZUKA ZONE REQUIRES AN UN-NATURAL SPIN...
!
IF HE KEEPS USING IT, THE STRAIN ON HIS ARM WILL BE...

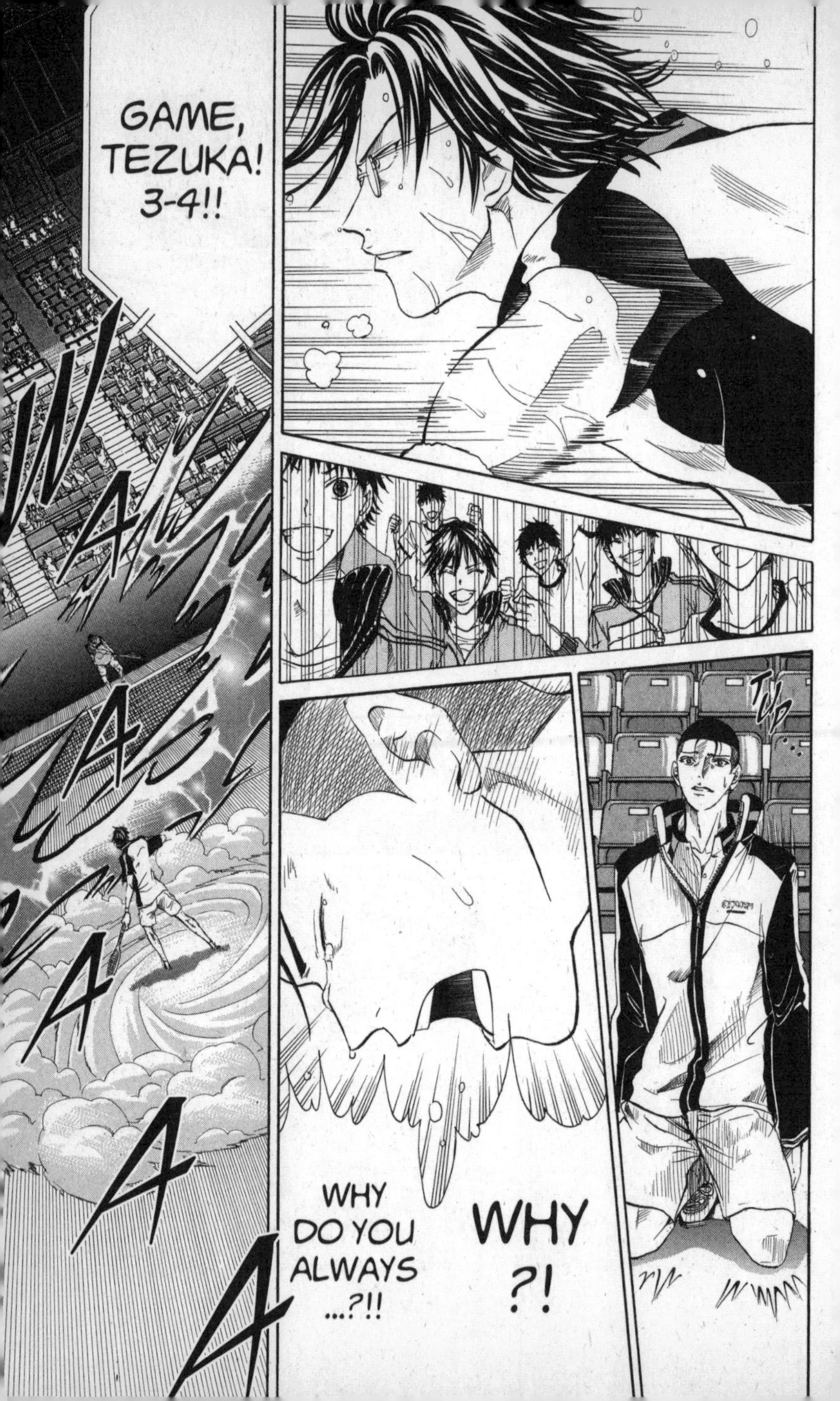
TUP
WHY
?!
WHY
DO YOU
ALWAYS
...?!!
GAME,
TEZUKA!
3-4!!
WAAAAA

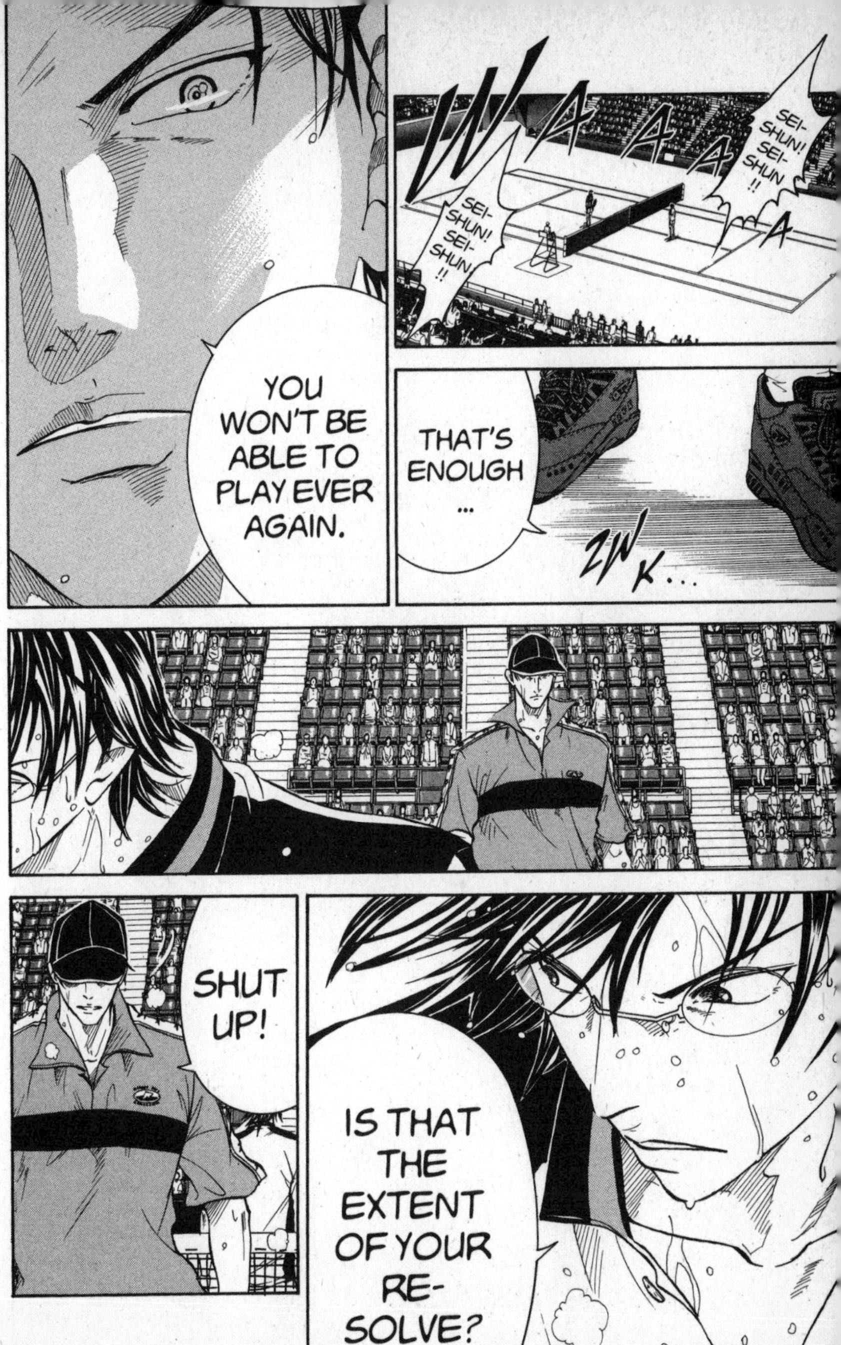
WAAAA
SEI-SHUN! SEI-SHUN!!
SEI-SHUN! SEI-SHUN!!
THAT'S ENOUGH ...
ZWK...
YOU WON'T BE ABLE TO PLAY EVER AGAIN.
IS THAT THE EXTENT OF YOUR RE-SOLVE?
SHUT UP!

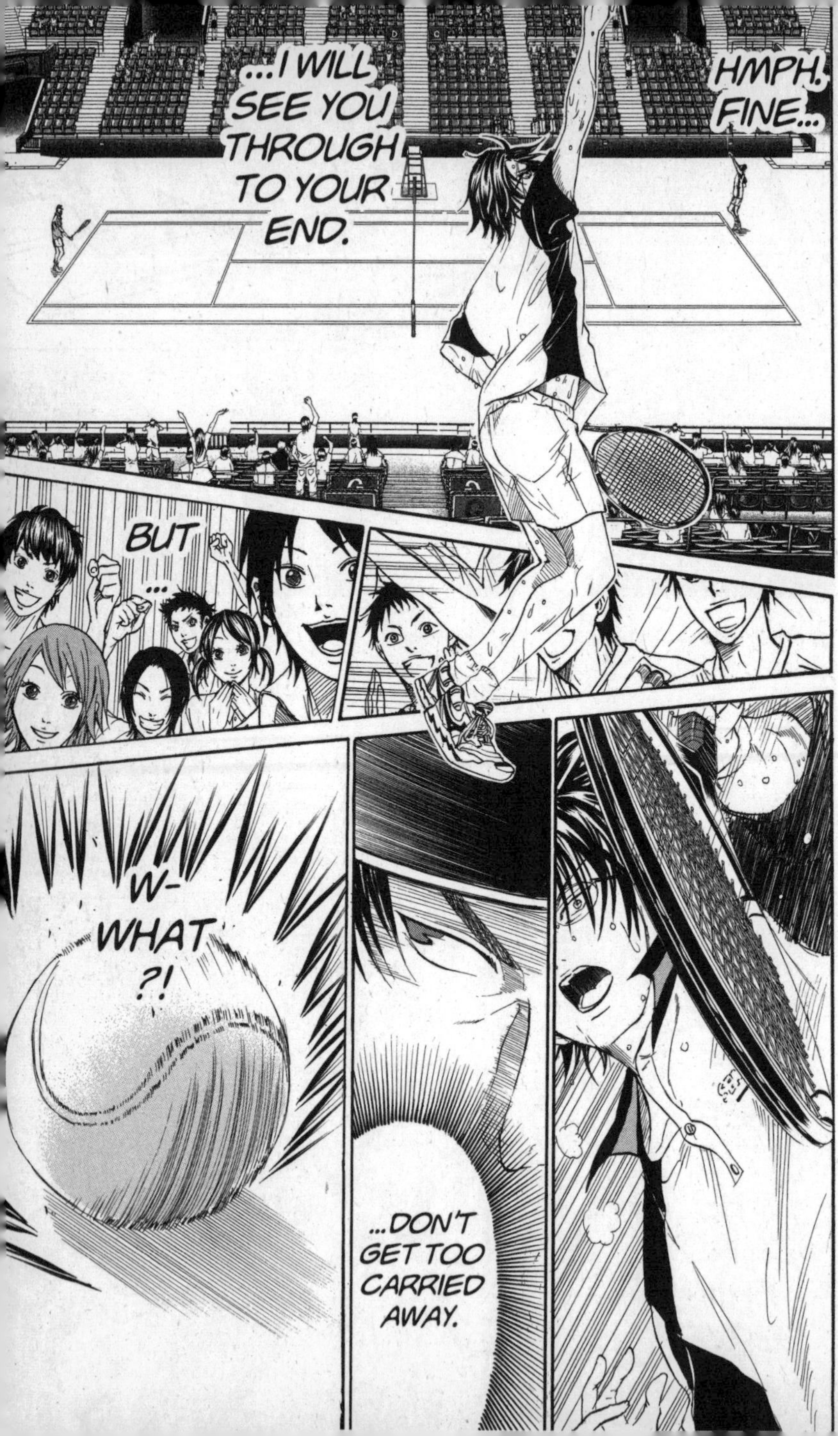
HMPH. FINE...
...I WILL SEE YOU THROUGH TO YOUR END.
BUT ...
...DON'T GET TOO CARRIED AWAY.
W- WHAT ?!

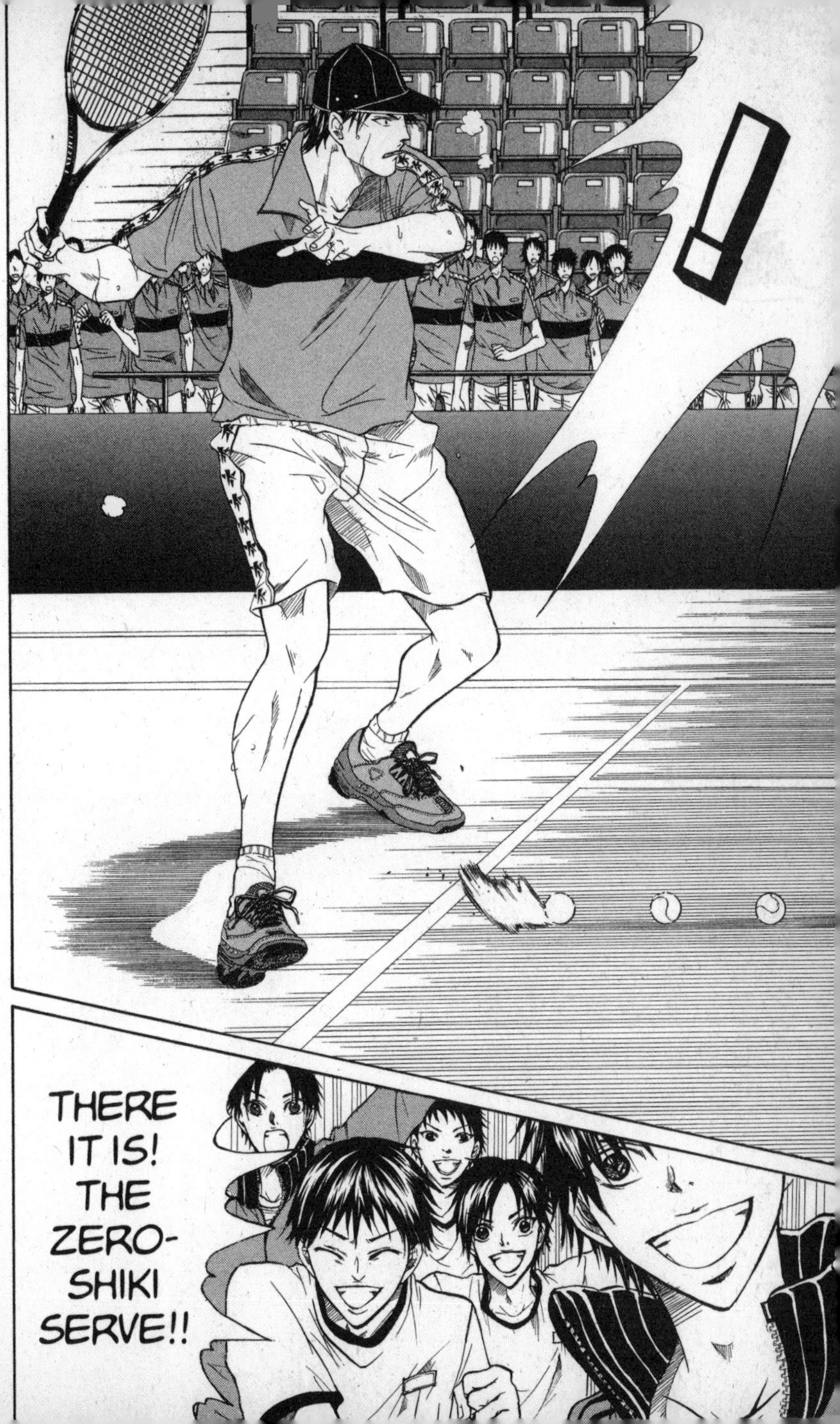
!
THERE IT IS! THE ZERO-SHIKI SERVE!!

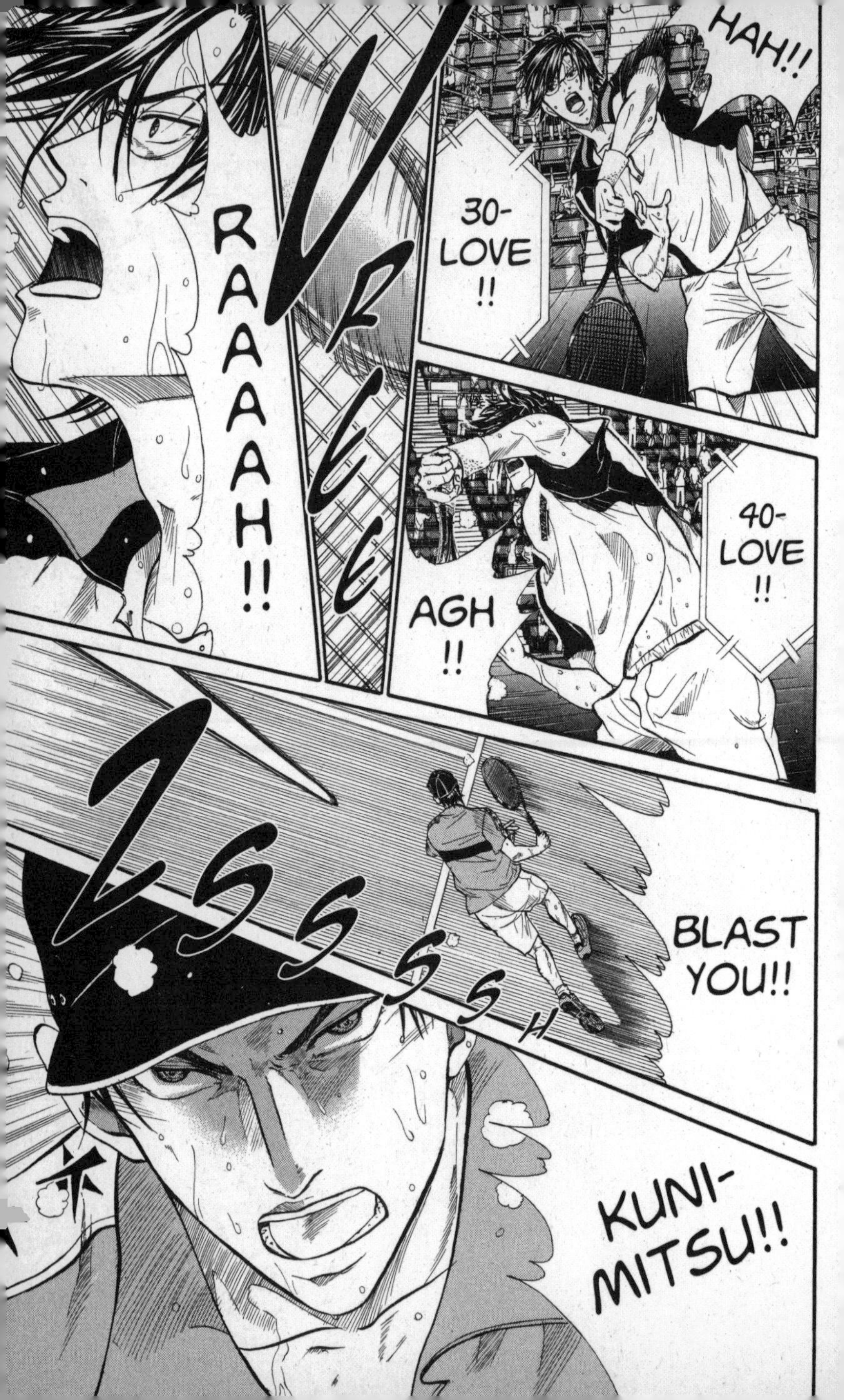
HAH!!
30-LOVE!!
40-LOVE!!
AGH!!
RAAAAH!!
BLAST YOU!!
ZSSSSSH
KUNI-MITSU!!

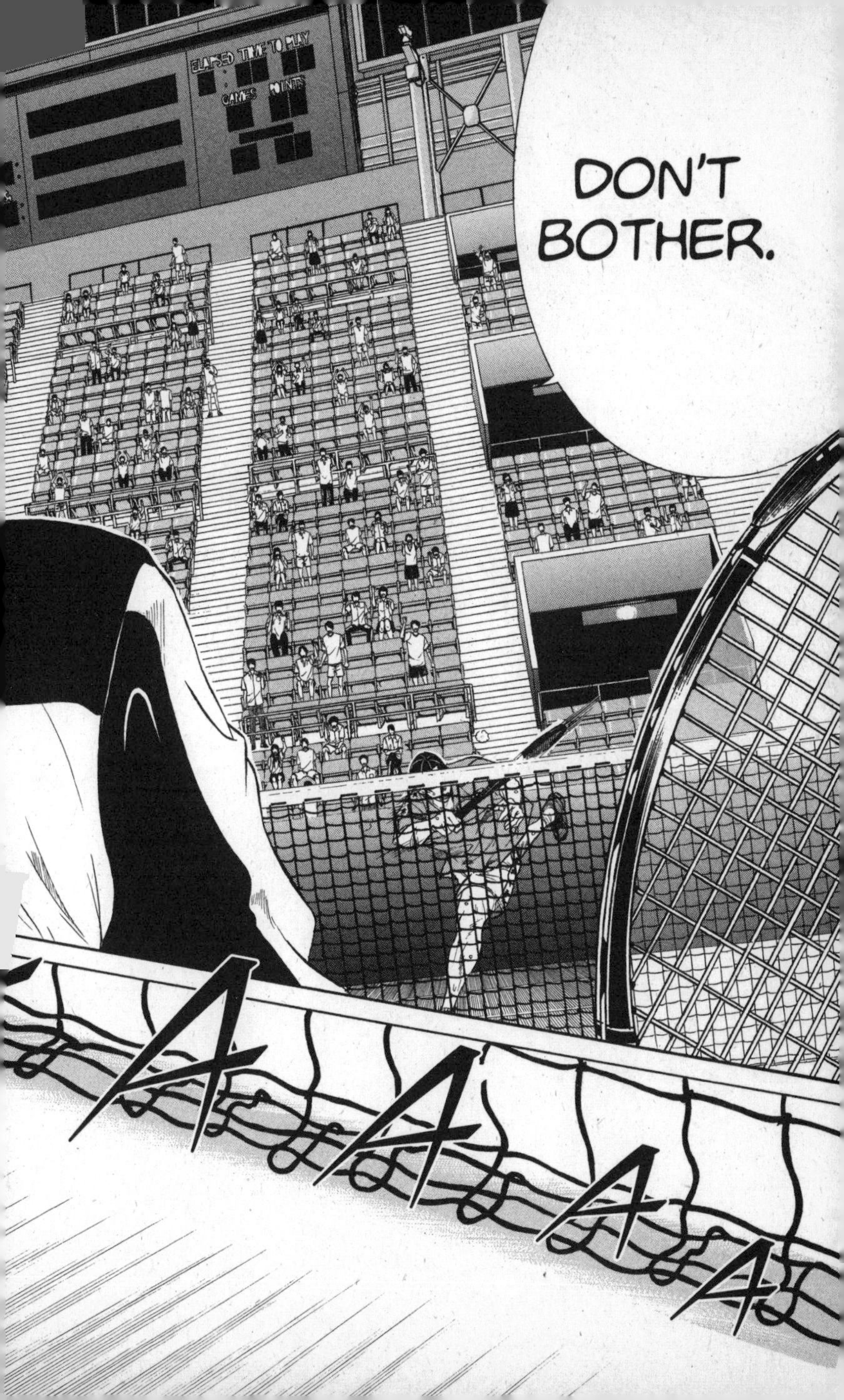
DON'T BOTHER.
ELAPSED TIME TO PLAY
GAMES
POINTS
AAAAA

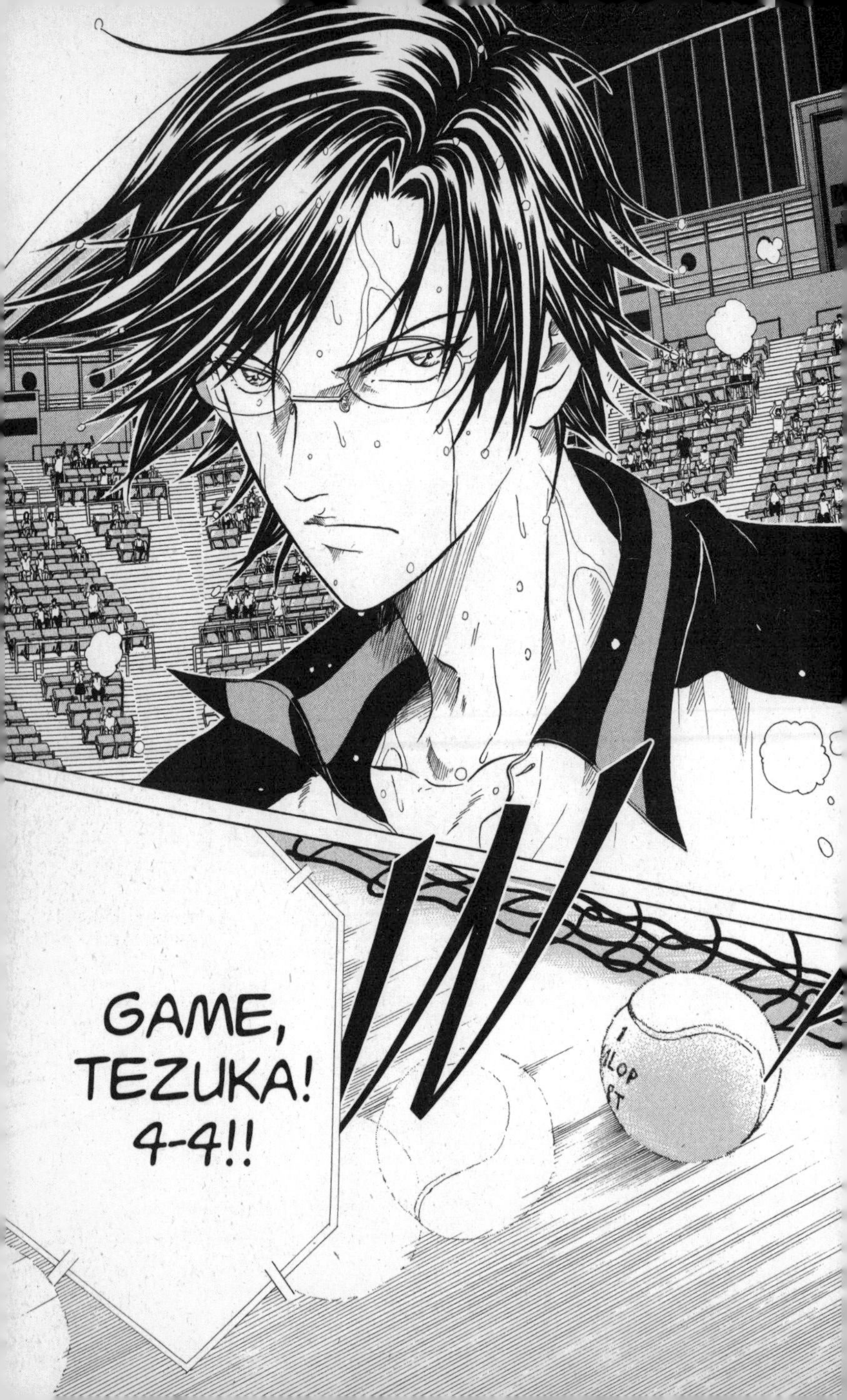
GAME, TEZUKA! 4-4!!

テニスの王子様

THE PRINCE OF TENNIS

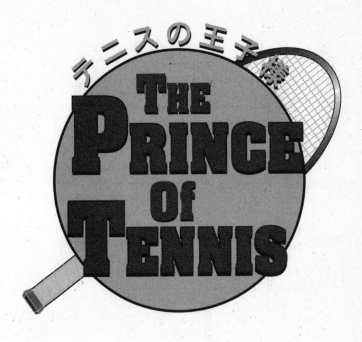

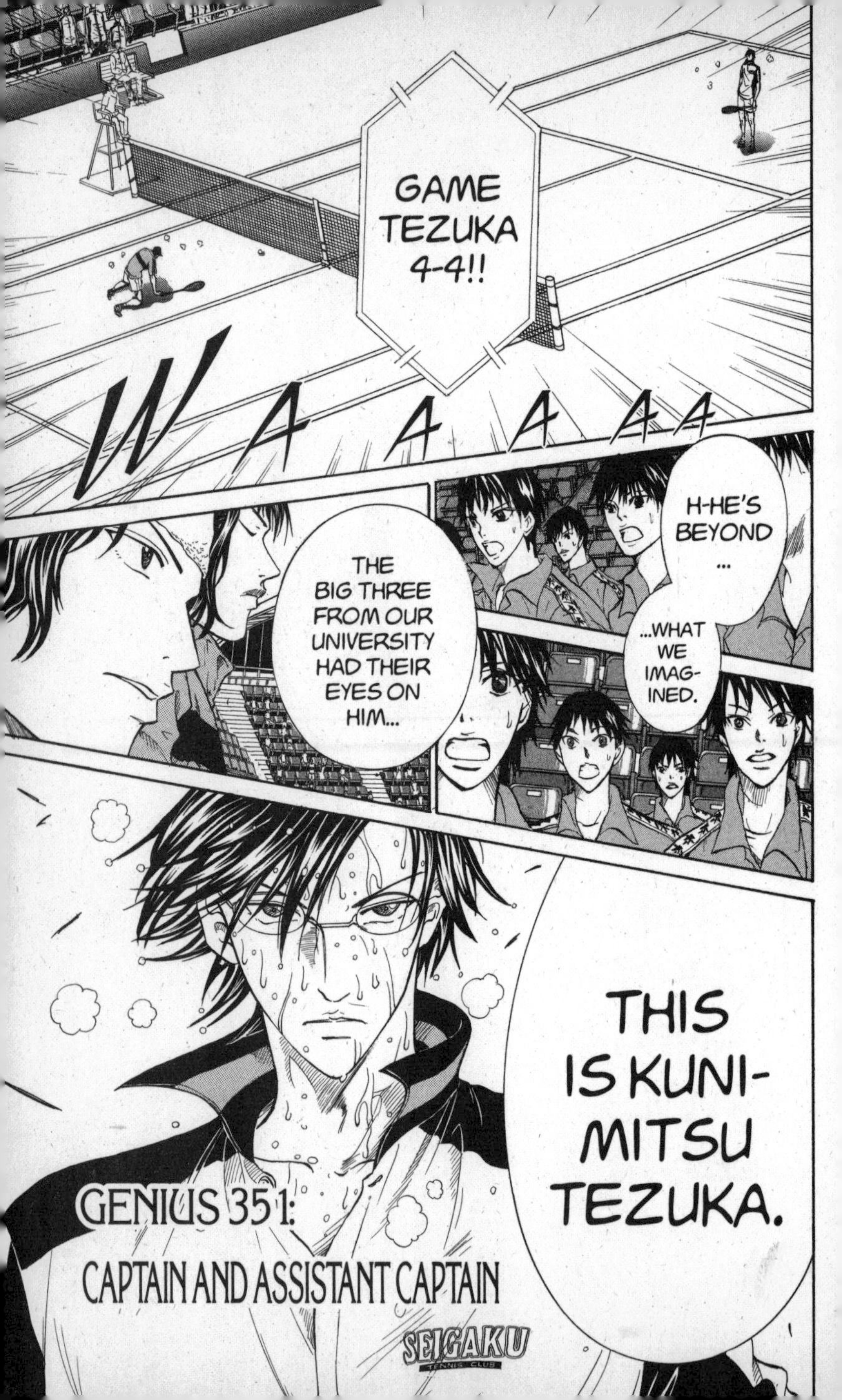
GAME TEZUKA 4-4!!
WAAAAA
H-HE'S BEYOND ...
...WHAT WE IMAG-INED.
THE BIG THREE FROM OUR UNIVERSITY HAD THEIR EYES ON HIM...
THIS IS KUNI-MITSU TEZUKA.
GENIUS 351:
CAPTAIN AND ASSISTANT CAPTAIN
SEIGAKU
TENNIS CLUB

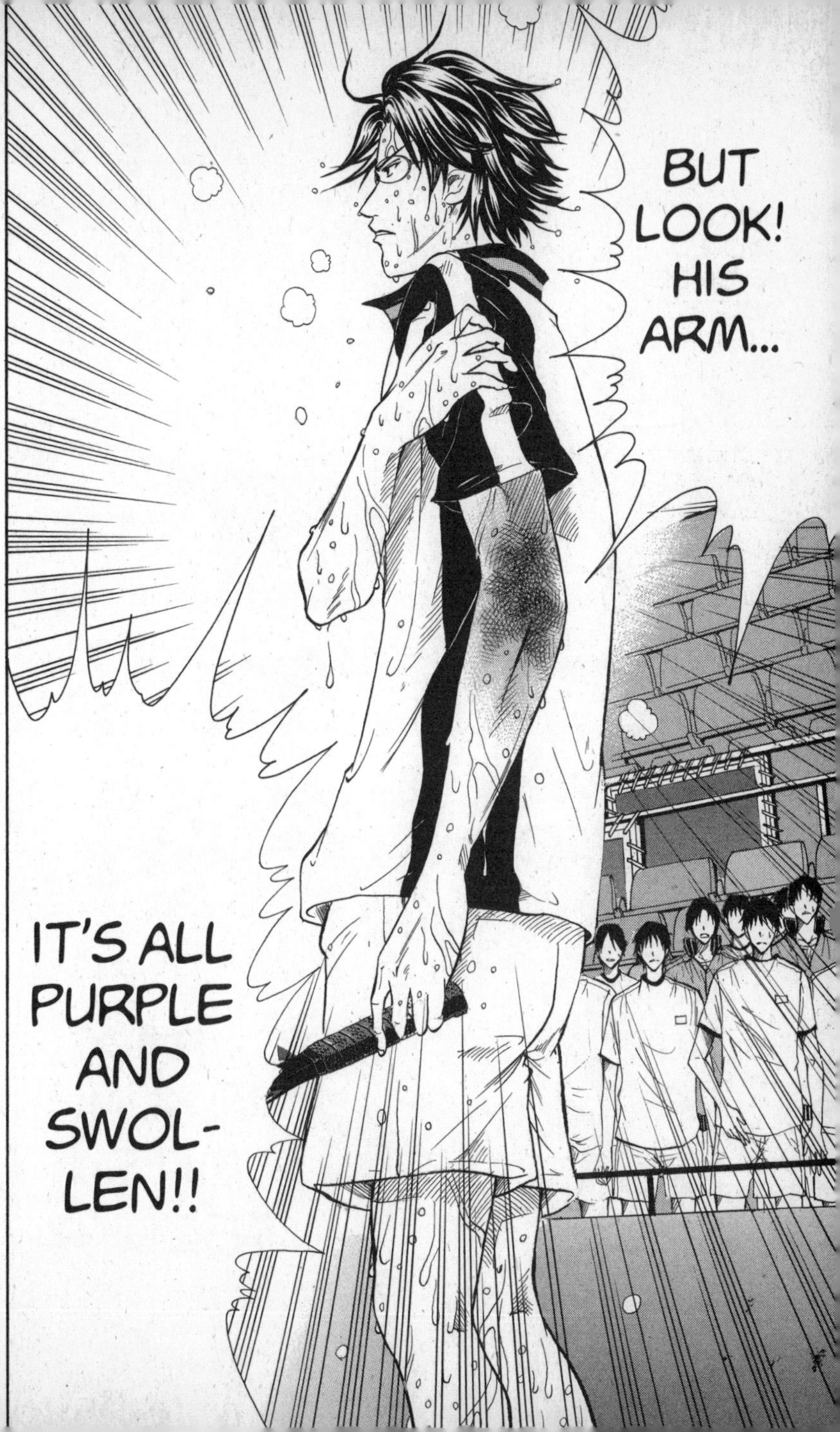
BUT LOOK! HIS ARM...
IT'S ALL PURPLE AND SWOL-LEN!!

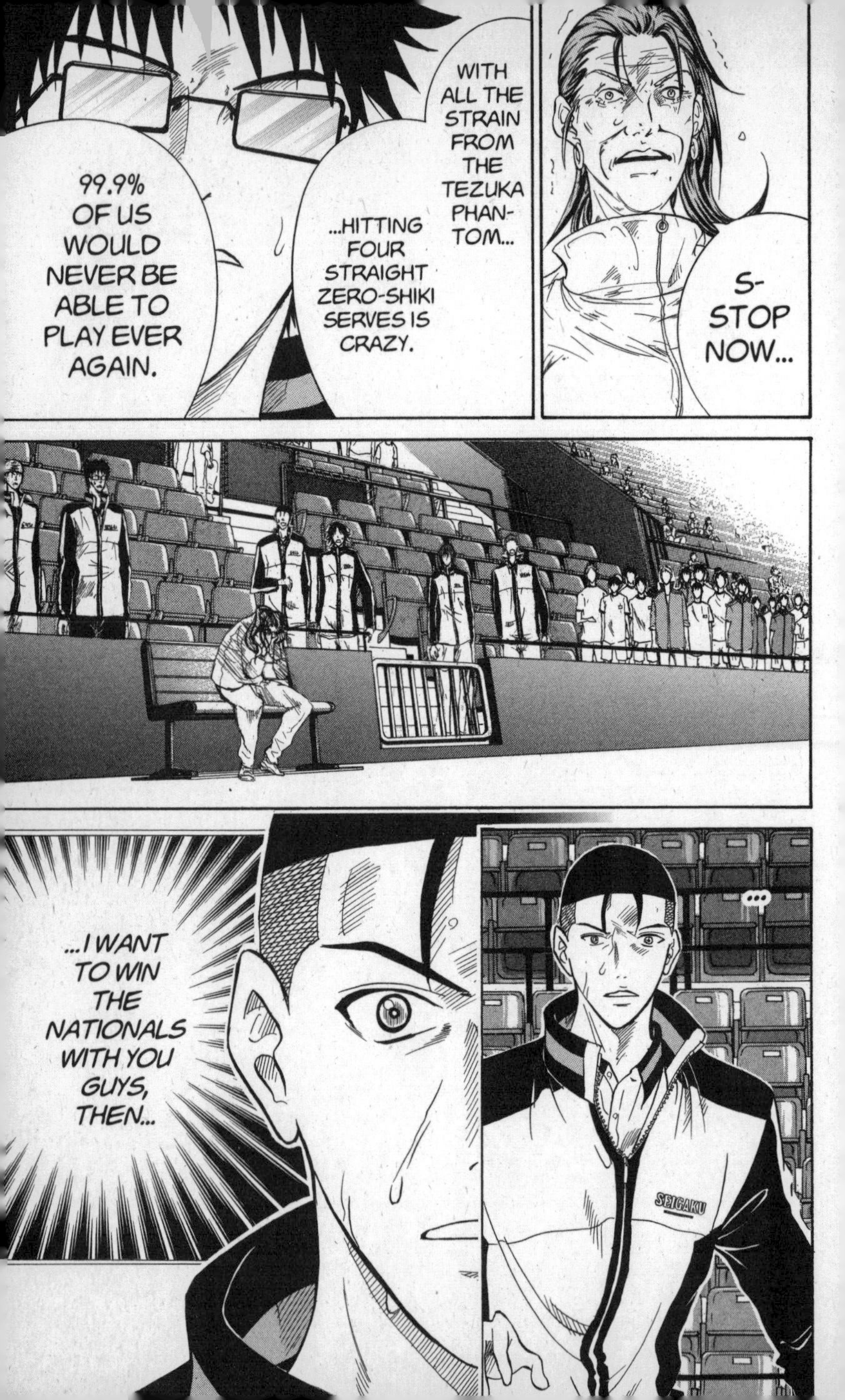
S-STOP NOW...
WITH ALL THE STRAIN FROM THE TEZUKA PHANTOM...
...HITTING FOUR STRAIGHT ZERO-SHIKI SERVES IS CRAZY.
99.9% OF US WOULD NEVER BE ABLE TO PLAY EVER AGAIN.
...
SEIGAKU
...I WANT TO WIN THE NATIONALS WITH YOU GUYS, THEN...

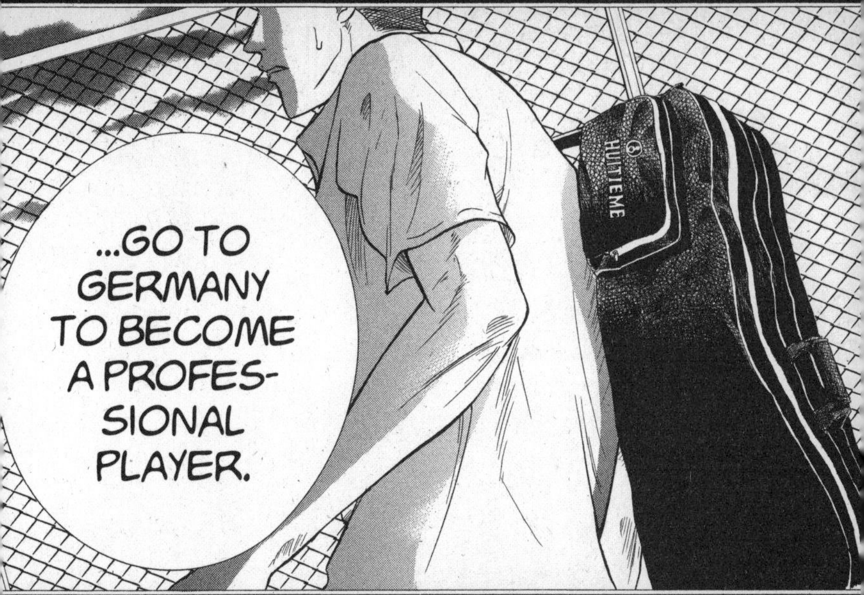
HUITIEME
...GO TO GERMANY TO BECOME A PROFES-SIONAL PLAYER.

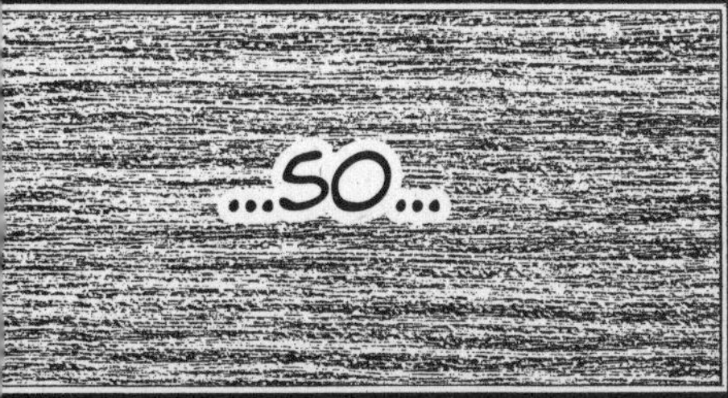
...SO...

GENIUS 351: CAPTAIN AND ASSISTANT CAPTAIN

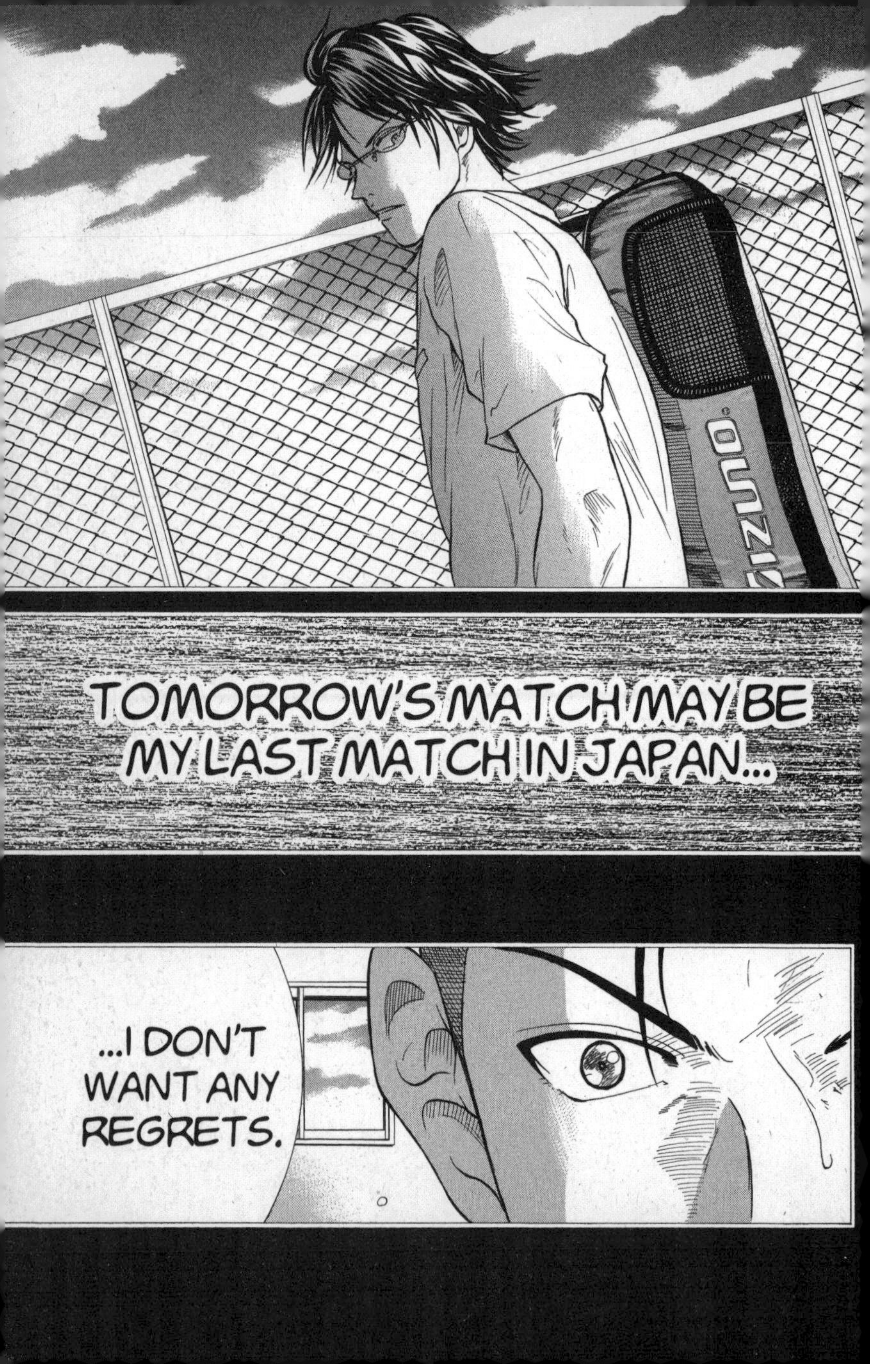
TOMORROW'S MATCH MAY BE MY LAST MATCH IN JAPAN...
...I DON'T WANT ANY REGRETS.

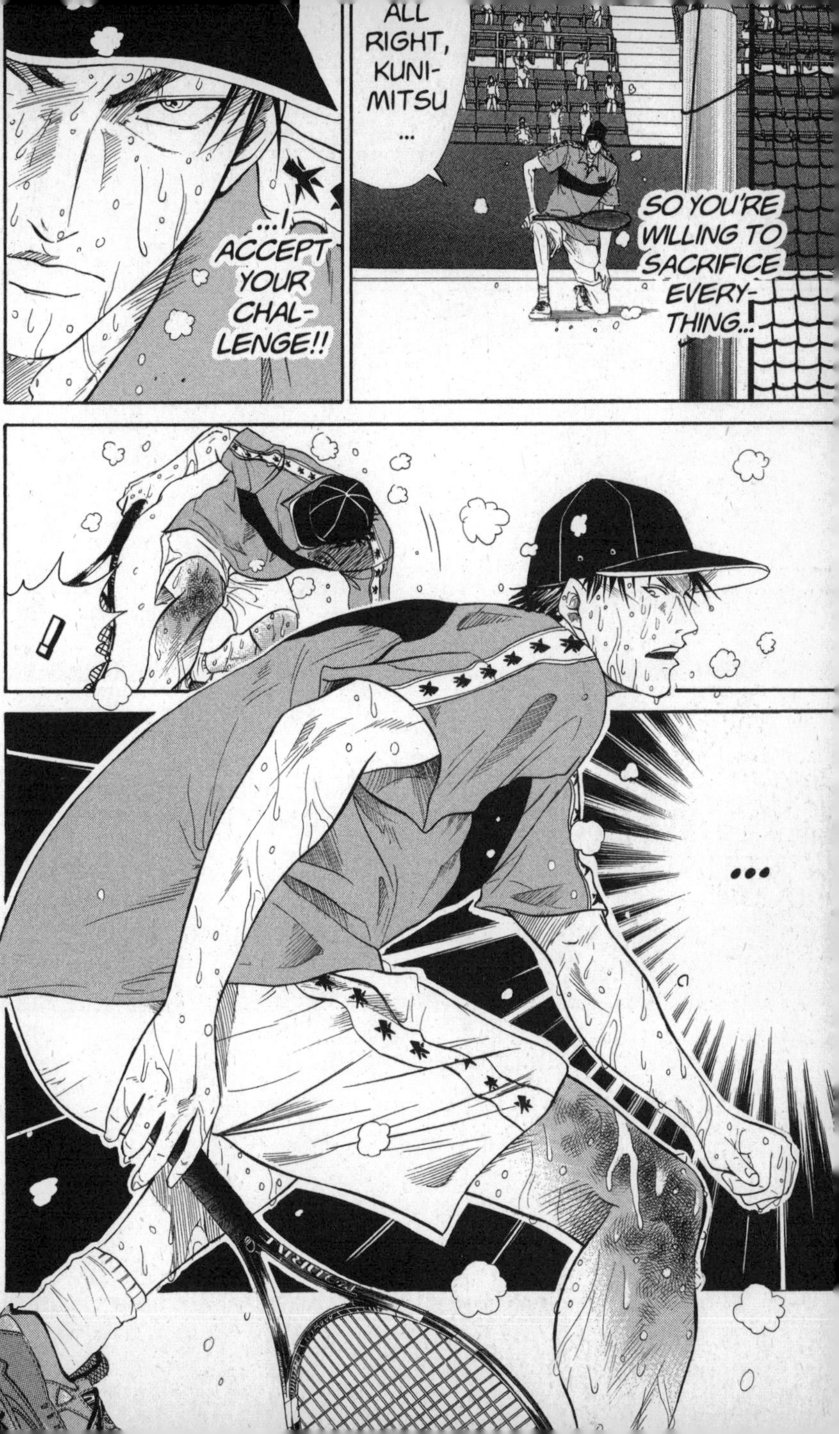
SO YOU'RE WILLING TO SACRIFICE EVERY-THING...
ALL RIGHT, KUNI-MITSU...
...I ACCEPT YOUR CHAL-LENGE!!
!
...

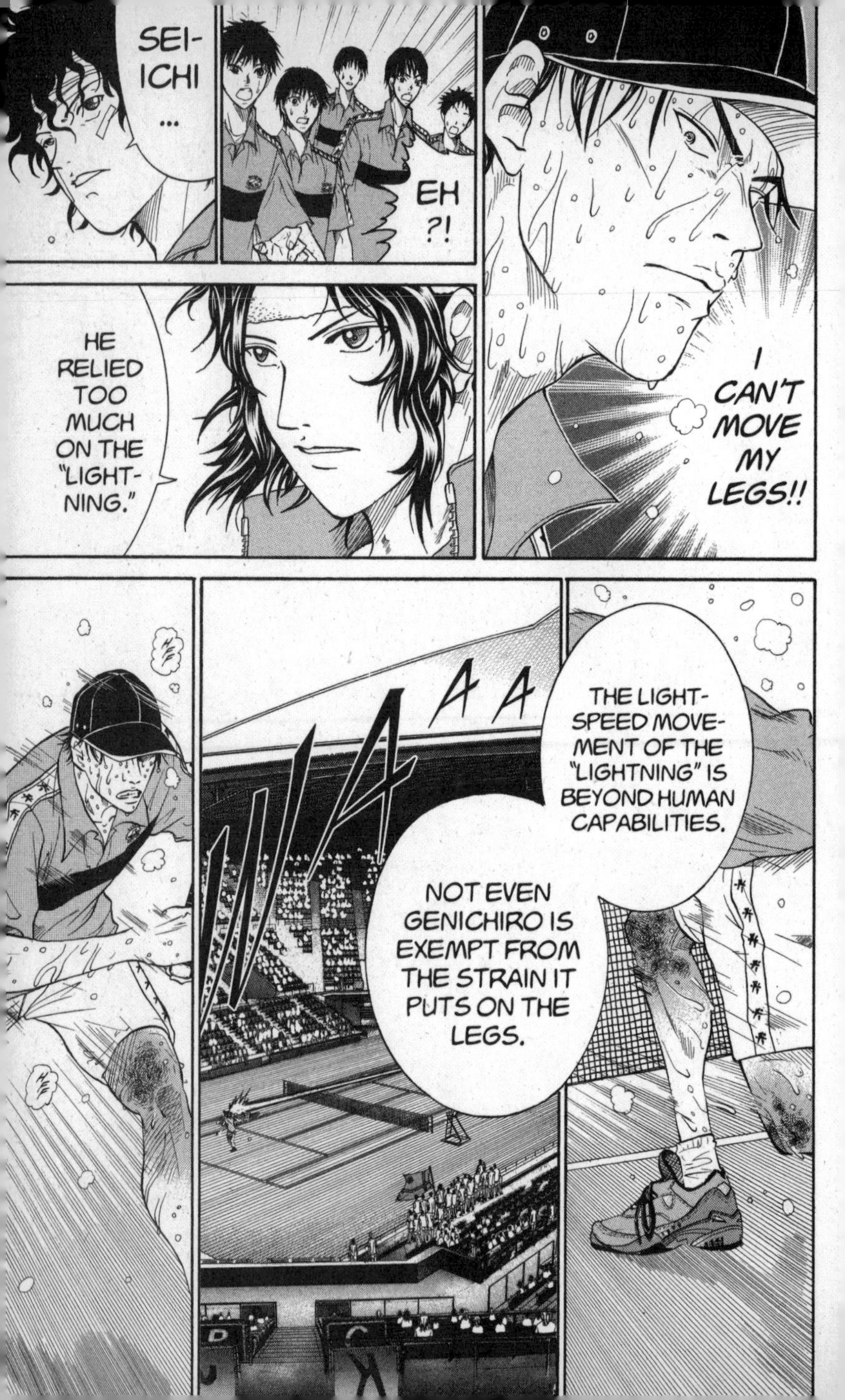

I CAN'T MOVE MY LEGS!!
EH ?!
SEI-ICHI ...
HE RELIED TOO MUCH ON THE "LIGHT-NING."
THE LIGHT-SPEED MOVE-MENT OF THE "LIGHTNING" IS BEYOND HUMAN CAPABILITIES.
NOT EVEN GENICHIRO IS EXEMPT FROM THE STRAIN IT PUTS ON THE LEGS.
WAAA

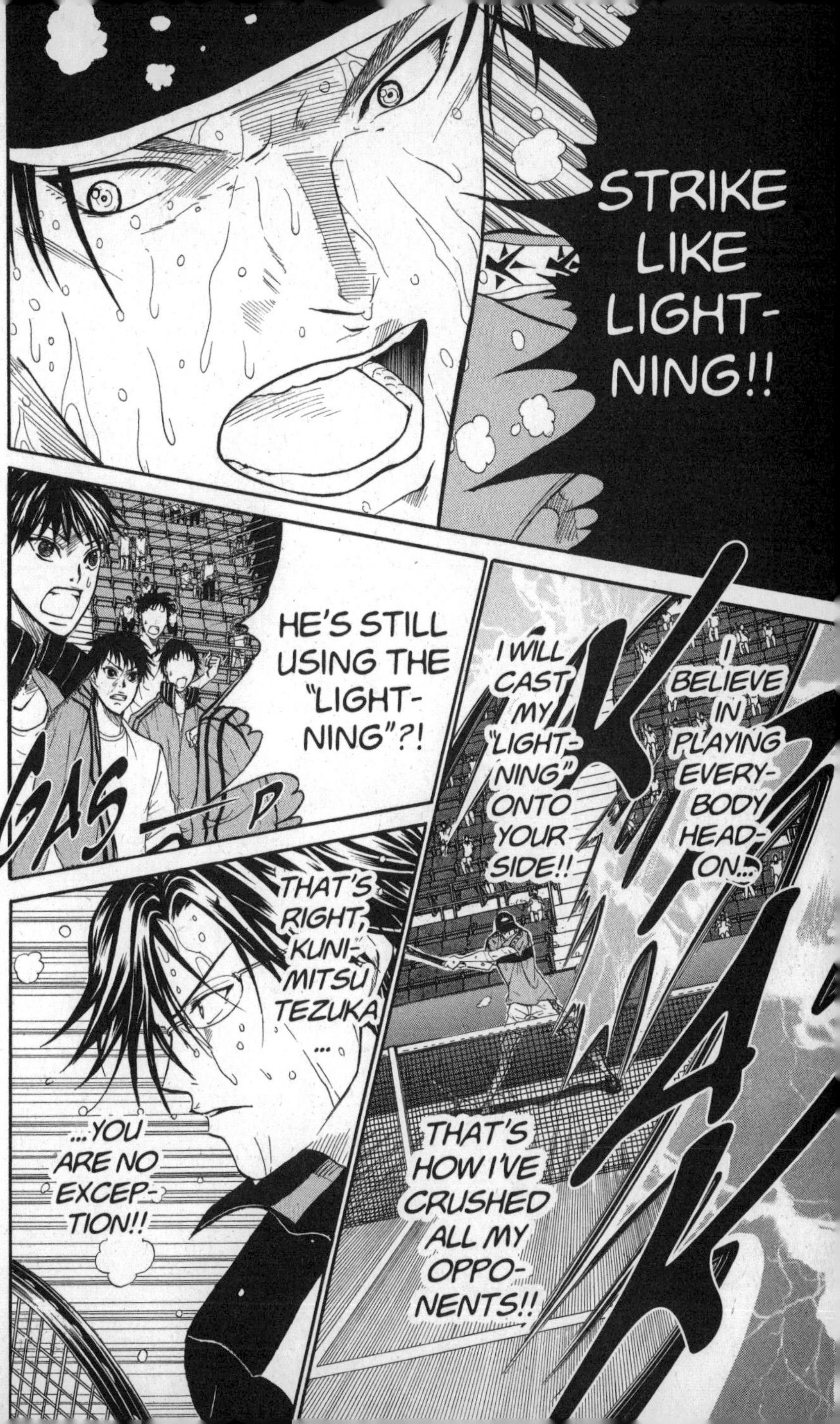
STRIKE LIKE LIGHTNING!!
I BELIEVE IN PLAYING EVERYBODY HEAD-ON...
I WILL CAST MY "LIGHTNING" ONTO YOUR SIDE!!
THAT'S HOW I'VE CRUSHED ALL MY OPPONENTS!!
HE'S STILL USING THE "LIGHTNING"?!
GASP
THAT'S RIGHT, KUNIMITSU TEZUKA...
...YOU ARE NO EXCEPTION!!

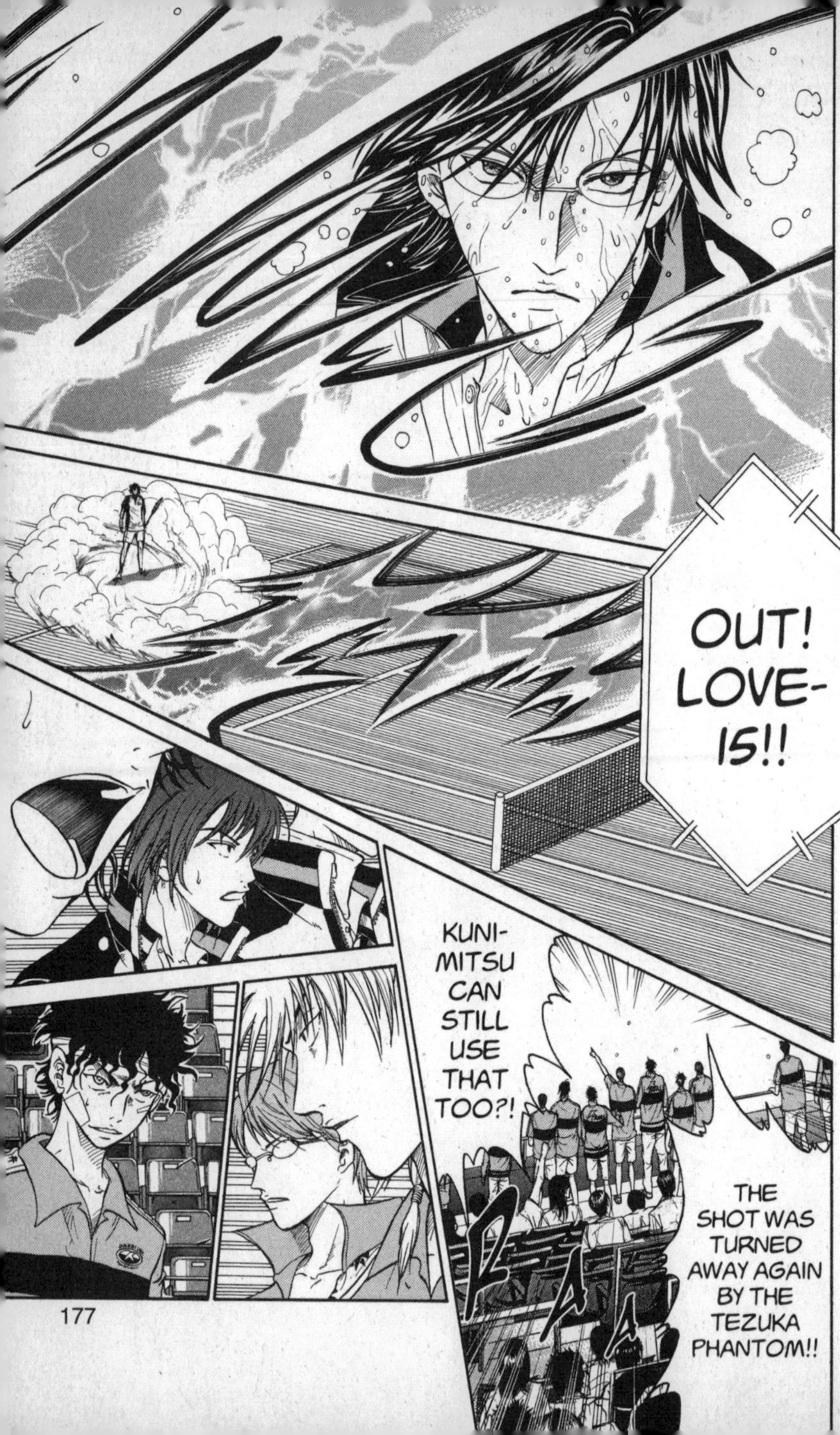
OUT! LOVE-15!!
KUNIMITSU CAN STILL USE THAT TOO?!
THE SHOT WAS TURNED AWAY AGAIN BY THE TEZUKA PHANTOM!!

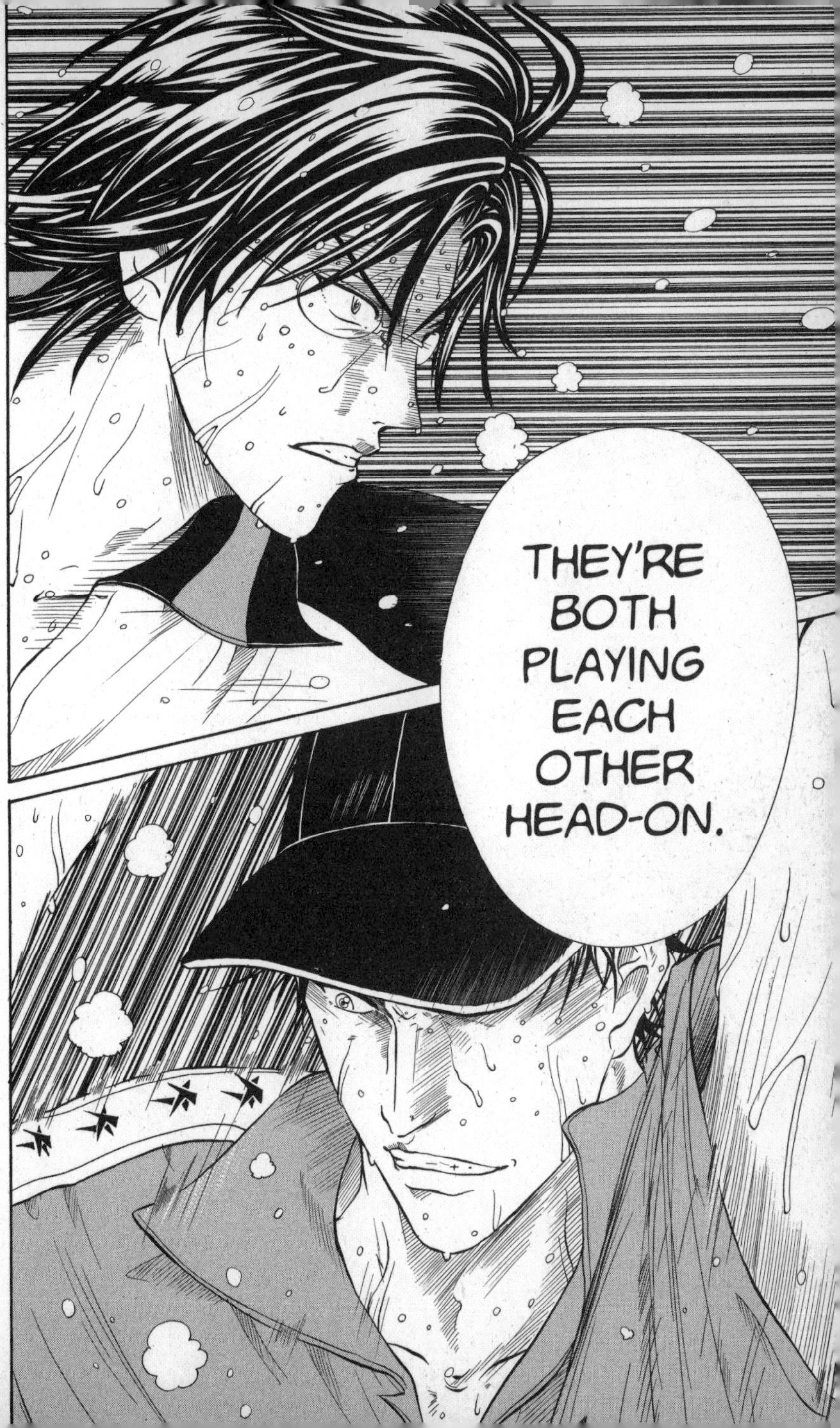
THEY'RE BOTH PLAYING EACH OTHER HEAD-ON.

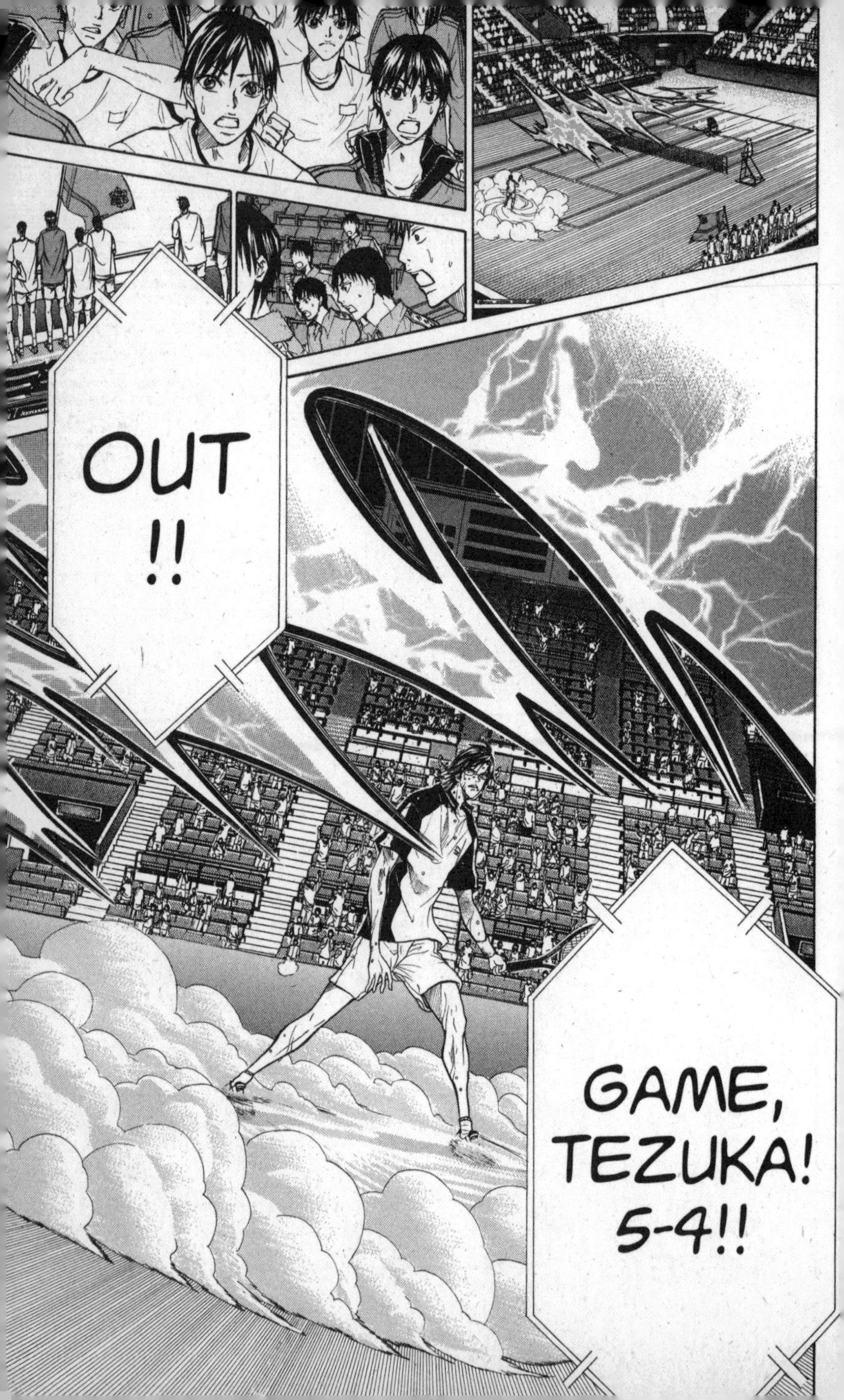
OUT !!
GAME, TEZUKA! 5-4!!

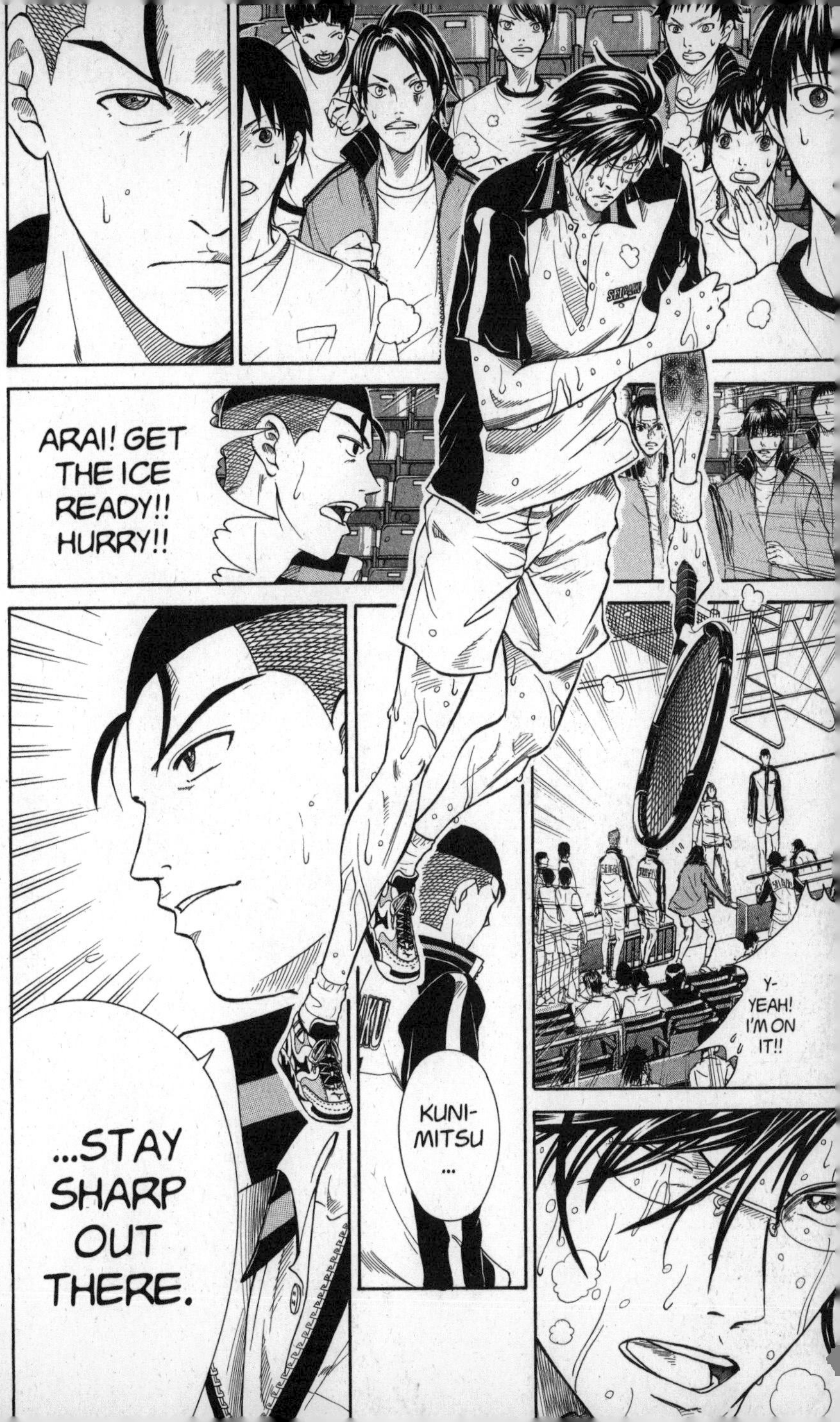
ARAI! GET THE ICE READY!! HURRY!!
Y-YEAH! I'M ON IT!!
KUNI-MITSU ...
...STAY SHARP OUT THERE.

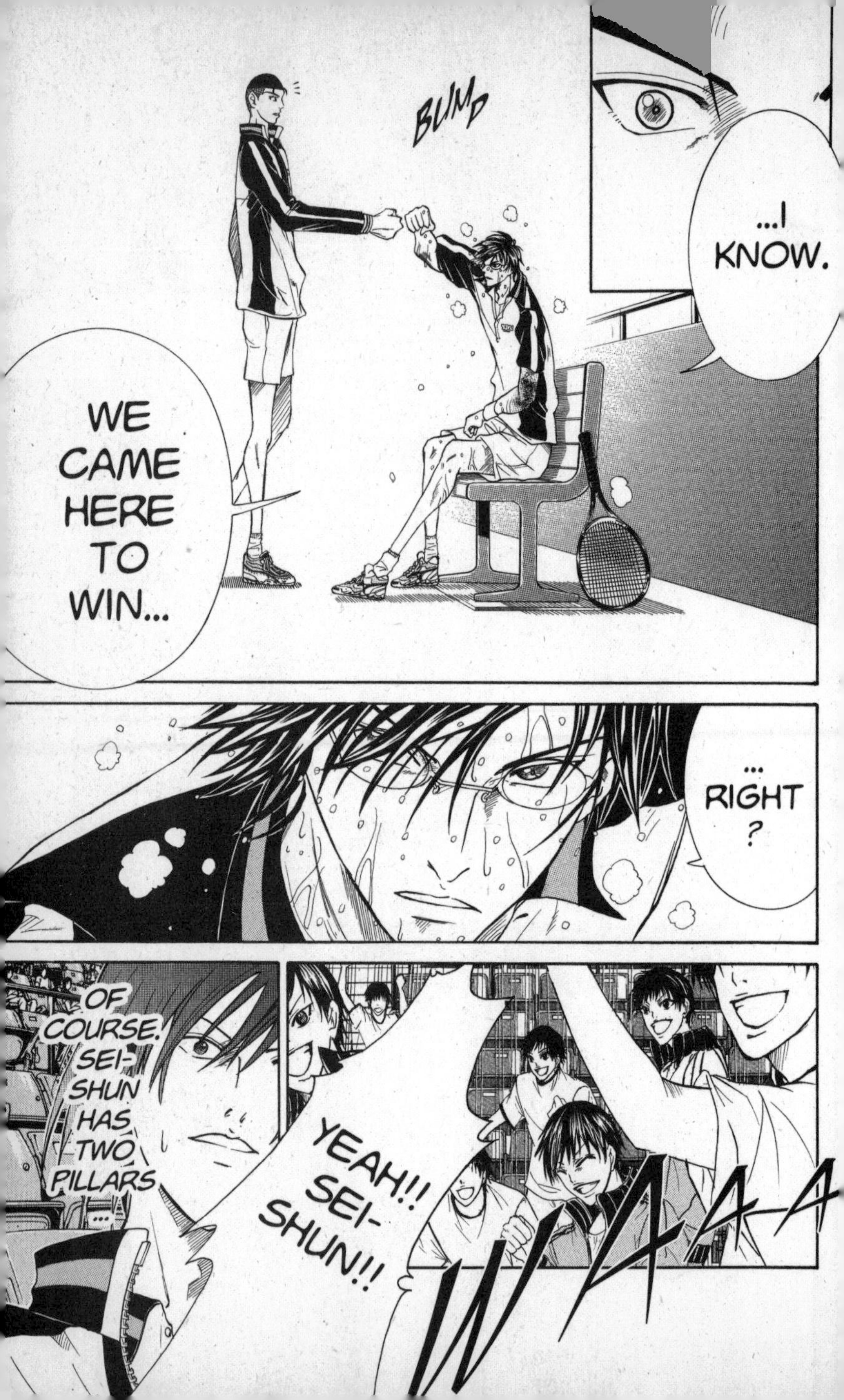
BUMP
...I KNOW.
WE CAME HERE TO WIN...
...RIGHT?
YEAH!! SEI-SHUN!!
WAAA
OF COURSE. SEI-SHUN HAS TWO PILLARS...

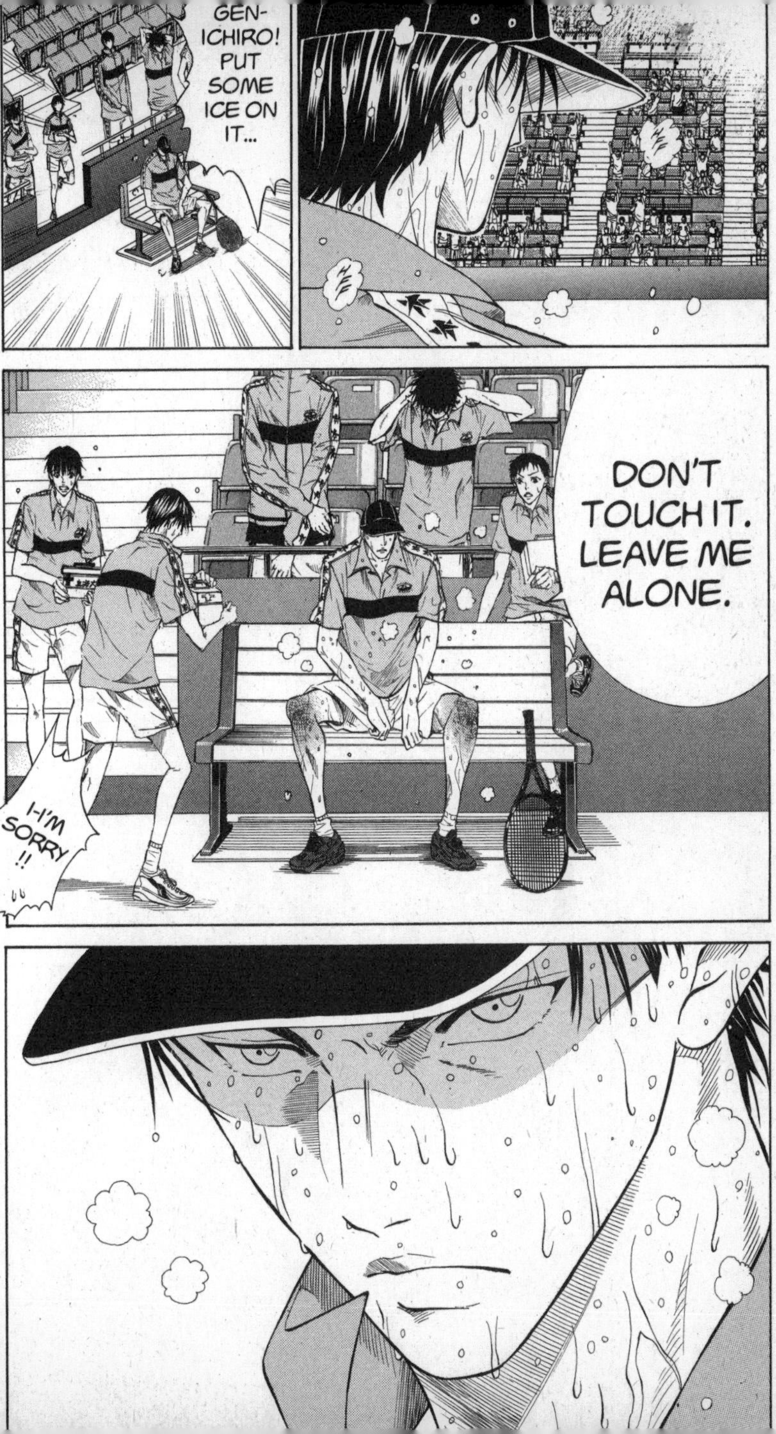
GEN-ICHIRO! PUT SOME ICE ON IT...
DON'T TOUCH IT. LEAVE ME ALONE.
I-I'M SORRY !!

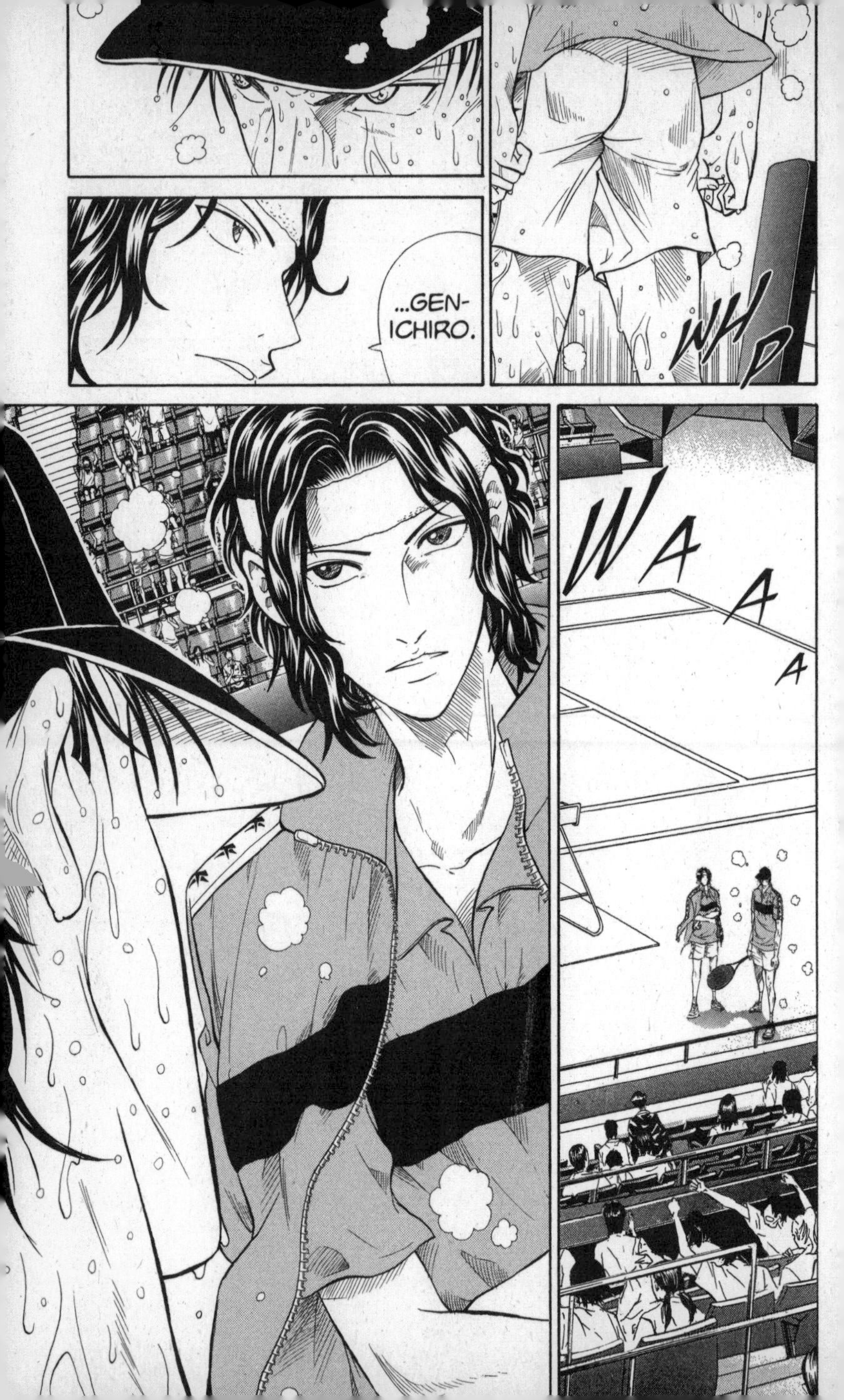
WHP
...GEN-ICHIRO.
WAAA

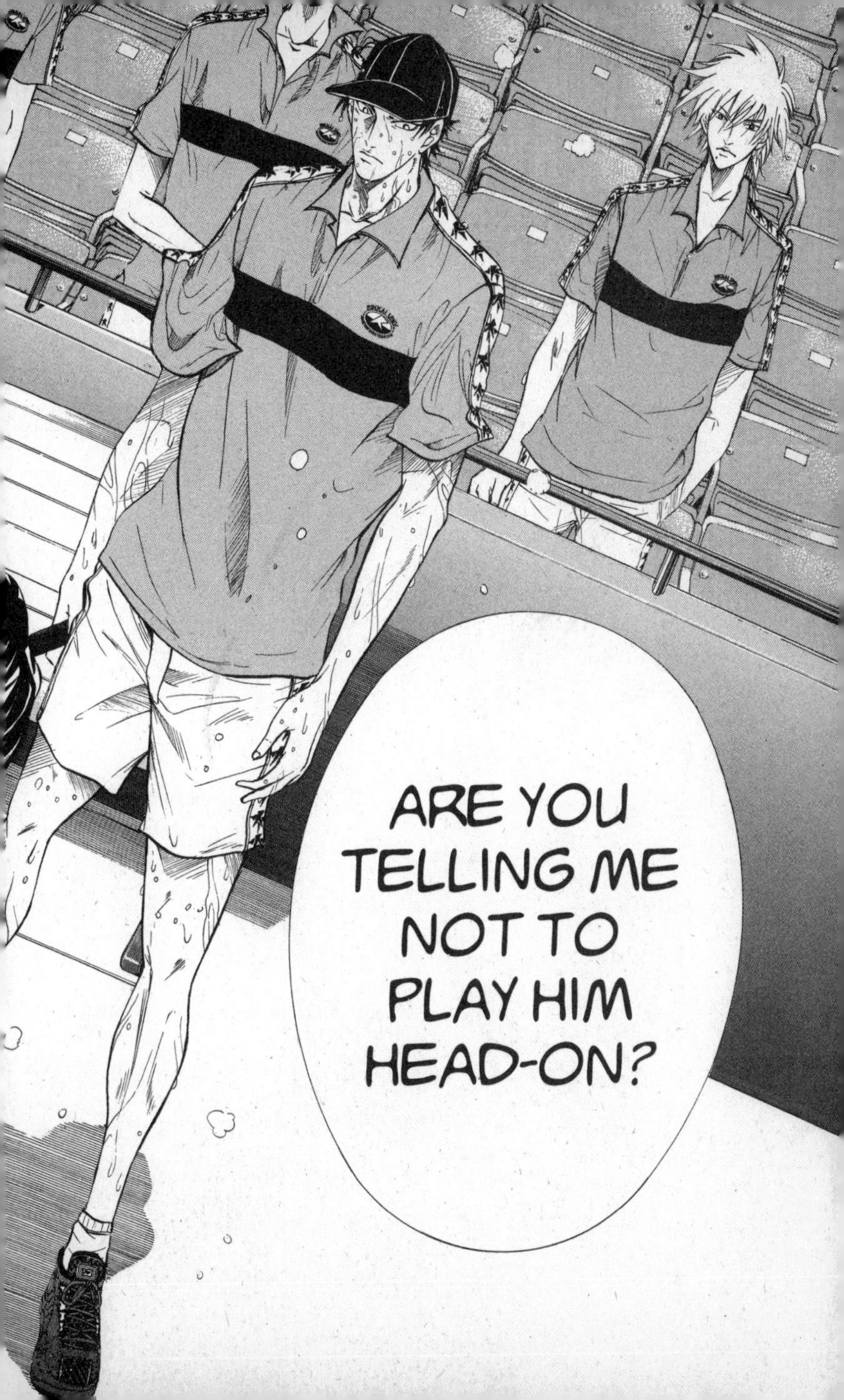
ARE YOU TELLING ME NOT TO PLAY HIM HEAD-ON?

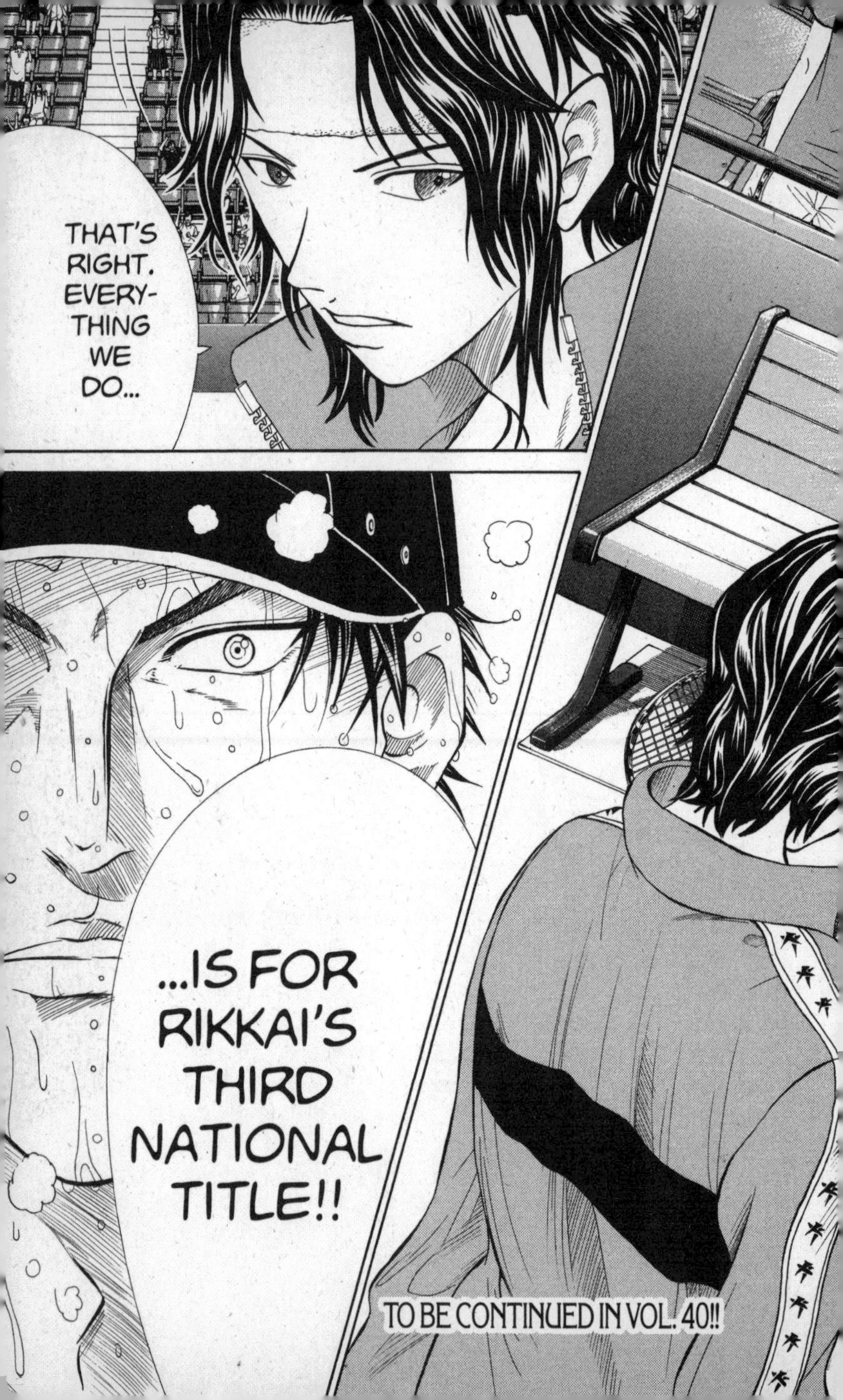
THAT'S RIGHT. EVERY-THING WE DO...
...IS FOR RIKKAI'S THIRD NATIONAL TITLE!!
TO BE CONTINUED IN VOL. 40!!

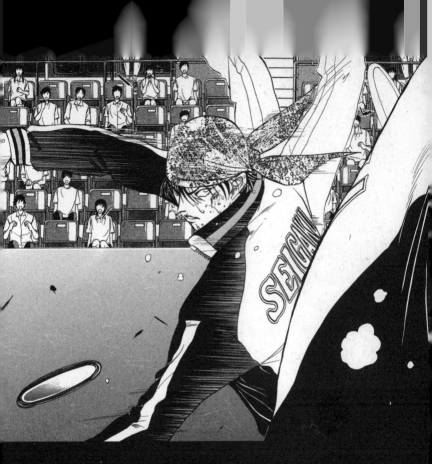

The Prince Who Forgot Tennis

The match between Seishun captain Tezuka and Rikkai's Sanada blares on. Sanada takes his captain's advice and attacks Tezuka where he's most vulnerable. Has the captain of Seishun finally met his doom? Next, Kaoru and Sadaharu take on Rikkai's lethal pair. When they target Sadaharu, Kaoru has to pull out his Gyro Laser Beam to save the match. And Ryoma finally arrives at the arena! Unfortunately for Seishun, he's got a wicked case of amnesia.

Available January 2011!

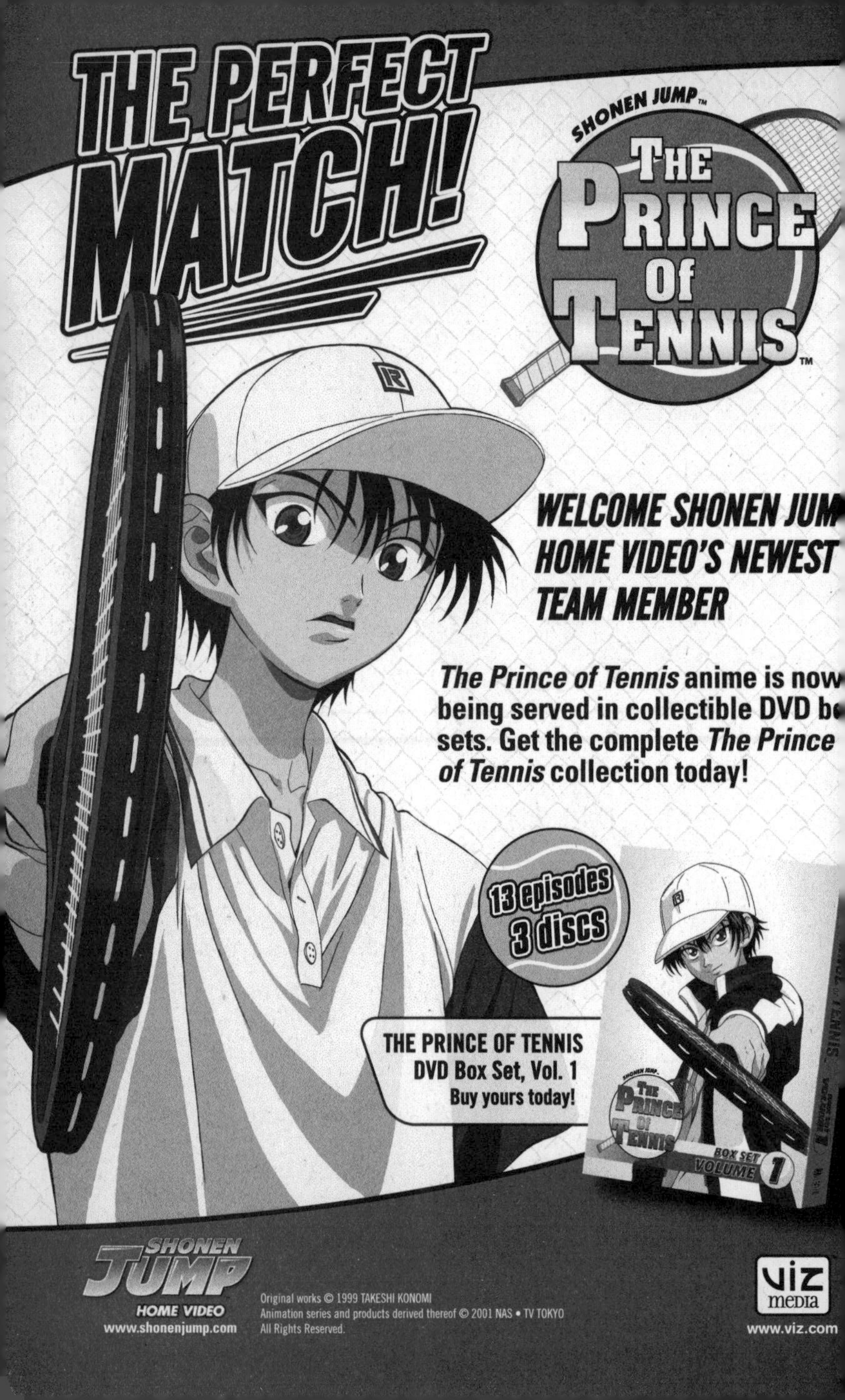
THE PERFECT MATCH!
SHONEN JUMP™
THE PRINCE OF TENNIS™
WELCOME SHONEN JUM
HOME VIDEO'S NEWEST
TEAM MEMBER
The Prince of Tennis anime is now being served in collectible DVD b sets. Get the complete The Prince of Tennis collection today!
13 episodes 3 discs
THE PRINCE OF TENNIS
DVD Box Set, Vol. 1
Buy yours today!
BOX SET VOLUME 1
SHONEN JUMP HOME VIDEO
www.shonenjump.com
Original works © 1999 TAKESHI KONOMI
Animation series and products derived thereof © 2001 NAS • TV TOKYO
All Rights Reserved.
VIZ media
www.viz.com

hange Your Perspective

om Akira Toriyama,
e creator of Dr. Slump,
OWA! and SandLand

✳ ✳ ✳ ✳ ✳ ✳ ✳ ✳ ✳ ✳ ✳

live Goku's
est with the
w VIZBIG
itions of
agon Ball and
agon Ball Z!

ach features:
- Three volumes in one
- Exclusive cover designs
- Color manga pages
- Larger trim size
- Color artwork
- Bonus content

DRAGON BALL
ZBIG Edition, Volume 1

DRAGON BALL Z
VIZBIG Edition, Volume 1

Get BIG

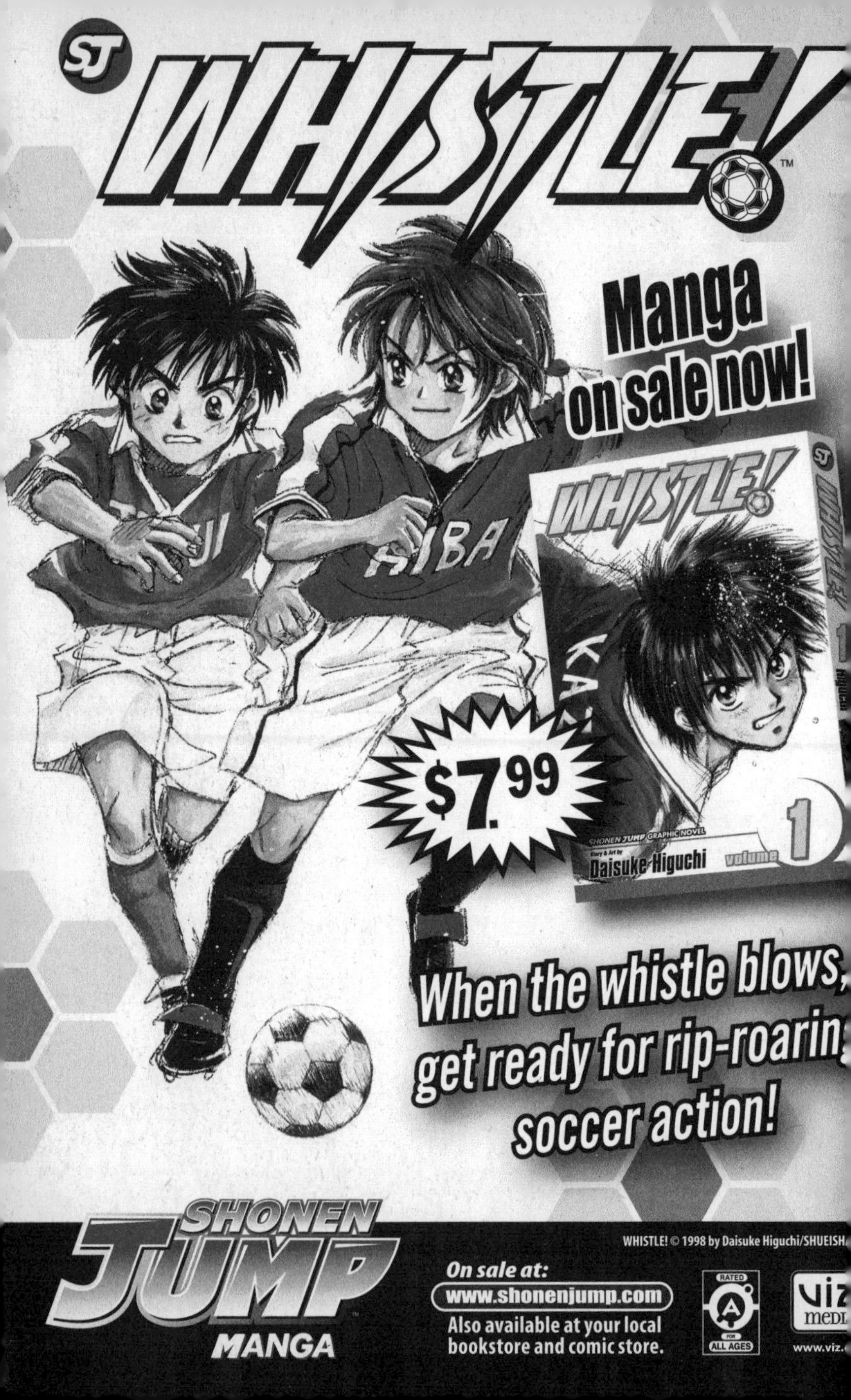
SJ
WHISTLE!™
Manga on sale now!
WHISTLE!
SHONEN JUMP GRAPHIC NOVEL
Story & Art by
Daisuke Higuchi
volume 1
$7.99
When the whistle blows, get ready for rip-roarin soccer action!
SHONEN JUMP MANGA
WHISTLE! © 1998 by Daisuke Higuchi/SHUEISH
On sale at:
www.shonenjump.com
Also available at your local bookstore and comic store.
RATED A FOR ALL AGES
www.viz.

SHONEN JUMP

THE WORLD'S MOST POPULAR MANGA

BLEACH

STORY AND ART BY
TITE KUBO

ONE PIECE

STORY AND ART BY
EIICHIRO ODA

Tegami Bachi
LETTER·BEE

STORY AND ART BY
HIROYUKI ASADA

JUMP INTO THE ACTION BY TELLING US WHAT YOU LOVE (AND WHAT YOU DON'T)

LET YOUR VOICE BE HEARD!

SHONENJUMP.VIZ.COM/MANGASURVEY

HELP US MAKE MORE OF THE WORLD'S MOST POPULAR MANGA!

SAVE 50% OFF
THE COVER PRICE!

IT'S LIKE GETTING 6 ISSUES

FREE!

OVER 350+ PAGES PER ISSUE

This monthly magazine contains 7 of the coolest manga available in the U.S., PLUS anime news, and info about video & card games, toys AND more!

❏ **I want 12 HUGE issues of SHONEN JUMP for only $29.95*!**

NAME

ADDRESS

CITY/STATE/ZIP

EMAIL ADDRESS   **DATE OF BIRTH**

❏ YES, send me via email information, advertising, offers, and promotions related to VIZ Media, SHONEN JUMP, and/or their business partners.

❏ **CHECK ENCLOSED** (payable to SHONEN JUMP)   ❏ **BILL ME LATER**

CREDIT CARD: ❏ **Visa**   ❏ **Mastercard**

ACCOUNT NUMBER   **EXP. DATE**

SIGNATURE

CLIP&MAILTO:
SHONEN JUMP Subscriptions Service Dept.
P.O. Box 515
Mount Morris, IL 61054-0515

P9GNC1

* Canada price: $41.95 USD, including GST, HST, and QST. US/CAN orders only. Allow 6-8 weeks for delivery.
ONE PIECE © 1997 by Eiichiro Oda/SHUEISHA Inc. BLEACH © 2001 by Tite Kubo/SHUEISHA Inc.
NARUTO © 1999 by Masashi Kishimoto/SHUEISHA Inc.

RATED FOR TEEN
ratings.viz.com

VIZ media
www.viz.com